BLUEBEARD GOTHIC

Heta Pyrhönen

# Bluebeard Gothic

## *Jane Eyre* and Its Progeny

UNIVERSITY OF TORONTO PRESS
Toronto Buffalo London

© University of Toronto Press Incorporated 2010
Toronto Buffalo London
www.utppublishing.com
Printed in Canada

ISBN 978-1-4426-4124-2 (cloth)

Printed on acid-free, 100% post-consumer recycled paper with
vegetable-based inks.

---

**Library and Archives Canada Cataloguing in Publication**

Pyrhönen, Heta
    Bluebeard gothic : Jane Eyre and its progeny / Heta Pyrhönen.

Includes bibliographical references and index.
ISBN 978-1-4426-4124-2 (bound)

1. Brontë, Charlotte, 1816–1855. Jane Eyre.   2. Bluebeard (Legendary
character) in literature.   3. Religion in literature.   4. Sacrifice in literature.
5. Scapegoat in literature.   I. Title.

PR4167.J5P97 2010      823'.8      C2009-906577-0

---

University of Toronto Press acknowledges the financial assistance to its
publishing program of the Canada Council for the Arts and the Ontario
Arts Council.

University of Toronto Press acknowledges the financial support for its
publishing activities of the Government of Canada through the Book
Publishing Industry Development Program (BPIDP).

# Contents

# Acknowledgments

I started collecting material for this book in the summer 2002 while participating in a seminar by Sander Gilman at the School of Criticism and Theory at Cornell University. I wish to thank Sander Gilman for his useful feedback on my first attempts to get a handle on my topic. That he read the completed manuscript was an unexpected act of kindness for which I am truly grateful. I would also like to thank Dominick LaCapra for his inspiring talks on trauma theory that gave me insight to *Jane Eyre* and the fairy-tale material with which this book deals.

A three-month stay at the University of Toronto in the summer of 2004 made it possible for me to start writing this study. I am thankful to Linda Hutcheon for arranging for me to have a tiny office on the fourteenth floor of Robarts Library. She kindly set aside time in her busy schedule to talk with me about this project. Some ideas presented in this book were first tried out as talks at the conferences of the International Society for the Study of Narrative, but the actual 'guinea pigs' who have graciously read various chapter drafts are my colleagues Klaus Brax, Teemu Ikonen, and Kristiina Taivalkoski-Shilov, participants in the project 'Narrating the Self' at the University of Helsinki. I greatly appreciate the feedback I got from them and, especially, the camaraderie.

Warm thanks go to Suzanne Keen for her valuable suggestions during the final stages of writing. The staff at the University of Toronto Press has proved as supportive as the previous time. Thank you, Richard Ratzlaff, Barb Porter, and James Leahy, for all your help. Finishing this book would not have been possible without a grant from Finland's Academy (grant no. 111 9702), a fact that I gratefully acknowledge.

Parts of chapters 3 and 4 appeared, in shorter versions, in *Mosaic: A Journal for the Interdisciplinary Study of Literature* (vol. 38:3, 2005) and

*Contemporary Women's Writing* (vol. 2, 2008). I am grateful to the editors of these journals for their permission to reprint.

I would also like to acknowledge Paula Rego's gracious permission to use her painting as the book's cover.

I have relied on the support of my husband, Markku Ollikainen, who has generously encouraged and spurred me on. This book is for our children, Pielpa and Paulus, with whom I have rediscovered the wonderful pleasures of reading aloud.

BLUEBEARD GOTHIC

# Introduction

In the 'Bluebeard' tale a young woman marries a rich blue-bearded widower. He forbids her to enter his locked chamber, proclaiming that disobedience will result in her death. The defiant wife enters the room, finding there her murdered predecessors. Frightened, she drops the key into a pool of blood. Because the key is permanently stained, Bluebeard finds out about her disobedience. He is about to execute her, but she is saved in the nick of time. In a related tale, 'The Robber Bridegroom,' a father promises his daughter to a rich suitor. The bridegroom invites his fiancée to visit his house in the woods. During a surprise visit she witnesses the groom, a leader of a robber gang, kill a woman. She manages to escape, and during their wedding feast she narrates the events as though they were a dream. When the groom hotly denies her accusations, she produces the finger of the murdered woman as proof. The wedding guests then kill the groom. In 'Fitcher's Bird,' yet another variant of this tale group, a wizard steals three sisters one after the other in order to find an obedient wife. He tests them by giving each an egg to protect and by forbidding them entry to a room in his house. Defying the wizard, the two eldest sisters drop the egg in fright upon discovering a basin of murdered women in the room. The sullied egg discloses their transgression, and the wizard kills them. The third sister places the egg in a safe place before opening the door. She resurrects her sisters and tricks the wizard by hiding the sisters in a basket of gold, which she makes him carry to their home. She dresses up a skull as a bride, placing it in a window, to look as if she were waiting for his return. In the meanwhile, she disguises herself as a bird, managing to escape. Learning of the wizard's wickedness, the sisters' relatives lock him in his house and burn it up. Together these variants form what is known as the 'Bluebeard' tale cycle. They share an emphasis on the mystery posed by the Bluebeard figure and the woman's curiosity to probe this mystery.

The textual identity of this tale cycle is a complex matter. Typically for fairy tales, there is no single authoritative version but a shifting constellation of stories gathered under this label. The recent studies by Casie Hermansson and Maria Tatar (*Secrets*) refer to the Aarne-Thompson (AT) system in *The Types of the Folktale* (1961) that identifies three main types as comprising the 'Bluebeard' tale cycle. These types themselves have variants. They are 'Bluebeard' (AT 312), 'The Robber Bridegroom' (AT 955), and 'Fitcher's Bird' (AT 311; the heroine rescues herself and her sisters). The two latter are best known from the Brothers Grimm collection *Kinder- und Hausmärchen* (1812) as 'Der Räuberbrautigam' and 'Fichter's Vogel,' respectively. In Britain, 'The Robber Bridegroom' has a parallel variant of 'Mister Fox,' also known as 'Mister Fox's Courtship.'[1]

In Charlotte Brontë's *Jane Eyre* (1847) the protagonist Jane lives in a series of households steered by a stern master figure. At Gateshead Hall, Aunt Reed keeps Jane apart from the Reed children, thanks to what the Aunt thinks is the girl's disgraceful background. This supposedly discreditable family legacy is the secret Jane is forbidden to explore at Gateshead. Given that Jane lacks knowledge of her immediate family, she finds it difficult to form a sense of identity and belonging. Angered by her cousin's act of cruelty against her, Jane defies this imposed silence by asserting her equality with the Reed family, an act of disobedience the domineering Aunt cannot forgive her. As punishment, she hands Jane over to the care of Mr Brocklehurst, who acts as the head of a charitable institution, the Lowood School. The regime at Lowood amplifies the restrictions placed on Jane at Gateshead, as human corporeality becomes the source and target of injunction. Anything and everything associated with the body is forbidden. Mr Brocklehurst imposes this stricture on the pupils by nearly starving and freezing them to death. While Jane escaped from Aunt Reed by rebelling, she learns another tactic at Lowood, one based on duplicity. Outwardly she conforms to the institute's strictures, while inwardly she disagrees with and criticizes them. This strategy ensures Jane a measure of personal space and a degree of internal independence. It enables Jane to survive her stay at Thornfield during her commission as a governess to Mr Rochester's ward. While Jane appears composed and resigned to her lot, in her thoughts she revolts against her station, for she has fallen passionately in love with her employer. Mr Rochester combines and condenses the strictures formerly placed on Jane: he entices Jane to explore bodily and intellectual pleasures in a love relationship, while continually hinting at the forbidden nature of such pleasures, thanks to some terrible secret he harbours. This mystery has a concrete location in a room in the attic. Learning of Mr Rochester's secret, Jane recognizes that he would annihilate her socially and spiritually by engaging her in a bigamous marriage. Jane escapes during the night, only to land at the doorstep of yet another unyielding man with whom she has to contend, the Reverend St John Rivers. While Mr Rochester tempted Jane with promises of initiation into erotic delights, St John Rivers entices her with an eroticism based on self-denial in the name of missionary work enacted for the glory of God. Succumbing to this latter appeal would also destroy Jane by requiring her to deny her needs for bodily and interpersonal intimacy. Jane again flees at the last moment. Ultimately her perseverance enables her to forge an identity, find a place in the world, and achieve happiness with the man she loves.

Summarizing the plot of *Jane Eyre*, one notices the similarities the novel shares with 'Bluebeard': an older man in search for a new companion, his hints of a secret plaguing his house, a wife incarcerated in a secret chamber of whose existence no one may know, the heroine's last-minute escape, to name a few of the most obvious. Charlotte Brontë supplies an explicit but subtle hint of the significance the 'Bluebeard' tale cycle plays in her novel soon after Jane has arrived at Thornfield. She visits the leads with Mrs Fairfax, lingering afterwards in a passage in the third story: 'narrow, low, and dim, with only one little window at the far end, and looking, with its two rows of small black doors all shut, like a corridor in some Bluebeard's castle' (JE 91). Today the close link between this novel and the tale cycle has become an established fact in Brontë studies. 'The echoes of "Bluebeard" in *Jane Eyre* are obvious,' states John Sutherland (69), while Patricia Ingham observes that 'it becomes apparent that Rochester is the Bluebeard-sultan with Jane as the Scheherazade of this story' (141). Stephen Benson (233) adds that *Jane Eyre* is a prime example of the fusion of Gothic romance and the fairy tale, in particular 'Bluebeard.' In spite of this consensus, this connection is seldom examined in detail. The notable exceptions are Sandra Gilbert's essay '*Jane Eyre* and the Secrets of Furious Lovemaking' and Maria Tatar's analysis in her *Secrets beyond the Door: The Story of Bluebeard and His Wives* (ch. 2). The link between these two narratives, however, may be indirectly discussed whenever *Jane Eyre* is placed in context of the Gothic genre, for, as Victoria Anderson says, there is 'no denying the close correlation between "Bluebeard" and the general trajectory of the Gothic novel' ('Investigating' 111).[2]

Anne Williams (ch. 2) argues that 'Bluebeard' condenses all the central generic conventions of the Gothic: a vulnerable and curious heroine; a wealthy, enigmatic, and usually older man; and a mysterious house concealing the violent, implicitly sexual secrets of this man. Like Bluebeard's mansion, Williams observes, the Gothic house always reflects its male owner. Not only does the chamber mirror his guilty secret, but also the layout of the house echoes his duplicity. The public spaces of his mansion proclaim his wealth and respectability, while the secret closet refers to the crimes he commits in private. Thanks to the sexual nature of his secrets, the heroine has to resolve what her relationship is to the other women who play or have played a role in the hero's life. It is the eerie setting of the hero's home that changes the other elements unmistakably into Gothic. As Michelle Massé points out, the Gothic heroine hopes that marriage to this man gives her voice (because she is listened to), movement (because she is an adult), and a house of her own (because she is now married). Contrary to her expectations, however, the fiancé's or husband's conduct and home only confuse and intimidate her. Like Bluebeard, he tempts her with the secret of a forbidden chamber. Defying his test of obedience instils in her a guilt-ridden anxiety, resulting in a paranoid uncertainty about the nature of reality. The general oppressiveness of her environs is enhanced by a dread of danger (Massé 20). In such instances we can justifiably speak of Bluebeard Gothic, a term I use throughout this study for such Gothic novels.

In her 'Introduction' to the Virago Modern Classics edition of *Jane Eyre*, Angela Carter characterizes this novel as being 'the most durable of melodramas, angry, sexy, a little crazy, a perennial bestseller – one of the oddest novels ever written, a delirious romance replete with elements of pure fairy tale, given its extraordinary edge by the sheer emotional intelligence of the writer, the exceptional sophistication of her heart' ('Introduction' v). Lucasta Miller (1) says that Charlotte Brontë has by now achieved the status she dreamed of: 'to be for ever known.'[3] The Brontë name, Miller (ix) goes on to observe, refers both to a collection of literary texts and to an actual literary industry. *Jane Eyre* and *Wuthering Heights* are not just literary classics but also modern myths. Cora Kaplan agrees, remarking that today *Jane Eyre* is part of the psychic vocabulary of individual and collective culture. That is to say, this novel is what Cora Kaplan calls a collective mnemonic symbol, the function of which is to enable readers to process private and public experiences. As a mnemonic symbol, she continues, '*Jane Eyre*'s narrative and its mode of telling memorialize no single event but a shifting constellation of stories, images and interpretations' (Kaplan 17; see also Schaff). Carter identifies elements of fairy tale as one factor accounting for *Jane Eyre*'s staying power, for classic fairy tales such as 'Beauty and the Beast,' 'Cinderella,' and 'Bluebeard' – each of which is included in *Jane Eyre* – have this same ability to stick with successive generations of readers. Fairy-tale scholar Jack Zipes (1) claims that these tales have become mythicized as natural stories, as second nature. They have this function, thanks to their abstraction from a specific context: their characters and settings exist nowhere and yet everywhere in terms of applicability and relevance.

It is nevertheless odd that the presence of 'Bluebeard' in *Jane Eyre* has received so little explicit and sustained critical attention. The purpose of this study is to change this situation by engaging in a detailed examination of *Jane Eyre* as a 'Bluebeard' story. I argue that *Jane Eyre* provides a major reading of this tale, one that has greatly influenced the work of subsequent female authors. How does interpreting *Jane Eyre* in light of 'Bluebeard' affect our understanding of Brontë's novel? We may word this question in another way: What is *Jane Eyre* like as an adaptive rewriting of the 'Bluebeard' tale? And vice versa: What does 'Bluebeard' look like when it is read in the context of *Jane Eyre*? In this study I read these two narratives in conjunction, examining the multiple ways in which they interact with each other. I show that the story of Jane Eyre becomes so intermingled with 'Bluebeard' as to be inseparable, an observation that also applies to the adaptations of *Jane Eyre* that I examine during the course of this book. My research is motivated by the cultural standing both narratives share. If, as scholars of *Jane Eyre* and of the fairy tale claim, both serve as cultural myths and mnemonic symbols, then they cannot help but address readers in powerful ways. Zipes maintains that narratives in such a position 'have become formative and definitive, and they insert themselves into our cognitive processes, enabling us to establish and distinguish patterns of behaviour and to reflect upon ethics, gender, morality, and power' (26). Given the continued relevance of narratives with staying power, he even claims that they are crucial for understanding social relations, for adapting to changing conditions, and for altering the sociocultural environment (127). I argue that, read as a 'Bluebeard' tale, *Jane Eyre* invites us to review questions of 'ethics, gender, morality, and power' in ways not formerly perceived either in the Brontë or 'Bluebeard' critical legacies. Reading these two narratives together thus promises to deepen our understanding of how exactly such questions are tackled when *Jane Eyre* is treated as a 'Bluebeard' tale. This endeavour means stepping into a contested interpretive arena, for 'Bluebeard' alone has received multiple interpretations. They range from an emphasis on the difficulties and dangers of intimate relationships (Tatar, *Secrets*), to a focus on the suppressed secret of patriarchy's ultimate impotence (Zipes), to a stress on mimetic doubling and rivalry provoked by phallotocracy (Lewis), to a concentration on the tale's self-reflexive narrative and intertextual strategies (Hermansson). Such interpretive richness characterizes *Jane Eyre* to an even greater degree, given the century and a half that it has invited critical scrutiny.

While literary and cultural critics have acknowledged, yet not really explored, *Jane Eyre* as a 'Bluebeard' tale, authors rewriting this novel have either intuitively or intentionally seized on this dimension. In other words, in adapting *Jane Eyre* they have simultaneously adapted the 'Bluebeard' tale. What this means is that their novels are revisitations of *Jane Eyre* as a 'Bluebeard' tale – which is, in itself, a clear indication of the intricate intermingling of these two narratives. Given the status of *Jane Eyre* as a mnemonic symbol, it is only to be expected that it has spawned numerous adaptations over time. The second purpose of this study is to examine these rewritings and their range. How have novelists interpreted the status and meaning of 'Bluebeard' in Brontë's novel? What clusters of meanings in these two texts have caught their attention? To what creative purposes have they put these narratives in their own adaptations of *Jane Eyre*? Besides a focus on *Jane Eyre* as a 'Bluebeard' tale, this study thus also examines the afterlife of Brontë's novel as a means of probing its literary and cultural significance. The adaptations tell us more about the kind of mnemonic symbol the novel has become over the decades than if we discussed solely the novel and its scholarly history. As we shall see, however, frequently the adaptations have been influenced by the tenets of various theoretical and intellectual movements such as feminism, poststructuralism, postcolonialism, and postmodernism (Schaff 26).

Stories of forbidden knowledge gained at great cost have circulated orally from time immemorial, as the biblical story of the Fall and the myths of Pandora and Psyche illustrate.[4] The first known written version of 'Bluebeard' is by Charles Perrault in his collection of fairy

tales, *Histoires ou contes du temps passé*, published in 1697. It was translated into English in 1729 by Robert Samber. This collection and *The
Arabian Nights* were well known all over Britain and much beloved
reading material of the Brontë family (Anderson; Ingham; Sutherland).
Charlotte Brontë published *Jane Eyre* in 1847 under the pseudonym of
Currer Bell. By that time the tale had already found its way into English
literature; for example, W.M. Thackeray used it as an intertext in such
stories as 'Bluebeard's Ghost' (1843), *The Memoirs of Barry Lyndon, Esq.,
of the Kingdom of Ireland* (1844), 'Barbazure' (1847), and 'Bluebeard at
Breakfast' (an unpublished manuscript, 1971). In fact, Charlotte Brontë
dedicated the second edition of *Jane Eyre* to Thackeray, whose literary
input includes a sustained interest in 'Bluebeard.'[5] It is also significant
that Jane Austen's parodic *Northanger Abbey* (1818) established an intimate link between this tale and the Gothic, a link that Brontë takes
advantage of specifically in the Thornfield section of her novel. While
this tale has a rich and varied history in British, American, and Cana-
dian literatures with such authors as Peter Ackroyd, Margaret Atwood,
Donald Barthelme, John Fowles, Henry James, L.M. Montgomery, Kurt
Vonnegut, John Updike, and Sylvia Townsend Warner writing versions
of 'Bluebeard,' I am only interested in works that draw on *both* this tale
and *Jane Eyre*. Thus I stay within the anglophone literary tradition that
echoes *Jane Eyre* as Bluebeard Gothic; the Continental tradition does not
include this connection, as, for example, Béla Bartók's opera *Duke Bluebeard's Castle* (1911) and Anatole France's 'Seven Wives of Bluebeard'
(1909) demonstrate. The narratives that I study are predominantly
adaptations in Linda Hutcheon's (3) sense; that is, they have an overt
and defining relationship to these nameable, prior texts. Adaptations
are blatantly intertextual, or, in Hutcheon's term, '"palimpsestuous"
works, haunted at all times by their adapted texts' (6). She explains
that adaptations have three dimensions: as products, they are acknowledged transpositions of recognizable other works; as processes, they
are interpretive and creative acts of either appropriation or salvaging;
finally, seen from the perspective of reception, knowledgeable readers
experience them as palimpsests through which their memory of these
other works resonates (8).

Although all the rewritings that I discuss may be read as autonomous works, in this study they are placed in the context of *Jane Eyre*, the
'Bluebeard' tale, and the generic conventions of the Gothic. It needs to
be emphasized that the term intertext is not used in terms of valorizing
priority. To be sure, many variants of 'Bluebeard' were in circulation

at the time Brontë wrote *Jane Eyre*; similarly, this novel is the historical predecessor of the adaptations. Yet, as Hutcheon emphasizes, 'to be second is not to be secondary or inferior; likewise, to be first is not to be originary or authoritative' (xiii). In reworking *Jane Eyre*, adapters have been motivated by a variety of purposes: imitation, homage, critical revision, contestation, and even the wish to destroy the adapted text altogether. Neither *Jane Eyre* nor 'Bluebeard' is used here as a yardstick for what novelists should have done; instead, I am interested in what they have picked from these narratives and what they have done with the materials they have chosen. To borrow Maria Tatar's fitting formulation, my goal is to study how *Jane Eyre* as Bluebeard Gothic 'has changed, created new versions of itself, and joined up with other stories to become yet other stories' (*Secrets* 7). As we shall see, *Jane Eyre* has become so intertwined with 'Bluebeard' as to form a master trope dominating subsequent adaptations. Thus it is often impossible to untangle these intertexts from each other. In some cases, however, an author may emphasize one intertext more than others, an emphasis that affects my discussion of a given text. Yet the master trope of *Jane Eyre* as Bluebeard Gothic runs through this book, forming the red thread of its discourse. Whenever Brontë and the other authors studied in this book refer to a particular variant of this cycle, I identify it, but otherwise I simply allude to 'Bluebeard' as a shorthand expression of the whole tale cycle.[6]

The textual identity of *Jane Eyre* is a relatively straightforward matter: its first edition purported to be the autobiography of Jane Eyre, edited by Currer Bell, while the subsequent editions deleted the mention 'edited by' to make the work look more directly that of Currer Bell. Later on, Charlotte Brontë herself conceded that she was the author behind the male pseudonym. Today, this pseudonym is read as a reference to the difficulties female authors faced during the nineteenth century when trying to get their work published.[7] I use the third edition of the novel, published in 1848, which is the text of the third edition of the Norton Critical Edition series (edited by Richard J. Dunn). As regards 'Bluebeard,' I cite the versions Maria Tatar appends to her *Secrets beyond the Door*, because of their representative nature and easy accessibility. Besides *Jane Eyre*, a specific corpus of short stories and novels provides the material for this study. It consists of the following texts that I group here thematically in order to provide a preliminary road map of the book's organization: after discussing *Jane Eyre* as a 'Bluebeard' narrative, I examine a group of narratives focusing on aspects of trauma in their joint intertexts of 'Bluebeard' and *Jane Eyre*: Anna Leonowens's

*The Romance of the Harem* (1872), Jean Rhys's *Wide Sargasso Sea* (1966), and Emma Tennant's *Adèle: The Hidden Story of Jane Eyre* (2002). I then consider novels that emphasize love and romance in these intertexts, namely, Sally Beauman's *Rebecca's Tale* (2001), Daphne du Maurier's *Rebecca* (1938), Diane Setterfield's *The Thirteenth Tale* (2006), and D.M. Thomas's *Charlotte* (2000). Looking at Sarah Waters's *Fingersmith* (2002) and Jeanette Winterson's *Oranges Are Not the Only Fruit* (1985) enables me to treat novels that underline the conjunction of religion, sacrifice, and scapegoating in each intertext. Finally, Angela Carter's numerous 'Bluebeard' stories such as *The Magic Toyshop* (1967), *Heroes and Villains* (1969), 'The Bloody Chamber' (1979), *Nights at the Circus* (1984), and 'The Fall River Axe Murders' (1985) provide a corpus in the light of which it is possible to zoom in on meta-intertextual themes that Carter picks from the two intertexts of this study.

All these chosen texts are, each in a different manner, spin-offs of *Jane Eyre* as a Gothic 'Bluebeard' tale. What is more, the historically later texts are spin-offs of the earlier spin-offs. Julie Sanders observes that what she terms 'filtration effect' is typical of adaptations: they tend to adapt other adaptations, thus forming complex intertextual webs (13, 24, 62). Admittedly, this book's emphasis lies on contemporary renditions, but its corpus nevertheless covers the whole time span from the publication of *Jane Eyre* up to the present day. That many of these texts are (semi)autobiographical strengthens the connection between character and writer in these novels. These close intertextual links give the corpus a focused yet varied consistency, enabling a detailed discussion of the ways in which *Jane Eyre* as a Gothic Bluebeard tale has been adapted in British literature over the years. Unlike Hutcheon, who studies adaptations across the media, I stay solely within narrative fiction.[8]

What lends further consistency to the chosen corpus is its Britishness. Like other literary classics, *Jane Eyre* has trotted the globe, leaving non-English adaptations in its wake. This same observation applies in an even greater degree to 'Bluebeard,' as it has numerous indigenous versions worldwide.[9] Although authors and readers all over the world have responded to both these narratives in ways ranging from affection to scorn, *Jane Eyre* undoubtedly belongs squarely to Britain's national heritage. The selection of my corpus reflects this fact. I have stayed with either British authors or with authors who have close ties with the country (Anna Leonowens) or who have made it their home (Jean Rhys). If *Jane Eyre* serves as a cultural myth and mnemonic symbol, it does so first and foremost on its home turf. Thus, instead of tracking its global itinerary, I have chosen to examine the ways in which it has invited, for example, emulation, critique, and ridicule at home. One might say that the novel serves as a test bed for analysing the range of meanings a literary classic has invited from authors within one cultural context. Such meanings have frequently been absorbed from adaptations written elsewhere. Staying within one cultural context elucidates the role repetition on one hand and variation on the other play in adapting a national classic. Simultaneously this focus throws light on the process whereby folkloric themes are read through high culture, forming ultimately a new dominant master trope that, over the decades, also leaves a lasting influence on popular literature.

Carter observes that 'the archaic subliterary forms of romance and fairy tale are so close to dreaming they lend themselves readily to psychoanalytical interpretation ... *Jane Eyre* is a peculiarly unsettling blend of penetrating psychological realism, of violent and intuitive feminism, of a surprisingly firm sociological grasp, and of the utterly non-realistic apparatus of psycho-sexual fantasy' ('Introduction' vi). Tatar ('Bluebeard' 20) adds that 'Bluebeard' reveals how psychoanalysis serves as an analytic investigative move that uncovers and elucidates spaces containing forbidden impulses. Williams concurs, remarking that psychoanalysis is useful for critics of the Gothic, since the genre is so close to (psychic) fantasy. Psychoanalysis provides the model of interpretation in this study with whose help I examine *Jane Eyre* and its adaptations as Bluebeard Gothic. This approach discloses narrative and thematic structures that unite the chosen corpus, motivating their study in relation to one another. Simultaneously I am responding to Williams's wish that psychoanalysis be used for purposes of close textual analysis, instead of social diagnosis in historical contexts (136–8).

The notion of psychic fantasy plays a major role in this study. In particular, I refer to the primary fantasies that Sigmund Freud identified as shaping the subject's identity formation: castration, seduction, and family-romance fantasies. Briefly put, the castration fantasy grounds sexual differentiation; the seduction fantasy assigns the father a special place in the origin of (sexual) desire; and the family-romance fantasy concerns the subject's understanding of her or his own origin. In each case, the given fantasy refers to an imaginary scene in which the fantasizing subject acts as protagonist. The fantasy represents the fulfilment of an unconscious wish in a manner distorted by defensive processes such as negation, projection, or reversal into the opposite. What makes psychic fantasies a useful tool for literary analysis is the fact that they are *narrative* scripts in which the fantasizing subject has a role or roles to play; these roles and their attributes are open to permutations. It is the task of analysis to explicate these variations. Furthermore, the usefulness of these fantasies as an analytic tool is enhanced by their applicability to examining intrapsychic and interpsychic phenomena within fictional worlds as well as to analysing narrators and narration. Both levels figure strongly in my analyses, and I typically relate phenomena at fictional worlds to phenomena at the narrative level. In examining narration, narrative structures, and a given adapter's relationship to the literary legacy, whenever necessary I supplement psychoanalysis with narratology.

Employing Julie Sanders's (47) formulation, the corpus of this book illustrates the ways in which *Jane Eyre* has invited 'collaboration across time.' The chosen texts stay within *Jane Eyre*'s indigenous culture, a choice that amounts to keeping within a family circle. This family metaphor is intended, thanks to the aim of studying the adaptations that *Jane Eyre* as Bluebeard Gothic has prompted in Britain. This corpus enables the treatment of this novel from the perspective of a familial dynamic, and it evinces the kind of intimacy, in both good and bad, typical of families, including cross-generational relationships. Within the British literary canon the novel enjoys the status of a revered great grandmother, inviting such reactions as imitation, emulation, rivalry, and even matricide. What is more, the psychoanalytic approach of this study suggests that authors may be guided by various psychic fantasies in their relationship to the intertexts they adapt.

Specifying the main approach of this study as psychoanalytic elucidates further its focus on the literary legacy of *Jane Eyre* as Bluebeard Gothic. Given the novel's status as a national mnemonic symbol, scholars have related it to its ideological, social-historical, and cultural contexts. My interests in this book lie elsewhere, for I am primarily intrigued by what might be called the *Brontë effect* of the *Jane Eyre* legacy. This expression refers to Shoshana Felman's analysis of the Poe-etic effect that Edgar Allan Poe's short story 'The Purloined Letter' (1844) has had on literary criticism. Felman states that the critical discourse about Poe is one of the most visible effects of his short story, in particular, of its poetic signifier. She suggests that the peculiar effect of Poe be dealt with (psycho)analytically by 'locating what seems to be unreadable or incomprehensible in this effect; by situating the most prominent discrepancies or discontinuities in the overall critical discourse concerning Poe ... and by trying to interpret those contradictions as symptomatic of the unsettling specificity of the Poe-etic effect, as well as of the contingence of such an effect on the unconscious' (50). While I draw on critical studies of *Jane Eyre*, I am mostly interested in the Brontë effect that this novel has had on the adaptations it has spawned, because I claim that they provide the first-hand critical reception where the workings of this effect are best evident. In anticipation, adaptors tend to seize on what they think are the blind spots, contradictions, and discrepancies in *Jane Eyre*, thus demonstrating the effects it has on them and on their culture. We may in advance wager that these effects are precisely what have turned *Jane Eyre* into a mnemonic symbol not only in Britain but also worldwide.

In analysing *Jane Eyre*, I suggest that Jane's narration consists of a discursive layering in which what Lacanian psychoanalysis calls the symbolic, hysteric, and analytic registers play off against each other ('Seminars' XVII and XX). Without yet defining these terms, it suffices to observe here that each register provides a different understanding of the events depicted and their significance. It is as if these registers were differently cut windows onto the fictional world whose particular prism moulds the narrator's comprehension. Consequently, Jane's autobiography is internally discordant, which not only explains the existence of lacunae and silences within it but also largely accounts for the particular shapes the Brontë effect has taken over the decades. Another factor contributing to such internal dissonance is the presence of the 'Bluebeard' tale, for, as I show, the novel and its fairy-tale intertext do not fit each other seamlessly.

As regards the adaptations *Jane Eyre* has invited, one of the guiding ideas in this book is that authors rewriting this novel have paid attention to different discursive registers, which explains the divergences among the adaptations. An adaptation emphasizing the symbolic register in *Jane Eyre* shows a different stance to the adapted text than, for example, one seizing on the discourse of the hysteric in the same book. Thus Tennant's *Adèle*, for instance, positions itself in another way than du Maurier's *Rebecca* does vis-à-vis their shared intertext. It needs to be mentioned here, however, that what is at issue is emphasis: a narrative stressing the symbolic register also makes use of the other two discourses, but their import is less noticeable.

Saying that this study concerns *Jane Eyre* and its adaptations as 'Bluebeard' Gothic does not yet clarify what features in this process of adaptation are examined. In organizing my discussion, I take my cue from the thematic structures of Bluebeard Gothic. The notion of thematic structures refers to an amalgamation of form and meaning; that is, to the ways in which narrative structures highlight meaning clusters as pertinent for understanding. These structures include the plot and the motifs which it comprises; the so-called narrative situation consisting of the narrator's position vis-à-vis the story she narrates; the narrator's visibility and reliability; and the narrator's relationship to the narratee. The notion of thematic structures implies relative stability across tale variants; that is, certain issues are typically dealt with in Bluebeard Gothic. I next clarify the thematic structures that I probe in this study.

Bluebeard and his house mirror each other; thanks to this intimate connection, his domestic architecture echoes his psyche, including his plans, goals, and needs. He makes certain that any woman in the house comes in conflict with his law. A central presupposition of this law is female curiosity. Although he forbids her to probe his secrets by entering one specific room, he actually *wants* her to disobey him. In reading *Jane Eyre* as a 'Bluebeard' tale, however, Tatar emphasizes Jane's unwillingness to explore Rochester's secrets: 'Rochester's secret may be out in the open, but it is none of Jane's doing' (*Secrets* 73). Contrary to Tatar's claim, Jane actually causes the revelation of this secret by writing Uncle Eyre about her approaching wedding.[10] I show that Jane in fact actively probes Bluebeard's secrets, but her explorations take another form than the concrete opening of doors. Her quest for knowledge relies on relating material spaces to mental states, a strategy that derives from her worst fear, the dread of being enclosed. Her experience of imprisonment in the red room at Gateshead makes her act out her anguish, even against her will, whenever she feels threatened with physical or psychic incarceration.

Transforming psychic suffering into various bodily symptoms is the hallmark of hysteria. In chapter 1 I show how Jane's curiosity emerges through a hysteric dynamic, one that propels her to read spaces as a means of probing interpersonal relationships in order to discover Bluebeard's secret. I thus treat the spaces of *Jane Eyre* as analogues of the human body and psychic structures. This means examining the exchange between spatial and bodily topography, which I at every point relate to the mind's topology. This approach enables me to analyse the manifold links between space and psyche that 'Bluebeard' prioritizes in order to show how these links are made to play a specific role in *Jane Eyre*. Their function is to explain the genealogy of Bluebeard's chamber on one hand and, on the other, Jane's suitability for probing its secrets.

The conclusion of Jane's narrative shows that she has found sufficiently satisfactory answers to the questions troubling her. Yet she nevertheless feels compelled to tell her story. Elisabeth Bronfen observes that Gothic heroines often discover that they find the ideal family bond only by narrating and writing it (152). Also 'Bluebeard' places a premium on narration, as the heroine discovers that narrating her frightening experience enables her to escape from Bluebeard. Therefore, I consider how the psychic dynamic that guides Jane's actions in the fictional world carries over to her narration. Exploring the connections obtaining between physical and psychic space and narration in *Jane Eyre* illustrates how this novel expands and elaborates on a central structural thematic of the 'Bluebeard' tale cycle.

Jane is one among Bluebeard's women whose threshold experience depicts a moment of grisly revelation when she sees the murdered women and understands Bluebeard's true nature, a realization that spells out her own impending fate. Yet thanks to the overwhelming nature of her discovery, she is not able to integrate this traumatic event in its entirety into consciousness. Therefore, it is not fully experienced as it occurs. Both Jane and the tale's heroine assume the role of witness to female anguish. That both women address their testimonies to another – 'dear reader' or wedding guests – indicates that witnessing requires a recipient. The process during which a traumatized person narrates harrowing events is called witnessing or giving testimony. Because the events defy the victim's cognitive and emotional capacities, narration often falters.

While I do consider the nature of Jane's testimony in chapter 2, the main focus nevertheless shifts to *Jane Eyre*'s progeny. Can we say that the adapters of the novel have served as witnesses to Jane's narrative of trauma? I explore this possibility, paying attention to what these authors as co-witnesses hear in Brontë's narrative and how they conceive their role. I am interested in examining how adapters as witnesses not only talk *with* but also talk *back* to their literary heritage. In this capacity they may tell their readers another kind of story, one that includes identifying the adapted narrative itself as somehow traumatic for later generations. In such instances as these we are dealing with cultural trauma involving the adapted narrative under scrutiny as a symptom of cultural haunting. Such criticism is, of course, typical of postcolonial and trauma fiction, for in both genres authors let formerly silenced, ridiculed, or maimed characters to tell their own stories. The books that I discuss in this chapter have been chosen with the view of demonstrating the range of issues testimony raises and the modes of reception that authors have assumed in serving as co-witnesses to Brontë and her narrator Jane. They are Leonowens's *The Romance of the Harem*, Rhys's *Wide Sargasso Sea*, and Tennant's *Adèle: Jane Eyre's Hidden Story*; as I subsequently show, these books illustrate a continuum extending from treating trauma as an insurmountable psychic wound to a confident reassurance of the powers of working through.

Carter wryly observes that 'of all the great novels of the world, *Jane Eyre* veers the closest towards trash' ('Introduction' vi). One reason for the continued success of *Jane Eyre* is the passionate love story between Jane and Rochester. Gilbert (357) playfully observes that the novel is condensable to the tabloid heading of 'Cinderella meets Bluebeard!' Bluebeard Gothic includes two possible outcomes: either the master of the house is shown to be the evil source of the heroine's ordeal and is defeated by a poor-but-honest young man, who marries the woman; or the master of the house is cleared from suspicions of evil and he marries the woman (Massé 10). *Jane Eyre* departs from both standard conclusions, for Rochester is the source of Jane's suffering, yet she nevertheless marries him. Thanks to Rochester's repentance, Jane espouses, as it were, a 'new' man, with whom she is on equal footing. In many later spin-offs, however, mushy love eclipses *Jane Eyre's* spotlight on gender issues. They eroticize *Jane Eyre's* 'Bluebeard' dimensions: Bluebeard's sexually threatening cruelty turns out to mask a vulnerable, yet potent masculinity, one that a woman's patient love revives. Romance camouflages the fact that Bluebeard Gothic is entangled in perversity, understood in the sense of gaining sexual gratification with atypical means. The best proof is Bluebeard himself, who substitutes sex with murder.

Instead of looking at conventional romances that adapt *Jane Eyre* (in the vein of, say, Victoria Holt), I discuss a tradition among *Jane Eyre* spin-offs that has received less critical attention, one that has gained strength the closer we come to the present day. In chapter 3 I examine Bluebeard Gothics that fuse romance with various forms of perversity such as masochism, incest, and pedophilia. I start by analysing du Maurier's *Rebecca* as an example of a love story that relies on a masochistic fantasy. Sally Beauman resuscitates Bluebeard's first wife in her *Rebecca's Tale* by providing a prequel to *Rebecca*. She does so in order to review what counts as perverse in Bluebeard Gothic. My analysis targets Beauman's corrective handling of the elements that are identified as perverse. I also discuss Diane Setterfield's *The Thirteenth Tale*, which focuses on Bluebeard Gothic's perverting influence on narration, authoring, and reading. I conclude with D.M. Thomas's wicked adaptation, *Charlotte*, with its implication that today the cultural meaning of Bluebeard Gothic has been stripped of all other dimensions than perversion.

Rochester acts like Bluebeard in incarcerating Bertha. He sees in her the origin and cause of all that has gone awry in his life. Acting Bluebeard's role, Rochester's mode of thinking adheres to what René Girard (*Scapegoat*) calls the persecutor's mentality. Persecutors blame their victims for the loss of supposedly crucial distinctions and the lack of founding differences. The chamber is Bluebeard's site of ritual sacrifice, sustaining the order of his world. Bluebeard holds woman responsible for both sickness and cure, for her death redeems her transgression by asserting her fundamental difference from him. Woman is thus transformed into a sacred scapegoat. This structural mechanism of sacrifice generates the sacred through violence. 'Bluebeard' and *Jane Eyre* evoke the sacred in terms familiar from Christian theology. The tale echoes the biblical story of the Fall in the Book of Genesis. Just as God threatens the first couple with death if they disobey Him, so Bluebeard warns his wife of death if she visits his forbidden chamber. God's gender-specific punishment of Eve reinstitutes the hierarchy against which she transgressed; that is, it realigns Adam under God's supremacy and Eve under Adam. 'Bluebeard,' however, subverts this outcome, because the woman flouts patriarchal authority, acquires knowledge in the face of terrifying adversity, and is even rewarded for it in material terms (Davies, *Tale* 39–41).The temptations Jane faces prompt her to reconsider her religious convictions. Her suitors Rochester and St John Rivers expect her to sacrifice herself in the name of God for the good of either one man or the whole of mankind. Their demands, however, fly in the face of what Jane holds to be godly. The religious thematic of Bluebeard Gothic suggests two diverging perspectives, associated with Bluebeard's (the persecutor's) and the woman's (the victim's) positions respectively. In chapter 4 I examine two novels that view the religious thematic of Bluebeard Gothic from different angles. Winterson's *Oranges Are Not the Only Fruit* places its scrutiny of *Jane Eyre* and 'Bluebeard' within a Christian context, while Waters's *Fingersmith* illustrates the mechanisms of sacrifice in this textual legacy. I argue that in adapting *Jane Eyre*, both authors revise its 'Bluebeard' elements in order to reconfigure widely spread cultural notions of religious faith, sexuality, and literary creation.

Analysing the narrative pattern of 'Bluebeard,' Hermansson shows that it deals self-reflexively with the writing and reading of plots. Bluebeard is a criminal-author, writing his stories of murder in his secret chamber, while his latest wife is a detective-reader, whose reading enables her to write her way out of Bluebeard's deadly plot. The enmity between Bluebeard and his wife consists of a series of entangled writing and reading contests that are embedded within the global plot of 'Bluebeard' (5–6, 38–9). Metafictionally speaking, one might say that the tale illustrates the strife between a master poet and his successor. In her essays on Charlotte and Emily Brontë ('Introduction' and 'Love') Carter lauds them for creating heroines whose capacity for passion is unusual. The Brontë sisters struggled to find linguistic and narrative expression for sexuality, gender, and the emotions where no precedent models existed. In spite of professed admiration, Carter nevertheless sees Charlotte Brontë also as a negative model. Carter thinks that the author was unable to sustain her passionate vision, thanks to *Jane Eyre*'s conventional closure. Ambiguity as regards literary precursors is typical, argues Harold Bloom, of strong authors in particular. Such authors are endowed with an extraordinary artistic vision and an ambition to wrest the tradition from the precursors. In the Brontë essays Carter places herself as their descendant, but one who strives to succeed where she holds that Charlotte Brontë in particular failed. It is Carter's commitment to passion, pushing her to stretch the expressive capacities of language and narrative that gives her this position. Significantly, Carter identifies 'Bluebeard's' influence on *Jane Eyre* ('Introduction' vi), a tale she herself wrote time and time again during the course of her career. Carter thus explicitly recognizes the influence Brontë's novel has enjoyed as a master trope in British literature. The strongest link between these two authors is this shared intertext of Bluebeard Gothic, a fact that enables us to situate Carter within this literary tradition.

Carter's recognition of Bluebeard Gothic à la Brontë as a master trope explains the approach I take in the last chapter when I analyse Carter's relationship to literary precursors in light of Harold Bloom's mythico-psychoanalytical theory of literary anxiety. How and with what means does Carter swerve away from the preceding tradition? To what extent does she creatively misrepresent and misunderstand it in order to superimpose her own versions on the tradition? In this context the question of influence includes Carter's relationship to literary fathers and mothers. I show how her critical handling of Bluebeard Gothic bids farewell to the tradition associated with Brontë in order to steer the 'Bluebeard' literary legacy into new directions. No other British author, I believe, explores these new avenues in as sustained a manner as Carter does, thanks to her continued interest in Bluebeard Gothic.

The eminent fairy-tale scholars Cristina Bacchilega (106), Maria Tatar (*Off* 110–12), and Marina Warner (243–4, 246) draw attention to the long-standing interpretive tradition within Western cultures according to which 'Bluebeard' targets girls and women. It serves as a tale of warning, cautioning female audiences against curiosity and its dangerous consequences. As a cautionary tale it receives support from the biblical myth of the Fall: sin entered the world thanks to Eve's curiosity. As a version of 'Bluebeard,' *Jane Eyre* may certainly be called feminist in that it emphatically rejects this interpretation. Brontë does not scapegoat Jane for her desire to probe Bluebeard's secrets. The chosen corpus shows that *Jane Eyre* and Bluebeard Gothic enjoy special popularity among women authors, and many of the adaptations examined in this book subscribe to some notion of feminism. Thus I also use feminist approaches in my study. Hermansson observes that the adaptability of 'Bluebeard' to feminist rewriting has as much to do with this tale's self-reflexive and meta-fictional narrative form as with its potentially subversive content. The figure of the writing heroine, reflected and doubled by the female author, is linked with the fairy-tale tradition of female narrators such as Scheherazade in *The Arabian Nights* (a version of 'Bluebeard') and old Marie in the Brothers Grimm. The frame narratives depicting these narrators, however, are not straightforwardly empowering for women. Tatar (*Hard*) and Warner show that in nineteenth-century fairy tales either a female family member reads aloud to children tales written by men or a paid nurse tells them her own stories of wicked women. This polarization to good and bad women's narratives domesticated a female storytelling tradition that male authors of the period saw as frightening, unreliable, and of low quality. Hence when women today use fairy-tale material, they are working in a gender-marked genre, which in its familiar manifestations often promotes masculine ideology. Yet, as Davies (*Tale* 30) points out, the powerful fantasy of the female narrator and her submerged tradition survives.

This book probes how female writers of *Jane Eyre* as Bluebeard Gothic tackle this polarized, ambivalent tradition. Its narrative structure of embedding has enabled these authors to express and deal with their sense of Gothic imprisonment within male legacies of writing. In reading and writing a way out of Bluebeard's castle, woman authors, like the surviving wife, counter male models of creativity. They have used this tale in order to analyse and criticize the constraints of these models as well as to explore alternatives to them, as we shall subsequently see.

# 1 *Jane Eyre* as a 'Bluebeard' Tale

'I lingered in the long passage to which this led, separating the front and back rooms of the third story – narrow, low and dim, with only one little window at the far end, and looking, with its two rows of small black doors all shut, like a corridor in some Bluebeard's castle' (JE 91). Thus describes Jane Eyre her first eerie impressions of Thornfield's third storey. When a little later 'a curious laugh – distinct, formal, mirthless' (JE 91) echoes through the space, her apprehensions are increased. In keeping with the tradition of Bluebeard Gothic, Jane's new home contains a well-guarded secret, and the plot shows her to be the one whom it concerns. In Thornfield as well as in all of Jane's other homes her movements are restricted. There are places forbidden to her, and she is invariably shoved to the bystander's position. These restrictions affect Jane physically: her body absorbs impressions whose significance she must not probe openly. Jane's body, however, speaks for and in spite of her articulating her desires through dreams, melancholy, fits of anxious excitation, and absences of consciousness. During such moments, explains Paul Verhaeghe (18), 'something rises up, is refused access, and gets itself inscribed, together with the refusal, elsewhere on the body.' Jane's fits lead to uncontrollable bodily reactions during which desire bypasses censure. She observes, for example, that 'it seemed as if my tongue pronounced words without my will consenting to their utterance: something spoke out of me over which I had no control' (JE 22).[1] In these moments she does not know herself and yet is intimate with her desire. These fits arise from Jane's vulnerability, against which she cannot shield herself.

Transforming psychic anguish into somatic symptoms is the hallmark of hysteria. *Jane Eyre* pits a hysterical heroine against Bluebeard.

Such an encounter is typical of Bluebeard Gothic, whose heroine Elisabeth Bronfen (155) characterizes as a hysterical fantasizer par excellence. This heroine's fantasies concern problems of origin. Following Bronfen's wording, the hysteric probes three interconnected questions through her symptoms: Who am I in relation to my family heritage? What is the origin of my body's vulnerable and mutable anatomy? What is the cause of my drives, desires, and fantasies? (148). With the help of these questions the hysteric, observes Verhaeghe (64–5), commits herself to a quest for knowledge. I argue that Jane actively probes Bluebeard's secrets, but, given what might be called her hysterical dynamics, her explorations take another form than the concrete opening of doors. Her quest for knowledge relies on relating material spaces to mental states.

The intimate link between physical and mental space in the topography of Bluebeard Gothic motivates my choice of psychoanalytic theories of hysteria as the context for analysing *Jane Eyre* as Bluebeard Gothic. Bluebeard's mansion, Anne Williams (43) points out, always reflects the man himself. Not only does the chamber mirror his guilty secret, but also the layout of the house echoes his duplicity. The public spaces of his mansion proclaim his wealth and respectability, while the secret closet refers to the crimes he commits in private. The house is thus the external stage on which Bluebeard projects his inner drama. The chosen psychoanalytic approach reflects the emphasis Bluebeard Gothic places on the motivation of events, actions, and characters, for, as Winfried Menninghaus observes, 'in the gothic novel everything is significant and everything is motivated, even if (often enough) only virtually so and in the form of "suspenseful" mystification' (112). In contrast, claims Menninghaus, the fairy tale as a genre ignores meaningful motivations; 'Bluebeard' is his prime example of this genre's thorough indifference to each and every explanatory framework. For example, the tale neither motivates Bluebeard's atrocious deeds nor explains the existence of the forbidden chamber in any way whatsoever (see ch. 4). Menninghaus's insightful argument forms one background against which I examine Brontë's efforts to explore how Bluebeard's chamber came to be erected in the first place. She favours a psychological account, for she portrays this space as reverberating with traumatic experiences that woman and Bluebeard have undergone in childhood and early adulthood. She traces the genealogical narrative of the chamber's existence from Bluebeard's perspective, showing that the woman is particularly well suited for his sinister purposes, thanks to her intimate familiarity with houses resembling Bluebeard's mansion. Brontë thus serves as a significant precursor to a markedly modern tradition that rationalizes Bluebeard's behaviour by suggesting that it may have realistic motivation. On the whole, this current began to gain ground in the late nineteenth and early twentieth centuries, and it coincided, observes Meredid Puw Davies, with the availability of the new idiom of psychoanalysis ('Bluebeard' 40–2; Nungesser 224).

Bronfen (156–7) elaborates the Gothic heroine's suitability for Bluebeard by explaining that an unconscious legacy inherited from her parents feeds her hysteria. Jane is the orphaned offspring of a marriage that her maternal grandparents disapproved. Jane knows nothing of her parents, and if they are mentioned at Gateshead, this is done disparagingly. With the death of Uncle Reed, Jane's maternal uncle, dies her hope of gaining knowledge of her immediate family. Her parents' love story, which would elucidate the story of her birth, becomes a secret buried with the Uncle. Like many a Gothic heroine, Jane grapples with a foreign body of inherited, buried knowledge that has passed from her foster parents' unconscious to hers. Thus when she hallucinates that Uncle Reed returns in the red room, it is not the dead who haunt her, but the gaps left in her psyche by the secrets of others. Her unconscious fantasies largely stem from other people's unconscious fantasies (see Bronfen 156–7). As this description suggests, Jane has within her psyche a crypt-like space comparable to Bluebeard's vault: it is a traumatic, forbidden region. It is this space that makes Jane responsive to the enigma of Bluebeard's chamber.

The symmetrical construction of *Jane Eyre* emphasizes, however, that the person who primarily is plagued by destructive unconscious fantasies is Bluebeard. Jane's traumatic red-room experience at Gateshead is paralleled by Rochester's similar experience. His red-room incident takes place after four years of marriage to Bertha Mason. Awakened one night by Bertha's shrieks, Rochester contemplates suicide. Again, spatial representation provides a key to psychic topography. Diagnosed insane, Bertha Rochester is locked away in the couple's house in Jamaica: by this time, she is the secret he encrypts in his psyche. His oppressively hot room, painted red by a bloody moon, corresponds with his self-destructive psychic impasse. Evidently Rochester and Jane experience the red room's horrors differently, but it nevertheless marks for both the trauma repeated in their later lives. This explicit stress on the protagonists' psychic similarity is striking in Brontë's handling of 'Bluebeard,' and it is this likeness that Thornfield's attic chamber puts into play.

The topography of Bluebeard Gothic directs attention to the ways in which the protagonists project their mental distress onto external stages. Such projection is part and parcel of what Karen Chase calls *Jane Eyre*'s interior design in which 'heaven, earth, houses, and minds, all are visualized in terms of regions, and this spatial analogy lets Brontë establish provocative connections among them' (64).[2] The forbidden chamber emanates eerily into the whole of Bluebeard's house, activating the heroine's hysterical symptoms. Consequently, all means of approach such as stairways, doorways, and windows turn into sinister spaces. Brontë lifts out such objects as mirrors, portraits, closets, and caskets – everything that may potentially reflect or contain the chamber's secret – as suspect. Often these objects are gendered (Chase 62).

In what follows I analyse the furnishings of rooms as providing the physical stage that provokes the acting out of traumatic experiences. Everyday pieces of furniture such as beds, chairs, and cupboards supply the stage props that enable the examination of how Jane and Rochester attempt to construct fantasies that shield them from trauma. In treating the spaces of Bluebeard Gothic as analogues of the human body and psychic structures, I examine the exchange between spatial and bodily topography, at every point related to the mind's topology. My focus lies on spatial relations of meaning as they address psychic fantasies. I first examine the link between physical and mental space that emerges from the respective red-room scenes of trauma of Jane and Rochester. I then analyse the Thornfield episode that is explicitly shaped by the 'Bluebeard' tale. I begin by looking at the key Rochester hands over to Jane and at Jane's employment of it, and move on to explore how the concrete props at Thornfield furnish the stage on which both play out their psychic fantasies. The disclosure of the attic's occupant leads to the culmination of such acting out. The ending of *Jane Eyre* departs from the endings of 'Bluebeard' and Bluebeard Gothic, for usually the persecuted woman either recuperates in the arms of a new, decent lover, or the initially sinister-seeming master of the house is exonerated, which enables her to marry him. Jane, however, marries the villainous Bluebeard, and I conclude my analysis of the fictional world of *Jane Eyre* by discussing Brontë's uses of psychological motivation and the fairy-tale tradition, specifically fairy tales ending in marriage, as two explanatory frameworks for this ending.

Insightful as the analyses of *Jane Eyre* as a 'Bluebeard' narrative are, they do not consider how Brontë draws on this tale in Jane's first-person narration. Perhaps this oversight has to do with the fact that the tale cycle employs an impersonal narrator (one who is above the narrated story and does not appear in it as a character). Yet having Bluebeard's prospective victim narrate the tale is a remarkable change, one that needs closer examination. How do the psychic dramas enacted within the fictional world carry over to Jane's narration? What are the connections between psychic space, narration, and the physical text? Although the heroines of Bluebeard Gothic survive their encounters with the ogre, remnants of their brush with death persist whenever their stories are told. The narrators of these novels reopen this unsettling experience, inviting readers to relive it through imaginative identification with the heroine. Their narratives cannot contain the distressing impact of trauma. The result betrays a rhetorical tension between experience and its narrative and textual transposition. Narrating and textualizing trauma reveal what Bronfen calls an *omphalic rhetorical tension* involving a movement in two opposite directions: on one hand, the integration of the hysteric's experiences into the symbolic register, and, on the other hand, the dissolution of this register, thanks to the inevitable gaps remaining in the narrative (59). There is an additional reason for the existence of such gaps in *Jane Eyre* that is related to its 'Bluebeard' intertext. Menninghaus observes that the mere presence of this tale suffices to challenge narrative coherence. Bluebeard – and, in extension, the tale bearing his name – is someone who does not lend himself to full understanding and meaningful contextualization. As a monstrous anomaly, Bluebeard threatens the integrity of any interpretive scheme (Menninghaus 4, 8). Hermansson explains this unsettling effect by pointing out that 'the nature of the secret is textual, as is the nature of the breaches of confinement and the monstrous replication of the story once it has burst its textual enclosure' (101). By using the Lacanian notion of discursive registers as an aid, I explore how the narrative and discursive organization of Jane's autobiography affects our understanding of 'Bluebeard.'

I analyse Jane's retrospective narrative by paying attention to its motivation and its fluctuation between narrative coherence and any phantom texts revealing the inconsistencies of symbolic representation.[3] The balanced elegance of Jane's narration catches attention. It is replete with doublings, parallels, correspondences, and antitheses that together create a harmonious architectonic system. It is as if readers entered a textual space where all elements seamlessly interlock, reflect, or contrast with other elements. This narrative design seems insulated from disruptive tensions and lacunae. I first scrutinize Jane's efforts to master her narrative by conveying the sense to readers that it originates from her as a coherent subject. These narrative layers rely on the discursive means of the master's discourse. Second, I ponder the motivation of Jane's invocations to 'the reader,' arguing that this communication betrays her uncertainty about whether the past is definitively behind. Dialogue, embedded narratives, and reported speech retain signs of former difficulties with expression and verbalization, and often the narrator Jane draws attention to them by addressing readers. Finally, I examine the breakage points of Jane's narrative. What strikes the eye is its concrete layout: it is pockmarked with commas, semicolons, hyphens, and exclamation marks, suggesting the narrator's pauses, hesitations, and ellipses. Punctuation and pauses as textual indicators of rhythm highlight the textual side of Jane's narrative, which refers to writing as the medium of narration. By drawing on the so-called analyst's discourse I show how these textual markers enable Jane the narrator and readers to probe the unconscious foundation of Jane's 'Bluebeard' tale. In analysing the discursive layers of Jane's narration, I rely on the Lacanian discourse theory as elucidated by Verhaeghe.

### Scene of Trauma I: Jane in the Red Room

On a dreary afternoon Jane hides herself in a window recess, an enclosure that represents her situation at Gateshead Hall: the Reeds barely tolerate Jane; likewise, Jane wishes to be rid of them. John Reed gratuitously attacks her, and Jane retaliates, but Aunt Reed punishes solely Jane by imprisoning her in Uncle Reed's death chamber. In abusing the authority she wields, Aunt Reed is akin to Bluebeard. Brontë fleshes out the 'Bluebeard' tale by providing the kind of psychological-hermeneutic motivation for its two protagonists that Menninghaus claims this tale lacks. Given that the red-room incident provides an explanatory background for Jane's conduct with Rochester, I examine it at length. I analyse Jane's psychic distress by looking at this room's furnishing. Perrault's narrator in 'La Barbe Bleue' carefully lists Bluebeard's belongings such as beds, chairs, cabinets, and mirrors; I show that in *Jane Eyre* these pieces of furniture acquire a systematic meaning.[4]

Once locked in the red room, Jane sits on an ottoman, facing her uncle's deathbed, which is 'like a tabernacle in the centre' (JE 10). Near the head of the bed is a white easy chair, looking 'like a pale throne' (JE 11). To Jane's left is a wardrobe, in a secret drawer of which Aunt Reed keeps Uncle Reed's miniature. Gateshead Hall thus contains a

secret niche, which suggests similarity with Bluebeard's castle. To
Jane's right is a large mirror. Her gaze moves from the bed-cum-chair to
the mirror, which shows her a 'strange little figure' that looks like a 'real
spirit ... half fairy, half imp' (JE 11). The room's layout demonstrates
Jane's plight. It was while lying in the bed that the dying Uncle Reed re-
quired from his wife – most likely sitting in the armchair – a promise to
raise Jane as one of their own children. Aunt Reed obliges but later on
refuses to honour her promise. She indulges her children, especially her
son, while openly showing her dislike of Jane. Her defiance suggests
the disorder of family relationships at Gateshead as the reason for the
origin of Jane's red-room experience. Uncle Reed ought to represent the
symbolic dead father who ensures the integrity and justness not only of
the family structure but also of the symbolic order. Tellingly, Aunt Reed
has reduced his standing at the estate, for he is present only metonymically in the shunned death chamber and in the miniature hidden in the
wardrobe's secret drawer (JE 11). The miniature's placement implies
the impotence of the symbolic order. Normally, this order is flexible and
sturdy enough to endure inconsistencies of culture and sudden appearances of the traumatic (see Bronfen 162). The degraded patriarch demonstrates, however, that the symbolic father is not able to live up to his
name and mandate. The disorder at Gateshead stems from this suspension of the paternal function; the vacuum is filled by what Slavoj Žižek
(*Looking* 99, 103) calls the irrational maternal superego. Such a superego
is the reverse of the paternal function, for it is arbitrary, wicked, and
blocks 'normal' sexual development. Aunt Reed encourages cruelty in
her son, while disciplining Jane as a social failure, causing her 'fearful
pangs of mental suffering' (JE 16). Given that the resident of the 'tabernacle' lacks potency to steer his family, Brontë from the start associates
the 'Bluebeard' intertext with the weaknesses and pitfalls of patriarchy.
She thus places her finger on what Philip Lewis and Jack Zipes regard
as this tale's secret: the arbitrary nature of phallocratic power, the arbi-
trariness of which Bluebeard refuses to acknowledge. Furthermore, the
aunt's usurpation of the patriarch's place introduces the question subsequently plaguing Jane: ought she to identify with a man or a woman?

By suggesting the patriarch's impotence as the chamber's secret,
Brontë represents this space as a screen upon which both Bluebeard
and the woman may project their fantasies concerning sexual relationships. The narrator-Jane's choice of words ('tabernacle,' 'throne')
suggests that the red-room scene serves as the stage on which the child-
Jane projects questions of origin perplexing her. Children process such

questions in terms of so-called primary fantasies, and as they address the child's relationship to its own body as well as its place within the family structure, these fantasies are the child's first sexual theories. As the mirror implies, Jane needs answers to such questions in order to form a sense of self. Given the death of Jane's parents and father substitute, her task is particularly difficult. As there are no earthly parents willing to claim Jane, the only parentage she can envision is a supernatural, fairy-tale one.

In addressing the problems of origin, children gauge the sexual relationship from three different yet interconnected angles: castration, seduction, and family romance fantasies are the so-called primary fantasies. These fantasies provide explanations at the point where the symbolic order fails; that is, they supply signifiers for phenomena for which the child originally did not and could not have signifiers.[5] These explanations are built up with signifiers in the Imaginary, outside the realm of the Symbolic (Verhaeghe 162–3, 170–1). As a 'tabernacle,' the deathbed resembles the resting place of a holy patriarch, while the throne-like armchair implies a queen's seating. This characterization points to the child Jane's family-romance fantasy dominating her perception: Jane endows these pieces of furniture with a royal flourish. Indeed, in discussing this fantasy Freud remarks that children typically entertain the notion of being the offspring of exalted parents ('Family'). That these thrones are placed side by side implies a separate identity for each, as they belong to Man and Woman. Verhaeghe (171) explains that the hysteric interprets the family-romance fantasy as proof that an empathetic sexual connection exists between two differently sexualized subjects, each with his and her own sexual signifier. In the hysteric's fantasy, Man is a primal father who hands woman a separate discursive identity. If each has an independent signifiable identity, the hysteric reasons, these signifiers could be joined to one another seamlessly. This union would represent the longed-for return to the lost primary unity (Verhaeghe 142). Such a fantasy, however, is definitely not Bluebeard's, for the chamber's chief purpose is to proclaim his innate supremacy over woman. Bluebeard understands the phallic basis of the signifying system literally. He conflates the phallus with anatomy and metaphysics; only he has the physical body that God created as definitive proof of supremacy over woman and the natural world. Therefore, as Lewis (206) points out, 'Bluebeard' represents primary fantasies and the actual sexual relationships in terms of mimetic rivalry. Bluebeard seeks to retain his (supposed) superiority, while the woman wants to usurp it. As an elucidation of the genealogy of Bluebeard's chamber, the red room suggests that Jane's fascination with such a space arises from its promise of an essential equality: if man and woman had separate signifiers, then neither could be elevated above the other, and neither would have to submit to castration.

Jane thinks Aunt Reed's merciless behaviour an abuse of power and a miscarriage of justice. She intuitively clings to the ideal of the dead symbolic father who is fair, impartial, and disinterested. Insofar as the dead father signifies the law, he experiences no forbidden enjoyment (*jouissance*) in enunciating the law like Aunt Reed does. Looking at the deathbed and the armchair makes Jane remember the violated promise, which, in turn, provokes her to wish for Uncle Reed's return from the grave 'to punish the perjured and avenge the oppressed' (JE 13). Jane's wish that a revengeful dead father defend her represents what Bronfen (162) calls the *phantom romance*, a toxic, uncanny side effect of the family-romance fantasy. Although Jane identifies with Uncle Reed's vengeful spirit, she intuits that such vengeance is foreign to the notion of the symbolic father. She represses this desire and the enjoyment it entails: 'I wiped my tears and hushed my sobs, fearful lest any sign of violent grief might waken a preternatural voice to comfort me, or elicit from the gloom some haloed face, bending over me with strange pity' (JE 13). For the hysteric, Bronfen explains, this phantom romance and its paternal representative, Father-of-Enjoyment, thwart the heroine's successful invention of adequate parents, because this figure signifies impossible, lethal, and nauseous enjoyment. He is a materialization of trauma and an obscene, revengeful leftover of the father who has been sacrificed to become law (Bronfen 161). Jane's fantasy of Father-of-Enjoyment, who takes sadistic pleasure in the execution of justice, invests the father's privileged place, the bed, with forbidden enjoyment. Gateshead Hall represents a place where the patriarchal symbolic order has been replaced by its underside: the irrational maternal superego holding sway there can be coupled only with Father-of-Enjoyment.

Identification with the ghost's projected but forbidden vengefulness sets off in Jane a mechanism of repression and displacement that is typical of hysteria. Suppressing her grief, she displaces her desire into the bodily symptoms of hyperventilation: 'My heart beat thick, my head grew hot; a sound filled my ears, which I deemed the rushing of wings; something seemed near me; I was oppressed, suffocated: endurance broke down; I rushed to the door and shook the lock in desperate effort' (JE 14). Jane's bounding of the door is accompanied with a 'dreadful noise,' her frantic screaming. It represents an 'Ur-human' cry calling for response, uttered for someone to acknowledge her. Jane's screaming implies that her hysterical reaction arises from a psychic moment of loss, severance, and deprivation. Bronfen (8) calls this moment that of *denaveling*, the subject's belated and imperfect understanding of the cutting of the umbilical cord. The navel refers to the indeterminate impact of parturition involving a traumatic experience of fragility and vulnerability. It 'marks a moment of castration not only in the sense that it commemorates the loss of the mother but also in the sense that it marks our mortality, the vulnerability of our bodies, and thus radically protests against any phantasies of omnipotence and immortality' (Bronfen xiii).[6] Gleeful jubilation in vengeance combined with the forceful repression of this desire is also later on responsible for Jane's loss of consciousness. It is the repeated discovery of Father-of-Enjoyment's union with the irrational mother figure that prepares the ground for her death-like experiences of denaveling.

These experiences have an architectural representation. Jane associates the ottoman, on which the servants threaten to tie her, with utter social disgrace amounting to death. Aunt Reed's pitiless reaction provides the final confirmation of Jane's worst fears: there is no place whatsoever for her at Gateshead. Indeed, Bronfen (16–7) characterizes hysteria as death anxiety.[7] Sitting on the ottoman, Jane fantasizes about dying: 'what thought had I been but just conceiving of starving myself to death? That certainly was a crime: and was I fit to die? Or was the vault under the chancel of Gateshead Church an inviting bourne?' (JE 13). For Jane, the ottoman is a vault, a place of annihilation. The logical consequence of Jane's placement is 'a species of a fit' (JE 14), unconsciousness signalling the ego's dissolution and marking Jane's symbolic death. In Brontë's adaptation, Bluebeard annihilates a woman's psyche and soul instead of killing her physically. She becomes a revenant, a living-dead.

The direst consequence of the Aunt's Bluebeard-like punishment is that Jane has *no place from which to desire*. The red-room incident proves to her that hers is the place of death, a conviction confirmed by the fact that afterwards Aunt Reed shuts her out of the Reed family circle for good, and many of Gateshead's regions become forbidden for her (JE 22).[8] Survival, however, necessitates that Jane find herself a place in an earthly, human structure. Lacking a place in such a structure results in Jane's 'new way of talking,' characterized as 'venturesome and hardy' (JE 33). It surfaces in situations in which she 'misbehaves.' Desire bypasses censure, and either Jane is compelled to speak up ('*Speak* I must: I had been trodden on severely, and *must* turn,' JE 30) or something escapes her self-restraint ('it seemed as if my tongue pronounced words without my will consenting to their utterance: something spoke out of me over which I had no control,' JE, 22). She talks in this way whenever she finds herself once again in the red room, under unbearable anxiety, in the place of symbolic death. The red-room scene suggests not only that Jane's unresolved primary fantasies and her intimacy with death draw her to explore Bluebeard's vault but also that this experience invests her with the authority to speak and act beyond Bluebeard's intentions. Hysteria becomes a survival strategy that eventually enables her to choose life over death, as I subsequently show. But first we take a look at what happens to Brontë's Bluebeard in his red room.

### Scene of Trauma II: Rochester in the Red Room

Menninghaus (55) observes that fairy tales occasionally consider the reasons for their characters' deviant appearance and behaviour, but even then the explanations are pragmatic and not psychological-hermeneutic. Zipes (156) remarks that Bluebeard neither explains nor repents his actions; his wife does not expect him to do so. Bluebeard acts as he does because the terms of the plot decree such action. In contrast, Rochester's confession to Jane (ch. 27) after the interruption of the wedding ceremony includes a lengthy account of how and why he turned into a Bluebeard. His self-pitying account reflects a psychic trajectory gone awry since childhood.[9] Rochester, however, singles out one night at Jamaica as decisive. Awakened by Bertha's yells, Rochester gets up and opens a window. A red moon throws a 'bloody glance over a world quivering with the ferment of tempest' (JE 262). His ears are 'filled with the curses the maniac still shrieked out: wherein she momentarily mingled my name with such a tone of demon-hate, with such language!' (JE 262). Like Jane, the desperate Rochester entertains ideas of death and suicide. He takes two pistols from his trunk in order to shoot himself (JE 263). Although there are crucial differences between Rochester's and Jane's scenes of trauma, they have comparable props: a trunk (a cabinet), a bed, and a window. As at Gateshead, the trunk's contents refer to the symbolic father, and, again, he represents vulnerability and impotence: Rochester can turn the phallic pistols only against himself. Bertha's inherited degeneracy prevents him from dealing with her. Society does not hold Bertha accountable, thanks to her madness, which leaves self-punishment as Rochester's only way out.[10] As with Jane, the traumatic experience of vulnerability and helplessness, expressed in the death wish, threatens to flood him.

If the purpose of a boy's family-romance fantasy is to enable him eventually to adopt the father's place and role, then the ineffective pistols point to the failure of this fantasy in Rochester's case.[11] Bertha derides and abuses the male authority Rochester represents. He can exert power by incarcerating her, but he cannot get rid of her. This angry but impotent realization forms his traumatic kernel. His self-justifying account paints a picture of a husband who has fallen victim to his wife, thanks to a reversal of marital power. Bertha's placement in Thornfield's attic, instead of its cellar, reflects this reversal. Bertha holds this Bluebeard in thrall and hinders him from fully assuming the position of a gentleman and landed proprietor.[12] Rochester's self-pity shows him resorting to the strategy Zipes (180) holds typical of Bluebeard according to which male insecurities and vulnerabilities are blamed on women.

In handling 'Bluebeard,' Brontë focuses on the shortcomings of patriarchy. Although Rochester admits partial responsibility, he nevertheless holds his father accountable for his quandary. Stingy and ambitious, Rochester's father and elder brother, fully aware of the streak of madness in the Mason family, sell Rochester on the marriage market in order to avoid splitting the family estate (JE 260–1). Once Bertha's unsuitability as wife emerges, the father is just as desirous as Rochester to keep the marriage a secret (JE 263). The father refuses to honour such principles as acknowledging the truth and taking full responsibility for one's actions. Rochester follows his father's example by bypassing the law and by acting as if the strictures of the symbolic order did not apply to him. He believes he is justified in transgressing 'a mere human law' (JE 270): 'I had determined and was convinced that I could and ought [to marry again]' (JE 264). Because the (symbolic) father falls short of his name and mandate, Rochester replaces him by the obscene reversal, Father-of-Enjoyment. As at Gateshead, the bed emerges as the seat of this figure, a place of illicit enjoyment in defiance of and outside the symbolic father's law.

The family-romance fantasy is uppermost in Jane's case, while with Rochester the castration fantasy concerning sexual differentiation plays a central role. Both are shown to search for a(n assumed) re-experience of original unity, although under different terms. Father-of-Enjoyment, whom Rochester emulates, enables him to elude castration. In this context, castration would mean his acknowledgment of and submission to the purely symbolic nature of the phallus. Rochester, however, clings to the fantasy of Father-of-Enjoyment, because it enables him to entertain the notion that while all other men are submitted to the law of castration, this obscene father remains outside its reach: he is his own law. In order for patriarchy to function, it needs this concept of a primal father existing outside the system that applies to other men (Fink, *Lacanian* 109–11). Rochester's defiance of the symbolic order is expressed in the song he sings for Jane during their betrothal (JE 231–3). It illustrates his mutiny against the symbolic father's law: he refuses to give up enjoyment in the name of the Father – and his own father in no way exacts such a sacrifice of him. The song's last lines tout Rochester's defiance: 'My love has sworn, with sealing kiss, / With me to live – to die; I have at last my nameless bliss; As I love – loved am I!' (JE 232–3). The lines refer to a man's merger with woman outside language and the law, again signalling a denial of castration.

There are crucial differences in the material and psychic design of Rochester's red-room experience in comparison to Jane's: the room has no armchair, and the mirror is replaced by a window. With Jane, the chair is associated with the seduction fantasy handling the father's role in the origin of desire. This fantasy deals with the child's realization that it is not the mother's sole object of desire; the mother also desires the father. A way of processing this fact, the seduction fantasy encourages the child, too, to desire other objects beside the mother. The missing chair, however, indicates that in Rochester's case such desire is thwarted, because he actually has no object of desire. His marriage explains this situation. The paternal conspiracy between the Rochesters and the Masons places Rochester in a position in which *he* must play the object of desire, because marriage turns *him* into the object filling in the void in Bertha. He *is* Bertha's sanity, good blood, prestigious social standing, and social security (JE 261–2). To the subject's basic question 'What am I?' Rochester can only respond, 'I am that,' the something that Bertha lacks. Bruce Fink (*Clinical* 175–6) explains that this structure is typical of perversion. The pervert is barred from the position of a subject and pushed into the role of the object that fills in the void in the mOther. Fink (*Clinical* 174) emphasizes that this structure always results from the inadequacy of the paternal function.[13] Rochester's case stems directly from the actions of his and Bertha's father. Further, this structure explains the absence of a mirror: in perversion alienation from the mother has taken place, but not separation. Separation, in turn, grounds the self-reflexive capacity, the division between subject and object.

To be sure, at the fantasy level Rochester pursues obscene enjoyment, but perversion covers over anxiety relating to the law and separation. While Jane is plagued by the question of how she can please the Other, Rochester's question deals with *who will lay down the law*. Perversion is a strategy with respect to obscene enjoyment, observes Fink (*Clinical* 174, 181), as the pervert actually craves someone to set limits thereto. Because the father refuses to institute the law, the pervert attempts to make his partner pronounce it, or at least to show the place of the law so that the anxiety-relieving separation from the smothering m(O)ther can succeed. This situation explains – although it certainly does not justify – Rochester's callous treatment of Bertha. Brontë's Bluebeard does not recognize Bertha as a separate human being. Lewis (197) explains that Bluebeard initially separates his female victims, but only by recognizing them as the contents of his traumatic kernel. He then secrets them away by crushing their singular bodies into his own corporal mass, where they are reduced to undifferentiated, homogeneous components. The secret's preservation, however, depends on Bluebeard's ability to appear integrally normal. Indeed, in the eyes of his neighbours Rochester seems a paragon of social grace and polite culture who is made all the more marriageable by his wealth.

Menninghaus (61) maintains that psychologically the Bluebeard plot necessitates a reasoning according to which Bluebeard is always already a serial killer. In implying seriality and repetition, his action suggests the paradoxical figure of an originary repetition; that is, the tale withdraws the instance of Bluebeard's first, 'pure' killing. Brontë's exploration of the psychological-hermeneutic motivation behind Bluebeard's actions tallies partly with this notion, for she shows that there is no precise moment when Bluebeard's vault was erected. Brontë, however, links its gradual construction with the patriarchal system as the ultimate explanatory frame of reference. Rochester's life story illustrates that the malfunctioning of the symbolic system (the impotence of the dead symbolic father) breeds Bluebeards.

This lengthy account of the red-room incidents in both protagonists' lives elucidates Brontë's elaboration of 'Bluebeard' by providing the tale with psychological-hermeneutic motivation. The Thornfield episode demonstrates how Brontë emphasizes these incidents in their pasts as accounting for their responsiveness to each other. She makes this similarity the touchstone for two possible outcomes – either destruction or love – as we shall see.

## The Other Woman as Key to Bluebeard's Vault

Rochester and Jane meet for the first time by chance. She is sitting by the wayside when his horse falls down on ice. She offers the injured Rochester help; leaning on her shoulder he feels 'something new – a fresh sap and sense – [steal] into [his] frame' (JE 266–7). The meeting touches chords of yearning in both: disdainful of womankind, Rochester longs for a love that would reform him morally (JE 269), while Jane longs for 'real knowledge of life amidst its perils' (JE 72). She wants to participate in life fully and not to remain an onlooker. In retrospect, Rochester sees the hand of fate in this incident: 'I had ... no inward warning that the arbitress of my life – my genius for good or evil – waited there in humble guise' (JE 266). What he does not acknowledge is that he has actually set the terms of this meeting beforehand. He has forbidden Mrs Fairfax and the servants to say anything to the new governess about the mad woman in the attic, lest the governess turn down the job (JE 256). Everyone else at Thornfield knows about Bertha's existence – even if they do not know her identity – except for Jane (JE 140). In this novel, then, Bluebeard has indirectly issued his injunction to his next victim even before he has ever met her. In keeping with his orders, Jane has been told that the strange laughter and the mysterious voices she hears in the third storey issue from Grace Poole. Having laid down the groundwork, on his return home Rochester has already singled out the unknown governess as the person with whom he repeats his psychic drama.

From the very first meeting onward, Rochester displays an initiating and aggressive stance toward Jane. He insists on his right to be his grim self without much bother about civilities (JE 114). He tests Jane, for if she patiently bears his caprice, then she might be the woman he hopes to find. The burgeoning attraction between Jane and Rochester makes them spatialize each other's bodies: the body is an outer shell protecting an inner treasure. There is thus an analogy between Thornfield Hall with its secret navel and the lover's body with its inward treasure. This spatialized analogy is characteristic of Bluebeard Gothic in which the castle stands for Bluebeard himself. Jane, however, is uncertain about the nature of Thornfield's – and Rochester's – inner core. Scrutinizing Rochester's face she cannot say whether his body shields a terrible secret or a beneficial treasure. In a similar fashion as Bluebeard, Rochester feeds such doubts. On one hand, he explicitly forbids Jane the entry to his vault, for example, by cautioning her against probing his secrets: 'for God's sake don't desire a useless burden! Don't long for poison – don't turn a downright Eve on my hands!' (JE 223). On the other hand, he wants her to defy his injunction. Typically, Bluebeard supplies the woman with the actual means of disobedience. Instead of giving Jane a concrete set of keys, Rochester repeatedly points out Grace as the key to his mystery. Jane tries to turn this key in its lock, but to no avail, for Grace does not let herself be interviewed. Rochester, however, puts other similar keys to Jane's hands by detailing his amorous adventures to her. These confidences imply that his secret concerns women and femininity. For example, as a miniature version of Céline Varens, Adèle personifies Rochester's former mistress.[14] Rochester's identification of another woman as the key to his mystery is significant thanks to its consequences for Jane. Jane constantly tries to place herself in the role of this or that woman in order to find out what exactly it is that Rochester desires. Such a response, typical of hysteria, is called the triangulation of desire.

Bluebeard's crimes and guilt are indisputable, but, as Lewis argues, his wife also is guilty of transgression, thanks to breaking her promise of obedience. Bluebeard's secret scheme is matched with the wife's covert goal. She hankers not so much after his wealth as after his superior status, the sign of which is the chamber with its secret knowledge. This mutual rivalry over dominance turns husband and wife into each other's mimetic doubles. Both are autotelic, seeking their own satisfaction so as to integrate their worlds as extensions or images of themselves (Lewis 204, 206). While Rochester takes little pains to hide his self-serving interests, Jane's personal goals are more difficult to detect. She eagerly accepts Rochester's offer of a degree of equality, especially as it promises her knowledge about the wider world and, in particular, of sexual matters (JE 122, 125).[15] Her covert goal begins to emerge, for example, when she muses on Rochester's fine eyes, intriguing in 'a certain change in their depths sometimes' (JE 111–12). They serve as the gateway to the recesses of his soul, which Jane desires to divine:

> And as for the vague something ... that something which used to make me fear and shrink, as if I had been wandering amongst volcanic-looking hills, and had suddenly felt the ground quiver, and seen it gape; that something, I, at intervals beheld still, and with throbbing heart, but not with palsied nerves. Instead of wishing to shun, I longed only to dare – to divine it; and

I thought Miss Ingram happy, because one day she might look into the
abyss at her leisure, explore its secrets and analyse their nature. (JE 160)

Jane thinks that in Rochester she has found a master willing to share
the secrets of an erotic relationship.[16] Although the hysteric realizes
that the symbolic order has no separate signifier for woman, she cannot accept this situation. It is the unbearable lack of this signifier that
makes her search for an authoritative man, a master. Jane is engaged
in mimetic rivalry with Rochester as is the wife with Bluebeard. If
Jane were leisurely to examine Rochester's phallic power, she would
eventually crack the mystery of femininity. Thus she would learn to
know this secret signifier, which, in turn, would make her man's equal.
She further fantasizes that exploring the secrets of this power would
lead to a situation in which she could remedy the lack in the symbolic
order by becoming the missing signifier. The result would, of course, be
a complete, infallible, and invincible Other. The omnipotent nature of
this dream is enough to attest to its impossibility.

*Jane Eyre* juxtaposes Bluebeard's forbidden chamber, the traumatic
navel of both his abode and his body, with what Žižek (*Puppet* 59) calls
the lover's inner kernel. The navel is a concrete sign of an inner wound,
a mark of separation from the original unity with the mother. Lovers
typically fantasize that possessing the other's inner treasure would heal
one's traumatic wound. It is as if owning the other's treasure enabled
the lover to be born again, but this time without the painful parturition from the mother. In Rochester's phallic eyes Jane sees the master's promise to share unifying, complementing knowledge so that she
would not have to face the deficiency of the symbolic order (the missing signifier of Woman). Rochester, in turn, characterizes Jane's body
as a cage, a prison, and a clay-dwelling place (JE 271), housing a rich,
principled inner world. It is Jane's spirit of 'will and energy, and virtue
and purity' (JE 271) – her inner treasure – that draws him to her. He
plans, however, to use her as an instrument for his moral cure. Yet as
we know, his scheme of making Jane his wife is illegal; his means for
reformation defies the law. He fantasizes that Jane will institute the law
in such a way that he will never have to submit to castration. Mimetic
rivalry in Brontë's handling amounts to an attempt to snatch the love
object's coveted inner treasure and use it for one's own benefit. Paradoxically, observes Žižek (*Enjoy* 58; *Puppet* 59), this treasure becomes
the very thing that introduces violence into the relationship. A skewed

logic of destructive love accounts for this discord: 'Because I love you, I destroy you; or, rather, I destroy the treasure hidden in you.'

Tatar (*Secrets* 72–4) holds Jane as the epitome of the passive heroine, for, lacking curiosity, she never defies Rochester's strictures. The preceding examination shows, however, that although Jane would like to learn about the third storey, for her the real secret at Thornfield lies elsewhere. She is piqued by what it is that Rochester desires. His erratic behaviour keeps her wondering about the origin and aim of his desire. The mysterious something in Rochester, rather than the forbidden attic chamber, is the enigma Jane attempts to solve. Her frantic activity emerges best in her efforts to make the key – the figure of another woman – Rochester has handed over to her divulge his secret.

After Jane has saved Rochester from burning to death, she tries to question him about the attic's strange occupant. He leads her on to name Grace as this person (JE 128); then, next day, he leaves Thornfield, and everyone believes him to be engaged in wooing Blanche Ingram. Similarly, right after setting the test of obedience, Bluebeard embarks on a business trip. Jane is akin to Bluebeard's wife in that she tries to solve Thornfield's enigma during the master's absence. Given that Grace proves uncooperative, Mrs Fairfax's description of Blanche supplies Jane with a new avenue for her investigations. Jane imagines Blanche as an ideal love object for Rochester. In order to prepare herself for Blanche's arrival, Jane sentences herself to draw two pictures, one of herself 'disconnected, poor, and plain' (JE 137), and the other of Blanche, 'the loveliest face [she] can imagine' (JE 137). These paintings help her to reflect on her situation. In the red room Jane looked into the mirror in order to reassure herself of her existence; the pictures she paints serve also as mirrors enabling self-reflection. While painting her own portrait takes only an hour or two, painting Blanche's miniature takes almost a fortnight. Such concentration suggests identification: engrossed in her task, Jane puts herself in the model's place. This scenario shows Jane trying to fit the key into the lock. Painting the rival's portrait is Jane's means of trying to fathom Rochester's enigmatic sexual desire as well as the equally enigmatic object of his desire. While painting, Jane divides herself into two: she becomes Blanche as the assumed desired object and Rochester as the assumed desiring subject. This is the circuit of desire typical of hysteria: a woman desires through a man and as a man in order to find out about femininity. His supposed desire points the way for her desire (Fink, *Clinical* 124–5; Verhaeghe 61). Unlike the wife, however, in spite of her concerted efforts Jane is unable to crack Bluebeard's secret at this point.

Thornfield's architecture and furnishings play a major role in Jane's investigations. Its public settings serve as the stage for the awakening of love. Rochester first interviews Jane in the drawing room, where, recuperating from his fall, he reclines on a couch, while Jane sits in a(n arm)chair at his side (JE 102, 103). During subsequent meetings, too, he lounges in a master's comfortable chair and she in a chair close by (JE 111). This arrangement refers to the family-romance fantasy – father's bed complimented by mother's chair – whose fulfilment both desire. The evening meetings are chaperoned by Mrs Fairfax and Adèle, whose presence monitors burgeoning feelings.[17] Rochester's illicit designs on Jane emerge in the intimate spaces of bedrooms. The incident of Rochester's burning bed (JE 127–9) and the scene of the mutilated Richard Mason (JE 177–83) provide Jane with ample clues of Rochester's secret, thanks to her familiarity with the dynamics of these scenes.

When Jane saves Rochester from burning to death, the bed is again identified as the seat of obscene enjoyment. The bed literalizes Rochester's illicit desire, for he is already scheming a way to secure Jane. That he sleeps in his bed while flames lick him associates the scene with Freud's account of the dream of a burning child. In this context, the burning Rochester can be taken to plead unconsciously with the symbolic father. Žižek (*Enjoy* 125) translates the son's reprimand – 'Father, can't you see I'm burning?' – into a plea 'Father, can't you see that I'm enjoying?' The son appeals to the symbolic dead father to limit and regulate enjoyment, but as this does not happen, the obscene Father-of-Enjoyment reigns supreme. The scene dealing with the mutilated Richard Mason elaborates this set of connections. Situated in the antechamber of the forbidden room, it contains familiar props: a bed, an armchair, and a cabinet, whose front bears 'the heads of twelve apostles, each enclosed in its separate panel as in a frame; while above them at the top rose an ebon crucifix and a dying Christ' (JE 179). As at Gateshead, the wardrobe literalizes Jane's fear of the symbolic father's impotence, which precludes her from even imagining a satisfactory resolution to the family-romance fantasy.[18] At Thornfield the fate of this father figure is even worse, for the cabinet pictures him as a crucified Christ. Given this mutilation of the symbolic father, he can neither guarantee the consistency and coherence of the social fabric nor regulate sexual relationships.

In sum, Jane's researches always throw her back on the original key handed to her by Bluebeard – Grace Poole. Rochester intimates that there is a living woman with whom he shares the coveted secret about sexuality: Grace, who in her plainness and lowly position most resembles Jane. Jane cannot reconcile Grace's plain face and her angular body with the tragic laughter and the sound of strange movements issuing from the locked room. In her unsuccessful investigations Jane actually plays into Rochester's hand. He would make Jane the instrument and accomplice of his transgression, a goal that is typical of perversion (Dor 111, 143–5). Rochester's manipulation of Jane is evident when she tells him about Bertha's night-time visit before their wedding. The scene recalls the bride's confrontation of the groom in 'The Robber Bridegroom' tale: she uses her dream to refer to the truth, while he hotly denies her narrative. Rochester lets Jane understand that the secret is actually Grace's, but he shares it with Grace (JE 128, 178–9), encouraging Jane's estimation that Grace must be an enigma even to herself (JE 132–3).[19] Rochester constructs a structure with three positions: he is bonded to Grace, who (ostensibly) does not quite know all the ramifications of the secret, while he conditions Jane regarding its revelation. He makes Jane a witness to Grace's violent deeds, while emphasizing that uncovering her secret would be detrimental not only to Grace but also to him (JE 178–9, 243; see also Dor 143–5). Jane gets caught up in Rochester's game through his adroit insistence on the necessity and benefit of silence. Let us entertain for a moment the possibility that Rochester had succeeded in his planned bigamy. If he then let Jane in on the secret, as he promises, knowledge would put her in an impossible situation: she would either keep silent, feeling persistent guilt and remorse, or she would have to make the secret public, but feel just as guilty for having been an agent of the misfortune Rochester warned her about.[20] Like Bluebeard, Rochester aims at the secret's eventual uncovering, but he must ensure that it takes place under certain conditions: 'I wanted to have you safe before hazarding confidences' (JE 269). Preoccupied as he is with transgressing the law, Rochester arranges things in such a manner that Jane would bear the brunt not only for finding out about the secret but also for having to continue to keep it a secret. Instead of physically killing the curious wife, this Bluebeard would punish her by first making her privy to the secret and then by forever sealing her mouth about it.

The first proposal scene (ch. 23) would seem to put a stop to Jane's attempts to fathom Rochester's secrets. It repeats the couple's first encounter out-of-doors. There is a bench under the chestnut tree seating the king and queen of the family romance side by side on the same settee. The orchard suggests the existence of a natural bond between Rochester and Jane, based on equality of spirit. In actual fact, the proposal does nothing to expel the hysterical circuit of desire. Although Blanche no longer is a threat, there is now a new female figure with whom Jane must contend, namely 'Jane Rochester,' or 'young Mrs Rochester – Fairfax Rochester's girl-bride' (JE 220). This phantom figure appears disconcertedly similar to Blanche Ingram, bedecked as she would be with jewels and dressed in silk and satin. 'Mrs Rochester' would obliterate Jane, who is nothing like her. This figure makes the vexing problem of Bluebeard's previous women persist throughout the courtship.[21] The nature of his desire remains an enigma until the contents of the mystery chamber are revealed. There Jane encounters once again the seating on which she seems destined to sit until the end of her days: the ottoman, the place of death.

### In the Forbidden Chamber: Jane and Rochester Pay Symbolic Debts

Directly after Mason's mutilation, Jane is called back to Gateshead to visit the dying Aunt Reed (JE 235–8). Lying on her death bed, the reluctantly penitent aunt asks Jane to retrieve a letter from a drawer in her dressing case. It is from Jane's paternal uncle, John Eyre, saying that he wishes to adopt her. The aunt acknowledges having thwarted Jane's rise in the world, for she has lied to Uncle Eyre that Jane has died. By confessing, the aunt at last subjugates herself to the Father's law: finally the father figure is dug out of the drawer and put on display at Gateshead.[22] The letter proves to Jane that there actually is a father willing to own her, which kindles her faith in the symbolic order. When Rochester's possessiveness becomes overwhelming, she writes to this newly-found Uncle Eyre, hoping that he lives up to his word and makes her his legatee (JE 229). Her letter defies Rochester's plans of keeping their wedding as secret as possible, and by telling the Uncle about her marriage plans Jane causes the abortion of her wedding.[23] The church as a place of a higher law is a fitting stage for exposing Rochester as Bluebeard (JE 247–8). As in 'Bluebeard,' paternal relatives save both Jane and Bertha from being wronged.[24]

Brontë changes the 'Bluebeard' tale's order of presentation by bringing the chamber's occupant on stage before its door is opened (JE 241–3). Most important is Bertha's night-time visit to Jane's bedroom that re-enacts the red-room scene of trauma with its props of bed, chair, cabinet, and the mirror. Lying in bed, the place associated with the Father-of-Enjoyment, Jane is made to view her hysteric dynamic from the vantage point of the castration fantasy. Given that Bertha issues forth from the vault, the place of death, she occupies what was Jane's place in the red room (the ottoman). For the hysteric, the castration fantasy involves the notion of a master capable of supplying woman with a signifier of her own, one that complements and completes the father's signifier, the phallus. Thus when Bertha takes out Jane's wedding veil, a precious gift from Rochester, from the cupboard, the implication is that this veil might disclose this coveted sign. After trying the veil on, however, Bertha tears it in two and tramples on it. These actions demonstrate that the veil does not carry the specific sign for woman. To the contrary, it suggests that the symbolic system cannot furbish woman with such a sign. In the red room Jane fantasizes that Uncle Reed bends over her 'with strange pity' (JE 13). In fact, the only one ever to do so is Bertha, who with her cautionary charade warns Jane against Bluebeard by illustrating what marriage to him holds. Such a marriage begins with romance, which promises the bride a separate identity (Bertha's look in the mirror), but is followed by bitter disappointment (the tearing of the veil), and eventually leads to death (Bertha's extinguishing of the candle). Given that Bertha's visit pits Jane against her worst fear of (social) annihilation, she swoons as she did in the red room.[25]

From this point onward, the Thornfield episode focuses on three pieces of furniture only, the chair, the bed, and the mirror as the objects around which its drama evolves. 'Bluebeard' accords the mirror a significant role. When the wife's friends explore Bluebeard's house, the narrator specifically mentions the mirrors: 'There were looking glasses in which you could see yourself from head to toe. Some of them had frames of glass, others of silver or gilded lacquer, but all of them were more grand and splendid than anyone could have imagined' (Tatar, *Secrets* 176). The motivation for this attention emerges with the wife's visit to the forbidden chamber: 'it dawned on her that the floor was covered with clotted blood and that in those pools of blood were reflected the corpses of several women, hung up on the walls' (Tatar, *Secrets* 176–7). The gilded mirrors serve as prefigurations of the clotted mirrors, for Bluebeard intends to make the wife look at herself 'from head to toe,' as expendable, bloody matter. The red, indelible tarnish on the key serves as another mirror touting Bluebeard's notion of woman as gory waste. This context elucidates Brontë's conflation of the key with woman – or, rather, with a series of women such as Bertha, Grace, Céline, Adèle, Clara, and Giacinta – which I now explore.

Scholarship on *Jane Eyre* has presented Bertha Mason as Jane's dark double, the ferocious secret self she has tried to repress (Rich 475, Gilbert and Gubar 359–60, Gilbert 360). Lori Pollock (252) explains that these studies treat Bertha as a projection of Jane's negative qualities. Bertha is Jane's psychological double, who externalizes a free, uninhibited, and often criminal self. The context of the 'Bluebeard' tale, however, implies a reversed relationship. For example, when Jane paces to and fro in Thornfield's attic, she repeats Bertha's movements in the chamber. Further, Bertha moves on all fours; similarly, after her escape, the desperate Jane crawls on her hands and knees. Pollock concludes from such incidents that 'since Jane's dehumanization occurs after Bertha's, we can conceptualize Jane as a reflection of Bertha – which simultaneously accords Bertha agency' (266). In fact, for Rochester all his mistresses are reflections of the first wife. When Jane finally understands this reflective relationship, she is not only able to crack open Rochester's secret but also to modify her fantasies, which prepares her to stand her ground against him. What Zipes says about the tale applies to Brontë's rendition: the secret is not the woman in the chamber, but Bluebeard's 'deep knowledge that the grounds for [his] superior power vis-à-vis women, backed by laws and rules, are groundless' (164).

When Rochester opens the door to the attic chamber, the chair, comparable to the ottoman in the red-room, plays a key role. Jane witnesses Rochester tie Bertha to this chair (JE 250), thus actualizing the shameful fate which the servants threatened to inflict on Jane in the red room. This deed validates Bertha's charade in Jane's bedroom by confirming that woman's fate in Bluebeard's hands is death: incarceration signifies Bertha's social and psychic annihilation. In Bertha Jane sees her past fears realized and her future stretching out in equally grim terms (JE 242, 266). This recognition finally enables Jane to use the key Rochester has handed to her. She realizes that in Bluebeard's schemes any woman, regardless of her attributes, serves only as either an instrument or as matter enabling him to reach his goals. Each and every woman ends up as Bertha in his hands: rejected, derided, and annihilated. Even Grace has turned into Bertha, jailed as Grace is in the same cell and living the same life as Bertha.

After the wedding has been cancelled, Jane mourns her lost love and prospects. 'Mr Rochester was not to me what he had been; for he was not what I had thought of him ... I would not say he had betrayed me:

but the attribute of stainless truth was gone from his idea' (JE 252–3).
The psychological death Jane suffered in the red room is now repeated
at Thornfield:

> Self-abandoned, relaxed, and effortless, I seemed to have laid me down in
> the dried-up bed of a great river ... [Trouble] was near: and as I had lifted
> no petition to Heaven to avert it – as I had neither joined my hands, nor
> bent my knees, nor moved my lips – it came; in full, heavy swing the tor-
> rent poured over me. The whole consciousness of my life lorn, my love
> lost, my hope quenched, my faith death-struck, swayed full and mighty
> above me in one sullen mass. That bitter hour cannot be described: in
> truth, 'the waters came into my soul; I sank in deep mire: I felt no stand-
> ing; I came into deep waters; the floods overflowed me.' (JE 253)

Lewis explains that while the wife waits for the decisive blow from
Bluebeard's sword, her psychological death dissolves her dependence
on him. The threat of imminent death satisfies her death wish, relieving
her of her past image of herself. Thus her psychological death can be
understood as the death of her former autotelic self, delivering her from
the crisis of mimetic rivalry and unchecked doubling (Lewis 241–2).
Žižek (*Enjoy* 59) observes that during such a moment the subject relin-
quishes the presupposition of a natural and/or metaphysical grounding of the symbolic system. As an act of withdrawal from the symbolic
order, this moment of utter abandonment has no one as its addressee,
not even this said order. Because Jane does not seek support in anyone,
the burden falls back upon her. It is fitting that she describes her experience as lying in 'the dried-up bed of a great river' (JE 253). This bed
is the fantasized master's resting place, whose aridness illustrates his
impotence. Žižek (*Enjoy* 67, fn41) fittingly calls such a place the mute
position of death. Jane's biblical language implies that she dies to this
world, to human society. She still is supported by God; however, it is
Jane's realization of the fragility of the symbolic order as well as of her
lack of a place from which to desire in a *human* context that concern us
for now.

During this moment of psychological death Jane confronts what she
has known all along: the man she has regarded as master is not a master, but castrated, weak, and ineffective. Even worse, he is deceptive
and untruthful. Admitting the master's shortcomings forces Jane to
re-evaluate the status and nature of the symbolic order. The hysteric
intuits that the symbolic order has gaps and that no master really exists;

this order is the human presupposition of an immaterial order guaranteeing the meaning and consistency of the subject's experience. The incompleteness of this order is horrifying, because it means that no one has what the hysteric lacks. This is the realization Jane faces. She also understands that no remedy and no sacrifice can compensate for this lack. During this ordeal Jane undergoes a change that modifies her psychic makeup. Subsequent events show that she re-evaluates her responsibilities by identifying the anguished child and woman she has been as the one to whom she has a symbolic debt to pay – and this woman is not unlike Bertha.

The confession scene (ch. 27) in the library stages the confrontation between Bluebeard and the woman after his crime has been discovered. Rochester seats Jane in his chair. Given that it is Rochester's habit to lounge in it, this chair conflates with his bed, which, we remember, is the place of the Father-of-Enjoyment. Rochester's placing of Jane is significant. Because Rochester does not desire as a function of the law, he leads the dance. In insisting that they should live together he pretends to Jane that the symbolic father is laying down the law, although he has no intention whatsoever of submitting to the law: 'I should have appealed to your nobleness and magnanimity at first ... Then I should have asked you to accept my pledge of fidelity and to give me yours' (JE 269). He explains 'the real state of the case' (JE 260) – he was tricked into marriage; Bertha has always been morally corrupt while madness set in only later – trying to make Jane comply by 'marrying' him. This insistence on a sham marriage echoes Bluebeard's repeated threats to his wife: 'Madam, you must die' and 'Prepare to die' (Tatar *Secrets* 177, 178). According to Menninghaus (63), Bluebeard acts more like the representative of an anonymous law rather than a blood-crazed individual. Brontë interprets this law as the obscene underside of the symbolic father's strictures.

Rochester's reasons for sacrificing Jane stem from his determination to reform. Jane has what he lacks: he wants her to *be* his conscience, virtue, and purity. He understands Jane's inner treasure as the fortune-telling scene shows. Scrutinizing her face while masquerading as a gypsy woman, he ventriloquizes it: 'I have an inward treasure, born with me, which can keep me alive if all extraneous delights should be withheld, or offered only at a price I cannot afford to give ... The passions may rage furiously ... but judgment shall still have the last word in every argument ... Strong wind, earthquake-shock, and fire may pass by: but I shall follow the guiding of that still small voice which interprets the dictates of conscience' (JE 171–2). Jane is the sacrificial lamb Rochester would offer to the symbolic father. He would reform by proxy. If she agreed to be his instrument, however, the principles she holds dear would be thoroughly destroyed. This skewed logic elucidates Bluebeard's vicious love: 'Because I love you, I destroy the treasure hidden in you.'

Contrary to Rochester's expectations, Jane refuses to act as the partner to the Father-of-Enjoyment. Her refusal stems from what one might term her mirror experience, that is, her merger with Bertha in Bluebeard's chamber. Such identification marks Jane as someone who is in-between two deaths. As Bertha, she is already psychically and socially dead; as Bluebeard's next victim, she is waiting for the decisive cut. Consequently, Menninghaus (64) calls the latest wife a revenant who survives the deadline set upon her life. Brontë's interpretation of this figure is unique. In spite of Bertha's dire fate, she nevertheless is still alive. Although madness and incarceration have robbed her of speech and freedom of movement, she retains vestiges of subjectivity through her destructive actions. If Jane's slogan has so far been 'Speak I must,' identification with Bertha's position changes it into 'Act I must.' Thus Jane sets limits to Rochester's enjoyment and delivers judgment by laying down the law for him: 'I will keep the law given by God; sanctioned by man ... Preconceived opinions, foregone determinations are all I have at this hour to stand by: there I plant my foot' (JE 270–1). Jane provides Rochester with genuine separation in word and deed by quitting Thornfield. Her decision shows Rochester that he cannot reform through proxy: an internalized relationship to the law cannot be transmitted to another person. It can only be acquired by submitting personally to castration. Jane's actions also illustrate the hysteric's clear-sightedness of the symbolic father's position. Being forced into the position of the law-instituting father, the situation would appear to feed Jane's hysteric questioning of gender ('Am I a man or a woman?'). Jane's insistence on adhering to the law, however, signals a changed understanding: she now sees that the father's position is purely structural, not literal.

Refusing to play the sacrificial victim is Jane's gift of love to Rochester, which eventually compels him to face castration. This is the symbolic debt he has refused to pay, but which must be paid if he is to reform in any real sense. Rochester, however, reciprocates Jane's gift of love. By revealing the weaknesses of his father, brother, and himself as well as by detailing his amorous entanglements, Rochester confirms

Jane's repressed intuition of what the phallus is. The confession shows it as a *void* that no one possesses. Similarly, there is no specific marker for Woman. Jane sees that her hysteric striving to be The Woman (instead of a woman) has been mistaken. These reciprocal gifts, exchanged reluctantly under external force, echo the doubling between Bluebeard and woman: both must relinquish their secret schemes. At the same time, these gifts suggest an alternative basis for love, one that is not grounded in using the other for one's own ends.

*Jane Eyre* ends with Jane's marriage to Bluebeard, but its prerequisite is the inner change of both parties. Rochester's almost excessive castration in the end has been noted: the destruction of Thornfield in a fire and the loss of an arm, eye, and sight serve as outer markers of an inner change, the belated submission to paternal law. In concluding the examination of this relationship I briefly discuss Rochester's eerie call to Jane and the couple's eventual union. Bluebeard Gothic typically expels the dangers the heroine has encountered during the course of the plot either by ascribing evilness to the master of the house (a decent man then rescues the girl), or by proving the master's innocence and assigning guilt elsewhere (the girl then marries the master). *Jane Eyre* is exceptional, because the master is evil and guilty, but also worthy of marriage with the heroine.

## The Ottoman Turned into a Tree Stump

The three days Jane wanders on the moors after escaping from Thornfield realize her childhood fear of finding herself permanently in the mute position of death. She has no one in society who would claim her. Social death would result in physical death if the Rivers did not save her. They are responsible for the highly improbable, fairy-tale rescue of Jane. Finding her paternal cousins enables Jane to begin constructing a protective narrative to shield her against trauma. Learning about the Eyre family, being made the legatee of her paternal uncle, and being accepted as a family member make it possible for Jane to put together a narrative about her origins. Her success in this protective work is proved when she unexpectedly hears Rochester call for her. At first, she is unable to locate his voice. It is neither in the room, nor in the house, nor outside; neither does it issue from the air nor the earth (JE 357). On reflection, Jane concludes that 'it seemed in *me* – not in the external world' (JE 359). This voice opens the doors of her soul's cell, and her heart and spirit 'neither feared nor shook, but exulted as if in joy' (JE 359). Previously Jane has associated such an eerie sound with her (and Bertha's) Ur-human cry for recognition, issuing forth from the ottoman, the place of death. Having found a footing in the symbolic order she now has a place from which to desire, which gives her protective psychic coverage to recognize Rochester's plea without having to call forth hysteric symptoms to shield her. (Later on Jane learns that the cry condensed Rochester's acceptance of symbolic castration.) She answers his call by starting to look for him.

The scene sealing the couple's union brings the ottoman again on stage. This second proposal scene repeats the first one by taking place outside in an Eden-like spot, but instead of a bench, Rochester sits on a tree stump with Jane on his lap. (The stump refers to the lighting-struck chestnut at Thornfield orchard as well as to Rochester's diminished state.) While so far both their family-romance fantasies have revolved around the father's bed and the mother's chair, now only a single seating, the ottoman, remains. This prop testifies to the fact that the traumatic navel in the psychic lives of Bluebeard and Jane has been sufficiently covered over. As the past no longer holds sway over them, their mimetic rivalry has ceased. Identifying the ottoman as the basis of their union suggests that love can only be built on the reciprocity between wounded, lacking subjects who neither regard nor use the other as a filler of, and substitute for, personal shortcomings. To explain this outcome, *Jane Eyre* has been compared to such fairy tales as 'Cinderella' (Gilbert 1998), 'Sleeping Beauty' (Tatar *Secrets*), 'Psyche and Eros' (Chase; Williams), and 'Beauty and the Beast' (Tatar *Secrets*). Perrault's *Histoires ou contes du temps passé*, however, contains a fairy tale that Lewis (260) characterizes as 'Bluebeard's' romantic recasting, 'Riquet à la houppe,' known in English as 'Tufty Ricky.' I argue that this fairy tale illustrates the kind of reciprocity Brontë's novel envisions for the redeemed Bluebeard and wife.

Ricky is a horribly ugly, but very clever, prince who falls in love with a beautiful princess. She, however, is exceptionally stupid. A fairy presiding over Ricky's birth has promised that he may endow any person he likes with his cleverness. Ricky makes the princess promise to marry him in exchange for *esprit*, spirited cleverness. After having received Ricky's gift, the princess nevertheless wavers, for she finds him repulsive. Ricky gives her a year to think things over (as long as it takes Rochester and Jane to be reunited). Although in the meanwhile a perfect prince (St John Rivers) proposes to the princess, she eventually honours her promise to Ricky. As it happens, a fairy presiding over her birth has proclaimed that she may share her beauty with anyone she chooses. Deciding to endow Ricky with her gift of *beauté*, she sees him transfigured into a handsome man. Lewis points out that Bluebeard and his wife, Ricky and the princess, are mimetic doubles of one another, because each covets what the other has. He describes the resemblances between Ricky and Bluebeard in the following fashion: 'each is physically repulsive and overcomes the woman's revulsion by tactics that smack of temptation and entrapment ... Also the structure is similar, for in both tales there are two scenes of confrontation, the first establishing the contractual terms of the man's gift, the second addressing the woman's failure to keep her commitment' (Lewis 259).

Jane's particular brand of stupidity has nothing to do with her mental capacities. Rochester quickly perceives that she lacks vivacity, ease, and confidence in social situations. In a similar fashion as Ricky, Rochester gives Jane a gift of *esprit* by helping her release her inhibited capacities. The evening conferences show Rochester giving Jane encouraging attention that puts her in touch with her potential: 'The ease of his manner freed me from painful restraint; the friendly frankness, as correct as cordial, with which he treated me, drew me to him ... My thin crescent-destiny seemed to enlarge; the blanks of my existence were filled up; my bodily health improved; I gathered flesh and strength' (JE 125). Lewis (250) observes that the interpersonal mechanism Ricky uses is the exchange of desire. He integrates the princess's wish into his own activity as a goal he willingly seeks for her, as his desire for her to participate with him in the mutual exercise of esprit. So it is with Rochester and Jane, too. When he summons her to spend evenings with him, he treats her cordially, making 'me feel I really possessed the power to amuse him; and that these evening conferences were sought as much for his pleasure as for my benefit' (JE 125). Rochester's looks are not the issue for Jane, but his moral 'squint.' Their relationship would ideally be grounded in an exchange drawing on each character's strengths: Rochester gives Jane what she desires, *esprit*, and in return she gives him what he desires, *beauté*. As we know, their secret goals thwart such an exchange. As in 'Tufty Ricky,' the commitment with which these gifts are given is tested during the second proposal scene. At this moment Jane has both *esprit* and *beauté*, giving her an advantage over Rochester, who still lacks beauty; that is to say, his moral transformation has not yet been acknowledged. She nonetheless chooses to reciprocate Rochester's earlier gift.

Lewis remarks that while the secret of 'Bluebeard' breeds persecution born of an unequal exchange that does not let the wife to contribute anything of her own, 'Tufty Ricky' offers a happy alternative by promoting an authentic exchange. Ricky's gift of spirit involves real sharing by the two parties. In giving beauty in return for spirit, the princess is not giving back a borrowed phallus. The beauty she offers to Ricky is a quality belonging to her that he lacks and gratefully accepts. This marital union is grounded in reciprocity and interdependence (Lewis 260–1) – as is also Jane's and Rochester's.

## Covering over the Void: The Autobiographical I

Williams (*Art* 47) observes that the narrative voice in Bluebeard Gothic belongs to an impersonal narrator who speaks from the position of the symbolic. What would happen, she asks, if Bluebeard Gothic were narrated by a woman? This is, in fact, a strategy favoured by feminist rewritings of the tale, as Hermansson points out. Because they prize the heroine and her defiant activity, the moment that Bluebeard intends as one of closure becomes actually the point at which the tale is drawn inside out. While looking at the murdered predecessors, Bluebeard wants the woman to realize that this gory tableau reflects her imminent fate. By refusing to conform to his plan of murder, she revises the automatism built into his plot. This defiance represents, in Hermansson's (11, 46, 61) view, the first revision of Bluebeard's plot, and it is written into the tale itself. The woman's own plot thus unleashes a revisionist intertext that liberates not only her individual story but also the global narrative from Bluebeard's deadly clutches. 'Such revision,' Hermansson (11) writes, 'subjects Bluebeard's plot for the first time to question; the grounds on which it stakes its claim to exist become available to scrutiny as the reader creates her own story beyond this plot.' Most critics agree that *Jane Eyre* is a revisionist text, although they disagree as to the extent of its rebellious impact. I would now like to suggest that a complex narrative and discursive layering creates tensions within Jane's narrative. Such a layering illustrates Brontë's ingenuity in adapting 'Bluebeard.' As I subsequently show, it explains why one and the same narrative may exhibit such contradictory goals as conformity with and rebellion against the sociocultural status quo.

Lewis's (203–6) structural analysis of Perrault's 'Bluebeard' uncovers surprisingly many correspondences among the tale's embedded plots. The wife's plot responds point for point with Bluebeard's plot until these plots part ways in the end: Bluebeard's marriage to her is matched with her marriage to him; the wife's violation of his prohibition is matched with her violation of his prohibition; his attempt to repeat the punishment he has inflicted on his former wives is matched with her resistance to the fate he has designed for her; and, finally, his failure is played off against her success (Lewis 204). Each plot blends actants (subject, sender, and receiver) in the activity of a single character. Both characters seek the satisfaction to be derived from addressing oneself (as hero or heroine) from oneself (as sender) to oneself (as beneficiary) so as to integrate one's world as an extension of oneself. Their mutual rivalry arises from their shared interest in wealth, sex, and power. In the course of the tale, the wife turns into Bluebeard's double; yet this doubling is based on resemblance rather than difference, as the discovery scene suggests. It shows both as morally ambivalent figures. The wife is a transgressor of the marital edict, while Bluebeard has transgressed against the laws of society. From the discovery scene onward, husband and wife occupy symmetrical positions: he is the disobeyed husband, the victim of the wife's violation of authority, and a ruthless pervert; she is her tempter's next victim and the violator of her own promise. Further, the punishment that Bluebeard is about to deliver on his wife is identical to the one he undergoes. Bluebeard's execution substitutes one victim who is simultaneously wrong and wronged, guilty and aggrieved, for another (Lewis 205–6). The tale's end as a transformation of its beginning caps this symmetry: the woman, who in the beginning married a bad man, recuperates in the end in the arms of a good man.

Lewis's analysis suggests that the psychological-hermeneutical inconsistencies and gaps Menninghaus identifies in 'Bluebeard' do not affect its narrative structures. To the contrary, they remain elegantly balanced and symmetrical. The tale's presence may in fact have not only a disintegrative but also a cohesive effect. I argue that this cohesive impact exerts its influence on the narrative structures of *Jane Eyre* too. In fact, it appears that whenever the 'Bluebeard' tale is present, it has this organizing influence on the host narrative. This impact places a premium on relations of similarity, doubling, and antithesis among the global plot and embedded plots, narrative levels, characters, and settings. The particular content and mode of representing these elements is secondary; of primary importance is narrative organization. Charting all instances of symmetrical relationships would be an extensive task; instead, I take up a few representative examples to show the general drift in *Jane Eyre*.

I have already dwelt extensively on the correspondences and differences between Jane and Rochester. Relations of similarity and contrast extend to other characters as well. In accordance with the mirror motif of 'Bluebeard,' Blanche Ingram resembles the young Bertha, whereas Jane resembles the older Bertha. Rochester represents a pleasure-seeking male, while St John Rivers is his ascetic counterpart. 'Bluebeard' exhibits symmetry in its locations, building on the typical fairy-tale pattern of home–forest (Bluebeard's castle)–(new) home that stands in contrast to the childhood home. Similarly, in Jane's narrative major locations reflect one another either through similarity or difference. Gateshead and Ferndean are antitheses of each other as the loathed narrative starting point and the beloved narrative end point. In the series of houses where Jane lives (Gateshead – Lowood – Thornfield – Marsh End – Ferndean), Thornfield represents the navel moment, demarcating her life in its two major phases. Moreover, Ferndean serves as a corrective antithesis to Thornfield, putting right the wrongs that took place there. The ending is a transformation of the beginning. At first Jane has no home, no family, no place in society, whereas the end shows her having accomplished all this. Moreover, the suffering caused by three bad cousins and their mother is counteracted by the benevolence of three good cousins and their maternal housekeeper, as Peter Allan Dale (208) points out. The purpose of this list is to demonstrate the confident organization and well-balanced form of Jane's narrative. Jane creates narrative connections and narrative coherence either through similarity or difference. She communicates a controlled, consistent totality where all narrative elements interlock seamlessly. In Dale's (208) fitting formulation, her narrative exhibits an 'excess of order.'

What characterizes the fairy tale, argues Menninghaus (177), is the tension between a balanced and simple narrative structure and the unmotivated nature of characters and their actions. This tension generates the fairy tale's wondrous effect. The narrator-Jane, however, takes great pains *not* to cultivate this tension. Instead, she uses the structural symmetries of 'Bluebeard' in order to reinforce the rationality of her narrative and to encourage just the kind of motivational-hermeneutic paradigm that Menninghaus thinks alien to this tale in particular. Jane's means of accomplishing her goal stems directly from her role as the narrator of 'Bluebeard.' This tale employs a narrator who is both outside and above the narrated world and its events (a so-called extradiegetic and heterodiegetic narrator). In determining the impact this fairy-tale narrator wishes to make, the key question is: Whose voice do we hear when this narrator narrates? The fairy tale gives the impression of unfolding by itself, without the intervention of an overt narrator. This seemingly neutral and 'automatic' manner of narration supports the argument that this fairy-tale narrator enjoys a position of authority. The narrator is responsible for the whole tale as well as for its overall effect, including its moral points. Such moralizing points have typically been associated with either folk wisdom or middle-class instruction. For example, the narrator of Perrault's 'La Barbe Bleue' appends two moralities to his tale, thus showing that he speaks from the position of the symbolic system. Therefore, it is the voice of this system we hear in listening to the narrator's tale in 'Bluebeard.' Narrating from this position rather than any specific content determines the tale's general effect.

So it is with Jane, too, even though claiming that as narrator she is complicit with the symbolic system may be surprising, given the novel's current status as an unruly feminist classic. *Jane Eyre* would seem to prioritize the wife's embedded narrative over that of the anonymous narrator at the tale's global narrative level. Yet I would nevertheless insist that Jane places herself in the same position as the tale's narrator, organizing her narrative in accordance with symbolic authority. After all, as the surviving heroine, she installs herself as a new authority – at least as the authority of her own fate. The power she wields is supported by the larger community. Although the community has for a time tolerated Bluebeard's serial murders, there comes a point at which its members rally behind the heroine, putting an end to his killing. Davies (*Tale* 55) observes that 'Bluebeard' functions as 'a conventional instrument of civilization,' although it also exposes its scandalous workings. Therefore, I think it justifiable to claim that as narrator Jane draws on what Lacan calls the discourse of the master. This master discourse is whetted by the desire of being one and undivided. The formal terms of this discursive mode allow the speaking subject to present herself as whole. Its message can be formulated, for example, in the following ways: 'I am myself,' 'I know who I am,' and 'I am in control of myself.'

Contrary to Menninghaus's argument, this emphasis on mastery permeates his prime example, Perrault's 'La Barbe Bleue' as well. In paying exclusive attention to its nonsensical and self-cancelling elements, Menninghaus overlooks the fact that these elements in no way challenge the narrator's authority. Instead, if they are taken in Menninghaus's sense as reflexive investigations of the fairy tale (70), they in fact work to enhance narratorial authority. The discourse of the master suits Jane's goal; after all, she narrates an autobiography the purpose of which is not only to consolidate an identity but also to consolidate it as Jane Rochester. By downplaying the disruptive subterranean influence of 'Bluebeard' and by emphasizing its structural coherence, Jane narrates in unison with the master's discourse. She does so because it offers her a protective structure against her primary experience of nauseous pleasure, the life-threatening experience of dissolution of self in the various red rooms of her life.

Narrating from the master's position, Verhaeghe observes, creates a specific social bond that is intimately tied with its goal of totalizing self-representation. Such a goal involves the fantasy that one's being oneself is not tied up with language. For example, the signifier 'I' is taken to refer to an identity in one's own right (Verhaeghe 105). In the context of narrative, the kind of social bond the master's discourse creates is best approached in terms of the narrator's relationship to the reader. This textually embedded recipient is explicitly present in Jane's narrative, thanks to her frequent and direct addresses to the 'gentle reader.' Following Carla Kaplan (9), Jane's autobiography may be described as 'the story of her own longing to talk, to find someone to credit her version of her life, to sympathize with her trials, and listen as a friend.' Looking at Jane's invocations helps us to sketch the bond she builds with her reader by using the discourse of the master.

Control of the overall narrative design is the hallmark of Jane's autobiography, and this feature extends to her relationship with the reader. She has a varied arsenal of means at her disposal in conversing with the recipient. The dominant feature in this relationship is the complicity narrator-Jane establishes with the reader over and above character-Jane. A good example of involving the reader in a complicit bond comes during all those moments when the narrator limits her perspective and understanding to those of the character. When Jane falls in love with Rochester, for example, the narrator takes care to record only the sensations and thoughts of her younger, ignorant self. Yet by reporting Rochester's abrupt and disrupted allusions to his interest in her, narrator-Jane makes sure the reader knows what is happening. The narrator thus invites the reader to watch over Jane in a mutual, sympathetic complicity. Further, by resorting to the use of the present tense at crucial moments in the narrative – for example, when Rochester proposes to Jane in the orchard, and after Jane's escape from him – narrator-Jane makes the reader relive what she then experienced. Yet as narrator, she presides over these emotionally charged scenes as the following example, taken from a scene after Rochester's return to Thornfield with the party including Blanche Ingram, shows: 'I have told you, reader, that I had learnt to love Mr. Rochester; I could not unlove him now ... because I saw all his attentions appropriated by a great lady ... There was nothing to cool or banish love in these circumstances; though much to create despair. Much too, you will think, reader, to engender jealousy' (JE 158). The narrator coolly reflects on the significance of the events, analyses her despair in a clear-headed manner, and even anticipates her recipient's reactions and thoughts. In so doing, the narrator coaxes the reader to make interpretations that fit the narrator's purposes: for example, to reject jealousy as an explanation of her response, but to choose despair, the nature of which the narrator then specifies. Anticipating the reader's reactions is a significant tactic in the narrator's arsenal, because it enables her to ward off erroneous judgments, to justify herself, and to drive home her points (see, for example, the scene where Jane announces her discontent and expounds on women's rights, JE 92–3).

Speaking from the master's position enables narrator-Jane to sustain the sense that she knows about herself and her story, is in control of her narrative's meanings, and self-reflexively presents the truth about her life and identity. Another way to put this idea is to say that the narrator represents herself as speaking a language instead of a language speaking her. The discourse of the master envisions a specific role for the reader: the interlocutor's task is to serve as the narrator's faithfully reflecting mirror. This notion is confirmed by the extensive scholarship on *Jane Eyre* where this role, observes Carla Kaplan (5–6), is described in terms of an ideal reader. Given that Jane conflates such an ideal listener with an ideal lover, this relationship emphasizes perfect concord between narrator and reader. Jane does not achieve such concord with Rochester, for she never fully confides in him. She keeps from him, for example, the fact that she heard his eerie summons. Carla Kaplan (18) claims that Jane's reticence explains why the reader's role in *Jane Eyre* has been understood as an invitation to complete Jane's narration by acting as her ideal interlocutor. We are Jane's intended confidantes, for we are more akin to Jane than anyone else. This is exactly the social bond the discourse of the master privileges. Instead of adding fresh insights to the narrator's interpretation, questioning it, or contesting it, the reader is meant to accept the narrator's version as it is – or, at the most, to elaborate it in harmony with the narrator's account. In this sense, the reader posits the narrator as the source of knowledge and authority. This is the fantasy of perfect communication where, in Jane's words, 'to talk to each other is but a more animated and an audible thinking' (JE 384). It is as if the medium of words were but an obstacle to conveying ideas directly from one mind to another.

To reiterate, by using the discourse of the master and by creating the social bond typical to it, narrator-Jane places herself in the position of symbolic authority typical of narrators of 'Bluebeard' and the fairy tale in general. This discourse secures her identity and wards off the influx of disturbing memories. Yet the maiden name Eyre in the title of Jane's autobiography implies Jane Rochester's continued need to keep on exorcizing the ghosts of her past as well as any elements threatening the identity that took such pains to achieve. In fact, no protective narrative offers complete security against hysteria whose traces manage to seep through all shields. Simultaneously the hauntingly disintegrative influence of the 'Bluebeard' intertext begins to emerge. By analysing in more detail Jane's relationship to the reader, I next examine how her traumatic experiences nevertheless break through her controlled narrative. Jane, too, like all speaking and writing subjects, is divided by language: beneath the master's discourse we hear the hysteric's questioning voice.

## Who Am I, Gentle Reader?

Although fairy tales tend to dispense with explicit and self-reflexive narrators at the highest narrative level, these narrators do occasionally signal their presence. The narrator of Perrault's 'La Barbe Bleue,' for example, occasionally makes his presence felt: he names, in parentheses, the wife's sister and appends two moralities to the tale. As an autobiography, Brontë's *Jane Eyre* understandably departs from such reticence. At the same time, it emphasizes the importance of the narrator's bond with the recipient. The first direct address to the reader in Jane's autobiography reads as follows: 'Let the reader add, to complete the picture, refined features; a complexion, if pale, clear; and a stately air and carriage, and *he* will have, at least, as clearly as words can give it, a correct idea of the exterior of Miss Temple' (JE 40; italics added). This is the only instance in the whole narrative in which the reader is gendered. Although the masculine pronoun may be taken to designate all readers generally, the reader has nevertheless been identified as male. Carla Kaplan even goes as far as to say that 'Brontë genders "the Reader" as male, positions him as a judge by representing Jane's discourse as a story wrenched from her not by affection or intimacy but in consequence of some moral or personal censure' (21–2). Thus it appears as if Jane presented her story to a master, seeking his approval. Yet, as Carla

Kaplan observes, readers universally think of the fictionalized reader as female (25). This association arises from the fact that Jane's most intimate and satisfying relationships are with other women, most notably with Helen Burns and Miss Temple, and Diana and Mary Rivers (Kaplan 18). In exchanges with them Jane finds the empathy she craves but which Rochester does not provide her.

What is remarkable in narrator-Jane's ambiguous gendering of the reader is that it replicates the hysteric's basic dilemma: 'Am I a man or a woman?' To be sure, a given subject seldom expresses this query in such blunt form. Jane articulates it in the following fashion: 'Why was I always suffering, always browbeaten, always accused, for ever condemned? Why could I never please? Why was it useless to try to win any one's favour?' (JE 11–12). When Rochester woos Blanche Ingram, Jane directs similar questions to Rochester in her mind: 'This was the point – this was where the nerve was touched and teased – this was where the fever was sustained and fed: [Blanche Ingram] *could not charm him*' (JE 159). Because Jane knows how to charm Rochester and has succeeded in doing so, the hysteric's dilemma plagues her. Why is she not enough of a woman to please Rochester? Do her poverty, plainness, and lower social standing preclude her from being an erotic object? This recourse to familiar terrain is needed in order to show how the questions that plagued Jane in the past seep into the narration of her autobiography. On a closer look, many of the communicative means she uses turn out to be double-voiced: they have an underside whose impact diverges from the explicitly intended one (see also Hennelly). A particularly good example is the advantage in knowledge and understanding the narrator Jane gives her reader as regards the character Jane during the Thornfield episode. By showing things from the character Jane's limited perspective, narrator-Jane elicits from the reader the assurance that she *is* the person Rochester loves. She repeatedly calls on the reader to confirm during reading that 'You, Jane, are the erotic object of Rochester's love.' Moreover, seeing through the character Jane's attempts to stifle her feelings enables the reader to reassure Jane also of the fact that Jane is, in fact, besotted with Rochester. In this way narrator-Jane places the reader in the master's position as someone who can supply her with knowledge about herself. Positioned thus, the reader now has the task to elaborate who and what Jane is. This placement of the reader divulges the persistence of the hysteric's discourse. It also reveals what Doreen Roberts (40) fittingly calls the 'tremendously centripetal, ego-centric reference' of the whole book.

Jane's wording of the question perplexing her from childhood onward – 'Why could I never please?' – supplies an additional clue of the way the hysteric's discourse subtends her narrative. In keeping with the self-reflexiveness of her character, she not only craves knowledge of her identity but also of the grounds for being what she is. The clear-eyed eagerness with which she analyses others she directs at herself as well. Therefore, by placing the reader in the master's position the narrator expects from her interlocutor elaboration on the reasons for the reader's reassurance: for example, 'What makes you say that Rochester loves me?' and 'Why do I please him?' In order to supply grounds for answers, the reader should review the information the narrator makes available, but, in this instance, the narrator's words are never enough. The reader must go beyond them, listening to and searching for details, information, and connections that escape the narrator's notice. If in the discourse of the master the reader is expected to serve as simply a reassuring mirror, the discourse of the hysteric demands much more: the reader must independently contribute to the narrator's self-understanding. It is in this sense that narrator-Jane expects the reader to provide her with substantial knowledge about herself.

The dilemma with such a bond, however, is that no reader can give the narrator a conclusive explanation to any of her questions. As Verhaeghe (110) observes, the hysteric's discourse is driven by the desire to make the master give a thorough account of the birth of herself as subject. In other words, the hysteric expects the master to explain how her parturition from the primary unity took place and how she then experienced and understood this unity, the trace of which she cherishes in a particular object – a voice, a look, a smell, or some such reminder of the lost wholeness. This is an impossible demand for two reasons. First, the master is able at most to say something general and theoretical about how humans become subjects; no one, however, can know the particulars affecting the formation of a specific subject. Second, primary unity and the object serving as its remainder (the so-called object a) can never be captured in and by language (Verhaeghe 110). The result is inevitably dissatisfaction for narrator-Jane, who does not find the ideal interlocutor in the reader. Moreover, the narrator's dissatisfaction involves an implicit reproach against the reader, whose inability to supply a definitive answer dislodges the reader from the master's position. The reader is but a sham master; actually, a castrated and limited being. Thus Carla Kaplan's conclusion appears to be correct: for all it may entertain the utopian notion of an ideal recipient, neither Jane as a narrator nor *Jane Eyre* as a novel will ever find such a reader. Lacanian discourse theory insists on the psychic beneficence of this outcome, for ideal reciprocity would actually result in the narrator's merger with the reader. Such a state would, in turn, stifle desire and lead to mutual paralysis (Verhaeghe 104).

In the end, then, the psychological-hermeneutical motivation that Jane as narrator fosters turns against itself. The disintegrative influence of 'Bluebeard' may be located in this self-reflexive turn of *Jane Eyre*. In Brontë's adaptation of the tale, the revisionist impact in Jane's narration springs from the persistence of the hysteric's discourse. She must supplement her self-understanding with the reflections offered by readers. Menninghaus says that Bluebeard's possible motives play no role, because they are superfluous to the unfolding of the tale's plot. While the modern period attempts to explain fairy-tale action in psychological terms, such explanations carry only so far. No 'Bluebeard' version is capable of wholly covering up the tale's inconsistencies (Menninghaus 63). This observation applies to *Jane Eyre* too. Although it succeeds in explaining away most of the unmotivated events of the tale, at least two lacunae remain; namely, the nature of Bluebeard's secret and the mystery of Bertha Mason's demise.

**The Pulsating Void**

By recounting at length the genesis of Bluebeard's chamber and the woman's suitability for the victim's role, *Jane Eyre* provides psychological motivation for what the tale leaves unexplained. Moreover, Jane's rescue from bigamy, for example, does not result from an ad hoc incident as the heroine's rescue does in the tale, but from her letter to her uncle. Exorcism of unmotivated fairy-tale elements, however, manages to create inexplicable events elsewhere in the plot.[26] Undoubtedly the greatest enigma of 'Bluebeard' is the vault. The mystery of this space is, in fact, that there is no mystery: it is an empty secret. If one thinks back on the first wife, then all she could have found there upon being the first transgressor is emptiness (Lewis 208–9; Menninghaus 60–1). Lewis remarks that Bluebeard links the woman's corpse to the emptiness of the original secret. His punishment literally inflicts on his wives 'the strangely unthinkable nothingness of the originally nonexistent secret that they violate and are then forced to embody; it deposits each victim's dead body in the empty room as the visible image, the tangible sign of the inaccessible nothingness that remains the core of the secret' (Lewis 209). And, as Hermansson (10, fn6) points out, such an explanation as Bluebeard's impotence – or the impotence underlying the patriarchal system – only introduces another absence as origin for Bluebeard's plot. Brontë adds to these enigmas the mystery of Bertha Mason Rochester. Bertha's actions show that she retains remnants of agency even in her madness, but her motives can only be guessed at. In particular, her demise presents an unsolvable mystery. If, as it appears, Bertha has a strange knack of knowing what is going on at Thornfield, why does she wait for two months after Jane's escape before setting the place on fire?[27] The innkeeper offers spite as an explanation (JE 364–5), but revenge seems a belated reaction. Does Bertha lure Rochester to the roof in the hope of making him fall down? Does she commit suicide as a leap to longed-for liberation or does she purposefully sacrifice herself in order to free Rochester? One can only guess at the answers. The only certainty is that Bertha's death miraculously enables Jane's marriage to Rochester – and Jane seizes this opportunity with both hands. In order to achieve a happy ending, this narrative must resort to the narrative logic of the fairy tale, glossing over any ramifications this miraculous event may have.

Treating Bertha's death in fairy-tale terms has at least one significant consequence: it breaks off the reflective relationship between Bluebeard's first and second wives. So far, this relationship has implied not only reflection but also mediation. In other words, the reflective bond has suggested Bertha as mediator with whose help Jane's transformation from a poor orphan child into a happy, fulfilled woman is achieved. Menninghaus clarifies this idea by saying that mediation works by providing a point of contrast that helps the subject to move from a negative (developmental) pole to a positive one. Such mediation, however, is alien to the fairy tale. He explains: 'The negative beginning of a fairy tale is thus not related to its positive conclusion like an unmediated opposition to a mediated one; rather, the transition from one to the other eliminates the negative elements for the benefit of the unadulterated triumph of the positive' (184–5). As in fairy tales, Jane does not return to the social circles from which she started out, but makes her fortune elsewhere, at Ferndean. In 'Bluebeard' the rescued wife forgets the bad time she spent with Bluebeard in the arms of a new husband. Similarly, the ending of *Jane Eyre* suggests that Jane's marriage demands a severing of the ties with the past – in particular, with Bertha, Bluebeard's first wife.

In spite of narrator-Jane's efforts, however, she cannot completely gloss over this traumatic core of her narrative. In fact, her narration contains ample signs that the painful events she recounts still exert an influence over her. She explains to the reader that she has chosen to 'invoke memory where I know her responses will possess some degree of interest' (JE 70). Jane's criterion for narrative interest, according to Bette London's wry remark (208), is painful sensation; she obsessively recounts scenarios of suffering. London argues that these scenarios serve to remake readers in Jane's image through identification; 'Jane's narrative strategies make readers replicate or replace Jane, to assume Jane's position as a suffering subject and invested observer of the spectacle she makes' (208). While *Jane Eyre* certainly is replete with distressful scenes, I would nevertheless maintain that the narrative and textual elements referring to traumatic experience serve another function than identification. Rather, I suggest that in recounting anxiety-provoking events and incidents, Jane frequently resorts to what is called the discourse of the analyst. This discursive mode calls upon narrator-Jane to recognize the enjoyment which landed her in a quandary. In a similar fashion as the other discursive registers, it constructs a special kind of bond with the reader, a bond whose goal radically departs from any notion of empathetic identification.

At times the narrator Jane deals overtly with the painfulness of her memories. Remembrance of the past inevitably results in anxiety, as the experiences themselves are articulated and given form in narration – perhaps for the first time. On three occasions Jane can barely contain the pain of her memories. First, remembering her childhood at Gateshead that culminated in the red-room incident, Jane cannot but hurl yet another accusation at Aunt Reed: 'Yes, Mrs. Reed, to you I owe some fearful pangs of mental suffering. But I ought to forgive you, for you knew not what you did' (JE 16; see also 30). Second, if the Aunt's cruelty is still able to stir feelings of resentment and anger, so also is Rochester's underhanded dealing with Jane. His mock courtship of Blanche and the revelation of the deceitfulness of his marriage proposal evoke anguish retrospectively. The narrator remarks, for example, that 'I hear their mutual whisperings; I recall their interchanged glances; and something even of the feeling roused by the spectacle returns in memory at this moment' (JE 158). The frequent use of the present tense in narrating these scenes enhances, of course, their agonizing effect on the narrator. So do the invocations to the reader such as 'Gentle reader, may you never feel what I then felt!' (JE 274). Finally, in concluding the narration of her three-day-long wanderings on the moor, the narrator remarks that she finds no enjoyment in recalling this incident: 'but at this day I can scarcely bear to review the times to which I allude: the

moral degradation, blent with the physical suffering, form too distressing a recollection ever to be willingly dwelt on ... Let me condense now.
I am sick of the subject' (JE 280). These explicit references to trauma
bring forth the limits of the narrator's autobiographical undertaking of
which she is aware. To be sure, the narration of her life story enables
her to organize, reflect, and express her experiences in and through narrative in order to consolidate her identity; yet it cannot conclusively
exorcize the ghosts of the past. There remain areas within this story out
of the narrator's verbal and cognitive reach – and this observation applies to the reader as well.

As narrator, Jane is verbose, eloquent, and poetic, but her torrent
of words is continually broken by the abundant use of dashes, exclamation marks, semicolons, and colons. Opening any page of *Jane Eyre*
shows the pockmarked nature of her text. These textual markers betray
the narrator's efforts to convey in language what language can only
insufficiently express. An example, describing Jane's anguish over her
choice to escape from Rochester, illustrates this claim:

> Meantime, let me ask myself one question – Which is better? – To have
> surrendered to temptation; listened to passion; made no painful effort – no
> struggle; – but to have sunk down in the silken snare; fallen asleep on the
> flowers covering it; wakened in a southern clime, amongst the luxuries
> of a pleasure villa: to have been now living in France, Mr. Rochester's
> mistress, delirious with his love half my time – for he would – oh, yes, he
> would have loved me well for a while. He *did* love me – no one will ever
> love me so again. (JE 306)

The present tense of the narration and the textual notation convey
Jane's out-of-breath meditation on her past choices. Doreen Roberts
(37) nicely characterizes such textual passages as this one by remarking
that they do not flow; rather, they are like a sustained series of small
explosions. The various textual markers punctuate Jane's frantic efforts
to verbalize what the choice she did not make would have meant for
her. The dashes and (semi)colons seem to serve a double purpose. On
one hand the textual markers, the dashes in particular, provide as it
were a safety line with the help of which to string words together. On
the other hand, they clearly identify the spots where the narrator Jane
has difficulties in expressing herself. Roberts (38) remarks that these
problems result from Jane's being acted upon by her emotions, which

Jane regards as external, alien forces. Thus even in her retrospective narration these difficulties refer to narrative lacunae.

The consequence of such continual textual gapping is that it changes the narrator's status: it places the narrator on a par with the reader. Consequently, the narrator becomes a recipient of and a listener to her own tale: Jane becomes one of her own readers. Autobiography actually includes this role, as this genre enables the narrating subject to review her life through narration. In *Jane Eyre* the textual markers serve as signals of the narrative's navel – the void pulsing in its centre, the traumatic enigma of Bluebeard's vault. Paying attention to this insufficiently articulated side of Jane's narrative elucidates how the discourse of the analyst functions (Verhaeghe 112–15). This discursive mode places narrator-Jane in the position of the lost cause of desire (the object a, the remnant of the lost original unity). By situating the narrator and the reader as recipients, this mode invites both to verbalize gropingly the lost object that grounds the narration of Jane's autobiography. In so doing, they must reposition themselves in relation to this object that recalls (lost) satisfaction. As regards Jane, narration probes such questions as 'Why did Bluebeard attract me?' and 'What pleasure did I derive from being caught by his game?' and even 'What satisfaction did I garner in loving Bluebeard?' As these questions indicate, the repositioning caused by the analytic discourse typically involves a subject's reassessment of the Other's desire, because internalized conformity to this desire hinders her from enjoying her object. Another way of putting this idea is to say that this discursive mode allows Jane the narrator to recognize herself in the pleasurable object that is amenable to language only with great difficulty (or not at all). The goal of analytic discourse is to enable a subject to reach a desire that is not swayed by the discourse of the Other. Instead, the freed subject pursues her desire without all the inhibitions deriving from internalized values and judgments (Fink, *Clinical* 211, 215).

Such liberating recognition appears to have taken place in Jane, for her selection of a love object repeats her mother's choice (who is her daughter's namesake, Jane Eyre, née Reed). Jane's mother defies her family and public opinion by marrying a poor curate, while the daughter opts for a life in the fringes of society with a social outcast. Yet as the effects of working through one's primary fantasies are largely affective, readers never learn what exact effect narration has on Jane. They do, however, hear the invitation narrator-Jane extends to them to join her in the exploration of that which she can never fully know. In the process, the analytic layers of this narrator's discourse turn the attention of readers on their own intellectual and affective responses. In this way, Brontë suggests that for Jane and readers a way out of Bluebeard's enclosure is provided by the opportunities the analytic discourse puts at their disposal.

This analysis of the ways in which 'Bluebeard' affects the narration of *Jane Eyre* suggests one weighty reason for the large range of variation among the adaptations of this novel: the adapting authors pay attention to different layers of discourse in this novel in writing their versions. That Jane is a protagonist of a 'Bluebeard' tale and the subsequent cultural standing Brontë's novel has come to enjoy in British literature explain the dominance of the master trope Brontë helped to form. The following chapters examine the diversity among the adaptations of this novel; I begin with the theme that has come up continually in this chapter, namely, trauma.

# 2 Testifying to Bluebeard's Atrocities: The Woman (Author) as Witness

All variants of 'Bluebeard' include the heroine's threshold experience of grisly revelation; and this moment, in Hermansson's words, 'solves immediately the supposed mystery of the previous women who ventured into Bluebeard's castle. In this interpretive instant, Bluebeard's true nature is also disclosed, but the role of the heroine is merely to read it and to realise that this is now her story also; if she was ever "outside" Bluebeard's plot, then she is no longer' (45). In Perrault's 'La Barbe Bleue' the effect of this scene is tremendous: 'She was sure that she would die of fright, and the key to the room ... dropped from her hand' (Tatar, *Secrets* 177). 'The Robber Bridegroom' depicts the fiancée's reactions upon seeing her bridegroom murder another woman in similar terms: 'The poor girl was trembling and shaking from her hiding place behind the barrel, for she now understood what the robbers had in store for her' (181). I elaborate Hermansson's insightful description by probing further the woman's reactions and its consequences. Evidently, the threshold moment is a traumatic experience for her, based on identification with her predecessors. The heroine, however, may turn fright into cunning action by, for example, narrating her experience to others. In so doing she recognizes herself in the dead women and acknowledges the pain they have felt in Bluebeard's hands, inviting the community to share this experience. At this moment she takes up the role of witness, giving testimony of female suffering. It is these notions of trauma and witnessing that I explore in this chapter in the context of Bluebeard Gothic.

The heroine's fright shows the shattering effect of the threshold moment. She is, after all, observing either an actual murder take place or its gory result. Her experience defies her emotional and cognitive capabilities, a characteristic typical of trauma. In other words, this event causes a psychic disorder and the resulting psychic state. Typically traumatic events involve threats to life and bodily integrity or a close personal encounter with violence and death (Kacandes 90). Cathy Caruth (17–18) explains that traumatic psychic disorder results from a disruption of history and temporality. What this means is that while traumatic events are taking place, the subject involved is not able to integrate them into consciousness. The event is not fully experienced as it occurs. Trauma has a haunting quality: the non-assimilated events possess the subject in such insistent repetitions as nightmares, inexplicable phobias, anxiety attacks, or compulsive behaviour. Recovery requires that the traumatized person review the shattering event in her mind, trying to give it narrative form. Irene Kacandes (91) neatly condenses views put forth in trauma research by stating that if trauma is a break in the mind's experience of time, then recovery necessitates the translation of that break into narrative memory, understood as the ability to construct mental schemas that make sense out of experience.

The process during which a traumatized person narrates traumatic events is called witnessing or giving testimony. Because the events defy the victim's cognitive and emotional capacities, narration often falters. It frequently necessitates searching for new modes of expression, for the experience proves familiar schemes insufficient. Often the witness encounters considerable difficulties in relating traumatic incidents so that she requires the support of another person in order for her to be able to give testimony. Anne Whitehead (7) explains the listener's role by stating that 'speaking beyond understanding, testimony requires a highly collaborative relationship between speaker and listener. The listener bears a dual responsibility: to receive the testimony but also to avoid appropriating the story as his or her own.' Dominick LaCapra (*Writing* 102–3) identifies what he calls empathetic unsettlement as the receiver's appropriate response. Empathetic unsettlement involves the receiver's feeling with and for the traumatized person without, however, losing her sense of (critical) distance. It is this distance that enables the receiver to help the trauma victim give form to experience by, for example, signalling her presence, offering encouragement, asking questions, or suggesting interpretive contexts. In fact, we may identify what Kacandes (95) calls circuits of witnessing in 'Bluebeard': at the inmost level, there are the murdered women whose mutilated bodies speak for them beyond death. The latest wife serves as a co-witness by recognizing their fate. At the next level, she herself is the victim under the threat of death who directs her narrative at another (sister Anne, wedding guests), asking for her support in helping this story emerge. Finally, at the utmost level, the tale's global narrator turns to us readers, inviting us to take the co-witness's role. What we then do with the story reveals the effects witnessing has on us. As Whitehead's characterization makes clear, witnessing causes various reactions in listeners; the extremes within this continuum are rejection and over-identification. Both turn a deaf ear on the witness, although in a different manner.

As the previous chapter on *Jane Eyre* made amply clear, Jane not only suffers from trauma but also serves as a witness to upsetting female fates. The allegiance Jane shows to victimized women demonstrates that she has taken up the role of an intrapsychic witness. This role, explains Kacandes, involves an individual's ability to bear witness to the self about traumatic experience by integrating aspects of it that have previously been missed. That Jane addresses her autobiography to the 'dear reader' indicates, however, that intrapsychic witnessing tends to require another person as a co-witness (Kacandes 99). Also Jane needs an empathetic other to help her give form to the painful experiences in her life. Given that Bluebeard Gothic is peopled by similar characters as Jane, this genre frequently reads like trauma fiction. In this chapter, however, my purpose is not to recover ground already covered, but to consider Bluebeard Gothic from the viewpoint of *Jane Eyre*'s progeny. This is to say, I explore the ways in which later writers have served as witnesses to Jane's narrative of trauma. What do these co-witnesses hear in this narrative and how do they conceive their role?

Identifying Brontë's progeny as co-witnesses to Jane's story means that the starting point of this chapter lies on the utmost circuit of witnessing, or, in Kacandes's terms, on the transhistorical and transcultural circuit. She explains that this communicative circuit involves understanding how a novel in its entirety testifies about the trauma-causing incidents to its later readers, and these readers, in turn, to their contemporaries about these same incidents (Kacandes 133). Although Kacandes talks about the activity of reader-scholars at this level, I believe that it also includes authors, enabling them not only to talk with but also to talk back to their literary heritage. The significance of this activity derives from its goal: 'In explicating other circuits as incomplete or failed testimonies,' writes Kacandes, 'the reader-scholar at a historical-cultural remove is herself telling a story of trauma ... and thereby facilitating the flow of testimony that the characters, text, and author try to give' (135). Authors as co-witnesses may tell their readers another kind of story, one that includes identifying the trauma narrative itself as somehow traumatic for later generations. This narrative functions as a symptom of cultural haunting. For example, *Jane Eyre* serves as a recurring symptom of wrongs in the past that must be reactivated and reconfigured in order to be transformed in the present or future. In *Jane Eyre*, these wrongs include harmful ideologies such as imperialism, colonialism, and racism. Wolfgang G. Müller explains this idea by saying that 'colonialism is a gap, a hole or a blind spot in the novel. A critical view of colonialism is simply not Brontë's declared or undeclared intention' (69). Postcolonial and trauma fiction typically require a critical mode of reception, for in both genres authors witness to trauma by letting formerly silenced, ridiculed, or maimed characters tell their own stories. Whitehead (82) elucidates the overlap between postcolonial and trauma fictions by pointing out that both are concerned with the recovery of memory and the acknowledgment of the denied, the repressed, and the forgotten.

The novels that I discuss in this chapter have been chosen with the view of demonstrating the range of issues as regards testimony and the modes of reception that authors have resorted to in acting as co-witnesses to Brontë and her narrator Jane. Anna Leonowens's *The Romance of the Harem* (1872) is based on her experiences in the Far East, on narratives recounted to her, and on invented material. An early example of *Jane Eyre*'s globetrotting, this book evinces a nascent awareness of the devastating consequences on local people by the presence of the British Empire in the Far East. Its main focus, however, lies on the damaging effects of indigenous culture: Siam's history and cultural traditions combine to imprison women in suffering and pain. The Siamese women's lot is physical and mental violence that damages them permanently. Their past resembles Bluebeard's chamber from which the present appears to offer no escape. Although Leonowens appears to recognize Western imperialism as threatening, she nevertheless believes that Britain's ideological presence is beneficial, because it keeps in view such notions as the abolishment of slavery, the ideal of personal freedom, and the rights of women. Like *The Romance of the Harem*, Jean Rhys's *Wide Sargasso Sea* (1966) insists on the conditioning influence of the past in the present: the shared experience of colonialism is identified as deeply disruptive and damaging for both the colonized and the colonizer. These authors envision their books as vehicles for dealing with historical trauma. Their narratives are testimonial accounts of historical circumstances causing trauma; they also insist that narrative fiction can address these circumstances. Another way of putting this idea is to say that these books rely on some notion of history as their reference point with the conviction that narrative fiction plays an important role in dealing with traumatic incidents. I conclude by discussing Emma Tennant's *Adèle: Jane Eyre's Hidden Story* (2002), which provides a useful point of contrast to the two other books examined in this chapter. Tennant is amply aware of the various dimensions of trauma in *Jane Eyre*; she, however, turns them into entertainment. *Adèle* thus demonstrates what tends to happen when a literary classic is adapted by popular genre literature. In this process socially and culturally pressing concerns are often trivialized and emptied out. While the thematic structure of witnessing runs through the chapter, the specific issues the authors deal with in their adaptations are introduced along the way.

### *The Romance of the Harem:* Anna Leonowens and the Burden of Testimony

What if Jane had married St John Rivers and had accompanied him to India? *Jane Eyre* keeps this alternative narrative line open for quite a while, presenting it, argues Jerome Beaty (ch. 7), as a viable and even desirable outcome for Jane. And if readers relate the novel to 'Bluebeard,' such a marriage seems expected, given the fact that Bluebeard's last wife recuperates in the arms of a new husband. Jane envisions St John's offer opening up two alternative narrative avenues: the first involves their marriage, while the second is based on her accompanying him as 'a curate' or 'a comrade' (JE 347). St John rejects the second option as indecent and unsuitable: 'How can I, a man not yet thirty, take out with me to India a girl of nineteen, unless she be married to me? How can we be for ever together – sometimes in solitude, sometimes amidst savage tribes – and unwed?' (JE 347). Approximately at the same time as Charlotte Brontë was writing *Jane Eyre*, an even younger girl than Jane (this girl was fourteen) went unchaperoned along with a thirty-year-old Reverend Mr Badger to the Middle East. She later married someone else and, after having been widowed, accepted a job as a governess in King Mongkut's harem in Siam. This woman was Anna Leonowens, who wrote two books of her experiences in Siam: *The English Governess at the Siamese Court* (1870) and *The Romance of the Harem* (1872). They seize on the suggested, but unrealized, narrative avenues of *Jane Eyre*, providing one version of what could have happened if Jane had opted for a life in the Orient. Anna Leonowens tried to live in Siam the life of what Susan Zlotnick (28) calls the maternal imperialist, a role consisting of a mix of domesticity, feminism, and imperialism. This role relied on a notion of female moral authority of supervision and surveillance (29).

Anna Leonowens worked in King Mongkut's harem for little over five years, from 1862 to 1867, teaching the king's children and any of their mothers and any other women in the harem who wanted to learn the English language, knowledge, and manners. The hybrid elements of *The Romance of the Harem* make it fit to be read in conjunction with *Jane Eyre* and 'Bluebeard.' It purports to be a factual, historical account of life in the Siamese harem, but large portions of it are actually fabricated. Susan Morgan observes that the book resembles a Victorian novel with 'its bizarre characters, its eerie atmosphere, its tales of social injustice, its villains and pure heroines, its pervasive focus on the sufferings of innocent children, and above all its sentimental language that would move us to tears' (xxxv–xxxvi).

While Jane fears Rochester's enslaving domination as a lover, Anna Leonowens experienced the threat of being turned into one of the harem women in her capacity as a governess at her workplace. *The Romance of the Harem* conveys her indignation and outrage at harem life. The king had forbidden her from attempts to convert the students to Christianity, a restriction which Leonowens had no difficulties accepting, as she did not see her assignment in religious terms. Instead, as Susan Brown (603–4) observes, she was motivated by abolitionist ideology: Leonowens 'positions herself as an abolitionist in the Siamese court, one whose primary concern is the sexual slavery of the women in the harem' (Brown 603). If she had a pronounced agenda, it was that of 'European feminist campaigns to "liberate" "other" women' (Brown 599). This set of connections forges the book's links with 'Bluebeard': Leonowens is akin to the tale's heroine in that she too witnesses female suffering and gives testimony of it. In *The Romance of the Harem*, the Bluebeard character is Mongkut, the king of Siam and Anna Leonowens's employer, who confines his wives and concubines in the city of Veiled Women or Nang Harm. In 'The Robber Bridegroom' tale, a father strikes the marriage deal with a suitor without asking his daughter. Similarly, most women were handed over to the king of Siam by their fathers in exchange for political favour. The women stayed there forever. Leonowens portrays the harem as a place of suffering and despair where women are spiritually and often also physically destroyed. Leonowens dedicates *The Romance of the Harem* to 'the noble and devoted women whom I learned to know, to esteem, and to love in the city of the Nang Harm.' Given that she recounts the violence these women encounter, the dedication identifies witnessing as the basis of Leonowens's narration. She is an outsider eyewitness to brutality, a witness who, unlike the fiancée in 'The Robber Bridegroom,' rarely has a personal stake in the events. The bride recounts the groom's brutality to the wedding guests. Her means of survival is narration: she must tell of the events in so convincing a way as to make her audience take action on her behalf. Similarly, Leonowens's book is motivated by the urge to reveal to the English-speaking reading public the lot of the Harem women. *The Romance of the Harem* may thus be regarded as an example of *testimonio*, a genre in which an educated person undertakes to record, transcribe, and edit the testimony of a witness (or witnesses) from another culture. Often such witnesses are illiterate and they narrate under the urgency of a pressing situation such as oppression (see Brooks 182).

*The Romance of the Harem* has no continuous, developing plot. The book consists of seven unconnected narratives of seven different cases of female suffering. It also includes expository material on Siamese life and customs. I examine how Leonowens understands her role as a witness and how witnessing affects her narrative testimony. How does it shape her narration and for what ends? I make extensive use of Kacandes's analysis of the circuits of narrative witnessing. These circuits can be distinguished both at the story and discourse levels of narrative; thus they enable the identification of the level(s) at which trauma incapacitates a person as well as of the level(s) where testimony takes place.

## Witnessing Violence against the Harem Women

Susan Meyer (105) points out that *Jane Eyre* compares its protagonist with an entire array of 'dark races' under the force of European imperialism in the nineteenth century such as Turks, Hindus, native Americans, and the generic heathen and savage. Rose Kamel (12–15) lists the many references associating Rochester with slave owners: he not only treats Bertha like a slave but also he has appropriated her fortune as slave owners do; Bertha's cell at Thornfield resembles the barns and cellars used to confine recalcitrant slaves; in the charades with the house guests Rochester plays an eastern emir; and once Jane has agreed to marry him, he tries to treat her as his favourite concubine. Rochester portrays 'a worldly man with pronounced orientalist inclinations that threaten the Euro-centric foundations of [Jane's] hard-won autonomy'

(Kamel 15). Meyer adds that 'when [Rochester] compares his relation-ships with women to keeping slaves ... the parallel is given a shocking vividness by his own history as a slave master' (107). Jane castigates Rochester when he claims that he 'would not exchange this one little English girl for the grand Turk's whole seraglio; gazelle-eyes, houri forms, and all!' (JE 229), half-seriously threatening him: 'I'll be prepar-ing myself to go out as a missionary to preach liberty to them that are enslaved – your harem inmates among the rest. I'll get admitted there, and I'll stir up mutiny' (JE 230). Rochester's eastern allusions bite Jane. She objects to such banter thanks to the age-old Orientalist construction of the harem as a place of fascinating and repellent sensuality. Her re-sentment also echoes the abolitionist discourse of Brontë's day. Laura Ciolkowski (341–2) points out that by 1830 there was virtually a national consensus in England concerning the immorality of slavery. English abolitionist discourse adhered to the rhetoric of Christian fellowship, human rights, and moral law. Zlotnick (43) calls Leonowens's approach maternal imperialism, a strategy she shared with Jane Eyre as a mode for female ascendancy. Zlotnick describes the ideas on which Jane's in-dignation is based by remarking that '[Jane] disclaims the principles of universal sisterhood on which her utterance seems to rely and trans-forms herself from a disempowered harem girl into a powerful mission-ary figure who will enlighten the new slaves of the empire, those natives shackled by the mind-forged manacles of their own heathenism' (35).

While Jane imagines what she would do in a harem, Anna Leonowens was actually working in one. Nang Harm, King Mongkut's harem, was a walled city housing about nine thousand women and children: the extensive royal family, consorts, concubines, officiating women such as guards and judges, and numerous slaves. Leonowens's assignment there began with a skirmish with the king who ordered her to live inside Nang Harm. She refused, obtaining after a struggle the right to a house outside the harem. The dispute shows Leonowens's dread of being taken for one of the harem women. With the king's eventual consent, she achieved general recognition as an outsider to whom the harem system did not apply. This position influences Leonowens's placing of herself in her book as regards the events she narrates. Kacandes (97) identifies altogether six circuits of narrative witnessing; the first three address the story level, while the subsequent three pertain to the discourse level. In this section I concentrate solely on witnessing on the story level. Of the three circuits at this level, two concern us directly: interpersonal wit-nessing in which 'two characters cowitness to trauma suffered by one of them'; and surrogate witnessing in which 'two characters cowitness to a third character's trauma' (97). Typically, Leonowens portrays cases in which she first acts as an interpersonal witness and then, to redress the situation, she moves into the role of the surrogate witness.

Here I examine the book's opening case concerning an adolescent called Tuptim, for it not only may be read against the background of 'Bluebeard,' but also it illustrates the limitations on Leonowens's witnessing. Suggestively, she characterizes this case as a tragedy. Generally speaking, she may take either the active role of a go-between or that of a passive bystander; Tuptim's case unites both these roles. Tuptim's tragedy is as follows: Tuptim's beauty catches the king's eye; later, her relatives offer her to him. Tuptim finds it hard to adjust to the harem life; in particular, she dislikes serving the king. One day she disappears and is found much later in a monastery disguised as a boy apprentice to a respected monk. Because women are not allowed in monasteries, she has defiled her teacher and the monastery. Both Tuptim and the monk are put on trial. It turns out that Tuptim was betrothed to this man before being given to the king. Both are tortured and sentenced to death. Tuptim defiantly faces death proclaiming her innocence.

'I can neither keep the tears from my eyes, nor still the aching of my heart' (RH 15), writes Leonowens on reminiscing about Tuptim. She regards this tragedy as an account of her own failure. She remembers having seen Tuptim's relatives bring her in as a gift to the king, but was then too numbed by the cruelty of the harem system to pay attention. Although she liked the girl, she never really tried to talk with her. 'If I had done this,' she says, 'I might have succeeded in winning her confidence, and perhaps have been the means of reconciling her to her life in the palace. That I did not, will ever be a source of poignant regret to me' (RH 18). The author's self-blame suggests a number of things: first, the lack of real options, for reconciliation with the harem life is the most positive outcome in Tuptim's circumstances. Second, it refers to the difficulty even Leonowens as an outsider had in the harem of rising above its quotidian systems and of viewing it from another frame of reference. Third, it implies that Tuptim's fate is traumatic not only for the girl but also for Leonowens.

Leonowens is drawn into the events, when Tuptim's slave girl seeks her out, begging her to help her mistress in any way she can. Leonowens reacts with unwillingness, fatigue, and fear, reactions which she explains as follows: 'I felt a strong reluctance to respond to the cry which had reached me from her, and wished I had never heard it. I was tired of the palace, tired of witnessing wrongs I could not remedy' (RH 21–2). Leonowens's position reminds us of that of the fiancée of 'The Robber Bridegroom' who watches the groom murder another woman. The fiancée's helplessness makes her merge with the victim. Looking on, she discovers what her fate will be were she to marry this man. Although Leonowens was a British subject, she nevertheless feared being made one of the harem women. After all, she was a widow financially dependent on the king and living alone without male protection.

Tuptim is tried twice, and the trial scenes usefully illustrate the roles Leonowens adopts as a witness. Despite her vulnerability, she decides to show loyalty to Tuptim by attending the first trial. This scene elucidates her relationship to the accused victim; it also illustrates her room for manoeuvre. Looking on at Tuptim's torture, Leonowens feels 'as if bound and lacerated' (RH 33). She serves here as an interpersonal witness. 'In this circuit,' explains Kacandes, 'which also occurs within the story level of the text ... a character tries to communicate to another character a personal trauma. That other character's listening, her cowitnessing, becomes the means ... by which the story comes to be' (105). As Leonowens's reactions suggest, she identifies with the victim to the point of merger. There is thus the danger that the impact of witnessing on the witness eclipses the actual victim's experience. What makes Leonowens's situation peculiar, however, is that usually only she can recognize that trauma-causing violence is being inflicted on someone. This is to say that she alone perceives that the treatment to which a woman is subjected in the harem wounds this woman not only physically but also psychically. In this particular case, Tuptim laments that she is punished for something she did not do, while Leonowens insists that the harem system and the Siamese law continually traumatize women. Given such non-recognition, Leonowens's identification with the victim turns her into a substitute victim who must first acknowledge the occurrence of a traumatic event intrapsychically and then adopt the role of an interpersonal witness.[1] Jane's proclamation that she would preach freedom in Rochester's harem (JE 230) implies a similar attitude: Jane envisions recognizing mistreatment on behalf of the harem women; she would then make them see that they are in fact mishandled so that they could demand freedom.

While in 'The Robber Bridegroom' the fiancée cowers behind a barrel fearing discovery, Leonowens's merger with Tuptim prompts her into action. She now acts as a surrogate witness. While surrogate witnessing typically raises social issues of testimony such as how and to what extent we can know another person's trauma (Kacandes 108), Leonowens faces the challenge of having to convince others that a third person's experience really constitutes trauma. She describes her actions thus: 'Losing control over my actions, forgetting that I was a stranger and a foreigner there, and as powerless as the weakest of the oppressed around me, I sprang forward, and heard my voice commanding the executioners to desist, as they valued their lives' (RH 33). In a similar fashion as Jane, who acts against Rochester when she is most vulnerable, Leonowens has the courage to speak out. By feeling with and as Tuptim, she lends her voice to the tortured girl. While Tuptim courageously insists on her innocence, Leonowens's ventriloquism on her behalf – and, by extension, on behalf of all the harem women – goes much further by insisting that no one be subjected to torture and slavery. This insistence stems from the frame of reference within which Leonowens places the trial. Judges, guards, and harem women attend it. Although many feel pity for Tuptim, they nevertheless think she is getting what she deserves. They do not regard her punishment as wounding her psychically. In contrast, Leonowens perceives the trial as essentially unjust; it is the culmination point of an injustice she identifies as having begun when Tuptim was made a present for the king. Leonowens's abolitionist frame of reference and her maternal imperialism make her distance herself from the event's dehumanizing and contaminating power.[2] The thread running throughout *The Romance of the Harem* is her conviction that all forms of enforced subjection and slavery are always wrong. In the harem context, this mode of thinking is new and radical. The book suggests that the lack of socio-political alternatives made it difficult for the harem women to identify trauma-causing incidents. Consequently, they could only seldom bear witness to themselves among themselves.

Leonowens continuously reminds readers that her witnessing was affected by the manifold restrictions placed on her. Because even her successful interventions, such as when she helps a woman called L'Ore gain freedom, remain isolated incidents without larger effects, she suggests that her real merits lie elsewhere. She presents interpersonal witnessing as her most important contribution. She lent an ear to the harem women's lament. Thanks to her anti-slavery ideology, she represents herself as seeing and hearing things in the harem that no one else notices. In her view, this context of general blindness and deafness arises from the women's mutual rivalry for the king's favour, concubinage, the harem's hierarchical system, and slavery. In most situations only she can recognize suffering and name its cause. She presents her listening activity as therapeutic in itself, for she feels with the distressed women, experiencing, if not always voicing, such emotions as pity, sorrow, and indignation at the cruelty they face. The therapeutic effect, she suggests, lies in her recognition of their suffering, which she often communicates by either word or gesture to the sufferer.[3] Even if she is unable to do anything, her responsive listening alleviates the sufferer's pain by verifying this person's experience. By extension, all those incidents of violence she impotently witnesses nevertheless benefit from her active observation, because she identifies the system's injustice, names events causing psychic injury as trauma, records the sufferer's courage, and verifies the existence of violent events. Jane Eyre is engaged in a similar activity at Lowood, where the official policy proclaims the institution's beneficence, while Jane recognizes the suffering the school causes. To be sure, however, this recognition is shared by most students.

In 'The Robber Bridegroom' the bride acts as a surrogate witness when she tells the story of the groom's murder to the wedding guests. She knows that if she manages to persuade them, she can count on this community to protect her. In contrast, in an attempt to save Tuptim, Leonowens confronts Bluebeard (the king) alone, trying to convince him of the wrongness of his actions. Her passionate intervention, however, is possible because she is an outsider and a foreigner. Ironically, the only action available to her is to refer to the king as the ultimate source of authority. Although she is motivated by anti-slavery convictions, the act of entreating him threatens to merge her with the harem women. She begins her defence speech briskly, but soon finds herself faltering. She recounts that 'My voice failed me, and I sank upon the floor by the king's chair' (RH 34). While it is typical of the harem women to lie prostrate before the king, Leonowens accosts him as an equal. This experience of finding herself at the king's mercy brings her to her knees in front of him. She finds she cannot justify her plea with abolitionist arguments, but has to couch them in terms of the harem system. Even so, the king thinks her mad and first rejects the petition, but then succumbs to it, only finally to go back on his word. He orders Tuptim's scaffolds to be erected outside Leonowens's windows, which Leonowens interprets as his revenge on her for daring to oppose his royal will.

The account of Tuptim's tragedy ends by reversing the final scene of 'The Robber Bridegroom.' The bride narrates the truth in the guise of a dream, while the bridegroom hotly denies everything she says. In *The Romance of the Harem* about a month after Tuptim's death, the king tells Leonowens that he dreamed about the dead girl, saying that this dream proved him wrong. Yet he insists that he nevertheless acted correctly, for he demonstrated to Leonowens the primacy of his own culture. He then decides to have an obelisk erected in Tuptim's memory. This conclusion to Tuptim's 'case' juxtaposes the king's memorial obelisk with Leonowens's testimonial narrative as two competing monuments to the unfortunate Tuptim. There is a further twist to this story. In 'The Robber Bridegroom' the bride manages to persuade the community of the truthfulness of her narrative and make it act on her behalf. Similarly, *The Romance of the Harem* ends on a hopeful note, for the whole book concludes with a manifesto issued by King Mongkut's son and successor in which he declares his intention of abolishing slavery in Siam. Given that this son was Leonowens's former student, the ending suggests that there was, in fact, a receptive audience to anti-slavery discourse in the court and that the future may look brighter for the harem women. Nevertheless, thanks to her limited possibilities to intervene in events and change conditions, writing the book is Leonowens's actual means of testimony. Therefore, I next examine the narrative and discursive circuits of witnessing in Leonowens's book.

## Witnessing Cruelty through Writing

Textual witnessing, explains Kacandes, concerns the narrator's communication of the traumatic experiences of characters within a text to its inscribed readers. In narratological terms, this level looks at a narrator's relationship to narratees. In the scrutiny of this level, the focus lies on the various strategies the narrator uses to relay the event and experience of trauma to receivers. Such strategies include, for example, pronouns of personal address serving as invitations to readers to become co-witnesses and rhetorical devices of mimicking traumatic symptoms (narrative indirection, gaps, repetition, and so forth) (Kacandes 111). I single out Leonowens's use of embedded narratives and her style of narration as the primary means through which she turns her narratees into co-witnesses. Kacandes observes that when a narrator does not explicitly identify the narratee, actual readers tend to insert themselves as the narrator's addressees. Therefore, in examining this circuit I speak simply of readers. In order to become co-witnesses, readers will 'need to interpret textual witnessing as the "statement" to which they are to respond' (Kacandes 111). These potential responses belong to the circuits dealing with literary-historical as well as transhistorical-transcultural reception, at which I look in concluding this section.

Although Leonowens functions as the narrator of her book, she includes lengthy embedded narratives that allow the Siamese women to recount their own stories. She also makes the women's bodies speak for them. Her observations of a wrongly slaved woman called L'Ore illustrate this strategy: 'The whole scene was startlingly impressive; the apathy, the deadness, and the barbarous cruelty of the palace life, were never more strikingly brought before me face to face ... this unhappy creature was suffering under some cruel wrong, which no one cared to redress. Naked to the waist, her long filthy hair bound in dense masses under her brow, she sat calmly, uncomplainingly, under a burning tropical sun' (RH 44). The listless body of L'Ore speaks for her, and as narrator, Leonowens makes readers hear the body's silent language of despair. Thus she gives the women room to express themselves on their own terms. The embedded narratives demonstrate the ability of the narrators to give intrapsychic testimony. What this means is that in these particular instances the women recognize that they are being hurt, and their narratives are pleas to Leonowens to serve as an interpersonal witness. Leonowens's listening helps them to articulate their stories – perhaps for the first time. By extension, her activity serves as a model for readers at the discursive level. This situation is typical of *testimonio*, which relies on collaboration in helping the witness's account emerge.[4]

Although narratives of trauma typically portray signs of difficulties with expression, the embedded stories flow with eloquence: 'I was surprised to find that [L'Ore] expressed herself so well, until I remembered that the princesses at Siam make it a special point to educate the slaves born in their household' (RH 50). Moreover, the women's narratives are usually coherent and well-formed. The teller, however, may be exhausted after finishing her story as is L'Ore (RH 57). Although as narrator Leonowens clearly wishes to evoke the admiration of readers for these courageous women, the effect of this strategy is curious. Kacandes (113) maintains that a victim's testimony invites the co-witness to help the victim's story come into being through the act of sharing the task of narration. It is as if the victim pleaded the co-witness to let her speak through the mouth of the co-witness. Yet when Leonowens embeds the women's distressing stories of violence and injustice, the melodramatic eloquence of narration does not seem to fit their experience. Further, the embedded narratives are stylistically uniform, making it hard to distinguish one narrator from the other. This discrepancy raises the question of whose voice we hear in reading these narratives – the women's or Leonowens's?

This melodramatic discrepancy imbues Leonowens's own narrative voice. Tuptim's second trial illustrates Leonowens's role as a textual witness. At this trial she pays attention to what she represents to readers as Tuptim's thorough transformation: the ordeal turns a troublesome child into a heroic woman who defends herself with courage and dignity. Narrating these events, Leonowens emphasizes 'the simple grandeur of that fragile child' (RH 31). While her narration conveys Tuptim's courageous conduct, her strategies of representation manage to distance readers from her by placing the girl in a flood of awe and fear. She endows Tuptim with a kind of sanctity which, while paying tribute to the girl, also avoids intimacy with her. This strategy admits the similarity Tuptim and Leonowens share as women who, although differently, are subject to the king's power. But Leonowens's narrative also underlines their difference: thanks to being an outsider, Leonowens knows she will never be made to find out how she would meet punishment and death. In fact, by dwelling on Tuptim's personal transformation in the face of adversity and by sanctifying it, she sets herself firmly apart from the girl. Consequently, she learns little of what the events actually mean for Tuptim or the other harem women. Instead, she characterizes Tuptim as 'calm and pure,' as someone who 'had already crystallized into a lovely statue' (RH 27), thus illustrating this awe-filled and protective distance. If testimony aims at discovering and creating knowledge about the traumatic event as Dori Laub (62) claims, this eyewitness account reveals little of how the Siamese women actually understood their lives. In Laub's characterization, 'knowledge in the testimony is ... not simply a factual given that is reproduced and replicated by the testifier, but a genuine advent, an event in its own right' (62). In contrast, for Leonowens the harem women's narratives serve as exotic illustrations of the universal wrongness of slavery as a social system.

While Leonowens's willingness to help, her concern, and sincerity are not to be doubted, her narrative testimony nevertheless falters. Discussing the taxing task that witnessing is, Laub (72–3) identifies the kinds of hazards co-witnesses encounter. These hazards may hinder them from properly hearing what the witness says; consequently, their testimony may become skewed. Leonowens's account includes many of the pitfalls Laub mentions. For example, she often reports a sense of paralysis, caused by the fear of merger with the victim; she frequently experiences a sense of withdrawal and numbness as well as hyperemotionality which looks like compassion and caring for the victim, but which in fact overwrites the victim's experiences with those of the co-witness. Although such reactions are surely understandable, they not only focus too much on Leonowens herself but also make it impossible to say what exactly are the events and their ramifications that she narrates. These difficulties, in turn, alert readers to historical and transhistorical circuits of witnessing.

The circuit of literary-historical witnessing concerns the ways in which a text communicates to the actual readers of the culture and time in which it was written. Often later readers have less information about this level (Kacandes 115). *The Romance of the Harem* was published in the United States in 1872 and in 1873 in Great Britain. It definitely did not target a Siamese audience, but was intended for the Anglo-American market. It supplemented financially the lectures in the United States with which Leonowens supported her family. Susan Morgan (ix–x) reports that the reception of *The Romance of the Harem* was mixed: some critics found the book interesting and even disarming, while others castigated Leonowens for ingratitude toward her employer, King Mongkut. Later on, experts on Siam have taken the author to task for factual errors, calling the book a deceitful fantasy (Morgan x–xi, xxxi–xxxii). As Morgan points out, however, settling the question of veracity is difficult, if not impossible, for the book is the only extant account of harem life from the period. Yet it is significant that Leonowens's contemporaries did not seem to regard the book as testimony to the harem women's suffering under slavery, even though its anti-slavery views are forcefully articulated. One would think that American readers in particular, emerging from the Civil War, would have seized on this aspect, but they did not. Thus there was no contemporaneous reception of these aspects of her book.

Transhistorical-transcultural witnessing deals with the outermost communicative circuit in which readers from a culture and historical period other than the one in which a text was written co-witness to the trauma articulated in and through this text (Kacandes 117). Thus present-day readers transact with *The Romance of the Harem* through this circuit. The few present-day commentators of Leonowens's book have recognized its testimonial character, but none have made it their focal point. Even today this dimension remains largely unheard. Kacandes remarks that successful co-witnessing calls for the reader's ability to point out the gaps and silences of the testimony and in the process to produce a narrative about the other circuits of witnessing to trauma (117). When this outermost circuit is 'flowing' then readers serve as co-witnesses. With a circuit's flow Kacandes refers to a reader's careful scrutiny of all the previous five circuits of the textual testimony and the difficulties (short-circuits) testimony may involve at these circuits. Such flow includes a reader's self-reflexive analysis of her own role. The transhistorical-transcultural circuit also concerns the attempt to understand how a particular text in its entirety can testify about trauma-inducing events. At this circuit successful witnessing demands that readers make sure they know what exactly took place (Kacandes 133). As was mentioned before, such confirmation is impossible as regards the events depicted in *The Romance of the Harem*. There simply is not enough data to check the veracity of Leonowens's book. Yet its mixture of fact and fiction (or fantasy) suggests that for Leonowens the onus of testimony lies not in a factual record but in emotional experience. The word 'romance' in the book's title implies that she places a premium on communicating the complex and heart-wrenching emotional experiences that harem life evoked in her. In fact, the genre of *testimonio* frequently displays discrepancies between witness accounts and historical facts. Brooks (182–3) explains that these gaps arise from *testimonio*'s goal of conveying the significance the narrated events have for witnesses. Consequently, transmitting this impact relies less on providing a factual autobiography than a 'vision' in which objective reality acquires a secondary importance. In the merging of fact and fiction, the events are presented from a highly subjective viewpoint in which the truth of memories is primarily emotional, not actual (Whitehead 40). One can also speculate that this merger was perhaps Leonowens's solution to finding an appropriate way to narrate trauma. Be it as it may, although Leonowens's testimony does not do full justice to the women whose stories and suffering she depicts, her book nevertheless serves as a powerful attack on the evils of slavery and, as such, a reinforcement of abolitionism.

When we compare *The Romance of the Harem* with *Jane Eyre*, there are telling differences. Although Jane recognizes Bertha's suffering, the first wife nevertheless remains an alien for her. On the whole, Jane is satisfied with Rochester's report of Bertha without any interest in probing what the disastrous marriage meant for the first wife. Meyer observes that Brontë was really only concerned with the damage that imperialist ideology wreaked on Britain. The author evokes this discourse only to inflect it back on British society, targeting with it such domestic problems as female subordination in sexual relationships and the lack of economic options of middle-class women without family ties. In fact, it is this group of women who resemble her that she most empathizes with. The women above her station in life, such as Blanche Ingram, or below her, such as the village girls whom she teaches, receive little understanding. Although Brontë identifies the similarities between the oppression of women at home and of, for example, black people abroad, she ends up marking all aspects of oppression as non-British, resulting from a damaging contact with other peoples (Meyer 94–7, 112–13).[5] Thus she not only represses the history of British imperialist domination but also represents racial oppression as something the British are 'in danger of being sullied by, something foreign and "other" to them' (Meyer, 113; see also Zonana 72). Zlotnick adds that the ideology of maternal imperialism enabled Jane to participate in the glories of the British Empire without leaving home. By rehumanizing Rochester, she can imagine herself to be indirectly at work for the public good in the privacy of her home. She emerges as St John Rivers's domestic counterpart, a missionary at the home front (Zlotnick 36, 41).

In contrast, Leonowens is much more sensitive than is either Jane or Brontë to the suffering of the various women she encounters. She lends an ear to slave girls and the high and mighty alike, recognizing that all positions in Siamese society involve women in trauma. She stresses that regardless of station, the concrete realness of suffering unites women. No one deserves such treatment and no one is more entitled than others to be freed from it. Therefore, Leonowens's testimonial account exhibits another perception of the mechanisms and effects of 'a sultan's harem' than does Brontë's novel. Although Leonowens depicts an indigenous system of slavery, she suggests that it is comparable to slavery everywhere, for example, in the United States. In this respect, the West is just as tainted as is the East. Furthermore, given that she had lived much of her life in the East, she had some understanding of cultural differences without immediately resorting to binary thinking according to which 'our' systems are automatically better than 'theirs.' In fact, her chequered background suggests a hybrid cultural identity without a clear-cut national heritage. Thus she often represents her observations of Siamese cultural customs without evaluating them; they are no better or worse than British customs, but simply different. One might characterize her attitude as that of an anthropologist, an approach typical of receivers of witness accounts in *testimonio* (Brooks 182).[6] Nevertheless, Leonowens' book, Zlotnick explains, cannot but reveal the serious limitations of maternal imperialism, thanks to the thin line separating the governess from the Siamese women. This proximity makes Leonowens retreat from her role as maternal imperialist and thus from her moral mission; in the end, all she can do is try to preserve her identity as an Englishwoman (Zlotnick 48–50).

## *Wide Sargasso Sea*: Jean Rhys's Caribbean Nightmare

The novel I discuss next is also situated in a context where colonialism, with its system of slavery, has wreaked havoc. Among its victims are those caught in-between cultures; in this instance, Creole women. Jean Rhys's *Wide Sargasso Sea* (1966) is beyond doubt the best-known adaptation of *Jane Eyre*. Rhys challenges Brontë's views on British colonialism in *Wide Sargasso Sea* by underlining the role 'Bluebeard' plays in *Jane Eyre*. This book is a prequel to Brontë's novel with the first Mrs Rochester in the limelight. It provides an alternative account of Rochester's confession to Jane after Bertha's presence at Thornfield has been revealed. To be sure, Rhys neither names the male protagonist Rochester nor his English mansion Thornfield; moreover, she calls the first wife Antoinette instead of Bertha.[7] Many details nevertheless forge a strong link between the novels: for example, the Mason family plays a decisive role in Rhys's novel; the husband renames the heroine Bertha; the heroine's life story tallies with Rochester's account of his first wife; both novels name Grace as the wife's keeper; and, finally, both depict the wife's escape from her solitary cell. The links between the two books include 'Bluebeard' as well. For the sake of simplicity I call Rhys's male protagonist Rochester and the wife Antoinette while talking about *Wide Sargasso Sea*, but I refer to her as Bertha while dealing with *Jane Eyre*.

In evoking *Jane Eyre*, *Wide Sargasso Sea* activates its ties to 'Bluebeard.' If a reader were not familiar with *Jane Eyre*, she could nevertheless spot the intertextual associations Rhys's novel has with this tale.[8] In this novel, as in 'The Robber Bridegroom,' a (step)father betroths his (step) daughter to a seemingly respectable man, whom she finds out to be crooked. Rochester not only robs Antoinette of her considerable fortune but also sets out to dismember her or, rather, to disintegrate her psyche and soul by imprisoning her in his mansion. The tale embeds the plots of Bluebeard and the woman, and Rhys elaborates this structure by letting both parties narrate the events from their perspectives. Further, she elaborates Rochester's self-pitying confession in *Jane Eyre*, rewriting it in terms of a testimony of the multiple wrongs he claims to have endured in the West Indies. Rhys juxtaposes Bluebeard's self-justifying narrative with Antoinette's associative autobiographical narrative about the violence she has suffered throughout her life, which culminates in Rochester's cruelty towards her. In a similar fashion as *Jane Eyre*, *Wide Sargasso Sea* dwells on the genesis of Bluebeard's vault by scrutinizing what accounts for Bluebeard's murderous impulse and what role the wife plays in this dynamic.

*Wide Sargasso Sea* employs repetition as a key narrative strategy. Repetition is a main device in trauma fiction, for it mimics the effects of trauma, suggesting the insistent return of the traumatic event(s) and the disruption of narrative chronology. Given the sustained evocation of *Jane Eyre* in *Wide Sargasso Sea*, it may appear that Rhys's characters simply repeat the actions of the earlier narrative: their decisions and fates seem predestined and known from the beginning (see Whitehead 89). Whenever repetition produces this effect of inevitability, it bears comparison with Freud's notion of the repetition compulsion. This is repetition in its negative aspect, as characters replay the past as if it were fully present, remaining caught within trauma's paralysing influence (Whitehead 86, 90).[9] Borrowing Whitehead's words from another context, *Wide Sargasso Sea*, however, attempts 'to grasp what was not fully known or realised in the first instance, and thereby to depart from it or pass beyond it' (90).[10] This is repetition in its positive aspect, as it works towards memory and catharsis. Repetition is inherently ambivalent, suspended between trauma and catharsis. I place my scrutiny of Rhys, Brontë, and 'Bluebeard' in this context of repetitive intertextual relationships as trauma fiction.

Patricia Moran identifies repetition as a key strategy in what she calls Rhys's aesthetics of trauma that, in her view, has its roots in the author's personal life. Rhys's mother neglected and severely punished her daughter; to this ongoing maternal abuse was later added the sexual abuse by a family friend. Writing supplied Rhys the means to confront these traumas (Moran 91). In Moran's analysis, the author and her fictional characters merge into one and the same 'Rhys woman' whose masochistic behaviour paradoxically aims at undoing and perpetuating the traumas that have convinced her of unworthiness. While Moran examines trauma by placing a premium on its infliction and behavioural consequences, I approach trauma in *Wide Sargasso Sea* by focusing on the effects it has on memory and narration. Instead of dwelling on the abusive mechanisms that cause trauma in this novel (or in Rhys's personal life), I concentrate on the repetitive patterns trauma creates and the traumatized subject's attempts to give testimony to painful experiences as a means of recollection and possible healing.

*Wide Sargasso Sea* consists of interconnected patterns of repetition: Antoinette's marriage replays her mother's marriage; the traumatic events of Antoinette's childhood are revoked during her honeymoon; in the novel's second part Antoinette recounts the events of its first part when she tells Rochester about her family's life. The third part, consisting of Antoinette's jumbled memories, repeats preceding parts; moreover, it recoils the narrative back to its beginning by recalling the burning down of Coulibri, the family home, thus raising the question of the ending's relationship to the beginning. Further, Rochester recounts the events in the West Indies that 'changed him out of all knowledge' (WSS 145). Couching my analysis in Kacandes's terms, I first look at the circuits of witnessing as they deal with patterns of repetition at the level of the fictional world, reflecting on how repetition affects Antoinette's and Rochester's narrative capabilities. I then examine Antoinette and Rochester as narrator witnesses who attempt to recall traumatic events in another key, one that endows repetition with cathartic elements. In concluding, I consider the (implied) author's role at the circuit of literary-historical witnessing, discussing the novel's overall design as an adaptation of *Jane Eyre* and 'Bluebeard.'

### Annette, Antoinette, and Bertha: Patterns of Destructive Repetition

Claire Kahane (335–6) draws attention to Bluebeard Gothic's portrayal of the heroine's predecessor in terms of the mother–daughter relationship. Her mother's namesake, Jane Eyre, insists on marrying for love as did also her mother. Both choose husbands to whom the *pater familias* objects (Mr Reed and St John Rivers, respectively). Similarly, in *Wide Sargasso Sea* the names Annette and Antoinette suggest doubling between mother and daughter, a kinship extending to their fates. While Jane's diminished circumstances result from a family dispute (Mr Reed leaves Jane's mother penniless), the poverty Annette and Antoinette suffer in the novel's opening is caused by the abolition of slavery that deprives the family of their former means of living. This change affects their social and racial status: although they are Dominicans, they are neither 'natives' nor 'proper' whites, but impoverished Creoles.[11] White colonial society does not wholeheartedly accept them, and they are not welcomed into native black society either. In Ciolkowski's words, 'not quite English and not quite native, Rhys's Creole woman straddles the embattled divide between human and savage, core and periphery, self and other' (340). This background leaves mother and daughter a constricted space of manoeuvre, and both try in vain to make their respective, European-born husbands understand this predicament. I now focus on the ways in which Antoinette's life repeats her mother's life, arguing that both are frustrated in their attempts to be heard. Both suffer from a sustained state of anxiety stretching over a long period of time culminating in a traumatic event that pushes each to a breaking point. In Kacandes's terms, mother and daughter try to find an interpersonal witness in their respective husbands, one who would enable them to act as intrapersonal witnesses to their distressing fates. I claim that the husbands' deafness to their wives' attempts at giving testimony sets in motion a dynamic that turns the husband into a Bluebeard and the wife into his victim. In this process Antoinette's fate is made to reflect her mother Annette's destiny. In focusing on relationships in the fictional world, my analysis stays within the circuits typical of the story level, namely intra- and interpersonal witnessing.

Widowed and impoverished, Annette Cosway is left with two children and a decaying house. She saves them by reselling herself on the marriage market to Mr Mason, a wealthy Englishman. Her rise from poverty, however, rekindles resentment among the local population, and Annette begs Mr Mason to move the family somewhere else. One night the locals set the Cosway home on fire, causing the death of Annette's disabled son, Pierre. For Annette, Pierre has embodied the family's vulnerability. His death hits directly at her sense of helplessness. Holding Mr Mason responsible, she is estranged from him. The trauma of her son's death unhinges her: she begins drinking and slides into madness. Mr Mason shuts her up in a house with abusive caretakers, while he himself travels widely. Such is the broad outline of a life that Antoinette appears set on repeating. Her adulthood too is shaped by the necessity of succeeding on the marriage market. She too marries an Englishman incapable of understanding a culture that is foreign to him. Once married, her life is also hampered by the gossip and ill-will of local people.

Antoinette recounts numerous quarrels between Annette and Mr Mason concerning Coulibri during which they 'always said the same things' (WSS 27). Once Annette openly declares that 'The people here hate us. They certainly hate me' (WSS 27), a statement that is met with Mr Mason's laughter. Annette tries to make him see the situation from her perspective: 'How do you know that I was not harmed? ... We were so poor then ... we were something to laugh at. But we are not poor now ... They talk about us without stopping. They invent stories about you, and lies about me' (WSS 27). Mr Mason thinks Annette dramatizes the situation, the worst of which is over. She comes from a slave-owning family and married into one; thus she is bound to evoke resentment in former slaves (WSS 27–8). Annette insists on the complexities of her situation. As long as she was destitute, she was tolerated, but now she has not only pulled through but also re-established her former standing as the wife of a slave owner. Although slavery has been abolished, Mr Mason plans to use coolies at his farms. His use of cheap imported labour shows to the locals that racial injustice and exploitation continue. Antoinette's iterative account of these quarrels describes a dead end with her mother speaking about going away 'persistently' and 'angrily,' and Mr Mason always replying 'I don't understand at all' (WSS 28). What becomes clear is his unwillingness even to try to understand his wife, a reluctance that leads to disastrous consequences. Time and time again Annette accosts Mr Mason, asking him to receive her account of the family's hardships, but to no avail. Thanks to his refusal to act as an interpersonal witness to his wife, she can neither organize past events in her mind nor ensure a safe future for her children. The end of the first marriage left Annette financially marooned, while the second marriage leaves her psychically isolated.

Antoinette's marriage repeats this same deadlock. Like the West Indies, Antoinette is an enigma to Rochester: she is un-English in looks, behaviour, and manner of speech. She does not even make sense, as he finds her explanations full of contradictions and uncertainties (WSS 73). For him, the incoherence of her explanations echoes the threat of miscegenation that lurks everywhere. The marriage rekindles old resentment, creating hostile tension between Antoinette, the servants, and the locals. Although Rochester is aware of these tensions, he, like Mr Mason, makes no effort to understand them. Instead of taking the role of a co-witness, he chooses to cultivate everything that supports his prejudice. Upon receiving a hate letter slandering the Cosway family from a local man called Daniel who claims to be Antoinette's half-brother, Rochester states that 'I felt no surprise. It was as if I'd expected it, been waiting for it' (WSS 82). This supposed confirmation of his prejudice and misgivings makes him reject the co-witness' role, leading to his first symbolic annihilation of Antoinette. He picks up a golden-brown orchid, associated in his mind with her, and tramples it into mud (WSS 82). From Daniel's letter onwards, Rochester always sides with biased and distorted information about Antoinette. His bigotry launches the gradual erection of Bluebeard's vault.

Believing Daniel's insinuations about miscegenation and madness in the Cosway family, Rochester begins to withdraw from Antoinette. In order to redress this situation, Antoinette begs Christophene, her former nanny and a family servant, to supply her with a love potion. The reluctant Christophene concedes, but makes Antoinette promise to try first to sort things out by talking. The confrontation scene (WSS 104–13) revokes the quarrels between Mr Mason and Annette. Parts of it are as if lifted straight out of their exchanges; for example, when Antoinette comments Daniel's letter, her words echo those of her mother: 'His real name, if he has one, is Daniel Boyd. He hates all white people, but he hates me the most. He tells lies about us and he is sure that you will believe him and not listen to the other side' (WSS 106). This scene explicitly focuses on Antoinette giving testimony to Rochester about the painful events in her life. Denying the existence of another side, Rochester, however, acts like Mr Mason. Rochester's mind is already closed against Antoinette, a closure that he understands as calmness and self-possession (WSS 105). He does not want to listen: 'Not tonight ... Some other time' (WSS 106), but she insists on telling him about her mother and their life.[12] This scene refers to Rochester's confession to Jane after his thwarted attempt at bigamy, an intertextual reference to which I return shortly.

Antoinette's narrative is replete with signals asking Rochester to receive it attentively. Like her mother, she asks the husband to serve as an interpersonal witness to the events she recounts. All are disturbing in nature: poverty, contempt, betrayal, rejection, abuse. Her story contains only a crude outline of the past and is full of gaps. Such lacunae are typical of trauma narratives, as they invariably testify to an absence, thanks to the fact that the trauma has not been witnessed yet (Laub 57). The following examples illustrate how Antoinette turns to Rochester. In describing the significance of Coulibri, Antoinette says, '"If I could make you see it, because they destroyed it and it is only here now." She struck her forehead' (WSS 109). She continually tries to make Rochester see the intimate connection of places with painful states of mind and memories. Further, she recounts the wound she got the night Coulibri was demolished: 'My head was bandaged because someone had thrown a stone at me. Aunt Cora told me that it was healing up and that it wouldn't spoil me on my wedding day. But I think it did spoil me for my wedding day and all the other days and nights' (WSS 110). Antoinette does not disclose that this someone was her one and only friend, but she does emphasize the lasting damaging effect of losing whatever trust she once had. To cite one more example, Antoinette reveals the depths of her mother's degradation when she relates seeing her mother made drunk and then taken advantage of: 'I saw the man lift her up out of the chair and kiss her. I saw his mouth fasten on hers and she went all soft and limp in his arms and he laughed ... When I saw that I ran away. Christophene was waiting for me when I came back crying' (WSS 111).

Kacandes observes that testimony flows at the interpersonal circuit whenever the co-witness understands the witness's account as a statement requiring an emphatic and respectful response from him or her. Moreover, testimonial flow requires that the co-witness be able to transmit this experience to another. This is to say, he or she can serve the role of a surrogate witness, relaying the received witness account to other persons (Kacandes 107–9). Consequently, Rochester's attentive listening would ideally become the means by which Antoinette's story is enabled. His first task would be to acknowledge the existence of hurtful incidents, thus making it possible for Antoinette to confront their shattering nature. Without such affirming encouragement, traumatized persons find it difficult, if not impossible, to approach these events, not to speak of forming a conception of them. Further, a co-witness helps the witness to give birth to the knowledge of the event. Such knowledge includes acknowledging the significance and effects the events have on the witness; this recognition is created together through narration and listening. Often it requires that the co-witness meet and bear the witness's silence, hearing its message of the difficulties of narrating trauma (Laub 62, 64). The beginning of Rochester's listening is actually encouraging. Obviously Antoinette finds it hard to begin her narrative, and he helps her: 'Then she was silent for so long that I said gently, "I know that after your father died, she was very lonely and unhappy"' (WSS 107). While listening he poses a few clarifying questions to Antoinette such as 'And who were they?' and 'What about you?' (WSS 108), but he also pacifies her with soothing, empty words such as 'put the sad things away. Don't think about them and nothing will be spoiled, I promise you' (WSS 110). After finishing with the incident of Annette's abuse and her own shock and grief, Antoinette remains silent for a long time. Her silence allows Rochester space to respond to her narrative with its ample signs of her need for a co-witness.

Rochester, however, says nothing whatsoever. His silence signals to Antoinette his refusal to hear and empathize with her. Rochester wants neither to invest emotionally in Antoinette's narrative nor to be actively present in the encounter in order to help her give testimony. A likely reason for this uncaring reaction stems from the effects of co-witnessing. Listening makes the co-witness a participant in trauma, which is potentially a frightening experience. As Laub (58) puts it, listeners have to be witnesses not only to the traumatized person but also to themselves. By preserving their own position and perspective, listeners are ideally able to distinguish their reactions from those of the witness. Feeling betrayed by his father and the Mason family, Rochester fears admitting similarity with Antoinette and merging with her. As Nancy Harrison (209) points out, Rochester intuits that by playing the part he was expected to play, he is a mere puppet with his father holding the strings. Hating his own vulnerability, he directs his feelings of resentment, blame, and anger at Antoinette. He turns down the invitation to co-witnessing, a fact Antoinette acknowledges by saying: '"I have said all I want to say. I have tried to make you understand. But nothing has changed." She laughed' (WSS 111). Her laughter expresses incredulity, contempt, and resignation, proving that she realizes Rochester will never serve as an interpersonal witness for her. As neither gestures nor words reach Rochester, laughter remains Antoinette's sole means of piercing through his armour.

Besides Rochester's silence, his refusal is indicated by his renaming of Antoinette as Bertha (WSS 94). Believing Daniel's insinuations, it is actually Rochester who is accountable for forcing Antoinette to repeat her mother's fate. The name Bertha condenses his hostile ambivalence. Having learned that Bertha was the name of Antoinette's mother, he merges the daughter with the mother by changing Antoinette's name. Antoinette is the successor to the woman Rochester first imprisons in Bluebeard's vault: fearful of the supposed truthfulness of Daniel's slander, he envisions Annette as the emblem of the Creole woman's unmanageable and threatening sexuality. What reinforces the daughter's merger with the mother in his mind is the white dress she wears; this garment is heavy with meaning. Rochester is aware of the dress's sexual connotations, knowing that Antoinette has put it on in order to seduce him.[13] Now, however, the dress repels him (WSS 105), thanks to his ambivalent hostility toward her. Daniel's insults have strengthened Rochester's views, according to which Antoinette is a Creole woman through and through: she enjoys having sex too much and is probably willing to have it with anyone regardless of colour or family ties. In order to prove his prejudice correct, he is bent on making sure that Antoinette replicates her mother, a goal Christophene sums up in the following fashion: 'It is in your mind to pretend she is mad ... The doctors say what you tell them to say ... She will be like her mother' (WSS 132). In Rhys's interpretation, then, Bluebeard's murderous impulse has its basis in his fear of woman as other – in this instance, a racial, cultural, and sexual other. Thus, when Rochester contemplates his future and draws a room on the third floor of an English house, placing a scribbled woman there (WSS 98), he is depicting both mother and daughter as prisoners of Bluebeard's vault.

As we have seen, Rochester's rejection of the co-witness's role forms the starting point in a process that turns him into Bluebeard and Antoinette into Bluebeard's wife. Dismemberment begins with Rochester's insistence to Antoinette that 'on this of all nights, you must be Bertha' (WSS 112). He first annihilates her on the level of language, an act of violence that he continues later in the night by calling her Marionette and Marionetta (WSS 127). Renaming serves the same function as Bluebeard's pronouncement to his wife: 'Madam, you must die ... Your time has come' (Tatar, *Secrets* 177). Thanks to Rochester's refusal to remember what happened (WSS 113), readers must fit together dispersed pieces of information from which they can nevertheless conclude that he makes such violent love to Antoinette that it resembles more a rape than an act of love. In the couple's bedroom he kills Antoinette in 'his way,' thus transforming this space into Bluebeard's vault. Afterwards he draws 'the sheet over her gently as if I covered a dead girl' (WSS 114). Convinced that there are two deaths – a psychic and a bodily death – Antoinette dies for the first time: her soul and mind are broken. Rochester's physical, linguistic, and psychic dismemberment of her turns her into a mechanical doll or a marionette that he can manipulate as he likes. His adultery with Amélie marks his flourishing touch. Lee Erwin (151) observes that by sleeping with the servant girl Rochester performs an act of purification the goal of which is to relay the sexual 'contamination' he has taken from Antoinette back onto her. Ironically, this act merges him with colonialist slave owners. From this point onward the couple is propelled by the kind of destructive repetition characteristic of Mr Mason's and Annette's marriage. Antoinette turns into Bertha-Annette, laughing crazily, drinking, abusing her husband verbally and threatening him. Hardening his heart, Rochester resolves to crush Antoinette's hatred with his own. In the end, he turns into a replica of Mr Mason by shutting his mad wife up, leaving her in negligent care, travelling here and there, and trying to forget about her.

As was suggested earlier, Rochester's refusal to serve as a co-witness to Antoinette refocuses Rochester's confession to Jane in *Jane Eyre*. Although Jane is exhausted from the day's ordeals, Rochester neverthe-less begs her to listen to him. She willingly acquiesces and throughout his account signals her encouraging presence in looks, gestures, and words. Jane accepts the role of an interpersonal witness, thus enabling Rochester for the first time to tell of his past and reflect on its mean-ing to another person. Yet Jane also fulfils her role in a manner un-foreseen by him, for she retains a healthy distance by not being drawn into the seductive dynamics of his confession. In other words, she ac-knowledges his trauma, but is also able to assess it critically without losing an empathetic understanding of his suffering. The dialogue Rhys establishes between the two texts shows Rochester enjoying the privilege of which he deprives Antoinette. Through this dialogue, *Wide Sargasso Sea* ponders narrative testimony as a means for seeking deliv-erance from destructive repetition. As is typical of postcolonial fiction, it fills in many gaps left in *Jane Eyre* by Rochester's sketchy account of his marriage. For example, it seizes on his allusions to Bertha's beauty and her similarity to Blanche Ingram to suggest his initial infatuation with her and to cast doubt upon him as a victim of paternal forces. By identifying such gaps and by representing them in terms that are alien to Brontë's novel, Rhys takes up the role no one is willing to take in *Jane Eyre*: the role of an interpersonal witness to Bertha. The results of Rhys's witnessing are recorded in the whole of *Wide Sargasso Sea*, an outcome that I discuss subsequently.

*Wide Sargasso Sea* shows that Rochester's confession is highly selec-tive; thanks to its crucial omissions, it fails to relieve his troubled mind. Rochester's failure is contrasted with what one might characterize as the success of Antoinette's testimony. I now move on to consider the circuit of textual witnessing in this novel, one that handles (embedded) narrators and their relationships to the narratee as a way of dealing with trauma. I first discuss Rochester's narrative testimony and then contrast it with Antoinette's testimony.

### 'But It Is Not So, Nor It Was Not So': Narrative Testimony as Self-Justification

Rochester's retrospective narrative takes place in Part Two of *Wide Sar-gasso Sea*, the longest of its three parts. It has been described as an older Rochester's self-pitying writing of his younger self (Harrison 237), an anti-*Bildungs* narrative of the young Edward Rochester (Kendrick), and a self-justification, an attempt at an analytic explanation of the breakdown of his marriage and of his wife that has the shape of a letter to his father that he will never send (Mezei 205). I treat it as an instance of textual witnessing in Kacandes's sense in which Rochester as a narrator tries to articulate his traumatic past experiences to a narratee. Significantly, Rochester's account shows him to be engaged in a search for an empathetic co-witness who would help him act the role of intrapersonal witness to himself; his plea for understanding from a responsive recipient thus resembles the one Antoinette futilely directed at him.

Part Two interweaves Rochester's and Antoinette's narrative voices, as his narrative is once interrupted by hers (WSS 89–98).[14] The resulting pattern echoes the textual and spatial architecture of 'Bluebeard,' for Antoinette's contribution in this second part is ensconced between Rochester's parts: Rochester–Antoinette–Rochester. This design illustrates woman as imprisoned within Bluebeard's plot.[15] I return subsequently to the book's total pattern, but for now I shortly dwell on the motivation and effect of Rochester's narrative. His haggard looks and haunted demeanour (WSS 145) imply that the time in the West Indies has wounded him permanently. His narrative confirms this implication, as it marks his repeated efforts to remember what took place in his past. From the start it becomes evident that his narrative recall is troubled and blocked: he may suddenly change tense (WSS 55), narrative chronology is jumbled (for example, he deals with his wedding before disclosing an incident preceding it, WSS 64–6), and he concedes that there are 'blanks in [his] mind that cannot be filled up' (WSS 64). Some of these blanks derive from Rochester's avowed determination *not* to remember what happened (WSS 113). The result is highly ambivalent: on one hand, Rochester narrates in order to understand what happened and why; on the other hand, by actively blocking memories, he eschews probing his past in depth. Kacandes (113) observes that in order for traumatized persons to begin the process of breaking out of inflexible traumatic recall, they have to recreate the traumatic scene in their minds and try to change at least one element in it. Rochester cannot succeed in loosening the stranglehold of compulsive repetition, thanks to his active refusal to remember the traumatic events in their entirety.

The clearest indicators of this compulsive repetition are what one may call the refrains from the discourse of other people echoing in Rochester's head. These refrains either modify or even contest what he says. They thus imply a nagging, unappeasable doubt on account of which his narrative fails to soothe him. Tellingly, the persistent refrains largely, but not solely, derive from Christophene's contesting replies to Rochester. An example illustrates how her words, given in italics, replay in his head and how he responds to this internalized voice:

> Pity. Is there none for me? Tied to a lunatic wife for life – a drunken lying lunatic – gone her mother's way.
> *'She love you so much, so much. She thirsty for you. Love her a little like she say. It's all that you can love – a little.'*
> Sneer to the last, Devil. Do you think that I don't know? She thirsts for *anyone* – not for me ... (WSS 135)

The excerpt shows Rochester juggling in his mind between what he knows to be just and fair (such as empathy and pity) and his self-serving and self-pitying justifications. Much of his narrative records similar internal dialogues in which he acts, as it were, as both a prosecutor and a defence attorney. The defence attorney, however, gains the upper hand, as Rochester always accepts the defence attorney's excuse for letting him off the hook. The confrontation with Christophene is particularly significant because she reminds him of his brutal acts against and violent passion for Antoinette, likening his conduct to the way native men mishandle their wives – and it is these memories that Rochester is determined to suppress. Instead of admitting his deeds then and as he replays the events in his head, he invariably finds ways to counter Christophene's arguments and ridicule her. Moreover, as Erwin points out, he occasionally misremembers what he has been told so that the refrain playing in his mind is more negative than the original phrase. Erwin's example (148) is Daniel's insulting greeting to Antoinette: 'Give my love to your wife – my sister ... You are not the first to kiss her pretty face' (WSS 104), words that Rochester later remembers as *'Give my sister your wife a kiss from me. Love her as I did – oh yes I did'* (WSS 130). While Daniel never says that he had an incestuous relationship with Antoinette, his words take this malignant twist in Rochester's mind; Rochester, however, is unaware of such biased changes.

These telling changes point to the ineffectiveness of the cultural categories with whose help Rochester tries to make sense of his experiences in the Caribbean. Winterhalter (223) explains that Rochester's pre-scripted, English concept of masculinity engages him in an attempt to reaffirm his manhood in the Caribbean world whose languages and culture are inhospitable to his desires (see Kendrick's similar account). Erwin (144) specifies Rochester's explanatory terms: Rochester interprets Antoinette and her culture in terms of sexuality and morality – miscegenation and contamination – while Antoinette accounts for her displaced condition in terms of historically specific shifts in class and economic power. The importance of the explanatory frameworks they apply is grounded in the nature of traumatic events. Given that trauma arises from painful experiences that the mind cannot account for at the instance of their occurrence, it draws attention to the discourses with whose help one tries to explain these experiences. The distinction between traumatic recollection and narrative memory (Whitehead 86–7) throws further light on Rochester's testimony that represents an effort to transform traumatic recollection into narrative memory. Traumatic recollection refers to the shock impact a traumatic experience has on a person. As was mentioned, in Rochester's case it arises from his inability to fit the events in the West Indies, including his own father's treachery, into prior frameworks of understanding. Consequently, he re-enacts these events in a disturbingly literal and precise manner, while the events themselves remain largely unavailable to conscious recall and control. Thus the ability to recover the past is closely tied up with the inability to have access to it – there is both too little and too much memory of the event. Whitehead observes that recovery requires changing traumatic recollection into narrative memory. The traumatic event should be fitted into a sufficiently expressive explanatory framework, and it also should be integrated into the individual's life history (87, 140–1). Giving testimony often requires stretching the expressive capabilities of language or even the invention of new linguistic means. Rochester never earnestly entertains the possibility that any other discourses than his colonial, white, British ones could account for his experiences. This reluctance has at least two consequences: on a personal level, his narrative testimony remains grooved in the same tracks, failing to enable him to act the role of an intrapersonal witness, while on a social level, social healing cannot begin to take place, thanks to Rochester's refusal to acknowledge his responsibility for and participation in the events.

This self-justifying nature of Rochester's testimony is highlighted through the links *Wide Sargasso Sea* shares with 'Bluebeard.' Rochester's narrative in Part Two is framed by Antoinette's narrative in Parts One and Three. Thus the overall narrative design of the book places Rochester's narrative ensconced between Antoinette's two narrative turns. This design recalls the exchange between Mr Fox and his bride at their wedding feast. In its defensive denial Rochester's testimony resembles the bridegroom's reaction to the bride's account of his cruelty. Everything she says Mr Fox counters with a pledge that 'it is not so, nor it was not so,' reassuringly adding 'And God forbid it should be so' (Tatar, *Secrets* 186–7). Playing both parts in his mind, Rochester invariably sides with Mr Fox. His choice of allegiance derives from the ultimate motivation of his testimony that is whetted by the desire to forget. In concluding his narrative, Rochester describes his motive as thus: 'I too can wait – for the day when she is only a memory to be avoided, locked away, and like all memories a legend. Or a lie ...' (WSS 142). Rochester wants his recurring memories to peter out in the deadening effect of forgetting. Achieving this goal requires that he turn Antoinette into one in a series of women, a goal that identifies Rochester as Bluebeard. He explains that 'very soon she'll join all the others who know the secret and will not tell it. Or cannot. Or try and fail because they do not know enough. They can be recognised. White faces, dazed eyes, aimless gestures, high-pitched laughter. The way they walk and talk and scream and try to kill (themselves or you) if you laugh back at them. Yes, they've got to be watched. For the time comes when they try to kill, then disappear. But others are waiting to take their places, it's a long, long line. She's one of them' (WSS 141–2). Rochester's fearful rejection of Antoinette results in a paranoid distrust of all women, whose 'true' nature he claims he now can recognize. Consequently, all women are one and the same mad Bertha, whose cunning, deceit, and murderous impulses require constant vigilance from Rochester. Such vigilance is best kept in a secluded place – a vault, in fact: 'I drew a house surrounded by trees ... I divided the third floor into rooms and in one room I drew a standing woman – a child's scribble, a dot for a head, a larger one for the body, a triangle for a skirt, slanting lines for arms and feet. But it was an English house' (WSS 134–5).

As it is, Antoinette remains a festering sore, forcing Rochester to replay his past. He is honest and self-reflexive enough to be aware of some of the reasons that account for his transformation into Bluebeard. He is cognizant of the disturbing effects the alien culture plays on him that he then deflects back on Antoinette. The decisive factor is his conscious choice to give in to hatred. This choice seems motivated by his belief that Antoinette was included in the plot against him for which he blames his father and Mr Mason. What is more, although he intuits that the magic of the West Indies islands that he associates with Antoinette is true and trustworthy, he nevertheless decides to give it up. He muses: 'It was a beautiful place – wild, untouched, above all untouched, with an alien, disturbing, secret loveliness. And it kept its secret. I'd find myself think-

ing, "What I see is nothing – I want what it *hides* – that is not nothing"'
(WSS 73). His testimony suggests that the reason for his not finding the
secret stems largely from his proclivity to explain everything in sexual
terms: 'I won't tell you that I scarcely listened to your stories. I was longing for night and darkness and the time when the moonflowers open'
(WSS 139). His turning a deaf ear on Antoinette's stories is revealing;
interpreting his longing as mere sexual lust, he nevertheless cannot but
record the entirety of the West Indian world, which consists of tales,
songs, sounds, and rich tactile and olfactory sensations. Together they
are the secret, but Rochester's narrow-mindedness precludes him from
understanding this. Consequently, Rochester concludes his narrative
with the repetition of the word 'nothing,' an indication that Antoinette's
idea of everyone dying two deaths applies to him too. While Antoinette,
however, is aware of her psychic death in Rochester's hands, Rochester,
in contrast, wards off such recognition by making woman represent
death. The reverberating 'nothing' refers to Bluebeard's vault as an externalized representation of an inner condition.

We are now in the position of perceiving another layer of meaning
that *Wide Sargasso Sea* adds to Rochester's confession in *Jane Eyre*. When
Jane defies the seduction of his confidences, he proclaims in desperation: 'I could bend her with my finger and thumb: and what good
would it do if I bent, if I uptore, if I crushed her? ... Whatever I do
with its cage, I cannot get at it – the savage, beautiful creature ... And
it is you, spirit – with will and energy, and virtue and purity – that I
want: not alone your brittle frame' (JE 271). *Wide Sargasso Sea* depicts
the first wife as everything Rochester claims Jane to be. Antoinette was
a 'savage, beautiful creature,' with energy, virtue, and purity, nestling
against Rochester's heart, but he crushed her body and soul. Rochester's traumatic recollection in *Wide Sargasso Sea* also works to highlight
his eventual similarity with Bertha in *Jane Eyre*: after Jane's escape, he
grows 'savage' and 'dangerous,' 'shutting himself up, like a hermit' (JE
364). Husband and wife become one in madness, both walking about
like ghosts in their shared prison, Thornfield Hall. Rhys's novel emphasizes, however, that Rochester has not managed to grind Antoinette
to nothing. Antoinette's testimony ultimately provides her with the
means of defying Rochester and flying away from his vault.[16]

### 'But It Is So, and It Was So': Narrative Testimony as Deliverance

In considering the circuit of textual testimony that occurs at the level of the novel's discourse, the crucial question to consider as regards Antoinette is when and where she narrates her story. The narrative situation in *Jane Eyre* and *Wide Sargasso Sea* is similar: Jane tells her life story in the secluded Fearndean after ten years of marriage, while the third and final part of *Wide Sargasso Sea* identifies the solitary attic cell at Thornfield as the place for Antoinette's retrospective narration. The nature of their narratives, however, separates the women. Jane's is a classical *Bildungs* narrative that records how she achieved maturity, independence, and a foothold in life, whereas Antoinette's narrative is an anti-*Bildungs* narrative, tracing a succession of losses and the difficulty of forming a coherent sense of self. It shows the protagonist-narrator slowly losing whatever grasp at life she may once have had. Yet while those very few who are in contact with Antoinette think she 'lives in her own darkness' (WSS 146), neither registering nor remembering things, she is actually trying to piece together her life story. Drinking Grace Poole's gin on the sly helps Antoinette to remember and think (WSS 147). Recollection is strenuous work – 'Quickly, while I can, I must remember the hot classroom' (WSS 44) – for the surroundings, the circumstances, and her illness do not facilitate it. Given her disturbing past and her even more difficult present, it is no surprise that her account exhibits typical signs of a trauma narrative: it is full of gaps, one-word sentences, and associative links between narrated items. Further, many of the narrated events are difficult to locate in time or space. Antoinette, however, desperately wants to put together a narrative that would explain why she is at Thornfield and what she must do there (WSS 146).

Besides questions addressing the location and time of Antoinette's narration, an equally pressing issue concerns the receiver of her narrative. As was previously discussed, Jane frequently turns to the reader for support and reassurance. It is worth quoting at length Hilda van Neck-Yoder's analysis of the narrative situation of *Wide Sargasso Sea*:

> Rhys invites us to imagine that Antoinette tells the 'real' story while speaking to no one, for no reason, as if in a vacuum. There is no fictional listener to Antoinette's voice, no 'you,' no 'reader,' no addressee to mediate between the nineteenth-century colonial 'I' and the twentieth-century postcolonial reader. The omission of a [a word is missing from the original article] and of a social context – a reason for speaking – may increase the illusion of Antoinette as a reliable, truthful witness, informing the reader of 'the other side' of Brontë's version ... Reading *Wide Sargasso Sea* as a representation of an explicit, purposeful act instead of as an informative

story, we can begin to recognise Antoinette's power over us, her power
to seduce us into believing that the Antoinette she tells is the 'real' Antoinette. (184)

This analysis is useful thanks to what I think are its erroneous assumptions about the recipient's identity and Antoinette's reasons for
narrating her story. The story level of *Wide Sargasso Sea* shows her reaching out to Rochester in the hope of finding a co-witness in him, but, as
was argued above, these attempts fail. Given that she has no address-
able other at Thornfield who would hear the anguish of her memories,
recognize, and affirm their realness, she is in danger of being altogether
annihilated. The absence of explicit addresses to a specified receiver
illustrates this threat. The difference as compared to narrator-Jane is
great indeed. Yet claiming that Antoinette has no motive and no addressee seems misguided, for she ultimately has herself as the person
to whom to turn. Her whole narrative serves, I argue, as her attempt to
bear witness to herself about her traumatic experiences. In other words,
her narrative belongs to the rare cases in fiction of intrapsychic witnessing. Kacandes points out that 'when violent events result in psychic
trauma, this [intrapsychic] circuit is broken. The healing of that trauma
involves integrating aspects of the experience that have been missed,
and this process seems almost invariably to require another person ...
Presumably, at some point during the witnessing process the self must
reintegrate the experience by testifying to the self about the occurrence'
(99). If we accept this notion of Antoinette's narrative as an attempt at
intrapsychic witnessing, then she does have an addressee in herself.
Such testimony depends on the ability to remember and to conduct a
dialogue with oneself about what happened. Throughout her narrative
Antoinette tries to create the internal 'you' who would help her to set
her past in motion and achieve distance to it. Laub (69) explains that
achieving distance is necessary, for the re-externalization of the event
occurs and takes effect only when one articulates and transmits the
story to another outside oneself and then takes it back again, inside.

The narration of *Wide Sargasso Sea* thus concerns the stage that occurs
directly prior to the witnessing to trauma. Kacandes (101) further explains this stage as the creation of the story of what has happened to the
self, when the mind heals by incorporating traumatic memories into
existing mental schemata that will guide future behaviour and contribute to the ongoing formation of a world view and a personal identity.
Therefore, readers of *Wide Sargasso Sea* cannot directly place themselves

in the addressee's position, but have to pay attention to the intrapsychic 'other' Antoinette tries to create. What Kacandes says of another 'Bluebeard' narrative, Margaret Atwood's *The Handmaid's Tale* (1986), provides an instructive point of comparison. Although the Handmaid has no actual receiver for her story, she creates this circuit of interpersonal witnessing through an act of will by strongly believing in the existence of an empathetic other who will one day read her narrative and pass it on (Kacandes 106). In contrast, Antoinette lacks such faith; at most, she can muster strength to create an intrapsychic witness in herself. Nevertheless, this intrapsychic circuit of witnessing has consequences for reading, because the implied author calls upon readers to function as interpersonal witnesses. This is to say that co-witnessing by readers requires them to position themselves as regards the internal you that the narrator Antoinette is bent on constructing. In this joint project between a traumatized narrator, the implied author, and readers as interpersonal witnesses, the latter accept the narrator's traumatic reality but also they enter into a commitment to accompany her for the duration of the narrative unfolding (Whitehead 36). Such is the invitation Rhys extends to readers; their response takes place at the circuits of five and six in Kacandes's scheme, namely, literary-historical and transcultural-transhistorical witnessing that is discussed in the next section.

Van Neck-Yoder (184) characterizes Antoinette's narrative voice as seductive. She argues that by making readers blind to rhetorical strategies, Antoinette cajoles them to accept her narrative version as the truth. Judging by the foregoing analysis, however, I maintain that as narrator Antoinette primarily pleads for a listener, for she needs an empathetic other whose affirmation and verification of the traumatic nature of the recounted events would enable both her narrative and the knowledge it bears to emerge. Testimonials are undoubtedly subjective; *Wide Sargasso Sea* prioritizes memory as narration over memory as truth-telling, because Antoinette's narration aims at making possible a form of self-understanding even in the absence of empirical verification. Dominick LaCapra ('Reflections' 195–6; *Writing* 98, 102–6) stresses that empathy does not preclude critical analysis; on the contrary, it is an affective response to trauma combined with cognition, argument, and critical judgment. Critical assessment, however, should not preclude the listener from hearing the witness's plea for being heard.[17]

What unites Rochester's and Antoinette's testimonies is their attempt to transform traumatic recollection into narrative memory; she fares better in this effort. In Part One Antoinette dwells on her childhood and early adulthood. In Part Two she gives Rochester a condensed account of these same events. This shortened version shows that she is able not only to recollect the events in different ways but also to take her listener into account. Whitehead (87–8) remarks that such flexibility is a sign of healthy improvisation and adaptation, as the narrator is not fixed on recalling the traumatic incidents in one and the same fashion. In Part Three Antoinette's narrative is the most jumbled in its non-chronological and wholly associative nature, yet paradoxically this incoherent account finally enables her to achieve enough personal coherence and agency that helps her to decide what it is she wants to do. Although Antoinette's distressing present defies narration (and she hardly dwells on it at all), she attains a sense of personal truth through narrative recollection that may even have healing components. I focus on her advancing self-understanding as it emerges from the way in which she elaborates her recurring nightmare. This nightmare illustrates how Antoinette manages to create an intrapsychic witness in herself. It needs to be stressed that referring to the success of Antoinette's testimony means the personal satisfaction she experiences as resulting from testimony. Once she acquires a sense that her testimony hits a personal truth, the narrative has performed its task. It does not, however, cure her 'madness.'

Antoinette's nightmare develops serially, occurring at the turning points of her life. She regards it as an enigmatic expression of an inner truth. The turning points provoking this dream are associated with danger from the outside breaking whatever status quo she is enjoying: the first time it is caused by Mr Mason's appearance; the second time by Mr Mason's plan to remove Antoinette from the convent school and prepare her for marriage; and the third time by Richard Mason's visit to Thornfield. A strong sense of preordained destiny pervades the dream. Each version depicts Antoinette accompanied by a man who desires to harm her, while she is petrified and unable to defend herself. The dreams supply further links between Rhys's novel, *Jane Eyre*, and 'Bluebeard.' Not only do they resemble Jane's recurring nightmares, but also they evoke the 'The Robber Bridegroom' tale with its undesired marriage and foreboding forest through which the bride must walk in order to reach an ominous house where her destiny will be fulfilled.[18] How does Antoinette eventually understand that destiny and what effect does her understanding have on her testimony?

I focus on the third, fullest version of the dream. In accordance with the associative logic of dreams, it merges scraps of the dreamer's current life situation with her past. The occurrence of this dream appears to tally with the events of *Jane Eyre*, for the dream's empty house implies that the house party has disbanded; perhaps also Jane has departed. (In *Jane Eyre* Bertha is surprisingly well informed about incidents in the house.) In the dream Antoinette recognizes the ominous house as her present abode and identifies her persecutor as her husband ('the man who hated me was calling too, Bertha! Bertha!', WSS 155). *Jane Eyre*'s Rochester wagers that Jane's wedding veil reminded Bertha of her own wedding (JE 264); this veil figures in Antoinette's dream too: 'A lamp and the dark staircase and the veil over my face. They think I don't remember but I do' (WSS 153). Further, the veil, as a bridal accessory, is associated with a white dress: 'Turning a corner I saw a girl coming out of her bedroom. She wore a white dress and she was humming to herself' (WSS 149). Rochester admired Antoinette's white dress; this dress relates Antoinette with the other women staying in the house, identified in *Jane Eyre* as Jane and Blanche Ingram, who both dream of marrying Rochester. These associations imply that any woman in the 'English house' becomes one in a series of Bluebeard's women. The white apparel also alludes to the ghost, later revealed as Bertha, who haunts the mansion in *Jane Eyre*, and this apparition plays a role in Antoinette's dream too: 'I never looked behind me for I did not want to see that ghost of a woman whom they say haunts this place' (WSS 153). This merger of a bride with a ghost strengthens the links the two novels share with 'Bluebeard,' representing in a nutshell the life story of any woman coming into contact with Bluebeard: from a bride to wife to corpse to ghost.

Typically, it is when the current wife recognizes herself in the former wives that she can distance herself from Bluebeard's bloody fantasies. Often this recognition takes place with the help of the mirror; for example, in looking at the clotted blood on the vault's floor, the wife understands that Bluebeard intends her to be soon what the former wives already are – dead. The mirror motif plays this role in Antoinette's dream: 'It was then that I saw her – the ghost. The woman with streaming hair. She was surrounded by a gilt frame but I knew her' (WSS 154). Antoinette has no mirror at Thornfield, but she recognizes herself in the dream's mirror: she is the ghost. After her face-off with her mirror image, Antoinette relates that 'I dropped the candle I was carrying and it caught the end of the tablecloth and I saw flames shoot up. As I ran or perhaps floated or flew I called help me Christophene help me and looking behind me I saw that I had been helped' (WSS 154). Antoinette's actions suggest that she rejects the ghost-like reflection as false; it is only in Rochester's interests to portray her thus. This rejection introduces a significant change into her dream, for she is freed from her former petrification: she now asks for and also receives help from the one person whom she has loved the most – Christophene. This change leads to an epiphany during which the pieces of Antoinette's life fall into place:

> Then I turned round and saw the sky. It was red and all my life was in it. I saw the grandfather clock and Aunt Cora's patchwork, all colours, I saw the orchids and the stephanotis and the jasmine and the tree of life in flames. I saw the chandelier and the red carpet downstairs and the bamboos and the tree ferns, the gold ferns and the silver, and the soft green velvet of the moss on the garden wall. I saw my doll's house and the books and the picture of the Miller's daughter. I heard the parrot call as he did when he saw a stranger, *Qui est là? Qui est là?* and the man who hated me was calling too, Bertha! Bertha! The wind caught my hair and it streamed out like wings. It might bear me up, I thought, if I jumped to those hard stones. But when I looked over the edge I saw the pool at Coulibri. Tia was there. She beckoned to me and when I hesitated, she laughed ... Someone screamed and I thought, *Why did I scream?* I called 'Tia!' and jumped and woke. (WSS 155)

The red sky and the pool of water become the one mirror in which Antoinette can truly recognize herself. They merge with her memories, and together they become the reflecting surface that enables self-recognition on her own terms. The panorama of her life takes Antoinette back to the West Indies with its abundant sounds, sights, and colours as well as the people she has cared for. Taking her life in her own hands – that is, determining its meaning – Antoinette envisions herself as a bird flying away from Thornfield. (The clever third sister of 'Fitcher's Bird' manages a similar escape by disguising herself as a bird; also Jane flies away in the dead of night from Thornfield.) When Antoinette upon waking says that 'Now at last I know why I was brought here and what I have to do' (WSS 155–6), she is referring to her resolve to become mistress of herself, decide upon her fate, and go 'home.' This resolve is certainly not sentimental; neither is it as straightforwardly celebratory as Sandra Drake suggests. Arguing that the dream awakens Antoinette from her zombie-like state so that she finally embraces her Caribbean heritage, Drake characterizes the novel 'as victory over death itself by changing the cultural and belief system from a European to an Afro-

Caribbean one' (Drake 205). In Drake's view, Antoinette's final actions verify her belief in the Afro-Caribbean notion of death as a change of state in the continuity of life so that she can begin her reverse trip back across the Sargasso Sea (201–3). While I agree with Drake's claim of Antoinette's liberation from Rochester, I doubt whether this protagonist's acknowledgment of her cultural heritage is as extensive as Drake claims. Antoinette has throughout been positioned in-between cultures without a framework she could really call her own. Thus Mary Lou Emery's and John J. Su's cautious conclusions seem more plausible. Emery emphasizes Antoinette's position as a double outsider who cannot be said to return 'home.' Rather, Emery (165–7) sees the ending as disclosing Antoinette's divided identity and the specific sociohistorical forces causing (female) homelessness. Su, in turn, points out that by depicting Antoinette's fantasy union with Tia the novel uses nostalgia for a lost past in order to identify the absence of empathy and to attribute it to colonialism. It is only retrospectively that the two girls feel an empathy born of identification. Thus Antoinette's nostalgia-tinged self-recognition is not really comforting, because it points to what might and should have been, but was not. Su (170) sums up this notion by saying that 'nostalgia is haunting in that it not only proposes alternative worlds but interweaves itself with memory so that life stories become saturated with those images of lost promise.'

Examining *Wide Sargasso Sea* as trauma fiction suggests that the significance of the final dream lies in Antoinette having succeeded in establishing an intrapsychic witness in herself. The first two times the dream has badly frightened her, and neither time has she been able to find a sympathetic audience to help her unravel its significance. This third time, however, the dream instructs her: she is able to form a coherent enough picture of her situation, decide upon the dream's significance, and act according to what she deems is best for her. In hitting upon an inner truth, the dream enables Antoinette to begin to deal with trauma. Su observes that Rhys represents Antoinette as a woman woken from a dream in which 'she recognises for the first time the magnitude of her loss: the friendship and home she never experienced' (170). Antoinette's realization of loss reverberates with Rochester's awareness of 'nothing' by the conclusion of his narrative. While the former is liberating in its frank admission of missed opportunities, the latter is imprisoning in its denial of them.

In 'Mr Fox' and 'The Robber Bridegroom' the bride tells the wedding guests the truth about the groom's atrocities in the guise of a dream.

Antoinette's retrospective narrative becomes a defiant contestation of Rochester's self-justifying denials of it 'not having been so.' Like the bride, Antoinette insists that 'it is so, and it was so,' and she has her whole narrative to prove it. By representing Antoinette's assessment of her situation as resulting from an achieved sense of self-recognition, Rhys endows Antoinette with agency, determination, and will. By departing from *Jane Eyre*, Rhys's intertextual repetition speaks of an attempt to grasp 'what was not fully known or realized in the first instance, and thereby to depart from it or pass beyond it' (Whitehead 90). This ending reverberates back on *Jane Eyre*, suggesting that from Rhys's perspective, Jane's return to Rochester represents her permanent and voluntary imprisonment with Bluebeard. Jane appears the weaker of the two women. I conclude my analysis of *Wide Sargasso Sea* by looking at the intertextual strategies Rhys uses at the literary-historical circuit of witnessing.

## Intertextuality as Rhys's Testimonial Strategy

In her letters Rhys reveals that she sees Antoinette's story as part of a larger phenomenon, for the daughters of the wealthy West Indian plantation owners were a good match for Englishmen. Many of these marriages were, according to Rhys, unfortunate and unhappy (Rhys 139, 144). As is well known, she was indignant at Brontë's portrayal of Bertha: 'Of course Charlotte Brontë makes her own world, of course she convinces you, and that makes the poor Creole lunatic all the more dreadful. I remember being quite shocked, and when I re-read it rather annoyed. "That's only one side – the English side" sort of thing' (144). From Rhys's West Indian perspective, *Jane Eyre* functions as a source of cultural trauma. Brontë's Bertha only growls and shrieks; her story is narrated by Rochester, an innkeeper, and Jane. Intertextuality is Rhys's means of letting this silenced Creole woman tell her own story. *Wide Sargasso Sea* depicts that which has been omitted, thanks to its having been suppressed, in *Jane Eyre*. By purposefully writing a prequel, Rhys insists that the events her novel narrates come first: they supply the necessary context and background to understanding Brontë's novel. In this section, I consider the intertextuality of *Wide Sargasso Sea* as the means of Rhys's testimonial statement. In so doing, I consider how the novel and its implied author (whom I call Rhys for the sake of simplicity) co-witness to the trauma in and of the novel. Given that I myself am a contemporary reader and one from outside the British Empire and the English-speaking world, my interpretation takes place at what Kacandes terms the transhistorical-transcultural circuit of reading at which the 'text and its later or foreign reader cowitness to the trauma of/in the text' (97).

Rhys explicitly identifies 'Bluebeard' as *Jane Eyre*'s intertext, using it extensively in shaping her own novel. In so doing she picks up on the thematic of cultural otherness typical of the literary and pictorial depictions of this tale ever since the eighteenth century. By placing the events in the Orient and by giving the protagonists such names as 'Barbazure' and 'Fatima,' these renditions served to distance domestic violence: unhappy marriages with domestic abuse and violence supposedly took place far away from home. (The illustrations Tatar has collected in her book verify this claim; see Tatar, *Secrets* ch 1.) By expressly treating *Jane Eyre* as a 'Bluebeard' tale, Rhys turns the mirror back on Britain and the British, arguing that Rochester is a Bluebeard thanks to his being an imperialist Englishman. Abuse and violence breed at home, spreading out to the colonies.

Given that *Jane Eyre* is the story of Bluebeard's second wife, as a prequel *Wide Sargasso Sea* promises to reveal what the first wife saw upon opening the door to Bluebeard's chamber. Given the probing of Rochester's and Antoinette's psyches, it may appear that this novel too emphasizes a psychological-hermeneutic exploration of this tale as does *Jane Eyre*. To be sure, *Wide Sargasso Sea* elucidates the protagonists from within, but I would nevertheless argue that for Rhys the motivation for using this intertext lies elsewhere than for Brontë. The manner in which the tale is introduced into the novel supplies a clue of its driving force: it arrives on the scene in the character of Mr Mason. It is his arrival that triggers Antoinette's first nightmare, the trajectory of which follows 'The Robber Bridegroom.' *Wide Sargasso Sea* begins in a state of disequilibrium, but the 'Bluebeard' tale cycle emerges as a narrative option only with the arrival of new British colonialists on the lookout for spoils after the official abolition of slavery.[19]

Mr Mason resembles the devious wizard of 'Fitcher's Bird,' whose appearance and demeanour suggest beneficence, but whose intentions are wicked. Instead of probing the 'Bluebeard' legacy psychologically, Rhys employs it and *Jane Eyre* in order to explore the cultural intrusiveness of these intertexts. In 'Fitcher's Bird' the wizard 'asked for something to eat, and when the eldest girl came to the door to give him a crust of bread, all he had to do was to touch her, and she jumped right into the basket' (Tatar 182–3). Admittedly, Annette has self-serving interests (as does the wife in 'Bluebeard'), but once married to Mr Mason, he owns whatever property she still has with her sitting tight in his basket. The wheel of repetition has been set in motion, identifying Antoinette, thanks to her status as family member, as the next victim comparable to the tale's second sister. After disposing of Annette, Mr Mason arrives at the convent school to fix Antoinette's future. Rhys explores the tale as part and parcel of the political, social, and cultural intrusion of British colonialism into the West Indies.

In 'Fitcher's Bird' the wizard forbids the woman to enter his chamber; instead of a key, he gives her an egg the whiteness of which she is to protect. Rhys extends the intrusive effect of her intertext to address also Bluebeard's chamber; furthermore, she associates the egg with the woman. At Granbois this room is just an ordinary bedroom without any mysteries whatsoever. In Rhys's interpretation, it is actually the woman who gives Bluebeard the egg to safeguard; that is, the white-clad Antoinette succumbs to Rochester with the expectation that he receive her lovingly. He not only rapes and abuses her but also blames her for his atrocity. In Rhys's adaptation, the chamber is a place of scapegoating: Bluebeard projects his own prejudice, insecurity, and violence on the cultural other, claiming that she is their fountain. In Rhys's hands, then, this intertext elucidates the victimization of a colonized subject by the colonialist perpetrator; victimization is grounded on the erotic demonization of this subject. Consequently, Rochester turns Antoinette into the 'infamous daughter of an infamous mother' (WSS 110), whose immorality is expressed by her red dress. Bluebeard alone is responsible for sullying the egg; in fact, the very notion of dirt derives solely from his binary modes of thought (the woman as either a virgin or a whore).

Rhys's rewriting of the tale's ending brings again to view Bluebeard's binary logic. In 'Fitcher's Bird' the clever third sister manipulates the wizard with two disguises: she places a skull, dressed up as a bride, in a window, while she makes herself 'a strange bird no one could have recognised' (Tatar 184). Yet upon meeting her on the road, the wedding guests, and even the wizard himself, identify her as 'Fitcher's feathered bird,' that is, as one of their own. Given the tale's archaic setting, this designation suggests that her success relies on her dressing herself up as a totemic animal familiar to the wizard's clan. Her escape goes unnoticed, because her two disguises proclaim allegiance to this clan. The skull admits woman's nothingness (castration), while the bird's outfit signifies clan membership. In *Wide Sargasso Sea* Antoinette's two disguises acquire similar meanings. Her living conditions at Thornfield have nearly reduced her to the skull in the window. Her resistance, however, emerges through the red dress. Rochester misrecognizes it, because he interprets this garment in the terms of his clan. He thinks it proclaims her status as 'the red whore,' confirming his notion of the Creole woman in particular. For Antoinette, however, the dress express-es her allegiance to her own culture, with its smells of the sun, the rain, vetivert, frangipani, and cinnamon. Seeing the dress makes her remem-ber her last kiss with her cousin Sandi; she wore it then. Together the revoked memory and the dress remind her that she belongs to the West Indies, the recognition of which enables her escape: 'But I looked at the dress on the floor and it was as if the fire had spread across the room. It was beautiful and it reminded me of something I must do. I will re-member. I will remember quite soon now' (WSS 110–11). In 'Fitcher's Bird' the woman's relatives avenge her by burning the wizard with his guests. In the dream that advises Antoinette, she encounters her relatives and friends, who encourage her return. In her dream she jumps to the pool at Coulibri, leaving behind a burning Thornfield. Rhys thus makes 'Bluebeard' signal the distance between two cultures with Antoinette resisting the self-sacrificial closure of her plot in *Jane Eyre*.

Rhys's use of this tale reverberates also to her use of *Jane Eyre*. The ending of *Wide Sargasso Sea* plays out twice Bertha's end in *Jane Eyre*: Antoinette first dreams of burning down the house, and then sets out to carry its incendiary act, but the actual deed is never depicted (Rody 302). By giving the force of the ending to the moment before the burn-ing, argues Rody, Rhys's unclosed end leaves Antoinette's death to the moments after readers close the book and muse in their intertextual memory. In this way Rhys forces (literary) history – Charlotte Brontë – to bear responsibility for killing Bertha. Brontë is made to re-extinguish a life we readers have come to value (313).[20] Rhys's narrative construc-tion of Antoinette departs from the preordained, constrained text origi-nating in Brontë's desires and needs (Harrison 136, 148). Although both writers bring the Creole to Brontë's England, Rhys's novel alone dis-covers her (133–4).

This discovery involves readers in a re-evaluation of Jane's narrative voice, in particular the manner in which trauma affects narration. The previous analysis of Jane's narration showed her using various discursive registers. As narrator, Antoinette has fewer options than Jane. Her narration is marked by the discourse of the hysteric, which, toward the end in particular, shows signs of psychosis such as the breakdown of temporal and spatial coordinates. If Jane's narrative communicates her eventual ascension, then Antoinette's may be characterized as a narration of disempowerment. If I am correct in assuming that Antoinette narrates her story in her solitary cell, then her placement largely explains the predominance of the hysteric's discourse. While Jane questions whether she is male or female, Rochester's cruel positioning of Antoinette forces her to question whether she is beast or human. The discourse of the master is foreclosed to her; in fact, narrating becomes a means of proclaiming her humanness against all odds. The effects of trauma thus pervade Antoinette's narrative more deeply than Jane's. While Jane's traumatic experiences primarily emerge through textual notation indicating difficulties with expression, Antoinette's narrative includes non-chronological narration, ellipses, as well as jumbled temporal and spatial indications. It is a performative narration, reflecting the traces of traumatic disruption and discontinuity. After all, the distressing events took place outside the parameters of 'normal' reality, such as causality, sequence, time, and place (see Laub 69).

Given the fact that ultimately Rhys is responsible for the aesthetic and formal whole of this novel, she herself is comparable to the third clever sister of 'Fitcher's Bird,' who cunningly tricks herself out of the wizard's den. The manner in which Rhys uses intertextuality as a testimonial strategy, however, indicates that she sees no such happy ending for her narrative, thanks to the effects of trauma. If I might borrow Whitehead's words from another context, Rhys understands enough in order to convey a forgotten and excluded history, but simultaneously resists understanding too much, so that her novel still conveys the disruptive and resistant force of traumatic historicity (Whitehead 160). Rhys asks her readers to approach this novel in this same respectful manner: to receive its testimony and to avoid appropriating the story as their own. This approach enables the circuit of transhistorical and transcultural witnessing to flow: readers become co-witnesses who talk with *Wide Sargasso Sea*. They should not render the story too familiar or indulge in too easy an understanding or identification (Kacandes 117; Whitehead 7–8). Should readers do so, they would miss identifying the ways in which *Jane Eyre* has perpetuated and kept alive the mechanisms of cultural scapegoating.

## Emma Tennant's *Adèle:* Trauma in a Narrative Hodgepodge

In concluding this chapter I turn to Emma Tennant's *Adèle: Jane Eyre's Hidden Story* (2002), a recent neo-Victorian novel in which *Jane Eyre* is explicitly reworked through 'Bluebeard.'[21] As its title suggests, *Adèle* is a rewriting of *Jane Eyre* whose purpose is to fill in one gap in Brontë's novel, the story of Rochester's ward, Adèle Varens. In the Preface Tennant first quotes Jane's summary in *Jane Eyre* of what became of the grown-up Adèle, then remarking, 'But perhaps, as is often found in the lives of girls as they grow into women, it was all a little more complicated than that. This is Adèle's story' (A x). In *Jane Eyre*, Jane views with disapproval her pupil's French ways and manners (JE 87–8), holding it as fortunate that as Adèle grew up, 'a sound English education corrected in a great measure her French defects' (JE 383). Tennant's book defends the girl. Focusing on Adèle reminds readers that there were actually two foreigners at Thornfield Hall during Jane's employment. As is typical of rewritings, this novel claims to disclose the true story, one that has been thus far hidden – like Bluebeard's first wife – among the ruins of Thornfield Hall. By placing Adèle centre stage, Tennant redeems not only her but also her mother, the French coquette whose manners Brontë rejected as unsuitable for British women. This adaptation enables me to examine what happens to the thematic structures of trauma and witnessing in the context of popular Bluebeard Gothic. By analysing this novel I hope to show how the pressing concerns a literary classic puts forth may be trivialized in popular adaptations.

Adèle's *Bildungs* narrative parallels Jane's: both act as narrators in order to come to terms with past trauma and construct their identities. The distressing incidents in Adèle's life include Céline Varens's tempestuous relationship with Rochester, Céline's abandonment of Adèle, the fire at Thornfield which Adèle believes she caused, and Adèle's search for Céline in Paris. As Adèle is the narrator, the novel focuses on the textual circuit of witnessing. The narrator Adèle demonstrates that, for her, working through trauma is a two-pronged process. She must first confront her parents' irresponsible behaviour and her misery at Thornfield in order to be able to work through the existential questions plaguing her. I ponder how Adèle's traumatic experiences affect the textual circuit of witnessing. I also consider the significance of Tennant's couching of Adèle's story in terms of trauma. I thus discuss the literary-historical circuit of witnessing dealing with the novel's contemporary meaning.

*Adèle* expands on Rochester's account of his amorous escapades in *Jane Eyre* by providing Adèle's version of his love affair with Céline. The novel's opening presents Adèle living happily with her mother. One day she is given a photograph of her father. Adèle recounts the photo's disturbing effect: 'I wanted to go home and dispose of this new invention, the evidence of my paternity. I saw myself, eyes closed, consigning the angry, darkly shadowed face – which reminded me of nothing so much as the illustration for Bluebeard, in my book of Perrault's fairy tales – to Tante Irène's willow basket' (A 10). Immediately afterwards, Rochester re-enters the life of mother and daughter (A 11), forcing Adèle to grapple with the question of her familial identity. Thanks to Rochester's long absence, Adèle suspects that he, like Bluebeard, has something dreadful to hide: 'The man I must love with filial devotion is a Bluebeard, and his castle, I have little doubt, has locked and forbidden rooms' (A 39). Rochester confirms Adèle's fears when he learns of Céline's infidelity and wrecks the Varens household. Adèle associates his jealous rage with Bluebeard: 'I ducked down the stairs again at the sound of his voice, the dreadful thought having come to me that the house was indeed empty except for a mad stranger milord, and that he might chase me right up the stairs and kill me like Bluebeard before locking me in a secret room' (A 24). After Céline elopes and abandons Adèle, the girl is sent to Thornfield Hall, where she is not wanted. Exploring the mansion, she by chance meets Antoinette and befriends her. (Following Rhys, Tennant calls the first wife Antoinette.) Totally forsaken, Adèle consoles herself by escaping into fantasies about Rochester's reunion with Céline.

Tennant's Adèle pays little attention to her governess, Jane Eyre, whom she finds mouse-like and authoritarian. As events proceed, Adèle's fondness for Antoinette turns into dislike and her resentment of Jane strengthens. Adèle witnesses two sequences neither of which she understands: the gradual diminishment of Antoinette from a mad yet spunky woman to a zombie; and Jane's growing love for Rochester with well-known consequences. After Jane's escape, Adèle's confusion turns into psychotic derangement so that she believes she shuts Antoinette on the roof, starts the deadly fire, and flies away from Thornfield. At this point it is difficult for both the girl and readers as recipients of her testimony to establish what really happens.

The story continues five years after the Thornfield fire, when Adèle goes to Paris to look for her mother. She is ready to face the traumatic incidents of her life. She eventually learns that Céline, in love with both

Rochester and a French viscount, was impregnated by both on the same day – Adèle has a twin brother by a different father. The now dead Céline has bestowed on Adèle a ring revealing this secret. The ring with its hidden compartment resembles Rochester's forbidden attic chamber: both of Adèle's parents have guilty secrets. This realization and the sight of a cruel spectacle of torture Adèle accidentally witnesses make suppressed memories emerge. She recognizes that the evil presence at Thornfield was not Rochester, but another who purposefully harmed her and Antoinette – the housekeeper, Mrs Fairfax (A 195–6). She realizes that it was Mrs Fairfax who kept her drugged, making her hallucinate psychotically. She also understands that the housekeeper manipulated her, making her believe she caused Antoinette's death and the fire. Recovering these memories enables Adèle to shed the past and look toward the future. Such is the broad outline of traumatic events in this novel.

Although Adèle's narration takes place retrospectively, as narrator she restricts focalization to her younger self so that her world is conveyed through the eyes and understanding of a child. The child's focalization is strengthened by the frequent use of the present tense, which makes the past feel as if it were the present. Such a strategy emphasizes the hurtful nature of the events recounted. Although the narratee of Adèle's testimony is nowhere specified, clearly her words are directed at an empathetic recipient. Whenever the interlocutor's place is carved out, but vacant, observes Kacandes (112), it prompts readers to take up the role of addressee and feel themselves accosted. Yet the curious effect of Adèle's retrospective narration is that she does not really seem to need an interpersonal witness to enable her story to emerge. As narrator, Adèle does emphasize the traumas she suffered, but the invocation to the addressee appears conventional rather than urgently necessary. This feature sets this novel apart from the books I have discussed earlier in this chapter. Thus we need to examine what causes this effect and what its consequences are.

A good example of Adèle's manner of involving readers as co-witnesses is her account of Rochester's jealous rage. The narrator-Adèle's representation of this scene is oddly deflated. Sticking to the child-Adèle's perspective creates a 'cutesy' effect that cuts the edge of the danger represented. This tactic turns the threat of violence of 'Bluebeard' into a conventional requirement to be fulfilled one way or another. Consequently, the narratee never earnestly considers the possibility that either Céline or Adèle could come to harm in Rochester's hands. The seriousness of the narrator's testimony is also punctured by the way in which she couples her fantasies at Thornfield with fairy tales. She describes to the narratee how she consoles herself by imagining that Rochester is like a king, Céline is his queen, while she herself is the cherished offspring of these exalted figures. This fairy-tale scenario tallies with Freud's notion of how very small children deal with the family-romance fantasy: the imagined royal status of the parents elevates the child's standing too, while making it easier for the child to bear the fact that she is left outside the parents' dyadic relationship ('Family' 239). Adèle's narration draws on a further feature of this fantasy by highlighting rivalry over father between mother and daughter: 'I shall show Papa that I know he loves me. I shall care for him for the rest of his days. And I shall also let him know his secret is safe with me: I have visited the chamber, and I hold the key' (A 116). In the end, *Adèle* vindicates Adèle's trust in Rochester by linking his violence against women to two sources: his unhappy childhood – his mother is described as being 'temperamentally incapable of love' (A 31) – and his capacity for great passion.[22]

This whitewashing of Rochester suggests the reason for the deflated impact of the narrator-Adèle's testimony. Tennant's disinterest in seriously probing the thematic structures of trauma and witnessing – both of which she continually raises – derives from treating *Jane Eyre* and 'Bluebeard' in solely romantic terms. Davies (*Tale* 88–9) observes that in romantic renditions blame for Bluebeard's development is typically ascribed to his mother or former lover. Such a shift, explains Davies, 'is necessary to distract attention from the male as oppressor and to direct it towards the male as victim who kills out of "verzweifelter Lieber" [desperate love], not hate, and deserves women's love and sympathy' (Davies 87). Once the traumatized Adèle is able to access suppressed memories, she recalls how Céline had returned from an outing with the viscount. The mother, with a look of satisfied desire on her face, had found a jealous Rochester there. He had chased her with a whip in hand, but this threatening scene had changed into passionate lovemaking. This story makes Adèle remember having witnessed the same chain of events repeated: 'Hadn't I covered my ears, praying the ogre would not kill [Céline] as her cries echoed around ... And hadn't those cries, as I had refused to accept then, turned to moans of joy?' (A 201). This recovered memory enables Adèle to see herself as resulting from passionate love. It also proves to her that Rochester's fault is possessiveness, but he is not, and never has been, a real Bluebeard. Rather, he is an unhappy and unsuccessful lover. Dealing with childhood trauma through narration consoles Adèle, not the least because it exonerates the still-living parent in her eyes. When Rochester acknowledges Adèle as his daughter and when he repents his treatment of Céline and even erects a shrine for her, Adèle absolves him fully. Facing the traumatic events in her life enables Adèle to resolve satisfactorily the plaguing uncertainty about her identity: 'If I am anyone, I am the daughter of Céline Varens and Edward Fairfax Rochester' (A 207). Finally, Adèle is told by a clairvoyant that her dead mother wants her to find a new maternal helper, a piece of advice that enables the girl to accept Jane as stepmother: 'Jane ... will be my companion and guide in life. That Papa loved Céline once is without doubt, and his remorse for his treatment of her will stay with him always' (A 209).[23]

The narrator-Adèle states in the novel's conclusion: 'So the family at Thornfield lived happily ever after' (A 224). Having faced her childhood traumas head on, she can confidently maintain that the past is definitively behind. She subscribes to the notion that both growing pains and actual traumatic incidents can be healed with no persisting scars left; thus it is possible to achieve full ego identity. This is to say that Adèle, in her double role of character and narrator, believes she is in full control of herself. Such confidence explains why she does not really need an interpersonal witness for her account: she can work things out all by herself, without help or intervention from another. Therefore, the thematic structures of trauma and witnessing serve mainly as predictable props to be routinely fulfilled in any popular adaptation of Bluebeard Gothic. Such a run-of-the-mill approach suggests that *Adèle* is a manifestation of what LaCapra calls contemporary wound culture. Today members of Western cultures are amply aware of various kinds of trauma; in fact, almost everyone claims to have some kind of a trauma to nurse. Consequently, trauma is everywhere and yet nowhere – the very concept and the phenomenon are watered down when all possible types of hardship are conflated under the same rubric (*Writing* 64).

This observation moves us to consider the literary-historical circuit of witnessing in *Adèle*. We may take notice of the fact that Tennant's novel represents Mrs Fairfax as the true madwoman in the attic. By identifying the housekeeper as an evildoer, this book alters the 'Mr Fox' tale in which the housekeeper sympathizes with the heroine, helping her to escape. These changes may be related to Tennant's goal of presenting a wholly new and unexpected twist to well-known intertexts. After all, previous adaptations have neglected both Adèle and Mrs Fairfax. Introducing novelty with the aim of reinvigorating a familiar narrative is a strategy typical of popular fiction, as John G. Cawelti (ch. 1) convincingly argues. Tennant's adaptation shows that today *Jane Eyre* belongs to genre fiction; as a household Gothic romance it requires what Cawelti calls narrative and stereotype revitalization in order to continue exerting influence on the popular imagination. Such a strategy relies on ringing variations – the more surprising, the better – on the thematic structures and characters of narrative formulas. Part of Tennant's revitalization concerns presenting the intertexts in terms of present-day concerns. Rochester and Céline resemble contemporary parents whose serial monogamy and love affairs pose problems for their offspring. Like many children currently, Adèle must come to terms with the breakup of her parents as well as the presence of step-parents and step-siblings.

Another significant factor in this circuit concerns Tennant's treatment of history. The events of *Adèle* are placed in the historical period of Brontë's novel, the first decades of the nineteenth century. The most straightforward markers of historical period occur in the sections taking place in Paris. Tennant situates the events by referring to such innovations as photography and to such cultural phenomena as vaudeville shows and symbolist poetry. She also evokes the 1830 French Revolution. The historical past, however, is solely relayed through textual sources: direct quotations, intertextual allusions, stereotypes, and popular images. The Thornfield section borrows heavily from *Jane Eyre*, *Wide Sargasso Sea*, and *Rebecca*, while the Paris episodes lean on literary depictions of Bohemian life in the artist and vaudeville circles familiar in such books as George du Maurier's *Trilby*, Djuna Barnes's *Nightwood*, and Angela Carter's *Nights in the Circus* and *Wise Children*. Whatever one may think of Fredric Jameson's wholesale analysis of postmodern culture, his argument about its cultural production applies well to Tennant's *Adèle*. All textual sources exist pell-mell in this book; no distinctions are made between older and more recent texts or between so-called high cultural and popular texts. Consequently, quotation becomes indigestive incorporation (Jameson 112). Unlike the examples Jameson discusses, *Adèle* is not a stylistic pastiche but what one might call a narrative pastiche in that it lifts out its plot lines, characters, and themes from previous fiction. To quote Jameson, *Adèle* speaks 'through the masks and with the voices of [the narratives] in the imaginary museum' (115); it self-consciously flaunts the various texts it employs in its construction. The result of this equalizing textual mix is that the period evoked exists nowhere; the novel has no reference point either in the historical past where the events are set or in the present day. Given this curious temporal flatness pervading *Adèle*, one may characterize it as an adaptation of *Jane Eyre* and its spin-offs that also severs the manifold links this textual legacy has with its various historical contexts. Such separation further explains the process by which the thematic structures of trauma and witnessing are thoroughly trivialized. Imported from intertextual sources and used mainly as a plot ploy, trauma becomes merely one of the set elements through which a culturally familiar narrative is told.

Jameson identifies nostalgia as one factor whetting postmodern fascination with historical fiction and film. Nostalgia in Jameson's sense does not really target a given past period but addresses cultural representations of this period that are actually beyond history (117). Besides being nostalgic in Jameson's sense, Tennant's book's relationship to *Jane Eyre* and its spin-offs is also playful: Charlotte Brontë and the Victorian period are set pieces of British cultural heritage. The book is engaged in playing a literary-cultural game the pieces of which derive from a variety of highly familiar texts that shape a shared cultural heritage. Unlike history, heritage is thought to allow more personal and factually less accurate representations of the past. In Suzanne Keen's (*Romances* 103) fitting formulation, heritage 'contributes to a prized collection of achievements.' Instead of addressing issues of history, Tennant toys with the collection of achievements known as Victoriana: *Adèle* is her move in this cultural game. In construing heritage as a collation of prized texts, images, and types from which one may pick and choose one's plateful, Tennant disregards the debates about (national) historical memory and the direction of political future that authors engaging with Victoriana have frequently evoked in the past decades. Simultaneously *Jane Eyre* and 'Bluebeard' are defused by Tennant of the painful thematic of trauma and witnessing, becoming merely empty chips in a trivial cultural game.

# 3 Romance, Perversion, and Bluebeard Gothic

A strong reason for the continued success of *Jane Eyre* is the passionate love story between Jane and Rochester. Although Jane cannot and will not accept a marriage based on inequality, deception, and exploitation, in later spin-offs romantic love has eclipsed the book's spotlight on gender issues. Daphne du Maurier's best-selling *Rebecca*, published in 1938, ninety-one years after *Jane Eyre*, has frequently been named as one such forgetful adaptation. In this novel, an orphaned girl like Jane falls in love with an enigmatic, haunted landowner whose estate contains a terrible secret. Unlike Jane, however, once this protagonist finds out about Bluebeard's wrongdoing, she fully supports him in order to make him love her. She willingly submits to his power, securing her status as his beloved wife. Diluting the gender issues of *Jane Eyre* goes hand in hand with turning 'Bluebeard' into a romance. As is well known, besides Jane Austen's oeuvre, *Jane Eyre* provides one of the most enduring intertexts for mass-produced romances. Feminist perspectives vanish altogether in these pulp novels.[1]

Michelle Massé holds this loss of awareness about feminist issues dangerous, because romance is made to hide the lot patriarchy preserves for women. She argues that romantic Bluebeard Gothic is about female masochism, as it portrays 'suffering women whose painful initiations provide some vague pleasure for women authors, characters, and readers' (1). Treating masochism and Gothic as mutually illuminative explications of women's pain, Massé analyses the genre in terms of what Freud ('Child') calls the beating fantasy, in which a spectator watches someone being hurt by a dominant other. Bluebeard Gothic highlights the danger of this fantasy by foregrounding what usually remains repressed: the beating itself and what it feels like to be the beaten. Freud holds that a girl identifies with the position of the beaten. Her fantasy of her father beating her confirms that she is loved, for his violence protects her against her forbidden incestuous desire: it equates being beaten and being loved. By depicting the fictional heroine's psychological development into a masochist who assigns subjectivity to another, argues Massé, Gothic romance persuades readers to accept this situation as describing normal gender relationships. In actual fact, she observes, this formation of female sexual subjectivity under patriarchy is abnormal, because it forces women to place themselves in positions and roles that are harmful to them. Yet patriarchy represents this subjectivity as both normal and natural (2–3, 7).

Bluebeard Gothic, however, acts not only as a means of disseminating patriarchal notions of sexuality and gender relationships but also as an exposition of the violence involved in these notions. By spotlighting Bluebeard and his crimes, this genre, maintains Meredid Puw Davies, 'breaks taboos on expressing profound doubts about the apparently rational, nominally masculine subject of Western civilization and the processes which produce it: in short, with the projects of modernity and civilization themselves, by revealing their deeply irrational and dangerous sides' (*Tale* 57). The exploration of this suppressed underside has steadily gained ground in adaptations of *Jane Eyre* the closer we come to the present day. This focus involves an awareness of the fact that the moment we designate something as 'normal' sexuality, we invariably also generate the complementary notion of 'perverse' sexuality in order to draw the contours of normality. The shift in focus has prompted a reconsideration of, for example, *Rebecca*'s classification as a romance and of its relationship to *Jane Eyre*. Nina Auerbach claims that 'the Brontës ... do inhabit Daphne du Maurier's romances, but in twisted, diminished shape,' adding that 'the forward thrust of *Jane Eyre* and *Wuthering Heights* becomes, in du Maurier's so-called romances, a strangled lunge into inescapability' (Auerbach 119).

This 'twisted shape' suggests a departure from what is considered socially and culturally normal. In this chapter I scrutinize a tradition among *Jane Eyre* spin-offs that highlights perversity as an inherent component of Bluebeard Gothic.[2] In keeping with the emphasis of these adaptations, I depart from Massé's approach by treating masochism as a sexual perversion. In so doing I take my cue from Gilles Deleuze, who argues in his *Coldness and Cruelty* (14) that literary representation is our primary source for understanding the specificities of such perversions as masochism and sadism. Speaking of perversion implies the existence of a norm against which deviance is perceived. J. Laplanche and J.-B. Pontalis (306–9) observe that psychoanalysis uses this concept exclusively in relation to sexuality. While infantile sexuality is polymorphously perverse (a child has not yet learned to direct the means of and objects for gaining sexual pleasure into socioculturally appropriate channels), adult sexuality, if it stays fixated in infantile or adolescent stages of sexuality, may be characterized as perverse. The notion of deviance is thus built into the very idea of personal psychosexual development. Laplanche and Pontalis (308) further explain that genital sexuality represents normal adult sexuality for Freudian psychoanalysis; this genital organization includes transcending the Oedipus complex, assuming castration, and accepting the incest prohibition. They also point out that, understood comprehensively, perversion connotes the whole of the psychosexual behaviour that accompanies atypical means of obtaining sexual pleasure (306). The narrow and broad senses of the concept are integral to my argument, for the textual examples discussed employ both meanings.

Perversions such as masochism play a role in many adaptations of *Jane Eyre*, but I treat them as *psychic fantasies*, not as means of consolidating a female gender identity as does Massé. A psychic fantasy, explain Laplanche and Pontalis (314–18), refers to an imaginary scene in which a subject acts as protagonist that represents the fulfilment of an unconscious wish in a manner distorted by defensive processes such as negation, projection, or reversal into the opposite. The structures of psychic fantasies, argues Meredith Anne Skura (88), invariably 'pull the [text's] surface elements into new patterns and reveal new emphases.' Psychic fantasies have this effect, because they are narrative scripts in which the fantasizing subject has a role or roles to play; these roles and their attributes are open to permutations. Therefore, fantasies have the power to reconfigure a narrative in surprising ways: we can never know in advance how exactly the set roles of, for example, the beating fantasy will be played – a claim that *Rebecca* effectively illustrates.

Given this chapter's focus on romantic Bluebeard Gothic, I start by analysing du Maurier's *Rebecca*. I examine the love story between the nameless protagonist and Maxim de Winter as relying on a masochistic fantasy, one that corrodes the genre from within. Massé emphasizes that female writers and readers must come to terms with Gothic romance's unhealthy representations of masochism. They must consider whether the spectator's position, which allows the pursuit of knowledge about the beating drama, is available for them. The spectator's role would enable them to recognize both their own and other women's suffering, to ask questions about it, and to make aggression work *for* the self, not against others (Massé 3, 239–40). In scrutinizing the spectator's position, Massé almost exclusively focuses on representations of fictional worlds and interpersonal relationships. In contrast, I pay attention to strategies of narration and the narrator's relationship to the narratee, because they directly involve readers in this process of scrutiny. I claim that du Maurier resorts to a masochistic art of narration that affects the novel's reading process.

Readers and critics of *Rebecca* replicate its protagonist's longing to be Rebecca, because the first wife is the novel's most memorable character. Yet we know little about this woman whose character we must put together from fragments of conversation, descriptions, and the second wife's fantasies. It is hardly surprising, then, that along comes an author who delves into the mystery of Rebecca as does Sally Beauman in *Rebecca's Tale* (2001). As the title indicates, this novel is comparable to Rhys's *Wide Sargasso Sea* in its resuscitation of Bluebeard's first wife and in providing a prequel to its primary intertext. This book's links to *Jane Eyre* and 'Bluebeard' are forged through *Rebecca*. Beauman criticizes interpretations of Maxim de Winter as a romantic lover and a wronged husband whose uxoricide readers should forgive, because then Rebecca is thoroughly demonized. *Rebecca's Tale* probes Rebecca's character through archival research, interviews with, and memories of, her contemporaries, and Rebecca's diary.[3] This process uncovers a history of many-faced perversity in its broader sense: obsession, degeneration, madness, and incest. My analysis targets what Beauman identifies as perverse in du Maurier's *Rebecca* and how she herself handles such elements.

I discuss *Rebecca's Tale* in conjunction with Diane Setterfield's *The Thirteenth Tale* (2006), which focuses on the activities of narrating, authoring, and reading Bluebeard Gothic. Besides *Jane Eyre* and *Rebecca*, *The Thirteenth Tale* includes a rich variety of nineteenth-century intertexts such as Mary Elizabeth Braddon's *Lady Audley's Secret* (1862), Emily Brontë's *Wuthering Heights* (1847), Wilkie Collins's *The Woman in White* (1860), and Henry James's *The Turn of the Screw* (1898). The novel takes place at two levels. Its framing narrative concerns a famous author, Vida Winter, telling her life story to an amateur biographer, Margaret Lea, whose task is to turn the author's oral narrative into a book. (Of course, Vida Winter's name echoes with death as does Rebecca de Winter's name.) The embedded level deals with the author's distressing childhood. Both Vida and Margaret have devoured nineteenth-century literature in order to escape life; Vida has made her escape effective by writing prolifically in this vein. *The Thirteenth Tale* is replete with metaphors for its intertextual relationship to the Gothic legacy: as an intertext, Bluebeard Gothic is the novel's dangerously deranged twin, or it is akin to a rotted ruin. Perversity addresses narrating, writing, and reading: Are Bluebeard Gothics healthy reading matter? If their effect is questionable, is there any other cure than to stop reading them?

I conclude this chapter with D.M. Thomas's wicked sequel to *Jane Eyre*, *Charlotte* (2000). By focusing on what really happened after Jane married Rochester, this book demonstrates that Bluebeard is incapable of change. In a similar fashion as in *Rebecca*, the deadly dynamic characterizing his first marriage continues in the second. While du Maurier's critique of romance in Bluebeard Gothic is subtle, Thomas, in contrast, revels in exposing its perversity. The novel's frame narrative makes his intention of blowing up the Brontë legacy even more evident. It concerns Miranda Stevenson, a Brontë scholar and fledgling author whose life is beset with mental breakdowns, thanks to her troubled childhood with a mad mother and a molesting father. Thomas makes Miranda's relationship to her father resemble Charlotte Brontë's relationship to Reverend Brontë, thus suggesting impropriety in the latter. By suggesting that the writing Miranda emulates Charlotte Brontë, Thomas tackles views feminist scholarship has presented as regards women authors. He makes fun of its arguments, implying that today the cultural meaning of Bluebeard Gothic *is* perversion. This chapter thus traces a trajectory starting with du Maurier's questioning of 'Bluebeard's' role in *Jane Eyre*, and ending in the full exposure of its perverting influence.

### First Wife, Second Wife in Daphe du Maurier's *Rebecca*

*Rebecca* seizes on the narrative paths that remain virtual – evoked but then firmly rejected – in *Jane Eyre*. It dwells on what could have happened if Jane had eloped with Rochester to his sunny Mediterranean villa, disregarding his marriage to Bertha. Had Jane agreed to become Rochester's mistress, the couple would have been condemned to the kind of cautious, muted exile without social contacts that characterize the life that *Rebecca*'s nameless protagonist-narrator and Maxim de Winter lead abroad. While Jane refuses such a shadowy existence, *Rebecca*'s protagonist-narrator welcomes it. Their different reactions partly stem from the diverging ways in which the respective novels handle the 'Bluebeard' intertext. More specifically, they treat differently the 'other woman' motif of this tale, that is, the current wife's relationship to her enigmatic precursor.

Jane's interest is piqued about Rochester's many mistresses, Blanche Ingram, and Grace Poole, but her centre of attention always lies with Rochester. Although she compares herself negatively with these women, Jane nevertheless believes in her own worth. To be sure, in *Rebecca* the protagonist's position is different, because she is Maxim's lawfully wedded wife. Young and unformed, she believes that marriage enables her to form a solid identity. As the female protagonists of Bluebeard Gothic such as Jane Eyre and Henry James's nameless governess in *The Turn of the Screw*, she thinks marriage has this effect, because it makes possible what Bruce Robbins (238) calls trans-class sexuality. In other words, marriage allows for the erotic transgression of class, solidifying an upper-class identity otherwise unavailable to the woman. Soon, however, du Maurier's protagonist finds that she is just as much fascinated by the first wife as she is by Maxim. In this regard she resembles James's governess, who is riveted by her predecessor, Miss Jessel. Random remarks about Rebecca initiate the fantasies of du Maurier's protagonist about the other woman as everything she herself would like to be (R 47–8). The inexperienced protagonist is in search of her self. In desiring Maxim, she actually desires herself *as* Rebecca. The protagonist's fantasies pivot on what she would like to be socially and sexually, mixing her idealization of Rebecca with rivalry. This ambivalence persists until she can resolve the conflict with the envied other. This emphasis on female relationships is typical of Bluebeard Gothic, in which the current wife's predecessors figure as one of the mysteries she must solve in order to achieve a mature sexual identity.

The second wife has doubts, thanks to the 'originality' of Maxim's proposal (R 61) that fails to include one word of love. This omission makes the protagonist compare the proposal with how she assumes Maxim proposed to Rebecca. This imagined vision is so torturous that it leads her to cut up and burn the title page of a book of poetry Rebecca has given Maxim. What begins in idealization ends in a symbolic disembodiment. Typically, idealization functions as a defence against destructive instincts, for it is a corollary of a split between an idealized good object and a bad object whose persecutory traits are of an extreme kind (Laplanche and Pontalis 203). The protagonist's envy makes her compulsively think of Rebecca so that she, the protagonist, feels persecuted by the first wife. Her fantasies of surveillance fit in with the typical signs of paranoia. This delusion serves as a defence against the realization of the object as the paranoiac's lifelike double. By external-izing an inner state of mind through projection, paranoiacs treat the outside world as an extension of themselves. Such an extension shapes the protagonist's tortured fantasies about her insignificance in the eyes of everyone else. Again, she seems closely related to James's governess, who is convinced of being persecuted not only by Miss Jessel, but also by Peter Quint, Miss Jessel's lover and her employer's former valet. Edmund Wilson's (172) characterization of James thus applies equally well to du Maurier: these narratives are insightful studies in morbid psychology.

Self-torture is typical of the traditional notion of masochism, and the novel's chronological beginning establishes the protagonist's masochis-tic position, which Bluebeard Gothic enhances. Its 'Bluebeard' intertext strengthens these expectations, for Bluebeard states that only total sub-mission will let the wife enjoy the marital rewards of knowledge, activ-ity, and sexuality. First, however, she must pass a test of obedience: she must not visit Bluebeard's locked room. Similarly as in *Jane Eyre*, the protagonist of *Rebecca* must not seek knowledge about the enigmatic hero's past (R 43), which, in *Rebecca*, has spatial correlates in the first wife's bedroom and boathouse.

Once at Manderley, the new wife unsuccessfully attempts to achieve marital happiness through submission. She begins to think that if she were Rebecca, then Maxim would love her. The couple is at odds with one another, for while she tries to merge with Rebecca, he tries to hinder such a merger – or so it overtly seems. According to the contradictory logic of 'Bluebeard,' the husband ensures that the stated goal of obedi-ence is never reached. In *Rebecca* Manderley continues to run accord-ing to Rebecca's instructions; no changes are made in the environs she designed; her study, bedroom, and wardrobe are left intact; and even the fancy dress ball follows her arrangements. By continuing his life at Manderley as if nothing had changed, Maxim prompts his second wife to ferret out his secret. When she seeks knowledge about Rebecca and imitates her, she acts according to his covert script.[4]

In order for the protagonist to reach the desired state of fusion (R 298) she must learn how to be the *real* Mrs de Winter. A chief means in Maxim's education is entrusting her to the tutelage of Mrs Danvers, an amalgam of Brontë's Mrs Fairfax and Grace Poole. The protagonist's presence forces the housekeeper to acknowledge Rebecca's death. En-raged, Mrs Danvers plots her revenge. Unbeknown to her, however,

Mrs Danvers helps Maxim to reach his covert goal. Brontë modified the 'Bluebeard' intertext by making the first wife an active agent in the narrated events. Du Maurier picks up this thread by making the dead first wife participate, first by proxy and then as a water-eaten body, in the drama being played at Bluebeard's house. Manderley is a den of plotting, as the participants strive to achieve their mutually contradictory goals. The fancy dress ball represents the first culmination of this plotting. Mrs Danvers uses the protagonist as the medium for Rebecca's return. The protagonist, in turn, hopes that the ball finally establishes her as the real Mrs de Winter. Following Mrs Danvers's suggestion, she is dressed as Caroline de Winter, but what she does not know is that Rebecca wore the same costume in her last ball. Dressing up, she believes she fuses with her ideal self: 'I felt different already, no longer hampered by my appearance. My own dull personality was submerged at last' (R 220).

The protagonist learns the full extent of her misguided detection when she joins Maxim. The ball scene builds on 'Bluebeard.' The protagonist's costume parallels the wife's handing the bloody key to her husband. In dressing up as Rebecca she admits defiance, for she has probed Maxim's past, but unlike Bluebeard's wives, she has *not* learned his secret. In fact, she understands nothing of the situation she is in. In this respect she resembles Jane, whose ardent wish to love Rochester makes her close her eyes from signs of warning and premonitions, including her dreams. In 'Bluebeard,' Bluebeard thinks that the wife's guilt justifies his punishment of her. Obviously, the protagonist's appearance in Rebecca's costume shocks Maxim. Like Bluebeard, he punishes his wife. Maxim symbolically destroys her by ordering her to put on an ordinary evening gown, which, for her, equals appearing as her insignificant self. This punishment teaches her that her role is *not* to strive for a merger with her ideal self. Maxim castigates her for misunderstanding their marriage contract. By suggesting that she dress up as Alice in Wonderland (R 204, 214), he has given her a clue to his covert goal, which reproduces the combination of innocence and knowledge that is the aim of his education. In Wonderland the absurd and the surreal reign, while in the looking-glass world Alice checkmates the Red King. The clue refers to two features of life at Manderley: the estate is a fantasy realm in which traditional expectations do not apply and the wife's role is to defeat the King.

Rebecca's return as a water-eaten body forces Maxim to confess his murder of Rebecca to the protagonist. Again, du Maurier follows

Brontë's modification of 'Bluebeard'; Jane never finds out Rochester's secret, but outside pressure forces him to confess. Similarly, in *Rebecca*'s confession scene (ch. 20) du Maurier's Bluebeard himself opens the door to his forbidden chamber by telling his secret to the second wife. He has only waited for an opportunity to confess (R 282–3). He then for the first time professes his love for her, beginning to kiss her 'like never before' (R 279–80; see also 371). Yet he continues to fail to show signs of traditional romantic love. Many interpreters have noticed the unsatisfactory nature of the heterosexual union and have pointed out that the confession changes the husband's and the wife's roles, for he becomes infantilized (Jagose 362; Horner and Zlosnik 123–5; Massé 189–90). (She reports, for example, that he 'held my hands very tightly like a child who would gain confidence,' R 282.) His dependency shows in his replies to everything she says – 'Yes' and 'I don't know' – that have so far been typical only of her. From now on, as critics point out, the protagonist takes full control (Horner and Zlosnik 123–5; Massé 189–90). This is certainly not romantic love, but possessiveness and domination with a distinctly motherly attitude: 'I woke Maxim. He stared at me at first like a puzzled child, and then he held out his arms' (R 373).

By confessing, Maxim achieves his covert goal: he finds himself in the same marital *structure* as before. He places himself in the protagonist's hands, for now *she* has the power to destroy him. Du Maurier's Bluebeard is in the same situation with his second wife as with his first, for both can bring him the public humiliation he fears. Unlike Bluebeard's wives, they have the power to undo him. Maxim's submission to his wives suggests that he yields them the traditional male position of domination. This shift brings the protagonist closer than anything else to a merger with Rebecca, because Rebecca had this same position in her relationship to Maxim. Her change of role from the beaten to the beater raises the question of the kind of masochism we are dealing with.

The protagonist's reaction to Maxim's confession shows another change in du Maurier's handling of 'Bluebeard.' Bluebeard's wife recognizes herself in the bloody spectacle in the forbidden chamber. So does Jane. The protagonist, in contrast, gloats over Maxim's confession, because it releases her from paranoia. 'I had listened to his story, and part of me went with him like a shadow in his tracks. I too had killed Rebecca, I too had sunk the boat there in the bay' (R 297). It allows her to finish what she started by burning Rebecca's dedication in the book of poetry: the symbolic murder of her double. After Maxim's confession, her fantasies almost cease, for now she wards off the discovery of her husband's lack, not her own. Being privy to Rebecca's 'immorality' enables the protagonist's identity to solidify at last: in her view, it justifies her English middle-class class-consciousness and authority over others.

When the protagonist becomes the real Mrs de Winter, the second de Winter marriage repeats the first one. In order to understand more fully the masochistic fantasy underpinning this marriage, it is instructive to explore the wife's role. The conditions of the de Winter marriage contract throw light on this matter.

## The de Winter Marriage Contract

In hindsight, Rochester claims he was trapped into marriage; this deception dawned on him soon after the wedding when, says he, Bertha no longer could hide her hideous nature from him. When Maxim de Winter marries Rebecca, everyone thinks him the luckiest man (R 284). During their honeymoon, however, Rebecca reveals to him her 'true' nature. We are not told what she tells him, but Maxim insinuates that she disclosed her promiscuity and bisexuality. While Bertha has few means to defend herself against Rochester, Rebecca is practical and calculating. She offers to make a deal with Maxim, granted that she can have her way outside his family estate: 'I'll look after your precious Manderley for you, make it the most famous show-place in all the country, if you like. And people will visit us, and envy us, and talk about us; they'll say we are the luckiest, happiest, handsomest couple in all England. What a leg-pull, Max,' she said, 'what a God-damn triumph!'(R 285) In choosing Rebecca, Maxim concedes, he chose something other than what she seemed, and this feature becomes articulated during this scene (R 284). Rebecca offers to disavow reality together with Maxim. Such disavowal means that they both know how things stand in reality but choose to disregard this knowledge in favour of fantasy. The aim is to secure an ideal that is suspended in fantasy. This type of disavowal consists in 'radically contesting the validity of that which is: it suspends belief in and neutralizes the given in such a way that a new horizon opens up beyond the given and in place of it' (Deleuze 31). Rebecca proposes that they create a perfect display of upper-class Englishness, an idyll with a lord of the manor and his lady presiding over a rural community.

Theorists of masochism agree that this fantasy is based on a private contract regulating a man's relationship to a woman. The first de Winter marriage is based on a contract whose effectiveness lies in the tension between public display and private knowledge. In *Rebecca* nothing clarifies better the tension behind the contract than Rebecca's 'perverse' duplicity (R 283–4). Dressed up as Caroline de Winter, for example, to everyone else she is the epitome of wifely femininity. Only in Maxim's eyes the pastoral costume is obscene, for he knows that Rebecca has hidden her lovers among the guests (R 287). Thanks to her promiscuity, Rebecca in her capacity as the 'angel-wife' mocks everything traditional marriage represents. The contract invests her with the symbolic power exerted in marriage, reversing the common power dynamic between husband and wife.

Maxim maintains that he sacrificed 'pride, honour, personal feeling' (R 285) in continuing his marriage in order to escape the humiliation a divorce would bring. Yet others point out that he was plagued by jealousy (R 256, 341, 347), which speaks of the suffering Rebecca inflicts on him, for the contract turns him into a voyeur who spies on Rebecca (R 287). He dreads exposure (R 289). Being found out would disclose Rebecca's promiscuity and his cuckoldry. This revelation would mark a re-evaluation of Manderley, showing that Maxim was the master neither of his wife nor of his estate (R 277, 282).

The fantasy has, however, gratifying aspects for Maxim. Rebecca turns Manderley into a perfect English country estate. Maxim's family has possessed it since the Conquest, and he places it above everything else (R 286). In his mind he himself and the estate are one. Yet neither his father nor he had the talent to make anything out of the place. 'Her blasted taste made Manderley the thing it is today ... it's all due to her, to Rebecca' (R 287). The theatricals they play allow him to reach for his ideal. Nothing stages it better than the costume balls at Manderley. 'I never dress up,' said Maxim, 'it's the one perquisite allowed to the host' (R 204). While everyone else, including Rebecca, wears a disguise, Maxim appears in his evening clothes, which suggests that only he is himself. To all the others the host's 'one perquisite' signifies Maxim's status as Manderley's master, indicating conventional connotations of the master's position: autonomy, domination, self-possession. The marriage contract allows *him* to strive toward *his* ideal ego. The estate, as a mythic realm of rural Englishness, and Maxim, as its master, converge in this ideal.

The husband's striving for his ideal ego, a fusion of the man and the estate, is the key to the fantasy being played at Manderley. By entering into a contract with Rebecca, Maxim hands over to her the position of domination. Rebecca's power to punish him – to expose his weakness – enables du Maurier's Bluebeard to project the superego's functions onto the woman. He externalizes these functions: the woman stands for the forbidding and punishing agency of the psyche. It then follows that the wife's lot in the de Winter marriage is to occupy the position of the beating woman, a role familiar from male masochistic fantasies. Maxim's confession includes the greatest surprise of the novel: the revelation of the romantic hero – *not* the female protagonist – as the masochist.

The goal of masochism, explains Deleuze, is to enable the masochist to reach for his narcissistic ideal ego. This ideal has as its pivot a specific belief about the mother image. She serves as a mirror to reflect and produce the ideal ego, the ideality of which derives from its being autonomous and independent of the superego (Deleuze 127). By projecting the functions of the superego on Rebecca, Maxim can entertain the fantasy of having an autonomous ego. According to Deleuze, this lack of restraint derives from the fact that in spite of the masochist's externalization of the superego onto the beating woman, she mocks and punishes everything the superego represents, because she – not the father figure – has assumed the functions normally associated with it (Deleuze 124).

Manderley is Rebecca's creation. She has designed the estate's grounds and its internal decoration; it runs according to her order; she organizes its social gatherings and presides over them. Her monogram exemplifies her rule with her sloping initial (R) eclipsing the initials of her surname (de W). In playing the master of Manderley, Maxim communicates his fantasy through the means created by Rebecca. These features fit in with Deleuze's analysis of the role masochism gives to the mother. The masochist magnifies the mother by insisting that symbolically she lacks nothing and, correspondingly, degrades the father by depriving him of all symbolic function. The symbolic order becomes a maternal order in which the mother generates the symbolism through which the masochist expresses himself (Deleuze 63).

Being the real Mrs de Winter means conforming to the role of the beating woman typical of male masochistic fantasies. This role, however, has its consequences, as the ending of *Rebecca* illustrates. The second wife realizes the meaning of her new role only after information about Rebecca's fatal cancer has cleared Maxim of suspicions of murder. On their way from London back to Manderley, she wakes up to a nightmare which alerts her to the cost of her role as Bluebeard's accomplice:

I was writing letters in the morning-room ... But when I looked down to see what I had written it was not my small square handwriting at all, it was long, and slanting, with curious pointed strokes ... I got up and went to the looking-glass. A face stared back at me that was not my own. It was very pale, very lovely, framed in a cloud of dark hair. The eyes narrowed and smiled. The lips parted. The face in the glass stared back at me and laughed. And I saw then that she was sitting on a chair before the dressing-table in her bedroom, and Maxim was brushing her hair. He held her hair in her hands, and as he brushed it he wound it slowly into a thick rope. It twisted like a snake, and he took hold of it with both hands and smiled at Rebecca and put it around his neck.

'No,' I screamed. 'No, no. We must go to Switzerland.' (R 395–6)

In the dream's first scene the handwriting startles the protagonist; looking into the mirror she finds herself confronting Rebecca. This scene merges into another one via the mirror with the protagonist standing behind Maxim and Rebecca and watching them look at each other in the mirror. The mirror motif ties the dream to 'Bluebeard' in which the latest wife sees her own reflection in the murdered predecessors. Jane understands fully what the consequences of becoming Rochester's mistress would be for her: she would be one in a series of his women. In *Rebecca* this realization comes only after the protagonist has secured her position as the real Mrs de Winter. The dream marks the moment she finally understands what she has consented to in becoming Maxim's accomplice. Rebecca's gaze reciprocates the protagonist's gaze, forcing the latter to recognize herself in the mirror image. The horror arises from her understanding of her place in Bluebeard's series: she merges with Rebecca. As a pre-scripted role, being Mrs de Winter condemns the protagonist to the repetition of the same, because it fuses all women with the mother figure of the masochistic fantasy. We never need to learn the protagonist's first name, because she *is* Rebecca.

The dream's second scene organizes the characters in accordance with the masochistic fantasy, showing Mrs de Winter's lot. That Maxim looks at Rebecca's reflection is significant, for, as the mother figure, she represents for him what Deleuze calls the 'maternal mirror of death' (131). This association of Rebecca – whose name in Hebrew signifies 'noose' or 'rope' (Smith 304) – with death is underlined by Maxim's submission to her phallus-like braid, which stands for the maternal phallus of the fantasy. The woman as an image of death paradoxically enables the male subject's rebirth, because his bondage to her ensures that his ego will be liberated from both the superego and genital sexuality (Deleuze 125).

The second marriage is Maxim's attempt to rebuild his fantasy (R 8). The novel's frame narrative, set ten years after the events recounted, shows that although the protagonist claims they share everything, both try to hide their inroads into the past from each other. The shared knowledge about Maxim's past – Rebecca's domination and sexual humiliation of him – explains the masochism of their fantasy. Being privy to these facts, the second wife is a living reminder of all that is humiliating to him. Also, her knowledge has the power to wound him. That the past is the second wife's 'secret indulgence' proves she enjoys her position of domination. In exile she has become the kind of Alice in Wonderland he had in mind, for she hurts him, as it were, innocently and unwittingly. 'Once there was an article on wood pigeons,' the protagonist narrates, 'and as I read it aloud it seemed to me that once again I was in the deep woods at Manderley ... How strange that an article on wood pigeons could so recall the past and make me falter as I read aloud. It was the gray look on his face that made me stop abruptly, and turn the pages until I found a paragraph on cricket' (R 10). By monitoring him and by conforming to his needs, she acts the same role as Rebecca: as Maxim's externalized superego. It is the wife's fine-tuned sensitivity to the husband's reactions that does not let him forget. The concluding irony of du Maurier's novel is establishing romantic love as a subtle form of torture.[5]

## Masochistic Art of Narration

Daphne du Maurier chooses a narrative strategy in *Rebecca* that we might characterize as a reframing tactic. Becky McLaughlin draws attention to the fact that retelling any narrative unavoidably reframes it. She notices that the moment we identify a given story as, for example, a repetition of 'Bluebeard,' we are dealing with literary disavowal, which she describes as a perverse act of telling and receiving a story whose end we already both know and do not know: 'Yes, this is the "Bluebeard" story, but ...' (McLaughlin 419–20). That du Maurier chooses to tell a familiar tale in the context of Bluebeard Gothic is a comfort to the reader. Yet by allowing what typically remains repressed to return in the rewriting, she turns this familiar world upside down, unsettling our assumptions about the genre. An important part of this rewriting is making the masochistic fantasy shape the novel's narration to the

extent that we may speak of a 'masochistic art of narration.' It is at
this level that she most radically parts ways with Brontë's *Jane Eyre*.
Throughout du Maurier places weight on the act of framing as a way
of looking at Bluebeard Gothic. As is to be expected, this strategy introduces a self-reflexive level to reading the novel.

It is instructive to compare *Rebecca*'s narrative framework to that of
Leopold von Sacher-Masoch's *Venus in Furs* (1870). Both are framed by
the narrator's dream about a woman torturer (Rebecca and Venus, respectively) followed by a return to the narrator's reality and reflections
on the dream's significance. The frame narrator of *Venus in Furs* confides in his friend, Severin, who reciprocates by letting the frame narrator read his manuscript. The rest of the novel consists of this embedded
narrative; only briefly do we return to the narrative framework with
the two friends discussing the moral of Severin's story. The manuscript
recounts how Severin became *disfantasized*: he says the moral of his tale
is 'that I was a fool! ... If only I had whipped her instead!' (von Sacher-
Masoch 271). In contrast, in *Rebecca* the narrator's account of becoming
Mrs de Winter signifies *becoming fantasized*, of assuming the position of
the striking 'hammer' through identification with Rebecca, the dream's
female torturer. This process draws attention to du Maurier's inversion
of the 'Bluebeard' intertext, which evokes the fairy-tale pattern of home
– forest (Bluebeard's castle) – home again. According to Skura (93), the
phase in the forest represents earlier psychic material than the framing episodes at home, which are closer to reality. *Rebecca* reverses this
pattern. At Manderley the protagonist has a chance of saving herself
from Bluebeard. Instead, she sinks deeper into fantasy: the narrative
framework testifies to her delusion. As she is locked in a masochistic
fantasy, her narrative has no destination or completion. It appears as
'a process of infection leading to illness' (Finke 125) – perhaps even to
repeated murder.

The motif of Bluebeard's forbidden chamber shows us how the men-
ace of his repeated violence is written into the spatial dialectic in du
Maurier's novel. According to Joan Copjec, this place is locatable in
the relation of Rebecca's boathouse, a scene of the breach of the marriage contract and of actual murder, to her bedroom, a scene of sexual
acts that, against appearances, never took place there (132–5). Significantly, this bedroom–boathouse dialectic continues in the second marriage, which primarily takes place in exile. The frame narrative shows
the now-mature second wife conforming to Maxim's needs in the dull
hotels they frequent (bedroom), but she reveals to us that she indulges

in 'things that hurt' (R 11) out of Maxim's sight. In the same fashion as Rebecca, she goes away (boathouse), and, after having satisfied herself, she can 'return, smiling and refreshed, to face the little ritual of our tea' (R 11). The juxtaposition of the first wife's extramarital liaisons with the second wife's indulgences in the past – of which the narrative we read is one – allows us to identify the motivation pulsing beneath the narrator's account. It suggests that the second wife's narration of the couple's story is comparable to the first wife's promiscuity: her narrative serves as her whip.

We can see the effects of the masochistic fantasy on narration most clearly in the repeated gestures of framing that comprise the whole body of du Maurier's novel. The following example elucidates this feature: 'I wanted to go on sitting there, not talking, not listening to the others, keeping the moment precious for all time, because we were peaceful, all of us ... In a little while it would be different, there would come to-morrow, and the next day, and another year. And we would be changed perhaps, never sitting quite like this again ... This moment was safe enough, this could not be touched. Here we sat together, Maxim and I, hand-in-hand, and the past and the future mattered not at all' (R 109). Jagose describes the narrator's 'inability to sustain herself in any temporal framing for long ... pitching back and forth between the scene she describes and those she fancies preceded or might follow it, as she is processed ... by the fantasies of an imagined past and future' (358). She argues that this plunging from one temporal frame to another is in radical counterpoint to the narrator's 'impossible and almost pathological desire to remain arrested in the present' (Jagose 358). The key words are 'impossible' and 'pathological.' What unites the narrator's temporal zigzagging and her desire to arrest time is the effort to frame events and thereby to aestheticize them. In other words, she keeps turning her fancies into frozen aesthetic tableaux. This movement from reality to fantasy reveals the basic thrust of masochism: a real event (or a live body) leads through the simultaneous acknowledgment of its status as reality and the disavowal of this reality to a suspension of reality that enables the construction of an ideal. (The memory of) sitting in the garden after lunch includes an awareness of the moment's transitory nature, yet this knowledge is disavowed and suspended. What rises in its stead is an arrested picture of a perfect after-lunch relaxation: a representation of an ideal non-reality. The recorded events and the narrator's attempt to describe Rebecca's body and characteristics do not in themselves really make up this narrative, but the way in which these 'real' elements can be turned into representations of an impossible and pathological ideal – a fantasy.

That *Rebecca*'s narrator obsessively disavows and suspends reality in order to construct aesthetic tableaux of an ideal reality – of which the fantasy of 'our Manderley' is the most conspicuous – suggests that the content of fantasy is less important than its mechanism (Finke 133). Indeed, Deleuze remarks that there is no specifically masochistic fantasy, but rather a masochistic *art* of fantasy (72). He even claims that the kind of disavowal in which the narrator is engaged is 'nothing less than the foundation of imagination, which suspends reality and establishes the ideal in the suspended world' (128). *Rebecca*'s narrator exhibits in a persistently explicit way the narrative mechanism of the masochistic fantasy that gives birth to a hallucinatory art, a mechanism that is alien to the narration of *Jane Eyre*. As is to be expected, this type of hallucinatory narration employed in *Rebecca* cannot but affect the reading process.

### Infecting Readers

The common assumption is that readers identify with the Gothic's heroine in order to experience suspense and romance vicariously. When the heroine is the narrator, this double role strengthens identification. As Marianne Noble explains, it is taken to suggest a sympathetic mode of reception in which we become another by making the other's agonies our own. It promotes unification by fostering the recognition of others' experiences as counterparts to our own, which wipes away the distance between individuals. Shared suffering is the mechanism that enables us to enter into another person (64–5). In Bluebeard Gothic, argues Massé, identification leads readers to adopt the position of the beaten heroine (3–5). Readers become party to the masochistic contract, for their identification with the beaten heroine lets them vicariously experience a loving fusion with the beating hero. This complicity questions neither the represented sexual relationships nor the ideology of love on which they are based. But what complicates this setup in *Rebecca* is that the beaten heroine, merging with Rebecca, ends up in the position of the beater. This change of roles places the typical masochistic reading contract under scrutiny: what role should readers assume?

In Gothic romances the protagonist wins the hero from a rival woman. This victory leads to a dyadic fusion of reciprocal nurture (Radway 146; Skura 92–3). Noble explains how this fusion ties in with notions of female masochistic submission, 'a state of "total subjectivity," in which the masochist is both an individual self *and* is merged with totality' (73). In this regressive fantasy the means to this goal is paternal discipline and punishment. By submitting to the husband's coercive but maternally protective rule, the woman returns to the mother *in* and *through* him (Noble 69–71). Because this union takes place through the husband, it disguises the woman's homosexual desire for her mother. This merger, as Massé points out, remains fraught with ambiguity in *Rebecca*, for the protagonist submits to Maxim, but will neither have Manderley nor be Rebecca (189–91). Depriving the protagonist of these two trophies suggests that the novel is what Radway calls a failed romance, for the readers' identification with her is not nurturing enough: they do not have the sense that, while reading, they have successfully become other and been happily elsewhere (184). In other words, the masochistic reading contract does *not* yield the expected outcome.

Given that identifying with the protagonist-narrator is fraught with ambiguity, does identifying with Rebecca bring satisfaction? Modleski observes that the novel's conclusion fails to resolve a woman's problems of overidentification with another woman (44; Jagose 362). Horner and Zlosnik join Light in arguing that the satisfaction associated with Rebecca's role is that of the 'mad woman in the attic' who acts out our desire, turning the narrative into a displaced revenge (Light 13, 20; Horner and Zlosnik 123–6). Identifying with Rebecca, Light (13) concludes, yields an ambiguous satisfaction, because it offers a deceptive control of the discourses defining femininity, which women, subject to those discourses, can never wholly enjoy.

Although romantic readings of *Rebecca* domesticate the cruelty of 'Bluebeard,' they are by no means alien to Bluebeard Gothic. Blaming the wicked first wife distracts attention from the male as oppressor and directs it toward the male as victim who deserves women's love. It is usually agreed that du Maurier meant us to forgive Maxim's murder of Rebecca (Light 1984; Smith 305; Massé 179–85). Yet by reconfiguring the traditional fantasy structure of Bluebeard Gothic, du Maurier's novel challenges romantic interpretations based on identification. In the male masochistic fantasy it portrays, the woman is not reunified with the mother in and through the husband, because this fantasy does *not* represent heterosexual marriage as the gateway to the pre-Oedipal union. Instead, it is incestuous in nature, for it dispenses with heterosexuality altogether in order to replace it with a pre-Oedipal union between mother (the beating woman) and child (the male masochist). Guilt and punishment substitute for reciprocal nurture. The male version of masochism does not disguise from a woman her (homosexual) desire for the mother, but forces it on her. This role allows her to hold on to the primitive notion of the mother as everything. From the woman's perspective, this symbiotic bond evokes both the illusion of the power of an absolute being and the fear of nothingness. The male masochistic fantasy plays on these extremes: when the woman identifies with the mother, she is able to entertain the illusion of being all. When, however, she realizes that the masochist forces this symbiotic identification on her, she must acknowledge that she is nothing, for the fantasy denies her a separate identity. The protagonist's desire for and merger with Rebecca are her ticket to a perverse sexuality. Because the male masochistic fantasy banishes genital sexuality, the novel's representation of heterosexuality remains passionless.

After learning she has cancer, Rebecca taunts Maxim into murdering her (R 390). This death has been interpreted as the 'madwoman in the attic's' triumph over patriarchal discourse. This act, however, illustrates the impasse the male masochistic fantasy entails for the woman. Maxim's attempt to reverse the balance of power backfires. Turning Maxim into a murderer is Rebecca's most successful form of torture, for murder has no statute of limitations. Slavoj Žižek draws attention to the moment when the woman's breakdown – Rebecca's laughter – shatters the fantasy's coordinates. She accepts, of her own free will, the facticity of death (*Looking* 66). In this sense, Rebecca's death is a victory over Maxim. But by embracing the emptiness of her subjectivity, Rebecca proves that she equals death – an equation that is central to the male masochistic fantasy. Rebecca's death merges her with its female role. The final irony of the novel is that Rebecca's triumph secures the continuation of Maxim's fantasy. Because Maxim is a murderer, he suffers to the end of his days a fear of exposure (R 8). Hence, although the power balance between the masochist and his master is reversed, there are limits to the master's role, because the master is the fantasy's enabling element, not a subject (Deleuze 42–3). Both Rebecca and the protagonist-narrator remain locked in Bluebeard's repetitious circuit. Although they differ in appearance and mentality, they are nevertheless caught in a fantasy that relies on destructive repetition emphasizing oversameness.

This interpretation of the fantasy material in du Maurier's novel suggests that the readers' identification with either the protagonist-narrator or Rebecca fails to provide a rewarding vicarious experience. Quite the contrary, it infects readers, simply causing the masochistic fantasy to repeat itself in them. Such projective identification is what the fantasy always aims at. Identification traps readers in Bluebeard's forbidden chamber: they become his latest victims. Given that within this fantasy there is no escape for Rebecca and the protagonist-narrator from Bluebeard's chamber, is there a way out for readers?

Casie Hermansson explains that new versions of 'Bluebeard' may either be recastings or reworkings. Recastings reject the tale's paradigm of escape and resubmit to Bluebeard's plot, thus rendering the new narrative another repetition of the Bluebeard material. They suppress the space in which readers may engage in resisting dialogue and alternatives to textual determinism. In so doing, they act like Bluebeard in relation to readers. In contrast, reworkings privilege the heroine's activity of rewriting by drawing on the tale's self-critical potential. Embedding 'Bluebeard' in a new fiction invites this potential to be actualized (Hermansson 7–8). Massé specifies that the heroine has three possibilities to work through the Bluebeard Gothic: the heroine's aggression against the dominator puts an end to the domination (Rhys's *Wide Sargasso Sea*); the heroine's self-conscious but covert subversion mimes expectations of femininity in order to achieve freedom (Atwood's *Lady Oracle*); and, finally, the heroine creates a utopian alterity, refusing to accept the binary options of oppressor versus subordinated as happens, for example, in Dinesen's *The Angelic Avengers* (Massé 240).

Insightful as these formulations are, they do not take into account that not all generic critique is tied to the consciousness of fictional characters or a (first-person) narrator. Linking the critical potential of 'Bluebeard' to the heroine's fate does not acknowledge the criticism that emerges through an author's use of plot, generic conventions, closure, and the reading contract he or she makes with readers. This is the level at which du Maurier operates. In her novel the male version of masochism seamlessly structures interpersonal relationships and narration, thus drawing the readers' attention to the writer's total destruction of romantic notions of love: only delusion and torture remain. *Rebecca* shows romance conventions as 'deceitful clues planted by the writer to rouse the attention of the reader before disappointing his expectations; conventions are paradoxically functional in the disintegration of the genre' (Tani 42–3). It is the reversal of the usual rendition of the masochistic fantasy in Bluebeard Gothic as well as generic dissolution that together create the critical distance in *Rebecca* to the preceding tradition.

My reading of the novel demonstrates that identification as a reading strategy involves entering into a masochistic contract that eventually traps readers in Bluebeard's chamber. It invites readers to review received notions about how we read Bluebeard Gothic. Consequently, reading becomes self-reflexive: what is at issue is no longer vicarious romantic experience but the ways in which and the purposes for which an author reframes and reuses the familiar tale. This readjustment of the reading strategy spotlights the representation of gender relationships and romantic love as ideological constructs of Bluebeard Gothic's world view. This creation of a self-reflexive distance to the legacy of romantic Bluebeard Gothic enables readers to escape from Bluebeard's clutches even if the female characters and the narrator remain imprisoned. Revisionist rewriting does not depend on the heroine-narrator's physical or psychic survival, but rather on this critical distance. As a destroyer of Bluebeard's romantic portrait and of the typical masochistic reading strategy, du Maurier plays a double role in the literary historical continuum. First, she partakes in the tradition in which the romantic Bluebeard Gothic gives way to overtly feminist generic reworkings, such as Margaret Atwood's *Lady Oracle* (1976) and *The Robber Bride* (1993), that explicitly call for a self-reflexive reading. Second, she plays an important role in lifting out such perversions as fetishism, masochism, and paranoia as central ingredients of Bluebeard Gothic. In this respect du Maurier's undertaking hearkens back to Henry James's parody of *Jane Eyre* in his *The Turn of the Screw*. Alice Hall Petry maintains that this novelette rests on James's presentation of the governess as an avid reader who mistakes herself for a heroine in Bluebeard Gothic. 'The governess,' writes Petry, 'has been unduly influenced by her reading of ... *Jane Eyre*; more specifically, that the tragic events at Bly are the direct result of her perceptions of herself, her employer, her situation, and of Bly itself having been hopelessly distorted by her pathetic attempt to emulate Charlotte Brontë's famous heroine' (61).[6] In a similar fashion as James's earlier ghost story, *Rebecca* casts a shadow on the literary precursor. Du Maurier figures in the gradual process in which Jane's and Rochester's cultural shares start to sink, while either Bertha or the position she occupies begins to be positively valued. In other words, Jane's love for Rochester appears in the sinister light of a dangerous delusion akin to the deranged devotion James's governess shows toward her bachelor employer, while Bertha emerges as an enticing beauty destroyed by her Bluebeard husband. It is the second wife who is mad, not the first one.

Auerbach describes *Rebecca* as a novel that seems 'to be about a *femme fatale*, but the woman is a cloudy catalyst for the narrative convolutions of a murderous man' (86). The link between the male creative imagination and sublimation of Deleuze's theory adds yet another layer of significance to these convolutions. The protagonist-narrator's narration, tied as it is to maintaining Bluebeard's masochistic fantasy, suggests that although the cruel mother occupies the father's place, she is incapable of imaginative power (the power of sublimation). Instead, she lends her voice to another's fantasy, speaking his words. Woman, as an independent subject, is totally effaced from the picture (see Stewart 54–5). This ventriloquism is du Maurier's scathing criticism of the Gothic legacy within which she worked.

## Sally Beauman's *Rebecca's Tale*: Marriage as Battleground

I now examine a contemporary novel that recognizes perversity as an inherent part of the *Jane Eyre* legacy. I discuss Sally Beauman's *Rebecca's Tale*, a recent example of a novel that celebrates the first wife – like Bertha, Antoinette, and Rebecca – as the real heroine. Beauman's novel is primarily an adaptation of *Rebecca*; its links with the *Jane Eyre* legacy are forged largely, but not solely, through du Maurier's book. *Rebecca's Tale* consists of contributions by four different narrators. Three of them narrate their stories in the book's present, in the months of April and May 1951. The fourth contribution is read by these three narrators during the two-month span covered by the novel, but it was written twenty years before, in April 1931. It is Rebecca's notebook written shortly before her death and addressed to the baby she assumed she was carrying. The diary is Rebecca's legacy to the baby (RT 256), written in eager anticipation of motherhood with the purpose of recording the twists and turns of Rebecca's life so far. Readers familiar with du Maurier's *Rebecca* have an advantage of knowledge over Beauman's Rebecca, for they know that Rebecca not only has a malformed womb but also that she has uterine cancer. This situation of romantic irony tinges the notebook with tragic colours. But it also satisfies readers' curiosity in fleshing out Rebecca's character and in painting a full picture of her marriage to Maxim. As in *Rebecca*, this marriage reveals Bluebeard's perversity in which he tries to make his wife partake.

In *Rebecca's Tale* Maxim's father, Lionel de Winter, seduces his wife's sister, Isolda, Rebecca's mother.[7] Isolda subsequently marries Jack Devlin, but it is never fully resolved whether Rebecca is Lionel's or Jack Devlin's child. Lionel's continued financial support of mother and daughter sustains these doubts about paternity. It is thus possible that

Rebecca and Maxim are half-siblings which would make their marriage incestuous. Rebecca never reveals to him the identity of her mother nor the uncertainty about her father. 'Dear fastidious Max would faint at the idea of incest' (RT 288), she writes, while this possibility only amuses her. Be it as it may, Rebecca and Maxim are first cousins. Rebecca holds Lionel indirectly responsible for her mother's death. His sudden discontinuation of payments to Isolda plunges mother and daughter into financial ruin and precipitates Isolda's death. Visiting Manderley as an adolescent, Rebecca is convinced of being its rightful owner, instead of the man who might be her father. She also realizes that the only way to make it hers is to marry the heir, Maxim de Winter. Even before they know each other, Rebecca is determined to have Maxim in order to wrest Manderley from him and be revenged on Lionel de Winter. Beauman's Rebecca thus replicates the wilfulness and vindictiveness of du Maurier's Rebecca. Moreover, Beauman makes her childhood echo with Antoinette's in *Wide Sargasso Sea*: in both cases, the first wife has suffered from contempt and poverty.

Rebecca's deep-seated grudge against the de Winter family does not explain, however, why her relationship with Maxim turns into a version of 'Bluebeard,' for at first they are besotted with each other. Du Maurier's *Rebecca* names as the beginning of trouble a moment in Monte Carlo when Rebecca confides in Maxim. *Rebecca's Tale* locates this moment earlier in time, identifying it as a scene on a beach in northern France when Rebecca tells Maxim a traumatic incident from her childhood. Unlike du Maurier, Beauman reveals what Rebecca confides in Maxim. It was on the same beach when she was nearly seven years old that she was raped by a local boy. These confidences have unforeseen results:

> I tried to make [Max] understand – but he didn't. His expression began to change. First I saw doubts, then that hideous fastidious distaste, and then – right at the very back of his eyes – a reluctant excitement, slowly deepening. You know what? His expression was the very *same* as that boy's – it was identical! That shocked me to the heart – and I will never, ever, forgive him. (RT 264)

Listening to Rebecca, Maxim merges with her rapist: behind the veneer of a gentleman lurks a primordial and violent lust that may take even a child as its object. This lust is highly possessive, leading to obsessive jealousy. Jealousy is heightened by Maxim's realization of Rebecca's acting skills, which make him doubt her earnestness and honesty. Soon the brand-new husband torments the wife with questions about her sexual past, expecting her to satisfy his curiosity (RT 265). Maxim's jealousy leads him to internalize the boy-rapist who becomes his closest companion, his double (RT 266). He turns the rape into Rebecca's fault, thanks to her 'bad blood and bad ways' (RT 266) – after all, in his eyes Rebecca is more French than English. While Rebecca has regarded Maxim as a typical restrained English bluestocking, she now begins to see him as Bluebeard, desirous of possessing the wife body and soul. The scene at Monte Carlo in *Rebecca* in which Rebecca reveals infamous things about herself to Maxim is reversed in *Rebecca's Tale*: in the latter it is Maxim, fearing that Rebecca has been licentious with men, who makes a scene. He is jealous to the point of wanting to murder her then and there (RT 266).

As in Du Maurier's rendition, so also in Beauman's interpretation Maxim is perverse. Beauman identifies this Bluebeard's deviance as stemming from extreme possessiveness and jealousy. A wife has no separate identity apart from her husband; she is a trophy who enhances a man's worth. Maxim holds women untrustworthy, sexually provocative, and immoral. His jealousy turns him into a voyeur spying on his wife. His excited identification with the rapist suggests not only that sexual relationships are grounded in male competition over women but also that he harbours a fantasy according to which a man can possess all women – mothers, sisters, daughters, and small girls – irrespective of the Oedipal prohibition. In fact, as Fink (*Lacanian* 109–12) points out, this is the basic fantasy underlying patriarchy. In order to function as a system, patriarchy requires the notion that there exists one man to whom the law of castration, including the incest taboo, does not apply. This man is the primal father of the primordial horde familiar from Freud's *Totem and Taboo* who is his own law. Thanks to not having succumbed to castration, the primal father controls all women. Moreover, only he can take his pleasure directly from woman, in contrast to all other men, who must content themselves to having a relationship with woman as object. That Maxim's sexual desire is kindled through identification with a pedophile-rapist implies that this fantasy of a primal father without bounds lives on in his unconscious. It suggests resistance to submitting to castration and accepting the incest prohibition. The fastidious man who would faint at the idea of incest actually gladly wallows in it. One of this Bluebeard's fatal shortcomings is his lack of self-reflexivity as regards sexuality and desire. His arousal requires hatred grounded in the desire to dominate. The terms in which Beauman models Maxim are familiar from Rhys's portrayal of Rochester.

Beauman's Rebecca enters marriage believing that ultimately she prevails. She is convinced of success in her plan of turning the estate over to her child and thus wresting it from the de Winter family. What she has not foreseen is the accuracy of the warning by Maxim's grandmother that a de Winter marriage requires sacrifices from the wife. On first hearing this warning, Rebecca has 'a vision of Manderley brides being led in procession to the ancestral altar; there, anointed and accoutred, with a patient acquiescence, they prepared themselves to be offered up to their wintry bridegrooms. Stifled? Strangled? Wedded?' (RT 324). Beauman follows Rhys in showing Bluebeard and the wife to be engaged in a battle over supremacy, with marriage as the ground on which this battle is fought. For the wife being wedded equals being stifled or strangled, unless she fights back, insisting on her separateness, independence, and full rights. In this novel, Rebecca's error is belief in her imperviousness (RT 324). Convinced that she has managed to turn herself into an effective weapon (RT 321), she has not anticipated the damage of being married to a 'wintry bridegroom,' that is, death.

Rebecca's clear-sightedness about her deathly husband makes her reflect on herself as one in a series of de Winter wives, leading to a striking premonition of her successor. Musing on this series, she suddenly sees the ghost of the nameless, second Mrs Maxim de Winter: 'Sweet as sugar, innocent as a schoolgirl, not a scrap of makeup, wearing no scent, lank hair – sly eyes ... I could smell emulation and rivalry; I didn't take to her, not at all' (RT 309). The girl's modest appearance and youth refer back to Jane Eyre, while her namelessness suggests to Rebecca that the girl incorporates Bluebeard's notion of a proper wife, 'the woman of eternal subservience who might have made the perfect Mrs de Winter' (309). A perfect wife, of course, has no other name than her husband's. On a closer look, however, Rebecca perceives that the successor's strength lies in determined stealth and passivity, which make the girl Rebecca's ally. 'She stepped in between me and Max; she held on to me for strength; I saw it was I who'd summoned her up, and I saw she could be my ally. I kissed her on the cheek, like an accomplice, and then on the mouth, like a lover. Blood rushed up into her bloodless cheeks. It was such a deep shocking kiss that we both shuddered' (RT 310). The premonition paints a picture of Rebecca as a sorceress whose skills affect the future. Thanks to her influence, even if Rebecca died, the girl she conjures up would carry on the battle, although with different means. By suggesting the continuation of marital strife Beauman casts doubts on romantic interpretations of the second marriage.

Thanks to the nature of Bluebeard's perversity, Beauman locates his chamber within Bluebeard's psyche. Rebecca has given Maxim 'the gift of tumult' and 'has put lightning in his hand' (RT 309), so he knows what may take place in the bedroom. Again, representing the first marriage as involving sexual passion is familiar from *Wide Sargasso Sea*. In a similar fashion as Rhys's Rochester, Beauman's Maxim fears that he is not the exclusive recipient of these gifts, which makes the bedroom an eventless place and turns the boathouse into a scene of assumed debauchery. His jealousy-ridden psyche becomes the chamber he carries with him everywhere: 'Whatever Max does, he'll *never* silence me. I'll talk on and on in his head and his heart and his guts, forever and ever' (RT 267). What amplifies Rebecca's persistent voice in Maxim's innards is the fact that he reads her notebook after having murdered her. Although it reveals the possible incest between the couple, it also testifies to Rebecca's earnestness.[8] This nagging inner voice resembles the refrains playing in Rochester's mind in Rhys's novel.

*Rebecca's Tale* concurs with the view suggested in *Rebecca* that Rebecca knowingly goads Maxim to kill her. Her murder is a form of gruesome suicide (RT 400). The three researchers into Rebecca's life differ on her ultimate goal. Ellie, who has the last word in the book, wagers that this Bluebeard's murder, manipulated by his wife, represents a *Liebestod* or a *folie à deux*: in her view, Rebecca would 'have meant Maxim to hang for the crime, or kill himself, or die of remorse; she'd have meant to drag him down to her underworld – and, of course, she did' (RT 342). The obvious conclusion is that one cannot prevail in such a marriage. The notion of a *Liebestod* nevertheless provides a romantic interpretation of Bluebeard Gothic by depicting an unforgettable love story that welds the partners together for eternity. And it is the ravishing, yet demonic, woman who keeps Bluebeard in thrall.

In her hallucinatory premonition of the future, the 'shocking kiss' Rebecca exchanges with her successor brings out a theme familiar from research on both du Maurier's *Rebecca* and Alfred Hitchcock's (1939) famous film of the same name. Critics have pondered on Rebecca's possible lesbianism as well as on the homosexual desire the second wife feels for her (Jagose; Modleski). In the historical period that serves as the setting for the novel, homosexuality not only was considered perverse but was also a hanging offence. In concluding my analysis of *Rebecca's Tale*, I consider briefly how Beauman tackles such other 'perversities' beside incest and obsessive jealousy.

The three characters doing research on Rebecca have diverging reasons for their undertaking. Ever since he met Rebecca, Colonel Julyan, an old friend of the de Winter family, has been besotted with her. Almost sure of Maxim's guilt, the Colonel is plagued by not having acted in Rebecca's interest at the time of her death. He now wants to find out the truth. Tom Galbraith arrives at Kerrith under the alias of Terence Gray to do archival research on Rebecca. Like Jane Eyre, he is an orphan brought up in an orphanage and a foster home. He has reason to believe he is Rebecca's illegitimate son. The third character is Ellie Julyan, who has grown up under the shadow of her father's suppressed infatuation with Rebecca. During the research process Rebecca's testimonial notebook reaches her offspring: Tom learns about his family legacy, and Ellie, whose name 'Ellen' is among the list of names Rebecca had drawn up for the baby, finds in Rebecca a mother substitute. It is fitting that Rebecca has two heirs, for she addresses her words to a boy-girl.

Knowing nothing of his background, Tom Galbraith feels he is nobody. A childhood memory of having once met Rebecca, who apparently knew who he was, has given him the idea that he is Rebecca's illegitimate son. Research into Rebecca's life enables him to find out about his family and consolidate an identity. Without going into the details of the concerted efforts of the three researchers, let it be mentioned that archival research and Rebecca's notebook enable them to conclude that Tom is Rebecca's half-brother. He too is Isolda's child; as with Rebecca, the identity of his father remains a mystery. This process frees Tom to have a life of his own, including living openly as a homosexual with a former fellow student. The issue of sexuality concerns Rebecca, too, for Ellie wonders about Rebecca's possible bisexualism. Bringing up the subject with her aunt Rose, Ellie finds out about Rose's lesbianism. Rose sums up the book's view on sexual orientation: 'Sexuality is a matter of taste. Some people like oranges, some people like apples, and some like both. You surely don't believe that morality is involved in that choice?' (RT 362). *Rebecca's Tale* rejects the voyeurism associated with Rebecca's sexuality in *Rebecca*. The novel also identifies Tom's and Rose's same-sex relationships as part of the romance it conveys.

Rebecca's notebook proves decisive for Ellie, who has lost her mother at an early age. Rebecca becomes Ellie's mentor in matters of love. When Ellie is courted by a local doctor, she cannot decide what to do. She seeks guidance from Rebecca's spirit; convinced that Rebecca has advised her, Ellie resolves not to marry, but to realize her dream of studying at Cambridge (RT 436). Tellingly, in clearing her father's library, she knocks over a pile of Austens and Brontës (RT 434), a further sign of conventional marriage as an unsuitable ending for a contemporary adaptation of Bluebeard Gothic. Thus both of Rebecca's legatees find the courage to pursue their interests thanks to the example Rebecca set in her life and written legacy.

The one person besides Maxim de Winter who is represented as a pervert in *Rebecca's Tale* is the second Mrs de Winter. She has initiated much of the research by sending Rebecca's notebook and belongings to Rebecca's various friends. Colonel Julyan and Ellie eventually meet her, and this encounter confirms the novel's portrayal of the second de Winter marriage in non-romantic terms. A brief quote illustrates this interpretation. The second Mrs de Winter says that she still imagines the now-deceased Maxim sitting beside her: 'I tell him little stories about the other guests, and he pretends to be bored, and gives me gruff answers just the way he used to do – but I know he's there with me in spirit, and he's not bored at all, he's just teasing me. He's happy, terribly happy, just as we always were' (RT 415–16). As in du Maurier's *Rebecca*, the second wife is unhealthily interested in Rebecca and seriously deluded about reality. Twenty years later, she still refuses to acknowledge Maxim as Bluebeard and she still rejoices in Rebecca's murder. Ellie wagers that the second wife is responsible for finally silencing Rebecca, for the third notebook delivered to the Colonel has only one word in it, 'Max,' while the rest has been torn away (RT 417).[9] Beauman presents the second marriage as plagued by delusion and denial on the wife's part, boredom and fixation on the past on the husband's part. The second Mrs de Winter resembles Jane Eyre, a fact that casts doubt on the happiness of Jane's marriage to Rochester in *Jane Eyre*.

Rebecca's notebook condenses what might be called the novel's policy of adaptation. In it Rebecca writes, 'This is my creed: *There is only one true legitimacy, and it is bestowed by love, not male lineage*' (RT 288). This creed applies to literary relationships as envisioned by Beauman according to which literary lineage is not grounded in patriarchal family legacies but in an author's love for certain books. It is this love that makes the author their legatee. Cherishing a literary legacy means having the courage to write in the predecessor's spirit, but not in its letter, as the choices Tom and Ellie make under Rebecca's influence demonstrate. Such a stance blends correctional criticism with paying a tribute. Beauman's corrective aim includes giving Rebecca a voice and elucidating her character as a way of doing her justice – just as Rhys did by portraying Antoinette. Yet by preserving much of her mystery, *Rebecca's Tale* is also a tribute to the achievement of *Rebecca*. It breaks into new ground by filling in many gaps left open by du Maurier, but in so doing it makes new gaps of its own.

## Diane Setterfield's *The Thirteenth Tale*: When Bluebeard Gothic Makes You Ill

I now move on to another recent rewriting of *Jane Eyre*, Diane Setterfield's *The Thirteenth Tale*. It too is a tribute to the legacy of Bluebeard Gothic; its focus, however, lies more firmly on the acts of narration and reception than in Beauman's book. They are shown to be wrought with the danger of making both narrators and readers fall ill, thanks to the narrated material. Somewhat surprisingly, the cure is found within the Gothic itself. Margaret Lea, the narrator-biographer of *The Thirteenth Tale* learned to read in her father's antiquarian bookshop: 'A is for Austen, B is for Brontë, C is for Charles and D is for Dickens' (TT 15). Associating the alphabet with the classical authors of the nineteenth century suggests, of course, that their books form the literary alphabet, the basis of narrative literature. And so it is for Margaret, who, until her commission to write Vida Winter's biography, reads only nineteenth-century literature. In order to be acquainted with her employer, she begins reading Vida's novels. To her amazement, Vida is capable of evoking the same charm and magic as the authors she reveres (TT 37). Margaret's literary alphabet is Vida Winter's too, as the author's library demonstrates. The Winter library is packed with the books that Margaret loves; for example, it has 'the collection of a fanatic' (TT 267) of *Jane Eyre*, with every conceivable kind of copy of this book. Yet this shared love has a harmful underside, for both author and biographer have made literature their escape from life. They have no other friends or lovers than those they encounter in books.

Once Vida's commission turns Margaret into a writer-biographer, she begins to be engulfed by Vida's life story: 'I was enclosed in the grain of the paper, embedded in the white interior of the story itself' (TT 90). Margaret's method of writing relies on imaginative identification. She first listens to Vida's oral narrative, taking down sparse notes, and then, by using the notes as memory aid, identifies with the narrating Vida, reproducing the author's voice, gestures, and intonation in her mind, in order to write out the story in detail (TT 62–3, 88–9, 178). Vida's narration of her life story and Margaret's listening to this story and writing it affects both women The impervious Vida becomes childlike and vulnerable; Margaret's anguish deepens as Vida's story progresses, until she falls seriously ill. Vida's personal physician, Dr Clifton, queries whether Margaret has compulsively read such books as *Wuthering Heights*, *Jane Eyre*, and *Sense and Sensibility* (TT 338). Margaret's positive answer has him conclude that she is 'suffering from an ailment that afflicts ladies of romantic imagination. Symptoms include fainting, weariness, loss of appetite, low spirits. While on one level the crisis can be ascribed to wandering about in freezing rain without the benefit of adequate waterproofing, the deeper cause is more likely to be found in some emotional trauma' (TT 339). The literature these women love feeds their trauma like it has fed the mental turmoil of many a literary Gothic heroine before them. What is it, then, that makes nineteenth-century Bluebeard Gothic unhealthy for writers and readers?

An obvious answer is that these novels verge on the perverse, for they deal with sensational and outrageous events. 'The centrality of usurpation, intrigue, betrayal, and murder to Gothic plots,' explains Fred Botting, 'appears to celebrate criminal behaviour, violent executions of selfish ambition and voracious passions and licentious enactments of carnal desire' (6). These characteristics shape the plot of *The Thirteenth Tale* too. The mad Bertha of *Jane Eyre* is replicated by as many as four persons in this novel: George Angelfield, incestuously attached to his daughter Isabelle; Charles Angelfield, the heir of the Angelfield family; his sister Isabelle; and their child, Adeline. Angelfield House harbours the secret of Charles's sadomasochistic incest with Isabelle and of the birth of the twins, Adeline and Emmeline, from this union. Another secret is Charles's rape of a local girl, the offspring of which is the twins' nameless half-sister. (As a child, she is called Shadow; later she adopts the name Vida Winter.) When Isabelle is taken to a lunatic asylum, Charles loses his mind, shutting himself up and venturing out once only – to commit suicide. Adeline is abnormal from birth onwards; besides having fits of violence, she kills the gardener and sets Angelfield on fire. Her Bertha-like incendiary act is caused by fierce jealousy. She is unable to distinguish herself from her twin, Emmeline. When Emmeline gives birth to a baby boy, Adeline is left outside this mother–child dyad. Enraged, Adeline tries to burn the baby, but Vida manages to save him. Vida then locks Adeline in the library in order to save herself, the baby, and Emmeline from Adeline's rage. Vida is motivated by love for Emmeline, with whom she plans to spend the rest of her life. Afterwards, however, Vida cannot say which of the twins she has saved, thanks to the loss of reason and badly burned face of the rescued person. Vida buries herself in a Gothic house on the Yorkshire moors; now the rescued sister becomes the secret Vida's house harbours. Vida feels her personal life has ended; this tragedy, however, marks the beginning of her life as a writer (TT 57–8). She writes compulsively and prolifically in the Gothic vein in order to escape from the traumas of her past (TT 130–1).

In spite of the implausible and transgressive nature of the events, *The Thirteenth Tale* nevertheless insists on an intimate link between life and literature. What Vida Winter writes about arises from her experience, even if in suppressed and distorted form. The Gothic genre acts a double role, for it feeds Vida's trauma while simultaneously allowing her to get a handle on it. This same observation applies to her biographer Margaret. *The Thirteenth Tale* represents the Gothic genre as having the status of *pharmakos*, a substance serving at once as a deadly poison and its cure. Taken in too great measures, such a substance kills the patient, but in moderate doses it fosters health. This notion is tied to the fluctuation in the genre between transgressing limits and re-establishing them, a two-way process that allows perversions to surface while ultimately curbing and containing them. *The Thirteenth Tale* illustrates the workings of this fluctuation, which explains why the cure it suggests to the illness caused by Bluebeard Gothic stays within generic confines.

In elaborating this notion of Bluebeard Gothic as *pharmakos*, Setterfield's novel presents the 'Bluebeard' tale in particular as having curative potential. Thanks to the inadequacy of the character placed in the wife's role, the tale at first fails to fulfil this potential. 'Bluebeard' is incorporated into the novel through James's *The Turn of the Screw*. After a local physician, Dr Maudsley, sends Isabelle to an asylum, he commissions a governess called Hester Barrow to take care of the twins. Hester occupies the role of Bluebeard's (first) wife. She also resembles both Jane Eyre (she is unattractive, intelligent, passionate, and determined) and James's governess. She is soon convinced of the abnormality of her beautiful charges. Adeline in particular baffles her, for the girl appears to be two persons in one: Adeline is mostly sunken in her incoherent private world but occasionally shows sharpness of mind. The ambitious Hester wants to solve the mystery of the twins, enlisting the help of Dr Maudsley, with whom she falls passionately in love. She, however, does not believe in ghosts and the supernatural as does James's governess, but puts her trust in medical science and the fledgling field of psychology. Together she and the doctor devise an experiment which involves separating the twins in order to see whether they learn to exist individually. For all her scientific aspirations, Hester is blind as regards her emotions and motives. (Readers, however, perceive her infatuation with Dr Maudsley.) After initiating the experiment Hester begins to suffer from what she fears are hallucinations: she sees apparitions, her things move about mysteriously, and she hears strange sounds in the house. James never divulges whether Flora and Miles intentionally trick their governess; Adeline, Emmeline, and Vida certainly play games with Hester.

All Hester's supernatural experiences have a perfectly rational explanation, but one that she never learns, for, unlike the heroine of 'Bluebeard,' she is unable to unravel the secret of the mansion. Her failure stems from misrecognizing her situation: had she realized that she is within a Gothic plot, she could have solved the mystery, which necessitates the ability to reason according to the logic of this genre. Hester does not understand that there is a Bluebeard present at Angelfield – the mad hermit Charles, who does not care a hoot for his family. It is he who occupies the structural role of James's gentleman, not Dr Maudsley. Instead of experimenting on the twins, Hester should have directed her researches on their degenerate parents. This direction would have enabled her to realize that she is actually dealing with three girls instead of two. Unlike James, Setterfield explains away both the governess's visions and the double nature of her charges. Hester's commission ends abruptly, thanks to her improper behaviour with the doctor, a reference to the love affair between Miss Jessel and Peter Quint.

Hester's failure places Margaret within the frame narrative as Hester's successor. Margaret's writing method, based on imaginative identification with Vida, soon makes her sense that Vida is not telling her biography in full. While Vida has promised to tell the truth, she does it evasively and elliptically. It is the ellipses and gaps that make Margaret fall ill, because they sensitize her to the secret Vida is hiding as well as activating Margaret's own trauma. Years ago, going through things in her mother's bedroom, Margaret has found a birth certificate revealing that she has lost her twin at birth. This twin is a strictly forbidden subject in the Lea family as is the existence of Vida in the Angelfield household. Margaret's Gothic frame of mind enables her to succeed where Hester failed. She first discovers the existence of the mad woman in Vida's Gothic mansion. Like Hester, she is then aided in her research by a doctor. When Margaret falls ill, Vida's personal physician, Dr Clifton, diagnosing the Gothic genre as the source of illness, prescribes as cure Arthur Conan Doyle's Sherlock Holmes stories. Devouring these detective stories has a salutary effect on Margaret. Given the Gothic elements of Doyle's stories, the cure stays within the Gothic world, but Sherlock Holmes introduces a sceptical perspective to it through his emphasis on rationality. He demolishes the supernatural by tracing it back to the dark desires of people. Holmes also insists on the capabilities of rationality to control the Gothic excess emanating from within. This perspective enables Margaret to act the heroine of 'Bluebeard.' The guiding influence of Sherlock Holmes is not far-fetched, because Bluebeard's wife is a detective uncovering past crimes and identifying the culprit. Margaret succeeds where Hester failed by carefully considering various clues, especially textual ones. Like a detective she has a moment of illumination when she finally sees the case right side up: the twins are actually three girls (TT 389). Doyle's detective stories have a salutary effect, because they instruct Margaret to treat the material narrated by Vida analytically and to dislodge herself from too intimate identification with the author.[10]

Presenting 'Bluebeard' in terms of a detective story and its heroine as a detective casts light on the status the Gothic intertexts enjoy in *The Thirteenth Tale*. *Jane Eyre* is a case in point. *Jane Eyre* runs as a leitmotif throughout the novel: it is present as copies (TT 118, 267) and as an example of the vital value of nineteenth-century literature (TT 266–73); Hester reads it aloud to the twins (TT 361); a scrap torn from this novel is found in the bag where Vida has placed Emmeline's baby (TT 260–1, 270, 428); and Vida herself gestures at the novel (TT 400). Ultimately, however, the significance of this novel's presence narrows down to a function as a clue that enables Margaret to 'crack' the case. All these references help her conclude that Vida is like Jane, a motherless, unwanted, and neglected child among indifferently hostile relatives. Like Jane, Vida is always pushed to the fringes of life, yet she is the only one with any moral backbone. This same mechanism of first invoking intertexts as having a thematically and structurally meaningful role, but then restricting this meaning to clues in a mystery, applies to all the intertexts the novel incorporates. If a reader is familiar with the legacy of Bluebeard Gothic, she may then act the role of Margaret, even beating her at this game. This narrative strategy empties out much of the meaning potential the intertexts have, reducing the weight of their presence. In this respect *The Thirteenth Tale* resembles Tennant's *Adèle*. As a writing of excess, the Gothic provides a counternarrative of modernity, dwelling on the underside of enlightenment and humanist values (Botting 1–2). The genre not only exposes that which must be suppressed in the project of modernity but also tries out ways to deal

with it. But when Gothic excess is treated simply in terms of clues referring to a crime story, then its cultural function is considerably diluted.
This is what happens in Setterfield's novel.

Associating 'Bluebeard' with a detective story strengthens the novel's emphasis on conventional narrative. The epitaph of Setterfield's
*The Thirteenth Tale*, taken from Vida Winter's *Tales of Change and Desperation*, reads: 'All children mythologize their birth. It is a universal trait.
You want to know someone? Heart, mind and soul? Ask him to tell you
about when he was born. What you get won't be the truth: it will be a
story. And nothing is more telling than a story.' The epitaph stresses
that narrative has its own ways of conveying the truth. But *The Thirteenth Tale* also underlines that any narrative whatsoever will not fit this
role. Vida Winter and Margaret Lea love nineteenth-century literature,
because it respects conventional storytelling: a proper narrative has a
beginning, middle, and a definite ending that ties all plot lines together.
Although a narrator may foreshadow events, helping readers to project
possible outcomes, the pact between narrator and readers forbids the
narrator to reveal the outcome prematurely and readers to peek at the
end. Vida and Margaret agree to stick to these conventions in their joint
biographical undertaking; the expectation is, of course, that readers of
*The Thirteenth Tale* respect this same pact. This emphasis on narrative
form also suggests that, for Setterfield, the only viable ideational basis
on which to ground her novel is supplied by narrative. Such grounding
derives, I think, from the notion that respecting conventional narrative
form extends readers an invitation to pleasure and excitement. It is this
emotional reaction, rather than, say, meditating on the ramifications of
exceeding limits, that the novel targets. The novel's return in its very
ending to the supernatural world of the Gothic confirms the genre's
emotional side as primary. Margaret has asked the dying Vida to deliver greetings to Margaret's dead twin; one day Margaret has a visita-
tion from her twin sister that puts to rest Margaret's longing and sense
of incompleteness. Ultimately *The Thirteenth Tale* ends up affirming
the supernatural as a distinct and unknown presence running parallel to realist representation (see Botting 126). The supernatural, purged
of perversion, provides whatever sense of unity, value, and spirit a
present-day Gothic may have.

## D.M. Thomas's *Charlotte*: Perversity as the Meaning of *Jane Eyre*

In concluding this chapter, I turn to an example of Bluebeard Gothic
that prizes perversion as the genre's contemporary cultural meaning.

In *Charlotte* (2000) D.M. Thomas purposefully leaves intact the perverse structures that are usually dismantled at the conclusion of Bluebeard Gothic. Through its embedded narrative recounting of what happened to Jane right after her marriage to Rochester, *Charlotte* insists that *Jane Eyre* is a 'Bluebeard' story, and Bluebeard never alters by simply chang- ing wives. In Thomas's book, Rochester's fixation on the first wife suggests that what is portrayed as romantic love is actually a hoax, camouflaging a game of domination and submission on the basis of which patriarchal marriage is instituted. Thomas extends his parodic treatment of Bluebeard Gothic to address the novel's frame narrative concerning Miranda Stevenson, the author of the embedded pastiche of Brontë. By depicting Miranda's troubled life, Thomas draws on its parallels with Charlotte Brontë's biography, suggesting that the perver- sity Brontë depicts in *Jane Eyre* had a real-life basis. In so doing, Thomas subjects the Brontë myth to a destructive treatment.

The events of *Charlotte* are briefly the following: the novel opens with the recently married Jane's growing uncertainty about her relationship to Rochester, thanks to his indifference and their sexual incompatibil- ity. An intimate talk with Mrs Ashford (former Miss Temple) reveals to Jane her sexual ignorance: she still is a virgin, for Rochester has used his finger to satisfy her. Realizing that Rochester is impotent, Jane confronts him. Rochester bolts out and is later found dead of a broken neck. Jane loses her faith in God and tries to commit suicide. She is saved by Grace Poole, who tells her that Rochester never gave up Bertha, with whom he had two children: Robert, left behind in the West Indies, and Adèle. Jane and Grace leave for Martinique in order to find Rochester's heir. The narrative then switches to the present day, depicting Miranda Ste- venson's conference trip to Martinique, filled with casual sex with vari- ous men. A conference organizer confuses her with Charlotte Brontë. This erroneous association proves fitting, for not only is Miranda giv- ing a paper on Charlotte Brontë but also it transpires that she has writ- ten the sequel to *Jane Eyre* that opens the novel. Details of Miranda's life are fleshed out when the novel changes narrators once again. Now the narrator is Miranda's aged, half-blind father, Ben, whose journal notes recount her visit to him. We learn of the manic depression of Mi- randa's dead mother, Emma, and of the mother's torrential relation- ship to Ben. In order to please Ben, Miranda occasionally impersonates Emma. Miranda decides to leave her husband and return to her father with her children and unborn child. The ending of *Charlotte* returns to Jane's story. It concludes with a letter from Robert Rochester to Mrs Ashford, conveying news of Jane's death. Robert writes about her brief life at Martinique during which she found love and sexual fulfilment with him.

Although *Charlotte* includes different narrators – Jane, Miranda, Ben, and Robert – it actually is the novel Miranda begins writing at Martinique.[11] The book's transitions from Jane's narrative to Miranda's, however, are written in such a manner as to confuse readers for a while about the narrator's identity. Miranda strengthens this confusion by presenting herself as a modern-day Charlotte Brontë. She writes the book in order to examine issues the original novel represses (C 174). As I show, Miranda targets Brontë's evasive handling of the 'Bluebeard' intertext that she intends to correct with her pastiche sequel.

Through the critical distance of parody Miranda's pastiche queries such issues as the following: Can Bluebeard give up his philandering, misogyny, and violence simply by falling in love with the 'right woman'? Can love put a definitive stop to years of abuse? If a woman falls passionately in love with Bluebeard, is not her love kindled by his being a Bluebeard? Does not his perversity strike a chord with hers? Miranda's pastiche answers each of these questions differently than does *Jane Eyre* by insisting that the dark, underside answer is the correct one: romantic love is an ideological illusion meant to hide what one might call the reality of desire, which explains why perversity and violence are closer to truth than are love and moral reform. This sinister 'truth' of desire emerges in multiple ways in the pastiche. Jane, in fact, has *not* explored Bluebeard's chamber thoroughly. Rochester's marriage forms just a part of his secret, the extent of which Jane learns only when Grace Poole tells her that Bertha and Rochester formed a masochistic couple: Bertha obliged Rochester by acting as his cruel Lady.[12] After Bertha's death Rochester makes Grace impersonate the abusive Bertha, for he needs a dominatrix to experience any sexual pleasure whatsoever. He also wants Grace to 'train' Jane to be 'more pleasing to him' (C 197).

Miranda exposes Rochester as a pervert, but her unflattering disclosures extend to Jane as well. In particular, she targets Jane's manner of narration as a means of disclosing Jane's sexual desire. Although the pastiche-Jane imitates the typical mannerisms of Brontë's Jane such as old-fashioned diction, frequent use of dashes and exclamation marks, and confiding tone, she does so quite badly. Miranda's pastiche resembles Harlequin romances more than Brontë's discourse.[13] The pastiche has both stylistically and thematically more to do with these run-of-the-mill romances than with *Jane Eyre*. This close link highlights the titillating and voyeuristic manner of narration in such romances, suggesting that getting sexually aroused is the real aim of Bluebeard Gothic. As narrator, the pastiche-Jane is forthcoming in her feelings, yet she expresses them through a coyness and modesty foreign to Brontë's Jane. An example illustrates this difference:

> It is not considered decent to express openly the fears which are bound to arise on a bride's wedding day; yet I possessed them in full measure. Reader, I was ignorant. I knew there were rites ... I even longed, for what I scarcely knew! ... When the holy mysteries of the marriage chamber were at last unveiled to me, I did not doubt he would be kind and patient. Yet I could not dismiss those apprehensions bred of my ignorance, and also my knowledge that he did not at all share my innocence. (C 13–14)

The address to the reader is, of course, a reminder of *Jane Eyre's* most famous sentence, but its repetition reveals a narrator other than Brontë's Jane. This narrator's mode of expression exaggerates the mixture of timidity, self-deprecation, and self-righteousness of *Rebecca's* protagonist-narrator. For all her propriety, uncertainty, and nameless longing, this Jane cannot wait to lose her virginity. The snugness of her narrative voice suggests that, specifically in mass-produced Gothic romances, all events aim at the romantic couple's sexual union, although the plot must first pass through detours that postpone this goal. The pastiche-Jane's narrative harps on this goal by dwelling on various sexual matters such as her fears, hopes, and yearnings. Brontë's Jane uses original metaphors and imaginatively mixes discursive styles; in contrast, pastiche-Jane resorts to hackneyed metaphors and clichés, which endow her narration with cheapness. These differences reveal Miranda's parody of *Jane Eyre*, especially its sugarcoating of sexual desire under the disguise of feigned propriety and romance. Given that Miranda thinks of herself as a contemporary Charlotte, the sexual frankness of her narrative amply 'corrects' the shortcomings of Brontë's Jane.

This notion of being true to sexual desire that Miranda understands as antagonistic to conventional morality further explains how she amends Brontë's supposedly erroneous depiction of sexuality within Bluebeard Gothic. Freud characterized desire as polymorphously perverse: we gradually learn to channel and express it in socially acceptable ways. Growing up is largely this process of internalizing social sanctions on sexuality. Miranda's pastiche, however, rejects such socialization, stressing polymorphous perversity as the reality of sexual desire. Miranda's outlook on life springs from her personal history of mental breakdowns and subsequent psychoanalysis; she appears to support a notion of sexual desire as the ultimate motivation for all human action. Bluntly put, 'fucking,' not 'making love,' equals being true to sexual desire, a reality which neither Jane Eyre nor Charlotte Brontë could voice, but which the contemporary Charlotte can.

Given Miranda's belief in the inability of Bluebeard to reform, she provides a new happy ending to Jane's story, one that allows the heroine a way out of Bluebeard's enclosure. First, however, Jane must reject Rochester as Bluebeard. Pastiche-Jane finds passion in the arms of Robert, Rochester's son with Bertha. Their union is unconventional: Jane is Robert's stepmother, he is black, and, in keeping with the book's general tone, a former catamite of the priest who brought him up. Moreover, the couple never marries. The sequel is a love story as is *Jane Eyre*, but it has an altogether different yardstick for love – the realization of sexual desire. The union of a white woman with a black man 'corrects' the racial prejudice of Brontë's novel, but it has an ideological mystique of its own, for Miranda holds that as Martiniquians, Bertha and Robert are less sexually repressed than are Rochester and Jane. Christian Gutleben concludes that pastiche works in *Charlotte* as a means of criticizing ideological choices and silences: 'What in the Victorian work is forbidden, repressed, rejected' he writes, 'becomes not only allowed, praised and cherished, it is presented as salvatory' (179). Miranda's pastiche provides a lurid, tabloid version of *Jane Eyre*'s 'Bluebeard' elements.

In order to understand this book's take on the *Jane Eyre* legacy more fully, it is useful to compare the pastiche with the sections in which Miranda writes about her life as a contemporary Charlotte Brontë. At the level of the frame narrative, Thomas raises questions about contemporary feminist interpretations of women authors and their sense of Gothic imprisonment within male legacies of writing. He also places *Charlotte* in the larger cultural context of canonizing authors and turning them into cult figures.

In her conference presentation Miranda argues that, like all great novelists, Charlotte Brontë was a big liar. Great writers take their material and subjects from their own lives and emotions: 'But they distort them, twist them, partly to make fiction, partly because they themselves are half-unconscious of the personal realities that the launch of a *roman*, a romance, allows them to explore' (C 137–8). One of the things Charlotte distorted was her father's role in her life. Miranda claims that Reverend Patrick Brontë was, in fact, Charlotte's first husband (C 138). The literary motif of an older man's attraction to a young woman in *Jane Eyre* actually hides the incestuous father–daughter relationship on which it is based. This biographical postulation of an intimate link between an author's real and literary lives applies at least to Miranda. The sequel is a poorly camouflaged probing of her troubled past, a life with a manic-depressive mother, Emma, and a pervert father, Ben. Her portrayal of Rochester's masochistic relationship to Bertha/Grace lends from Ben's masochistic relationship to Emma. Ben gets sexually aroused by Emma's fits of madness, during which she humiliates him by boasting of her sexual escapades. After Emma's death, Miranda installs herself in Emma's position, continuing these abusive rituals with Ben. She thus acts the role of Bluebeard's consenting second wife. Ironically, while pastiche-Jane escapes from Bluebeard, Miranda does not. Her choice to stay with her father leads to consequences that are by now familiar: the masochistic fantasy structures Miranda's life. Ben has taught her to eschew all sexual restrictions. For example, she tapes all her sexual encounters at Martinique as a gift for Ben. On the tape she babbles in her mother's voice and dialect while making love. Its purpose is to en-able Ben to indulge in his masochistic fantasies in Miranda's absence. The various sexual partners are mere props in her ongoing sexual re-lationship with the father. Miranda textualizes this fantasy by making the readers of her novel *Charlotte* engage in it. Made privy to scenes of seduction and rage between father and daughter, readers become (un-willing) participants.

In Gutleben's view, *Charlotte* rejects the forbidden and repressed ele-ments in *Jane Eyre*, proposing, instead, sensuality and free sexuality as curative (179). He further suggests that the goal of postmodern, neo-Victorian fiction is to seduce readers through mixtures of pornography, hagiography, and provocation (175). Part and parcel of this strategy is first to set up the rules of Victorian literature (*Charlotte* begins with a pastiche of *Jane Eyre*) and then dramatically to violate those rules, creat-ing thus a sense of subversion. Given that writers and readers are con-temporary, sexual considerations seldom appear scandalous. Gutleben remarks that '[sexual considerations] correspond to the set practices, and therefore to the expected practices, of the literature of their time … The subversion at play appears anachronistic, being directed at the past, not the present' (175). Incest and perversions may be the seductive bread and butter of present-day literature, but they play other functions too in *Charlotte*, for they seem to be part of what Gutleben calls the aesthetic project of revolt (175). If so, then it is instructive to examine the implied author's (whom I here for the sake of simplicity call D.M. Thomas) role in the novel.

Thomas appears to be tackling the feminist Brontë myth in particular. As author he hides behind the book's narrators: the female masks of Jane and Miranda as well as the male mask of Ben. At stake here is what Andreas Huyssen (45) calls the imaginary femininity of a male author. Miranda's conference talk postulates a correspondence between Charlotte Brontë's life and her fiction, a correspondence that applies to Miranda's life and fiction as well. Such a postulation is familiar from Sandra Gilbert and Susan Gubar's classic study *The Mad Woman in the Attic*, in which they argue that duplicity was the major writing strategy of female authors of the nineteenth century. Some form of the following argument is repeated throughout their study: 'These writers almost obsessively create characters who enact their own, covert authorial anger. They project what seems to be the energy of their own despair into passionate, melodramatic characters who act out the subversive impulses every woman inevitably feels when she contemplates the deep-rooted evils of patriarchy' (77). In *Charlotte*, Thomas exaggerates this claim to the point of parody. Gilbert and Gubar argue that 'Bertha does what Jane wants to do' (359) and that 'Bertha is Jane's truest and darkest double ... the ferocious self Jane has been trying to repress' (360); Thomas appears to be mocking these claims through Miranda's authorship. A present-day, liberated female author and feminist critic, Miranda supposedly need not repress anything. Miranda *is* Bertha: they act the same way – and both are utterly bonkers. Moreover, in her life and book Miranda banishes her husband David to a room in the attic. Taking Gilbert and Gubar literally, Thomas makes fun of their ideas, suggesting that it is difficult to see what artistic gain there would be if a female author actually took a mad woman as her aesthetic model. Further, if such models are the means of discovering and emulating literary mothers, how useful are they really aesthetically and psychically? Through pastiche *Charlotte* mocks not only feminist scholarship but also what many women like to read. Finally, the manifold associations among Charlotte Brontë, Jane, and Miranda highlight the confusion in these scholars' minds between fictional characters and flesh-and-blood authors. Thomas's target seems to be Gilbert and Gubar's notion of literary characters as personal extensions of authors, instead of imaginative creations.

Gilbert and Gubar, however, might retort that the images of women as either angels or monsters were created by male authors in the first place. *Charlotte* may be said to present the kind of male high-handedness typical of modernist literature analysed by Huyssen. One should not forget that Jane and Miranda serve as female masks of a male author. Although as literary characters Jane and Miranda function as beating women, each is ultimately the male author's puppet; he wields control over this masochistic fantasy. If Jane the narrator is under Miranda's control, Miranda the narrator, in turn, is subjected to the implied author. She stays within his fantasy: she can escape neither the Bluebeard father nor the Bluebeard author who has created her. The male author's cross-dressing as a female narrator is actually familiar from the history of the 'Bluebeard' tale. Victoria Anderson observes how Charles Perrault slyly usurped a markedly female narrative tradition in his *Histoires ou contes du temps passé*. By masquerading as Mother Goose, Perrault simulates the oral storytelling tradition and femininity. Yet given the allegiance of his stories to patriarchal ideology, his true role is that of the wolf in 'Little Red Riding Hood,' whose verbal dexterity makes a laughing stock of the female figures he tricks and murders. Anderson concludes that 'if one can discern the annihilation of the female storyteller ... then this annihilation becomes the literal cornerstone of Bluebeard's house, which then is symbolic of the system' ('Introduction' 12). To borrow Huyssen's words, the following evaluative move thus seems to take place in *Charlotte:* 'Woman is posited as reader of inferior literature, while man emerges as writer of genuine, authentic literature – objective, ironic, and in control of his aesthetic means' (Huyssen 46). If this interpretation is correct, then *Charlotte* suggests that not much has changed since the days that Gilbert and Gubar discuss in their book.

Contemporary renditions of Bluebeard Gothic are outspoken in identifying the 'kinkiness' of this genre: nothing is alien to it, as it covers everything from incest, pedophilia, sadism, and masochism to necrophilia. For some writers such explicitness serves no other purpose than providing titillating entertainment, while others cherish the classical narrative form of the genre. In the corpus of this study, *Charlotte* represents the clearest example of an attempt to destroy Bluebeard Gothic. Thomas exposes the mechanisms of repression in Bluebeard Gothic with vigour. *Charlotte* takes this legacy apart, but it does not propose new aesthetic or literary solutions in its stead. Cynical destruction of an old literary model is all that remains once the reading experience is completed. In this sense the contemporary cultural meaning of Bluebeard Gothic is perversion.

# 4 Faith, Ritual, and Sacrifice: Rewriting the Religious Foundation of *Jane Eyre*

The religious associations of 'Bluebeard' have typically been linked with what Maria Tatar (*Secrets* 1) calls the 'great mythical significance of prohibition,' that is, with the biblical story of the Fall. Meredid Puw Davies (*Tale* 39) observes that this tale echoes the book of Genesis. Just as God threatens the first couple with death if they disobey Him, so Bluebeard warns his wife of death if she visits his forbidden chamber. Bluebeard's understanding of the book of Genesis is paternalistic and misogynistic. In his view, when Eve gives into temptation and eats the fruit, she drags Adam and all humanity into disaster with her. Bluebeard holds God's gender-specific punishment of Eve as proof that the female body is a locus of suffering and cursed sexuality. While Adam has to sweat for his bread, Eve's punishment is instituted with these words: 'in labour you shall bear children. You shall be eager for your husband, and he shall be your master' (Gen. 3:16). This verdict shows that women are afflicted with sexual curiosity (Davies 40). The purpose of this passing of judgment is to reinstitute the hierarchy against which the couple transgressed; that is, to realign Adam under God's supremacy and Eve under Adam. 'Bluebeard,' however, subverts this outcome. Davies concludes that 'far from being a tale about feminine subjection and suffering, "Bluebeard" is a tale about a woman who flouts patriarchal authority, acquires knowledge in the face of terrifying adversity, and with the assistance of her sister and brothers, is rewarded for it. And, if Christian salvation is achieved only through the human sacrifice of Christ himself, in "Bluebeard" the agents of salvation, the brothers, survive unscathed' (41). The woman's reward is immediate and material to boot.

While the fact that the tale echoes the biblical myth of the Fall is generally recognized, what has received much less notice is that the tale also focuses on sacrifice. It presents the events from what René Girard (*Scapegoat*) calls the persecutor's and the scapegoat's perspectives. Persecution arises from Bluebeard's setting the chamber off limits to woman. In a manner typical of the persecutor's mentality, Bluebeard sees in woman the origin and cause of all that is harmful. Persecutors blame their victims for the loss of supposedly crucial distinctions and the lack of founding differences. Bluebeard's ominous phrase 'Madam, you must die ... Your time has come' (Tatar, *Secrets* 177) resonates with the persecutor's insistence that he simply acts reactively and passively to the evil the victim has brought upon herself. The chamber is Bluebeard's chapel, the site of ritual sacrifice, sustaining the order of his world. The woman's defiance of his injunction contests his notion of hierarchies; he must reimpose ignorance on her by confronting her with the irreparable difference of death. He claims the necessity of this deed for reinstituting his authority and reintroducing hierarchies based on (gender) difference. Bluebeard holds the woman responsible for both sickness and cure: her death redeems her transgression by asserting her fundamental difference from him. Woman is thus transformed into a sacred scapegoat. This is the structural mechanism of sacrifice, argues Girard (*Scapegoat* 21, 42–4), continuing that wherever and whenever it is working, it generates the sacred through violence. Given that 'Bluebeard' shows how this mechanism works, it also reveals that the woman is unjustly condemned and that she is without cause the object of hatred.

In this chapter I bring together *Jane Eyre*, 'Bluebeard,' Jeanette Winterson's debut novel, *Oranges Are Not the Only Fruit* (1985), and Sarah Waters's neo-Victorian novel *Fingersmith* (2002) in order to examine the religious issues raised by Bluebeard Gothic. Previous studies have explored *Jane Eyre*'s relationships to the Bible and to various theological doctrines (see, for example, Dale; Gallagher; Gilbert and Gubar; Lamonaca; Peters; Carolyn Williams). There is research on Jeanette's convictions in *Oranges* as well (Bollinger, Cosslet, Maagaard), while *Fingersmith* has not yet been related to this context. I argue that by rewriting *Jane Eyre*, *Oranges* and *Fingersmith* revise its 'Bluebeard' intertext in order to reconfigure widely spread cultural notions of sexuality, religious faith, and literary creation. I concentrate on this religious thematic from two angles: with *Oranges*, the focus lies on the significance of Christian theology, while with *Fingersmith*, it rests on the mechanisms of sacrifice. I next detail what these foci mean as regards each novel.

Winterson acknowledges her debt to Brontë on her novel's first page, and throughout, numerous intertextual links are obvious. Both novels are fictional autobiographies that focus on a young woman's *Bildungs* narrative. Winterson, however, departs from the heterosexual romance of *Jane Eyre* by replacing Jane's love for Mr Rochester with the love of a heroine having the same first name as the author – Jeanette – for Melanie. While this change surely is significant, what unites the novels is their shared emphasis on the religious and spiritual dimensions of love. Jane believes she is called to serve God as Rochester's wife; Jeanette too must decide what role God plays in matters of the heart. In both novels the body and sexuality form the secret of Bluebeard's chamber. In *Oranges*, however, God is associated with Bluebeard, whose self-appointed representative is the protagonist-narrator's (step)mother. A zealous member of a Pentecostal Christian church, the stepmother adopts Jeanette in order to raise the girl as a missionary. Since some of the church's missionaries have died while in service, it would appear that the mother intends to sacrifice the daughter. Winterson thus adapts the relationship of God the Father to Jesus His Son to the relationship between mother and daughter – biblical stories of origins thus address women and matriarchal history. The novel's Bluebeard, Jeanette's mother places Jeanette in the wife's position that in this novel corresponds to that of Adam/Eve and Jesus. The mother warns Jeanette against exploring the body, for she understands the Fall of Man in sexual terms. The mother's hatred of the body and of sexuality leads to conflict with Jeanette. Growing up, Jeanette realizes she loves women, a discovery that causes her expulsion from home and from her Christian sect. Like the first couple in Eden, Jeanette faces temptation and succumbs; she also turns out to be a Daughter of God in offering herself as a scapegoat, an act that leads to a kind of redemption. By using Slavoj Žižek's analysis of Christianity as my reference point, I examine how Winterson, in rewriting *Jane Eyre*, modifies the religious underpinnings of its 'Bluebeard' intertext.

These religious underpinnings address also the Freudian family-romance fantasy that I discussed in the first chapter. Reading *Jane Eyre* and *Oranges* through their shared 'Bluebeard' intertext shows that in all three texts, this fantasy represents the origin of sexuality as a Fall from grace. Both *Oranges* and *Jane Eyre* revise this fantasy; I analyse how Winterson alters the mother's fantasies of origins that the mother presents as being grounded in faith. I thus relate Winterson's activity as an author to Sigmund Freud's notion of *construction*, which refers to an analytic act of intervention aimed at the fantasies of origins that orient an individual and a whole culture. This link between private and public realms arises from Freud's premise that these fantasies are *in* an individual member of a culture, but they are not *of* him or her, because they are shaped by a culture's symbolic systems (*Moses* 169–71). Construction means a writer's tampering with a set narrative pattern by rearranging its components into another narrative order. Winterson's revision brings about such a reorganization, enabling Jeanette to escape from Bluebeard's chamber. Jeanette chooses the prophetic role of a writer for whom fiction, not the Bible, functions as scripture. Unlike Brontë, Winterson endows the writing of fiction with a spiritual dimension, which emerges from her novel's implicit link to 'Bluebeard.' At the highest narrative level, then, *Oranges* connects the question of origins with the writer's creative act. In this context, Bluebeard's crypt illustrates patriarchal notions of authorship associating the male author with God. In concluding my analysis of *Oranges*, I examine how the fantasies of origins that Winterson reconfigures reflect on her ideas of literary creation. I claim that she challenges established theories of literary creation and intertextuality as well as their heterosexual groundings. Her alternative creative strategy of prizing fragments enables her to 'find the balance between earth and sky' (O 165), that is, to unite body and spirit in writing.

I then move on to discuss how Waters's *Fingersmith* also draws on the religious associations of 'Bluebeard,' but in an instructively different manner than *Oranges*. By pointing out the purely material nature of the wife's reward, acquired here and now instead of in the afterlife, Davies says that the tale's ending subverts the religious associations evoked during the progression of its plot. This subversion remains partial, however, because Bluebeard's sacrificial cycle ends in the collective sacrifice of Bluebeard himself. In the tale variants, members of the community identify Bluebeard as a criminal and kill him in order to remove this festering sore from their midst. As has been previously observed, Bluebeard serves as the repressed, nauseous double of the 'normal' members of the community. They treat Bluebeard as a scapegoat, one whose murder cleanses all and sundry from forbidden desires. They cherish the notion that the scapegoat's sacrifice returns social cohesion and order. The victim thus plays a double role by being the source and remedy of trouble – and this is what makes him or her sacred (Girard, *Scapegoat* 55). Ritual and the sacred thus live on even in contexts that seem purely material. Brontë's handling of her intertext provides a good example within this framework. Not only does Jane claim that being Rochester's wife is the calling God has ordained for her, but also she gets the material rewards of social rank and wealth. Yet behind all this looms the one person without whose sacrifice these rewards would not be possible – Bluebeard's first wife, Bertha.

In *Fingersmith* Susan is her foster mother's, Mrs Sucksby's, special 'lamb' (F 4). Susan has her birthday at Christmas, for her real birth date is supposedly unknown. As in *Oranges*, this pet lamb is actually a fatted calf, pampered only for slaughter. In both novels the mother is ready to sacrifice the daughter to further her own ends, which in *Fingersmith*, however, are purely material. The implicit religious associations of this novel emerge from its complex and fast-moving plot that centres on sacrifice. Mrs Sucksby's self-serving ends reflect *Fingersmith*'s world of crooks and thieves, where everyone hankers after money and a higher place in the social hierarchy; the higher circles, however, are shown to be just as corrupt and mercenary as the lower ones. All social circles in this novel are affected by what Girard calls mimetic rivalry. Its communities fashion desire according to shared models that exemplify ways of both being and having. They take their cue for being and having from these models as well as emulating them. Strife ensues whenever imitators still believe in the hierarchical superiority of the model's position but refuse to grant the person(s) representing the model personal supremacy. While the idea of positional difference as the sign of arbitrary distinctions and of personal supremacy remains, few are willing to admit that someone else's characteristics are actually a better fit for this position than their own. In order to pacify the threateningly inflamed competition, the community resorts to the mechanism of sacrifice: it projects the mimetic rivalry tearing it apart on a scapegoat, believing that this person is the root cause of communal trouble (Girard, *Deceit* 101–4).

One of the settings of *Fingersmith*, the decrepit Lilly mansion, recalls the eerie Thornfield. Its association with *Jane Eyre* is strengthened when Maud and Susan, an unlikely and socially disparate pair, fall in love. Both are ready to sacrifice the other, but, as in *Jane Eyre*, a new understanding of love's meaning enables them to break from the stranglehold of Bluebeard's sacrificial practice. Reading this novel in the context of *Jane Eyre* and 'Bluebeard' enables me to examine the Girardian mechanism of sacrifice as an inherent part of the thematic structures of Bluebeard Gothic. The secular setting of *Fingersmith* exemplifies how this mechanism nevertheless creates effects of the sacred. The novel also deals with what it takes to break this mechanism. Unlike *Oranges*, *Fingersmith* is a pastiche of Victorian literature. As imitation, pastiche involves both emulation and ironic distance, which, in turn, suggests that mimetic rivalry may apply to intertextual relationships as well. In concluding this chapter I examine how Waters attempts to avoid the pitfalls of mimetic rivalry and the mechanism of sacrifice in her pastiche.

## Mother as Bluebeard God in Jeanette Winterson's *Oranges Are Not the Only Fruit*

The intentions of the Bluebeard-like Rochester seem straightforward: he wants a wife with 'virtue and purity' (JE 271), a 'better self' (JE 269). The intentions of Jeanette's (step)mother also seem straightforward: she wants a child. Like Bluebeard, however, Rochester has a hidden goal. Bluebeard tests the wife's obedience and, knowing that she will eventually fail, he plans to kill her. Murder is Bluebeard's ultimate aim. While Rochester does not intend to kill Jane physically, her acquiescence to his plea of becoming his mistress would destroy the purity he prizes in Jane. He would sacrifice her for his moral improvement. Similarly, St John Rivers, whom Gilbert (364) counts among the many Bluebeards in *Jane Eyre*, demands that Jane sacrifice herself for God's glory in missionary work in India (JE ch. 34). In *Oranges* Jeanette's mother adopts the girl in order to raise her as a missionary for the church. She too has a hidden agenda. She reads aloud to Jeanette her favourite book, *Jane Eyre*, but to support her notion of sexuality and sexual passion as sin, she alters the novel's ending. In this altered ending, Jane marries St John Rivers and accompanies him to India, although Jane knows that its harsh conditions will kill her (O 73). The ending reveals the mother's ultimate intention: she plans to sacrifice Jeanette.

The mother's hidden agenda arises from a tangle of religious faith and sexuality, which I will try to untangle here. In the mother's view, the body and sexuality are altogether sinful, as they are also for St John. If he married, he would, however, insist on fulfilling his marital 'duties' (JE 347–8, 350), while the act of adoption betrays the thorough dislike Jeanette's mother feels for sexual matters: 'She had a mysterious attitude towards the begetting of children; it wasn't that she couldn't do it, more that she didn't want to do it. She was very bitter about the Virgin Mary getting there first' (O 3). Adoption is the closest the mother can come to Immaculate Conception. She sees Jeanette as 'sprung from her head,' a child who is not the outcome of 'the jolt beneath the hip bone, but [of] water and the word' (O 10). When mother and daughter read the Bible, they encounter mentions of sexual matters, but the mother refuses to explain them. She warns Jeanette against 'Abominations and Unmentionables' (O 41), 'unnatural passions' (O 7, 83), and the like. Yet in a manner similar to Bluebeard, she continually piques Jeanette's curiosity. She repeatedly tells Jeanette the story of her own romantic conversion and she keeps Pastor Spratt's picture by her bedside (O 8). Together Jeanette and her mother leaf through a photo album of old flames. Among them is Pierre, a Frenchman, with whom the mother had an affair. The affair shows her confusion about the body, for what she thought was sexual passion – tingling in her stomach – turned out to be an ulcer (O 85–6). The mother's message is ambiguous in the same way as Bluebeard's: sexual knowledge is forbidden, but by its being forbidden, it becomes compellingly seductive – not only to the wife, but also to Bluebeard. The same kind of provocation takes place in Rochester's relationship to Jane. Rochester freely tells Jane of his sexual escapades (JE 120–4) and even makes Jane nurse the wounded Richard Mason in the anteroom to his forbidden chamber (JE 178–83). The inhibited St John also indulges momentarily in amorous reverie in gazing upon Rosamond Oliver's picture that Jane has painted, but then curbs his feelings. His conduct, however, makes amply clear to Jane his capacity for passion (JE 317–20). In all three texts under scrutiny, the Bluebeard figure's ambiguous message stems from an opposition between the symbolic law as a system and its obscene underside. St Paul points out that the law itself generates the desire to violate it. This dark underside of the law, observes Žižek (*Puppet* 105), splits every commandment into two complementary, albeit symmetrical, parts – 'you shall not commit adultery,' for example, is split into 'you shall not' and the obscene injunction 'commit adultery!'

In *Oranges*, the inability to handle this tension created by the symbolic law leads to a situation in which the Pentecostal church's attempts to mortify the flesh invest religious worship with perverted forms of sexuality. The worship relies heavily on fetishism, a feature familiar from *Jane Eyre*. At Thornfield, Jane fears that she has turned Rochester into an idol – a fetish, in fact (JE 234). One might say that *Oranges* demonstrates what happens to faith once fetishism gains a foothold.

The Pentecostal congregation's fetishism is propped up by concrete objects such as wipe-clean copies of the Book of Revelations, pictures of Jesus, cloths with biblical embroidery, and an elephant's foot Promise Box.[1] The investment in fetishism includes a ghoulish enjoyment of suffering. This enjoyment over suffering and pain is linked to what Emily Apter (127) calls *masofetishism* and *sadofetishism*. Both produce a state of excitation in which pain brings pleasure. Masofetishism is operating in the mother's identification with martyrs, whose suffering has proved their worth as Christian soldiers. The fetishes remind her that she must endure ridicule and exclusion, for as a believer she is 'called to be apart' (O 42). This masochistic position gives rise to sadofetishism whereby the fetish is turned outward against others rather than inward against the self. The religious objects serve as weapons with which to battle the irreligious and show sinners their horrific fate. When sounds of the neighbours making love, for example, are heard through the walls on a Sunday morning, the mother starts playing hymns on the piano, finally darting into the yard to shout scripture at them (O 53). The masochistic surrender to God enables her to identify with His wrath, which produces a pleasurable glee about the even greater suffering to which the unbelievers will finally be subjected.

The most significant fetish for the mother is the divine voice. In insisting that Jesus is the Word of God made flesh, she gives language an originating capacity. In order to be able to use language generatively and persuasively, she first has to listen to God. She starts each day in meditation. On Sundays she listens to the World Service devotional program on the radio. When she hears God, her mouth is filled with His Word. Devotional practice often relies on an exchange between the oral cavity and the biblical word and in particular, between a woman's ear and her mouth.[2] The mother's erotic organ is the ear filled by God's voice. Aural stimulation – a kind of 'orgasm of the ear' (Apter 138) – then turns into oral pleasure, into testifying and sermonizing. Apter explains that this notion of God's voice implanted in a woman's pliant body suggests that a woman's superego needs a symbolic prosthesis to hold itself up (141). In *Oranges*, however, this situation is complicated by the fact that strong women run the church. They function as role models who encourage Jeanette to have faith in the power of femininity (Keryn Carter 19). Apter maintains that although the female represents the body and the male the voice, the question remains whether the female believer retains the God-position in place or whether she uses God for her own pleasure (141). The latter option seems to be the case in *Oranges* until that is, the mother and the congregation find out about Jeannette's lesbianism. Then it becomes evident that they all wholeheartedly submit to patriarchal law in accusing Jeannette of usurping male prerogative. The mother can identify only with a vengeful, sadistic God. When Jeanette confesses her love for Melanie, the mother acts like Bluebeard. She annihilates Jeanette spiritually and socially by expelling her from home and church. She writes off Jeanette as one of the damned, refusing to have anything to do with her.

These observations throw light on the mother's Bluebeard-like intentions. Those intentions are not related to Jeanette's missionary education, because the mother would gladly sacrifice her daughter for the sake of redeeming pagans. Instead, they are linked to the turn of events that makes the mother renounce the daughter on their home turf. The mother's faith acknowledges only God's wrath and punishment. In *Jane Eyre* Rochester is ready to sacrifice Jane for his moral and spiritual redemption, while St John Rivers regards her as a sacrificial lamb whose voluntary death in India would prove that love and mercy exist. It is this latter motive that drives the mother in *Oranges*.

### Jeanette as the Wifely Christ

Unlike the wife in 'Bluebeard,' Jane never defies Rochester by furtively probing his secrets. Rochester's escapades make her suspect an involvement with illicit sexuality. Once the secret is out, Rochester's marriage to Bertha is less of a problem for Jane than his contempt for the sanctity of the institution of marriage. Rochester serves as a warning to Jane about earthly love that is out of bounds; hence, her fear of turning him into an idol. She searches for a way to reconcile sexual passion with spirituality. Peter Allan Dale (207) observes that this attempt feeds the tension beneath the story's progression between romance and religious structures. It also accounts for what both he and Doreen Roberts (40) characterize as Jane's blasphemous use of language that applies biblical terms and allusions to erotic contexts.

Similarly, Jeanette does not intentionally break her promise not to explore sexuality. Thanks to the mother's reticence, Jeanette does not even know exactly what is forbidden. Whatever she manages to learn of sexual relations mostly perplexes or disgusts her. In her teens Jeanette meets a girl named Melanie, whom she brings to church. Melanie is converted, and Jeanette is appointed her religious instructor. Together they read the Bible and attend services. When Jeanette falls in love with Melanie, Jeanette is convinced that it has happened with God's protection and for His glory. Unlike Jane, what Jeanette finds in the forbidden chamber is not violence and murder, but beauty and fulfilment. She describes her first lovemaking in the following fashion: '[Melanie] stroked my head for a long time, and then we hugged and it felt like drowning. Then I was frightened but couldn't stop. There was something crawling in my belly. I had an octopus inside me. And it was evening and it was morning; another day' (O 86). Jeanette's biblical language suggests that she understands her love for Melanie to be closely bound up with her love of God. Cindie Maagaard maintains that Jeanette sees the varieties of love and religious experience as necessary to each other. They coexist in her without conflict. Love dissolves tensions between spirit and body (152–3). In fact, the mother's hateful interpretation of the body and sex as forbidden becomes a source of horror for Jeanette. She feels the mother has betrayed her. In retrospect, for example, she understands that by changing the ending of *Jane Eyre*, the mother denies the passion that unites Jane and Rochester and that entwines their spirits and bodies. Furthermore, by pretending that Jeanette is her brainchild, the mother denies that her adopted daughter is the outcome of someone's bodily passion.

*Oranges* departs from *Jane Eyre* in its conceptualization of the meaning of the Fall. Reinterpreting the contents of the forbidden chamber in a positive sense, Jeanette describes her new understanding in this way: 'To eat of the fruit means to leave the garden because the fruit speaks of other things, other longings. So at dusk you say goodbye to the place you love, not knowing if you can ever return, knowing you can never return by the same way as this' (O 120). Jeanette's insight may be linked to Žižek's interpretation of the Fall. In this view, things did not first go wrong with Adam – or rather, with Eve – to be then restored in Christ: for Jeanette, Eve and Christ are one and the same. The Fall, Žižek argues, is revealed as a longed-for liberation: it is the emergence of freedom. By speaking of other longings, the Fall frees us to desire desirousness as the state that sustains life. The Fall is thus the right move, and misperceiving and representing it as a 'Fall' is actually where the true Fall takes place (*Puppet* 86–7).

Unlike in 'Bluebeard,' no human agent comes to Jane's or Jeanette's rescue. Natural forces, acting as God's mediators, aid Jane, but Jeanette has only herself to rely on. This change is in keeping with Jeanette's new understanding of the Fall according to which the task of humans is to transform our lives in this world. In *Oranges* this view is tested through events in which the role of Bluebeard's wife overlaps with Christ's role. Some time after the congregation has separated Jeanette and Melanie from each other, Jeanette falls in love with Katy. By accident their relationship comes to light. Jeanette willingly acts as the scapegoat by

taking all the blame and sparing Katy (O 128). The mother publicly betrays and then abandons her daughter (O 131–2, 134, 153). By accepting
the role of scapegoat, Jeanette is associated with Christ as the ultimate
Fool, deprived of all majesty and dignity. The experience leaves her in a
kind of limbo: old certainties no longer exist, and she belongs nowhere.
Žižek describes the consequences of such an experience: 'We are one
with God only when God is no longer one with Himself, but abandons
Himself, "internalizes" the radical distance which separates us from
Him. Our radical experience of separation from God is the very feature
which unites us to Him ... only when I experience the infinite pain of
separation from God do I share an experience with God Himself, that
is, with Christ on the cross' (*Puppet* 91).

Jeanette's understanding of the Fall and her identification with Christ
the Scapegoat shape her notion of love. Love reflects God's steadfast
loyalty: 'I want someone who is fierce and will love me until death and
know that love is as strong as death, and be on my side for ever and
ever ... Romantic love has been diluted into paperback form and has
sold thousands and millions of copies. Somewhere it is still in the original, written on tablets of stone' (O 165). This expression echoes Jane's
musings when she thinks of Rochester after she has left him: 'His idea
was still with me, because it was not a vapour sunshine could dispose,
nor a sand-traced effigy storms could wash away; it was a name graven
on a tablet, fated to last as long as the marble it inscribed' (JE 340). Jeanette not only proclaims the inseparability of physical and spiritual love
as does Jane, but, unlike Jane, she elevates a loving and thus an imperfect being to the place of God, the place of ultimate perfection. Žižek
explains that this is the mysterious paradox of love: only an incomplete,
vulnerable being is capable of love, because the mystery of love is that
incompleteness is higher than completion. We love because we do not
know or control all (*Puppet* 115). Yet in Jeanette's case, love does not aim
at erasing borders and being immersed in Oneness. Instead, it is a love
that needs distance because it thrives on differences. Jeanette's break
with her mother results in a belief in love that respects difference and
sustains desire without stultifying it.[3]

This notion is tested at the novel's end, when after a long time
Jeanette visits her childhood home. At first it seems that nothing has
changed except that her stepmother has gone electronic: she has a CB
radio and an electronic organ. She is still as active as ever in the church
and her views are just as black and white as ever. She has even started
a consulting service for parents with demon-possessed children such as

homosexuals. At home Jeanette realizes that she relates to her mother in a kind of loving frustration. This is how she describes her experience: 'Families, real ones, are chairs and tables and the right number of cups, but I had no means of joining one, and no means of dismissing my own; [my mother] had tied a thread around my button, to tug when she pleased' (O 171). Mother and daughter remain worlds apart, but by returning home, Jeanette affirms her loyalty and love, which keep the pair united. Significantly, the book's last chapter is entitled 'Ruth.' Laurel Bollinger links Jeanette's return to Ruth's loyalty to Naomi in the biblical book of Ruth. Jeanette expresses to her mother the same *hesed* Ruth showed Naomi. *Hesed* is more than ordinary loyalty, explains Bollinger (370); it imitates divine loyalty that comes without being deserved – it is a measure of divine mercy. Jeanette thus shows her mother the kind of love she hopes to receive from another (woman). Although the mother receives the daughter in a gruff manner, their relationship nevertheless teaches the mother to tolerate difference. She even changes her maxim: '"After all," said my mother philosophically, "oranges are not the only fruit"'(O 167).

The conclusions of *Jane Eyre* and *Oranges* portray a changed Bluebeard. Rochester learns that redemption cannot take place by proxy: he must humble himself before God. Jeanette's loyalty likewise helps the mother to rise above her own limitations. The closing words of the two novels, however, reveal a significant difference between them. The famous last lines of *Jane Eyre* are not Jane's words but St John Rivers's: 'My Master,' he says, 'has forewarned me. Daily he announces more distinctly, – "Surely I come quickly!" and hourly I more eagerly respond, – "Amen; even so come, Lord Jesus!"' (JE 385). *Jane Eyre* closes with St John's approaching death: his stern God will soon come for him. Jane may push St John outside to the edges of her narrative and anticipate his death, as Carolyn Williams (244) argues, but it is equally true, as Lamonaca (250) points out, that while Jane recognizes St John's personal shortcomings, she nevertheless admires his formidable Christianity. The book's last lines are ambiguous, Lamonaca argues, for by marrying Rochester, 'Jane has forfeited her ability to perform heroic, visible acts of self-renunciation. Deprived of this avenue of self-assertion and autonomous identity, Jane removes herself from the conclusion of her autobiography, ceding her place to one presumably worthier than herself' (258). Jane's spiritual integrity demands that she submit both passion and ambition to the constraints of Victorian domesticity (259). Jane's narrative retrospection takes place within this domestic framework.[4]

By contrast with *Jane Eyre*'s ending, consider that of *Oranges*: "'If I'm not sharp I'm going to miss my broadcast. Fetch the headphones." I passed them over to her, and she adjusted the microphone. "This is Kindly Light calling Manchester, come in Manchester, this is Kindly Light"' (O 171). *Oranges* gives the last word to Bluebeard, Jeanette's mother, but unlike St John, the mother is still in full swing. None of the many scandals her congregation has faced have shaken her belief in her god-given authority as a 'missionary on the home front' (O, 53). This is the positive legacy she passes on to Jeanette, although the latter understands it differently. The book's conclusion suggests a notable departure from the family-romance fantasy characteristic of nineteenth-century female fiction in which the female protagonist must replace maternal nurturance with a paternal bond in order to remain in the plot. Often the plot necessitates that the heroines be separated from the powerlessness and disinheritance that mothers transmit (Hirsch 168). Jeanette, however, need not forfeit her ambition: she becomes a prophet whose medium is writing fiction. For her, the prophetic quality of writing enables an author to scrutinize the myths of origins of a culture. She sees that writing opens up fissures there where the hold of these myths leads to psychic and social malaise.

How does Jeanette modify the family-romance fantasy and what relevance does her revision have for her views on faith and religion?

## Construction as the Prophet's Task

Marianne Hirsch argues that the usefulness of Freud's family-romance fantasy (Freud 'Family') derives from its intimate connection with the cultural plots of nineteenth-century fiction. Specifically, the fantasy emphasizes family as a set of relationships that an individual wants to manipulate. 'The constraints of family,' writes Hirsch, 'are precisely what motivates the desire for liberation, social transformation, even revolution' (167). Thanks to the different roles mothers and fathers play in reproduction, only fathers enter the Freudian family-romance fantasy as objects of a child's fictionalization. A child's imagination may alter a mother's status (by envisioning her as either a queen or an adulteress) and explore her sexuality, but it cannot change her identity. The uncertainty of the father's identity fuels fantasies of illegitimacy on whose basis boys can constitute a new self, free from familial and class constraints. Such fantasies include a religious dimension, for normally children envision their true father as a god-like being. In contrast, girls lack the ability to replace the same-sex parent imaginatively, a process on which, as this model insists, imagination and creativity depend. Freudian female family romances eliminate the mother and attach girls to the father/husband as their gateway to participation in the dynamics of power, success, and legitimacy (Hirsch 170–1). Hirsch maintains that nineteenth-century female fictions, including *Jane Eyre*, alter this model.

Relating *Jane Eyre* to its 'Bluebeard' intertext, however, shows that the family-romance fantasy vexes not only Jane, but also Rochester. Like Bluebeard, Rochester is fixated on examining the mother's sexuality. The chamber in the attic is the locus where he tries to unravel its mysteries. Bertha's sensuality first engulfs Rochester, but then fascination turns to abject horror. This sets up the pattern he follows in his subsequent relations with women: first enthralment, then revulsion. Lewis explains such repetition with the sameness to which the bloody chamber, and metonymically, Bluebeard's own body, testifies. Bluebeard initially recognizes his victims as separate from himself, but subsequently crushes 'their singular bodies into his own corporal mass, where they are reduced to undifferentiated, homogeneous components. Thus the secret is an effect of the sameness or oneness the incorporated bodies come to share with all parts of [Bluebeard's] body' (Lewis 197). In short, Bluebeard finds the fact of sexual difference intolerable: by destroying women, he annihilates that difference time and time again.

We have already seen that the family-romance fantasy is but one of three fantasies with whose help a child narrates its origins. In order to do justice to the richness with which *Oranges* deals with the issue of origins, I look at how Winterson handles all these fantasies: the castration fantasy, which grounds sexual differentiation; the seduction fantasy, which assigns the father a special place in the origin of (sexual) desire; and the family romance fantasy, which concerns the child's understanding of its own origin. The sexual relationship is thus examined from three different angles, providing three diverging, although complementary, answers to the problem of origins. The fantasies the book's Bluebeard, Jeanette's mother, unconsciously transmits to Jeanette illustrate malaise-causing forms the daughter needs to alter. These fantasies materialize the crypt in which Jeanette is imprisoned and which she must construct anew if she is to find her way out. In Kenneth Reinhard's formulation, construction represents 'a patently fictional narrative that is meant ... to get at the *cause* of [the desire of a patient's narrative], to encounter and reconfigure the *fantasy* at its core, *its fantasy of origins*' (paragraph 23).

One of the child's basic questions concerns distinguishing biological sex so that the child can answer the question, 'Am I male or female?' The castration fantasy addresses the mismatch between physical reality and the symbolic system. The phallic foundation of the signifying system places restrictions on our signifying capacity, because this system has no signifier for woman. In order to process this conundrum, the child elaborates fantasies 'in which a knowledge is constructed with signifiers in the Imaginary outside the realm of the Symbolic' (Verhaeghe 163). The child invents explanations to bridge the gap between physical reality and the symbolic system; for example, a woman's penis has been cut off or is hidden within. Of course, nothing of the sort has taken place, but the fantasy explains the baffling situation.

In *Oranges* the mother's sexual reticence orients Jeanette vis-à-vis sexuality. The mother is not just unwilling to discuss sexual difference, she is also unwilling even to acknowledge it, which leaves ample scope for fantasy. The following excerpt shows how she evades the issue: 'My mother had taught me to read from the Book of Deuteronomy because it is full of animals (mostly unclean) ... Deuteronomy had its drawbacks; it's full of Abominations and Unmentionables. Whenever we read about a bastard, or someone with crushed testicles, my mother turned over the page and said, "Leave that to the Lord," but when she'd gone, I'd sneak a look. I was glad I didn't have testicles. They sounded like intestines only on the outside, and the men in the Bible were always having them cut off and not being able to go to church. Horrid' (O 41). The Bible is more outspoken about sexual difference with its outward manifestations than is the mother, whose strategy is to skip all such discussions. This tactic is a sure way to rouse Jeanette's curiosity, and she indulges it by reading the left-out portions. It is also an effective means of passing on the mother's unconscious fantasies to the daughter. By remaining silent about sexual matters, Jeanette's mother cordons off certain areas as forbidden and transfers encrypted fantasy explanations onto the daughter's unconscious. This is the discourse of the Bluebeardish Other that shapes Jeanette's psyche. The mother's exhortation to leave sexual matters to the Lord results in a (shared) fantasy in which God emerges as the Great Castrator of men. He is a sublimated version of the totemic father, to whom everyone in the tribe – the biblical Jews and the Pentecostal congregation – is subjected. In this fantasy men are particularly vulnerable, because their genitals are located on the outside. By representing male genitals, the visible sign of sexual difference, as masculinity's weakest point, it emphasizes God's power of castration over all and sundry. By suggesting universal castration, the fantasy paradoxically enables the mother to entertain an idea of universal non-castration as her many fetishes suggest, for the fetish is a means of simultaneously acknowledging and disavowing (woman's) castration. Consequently, she can deny the fact of sexual difference – a strategy typical of Bluebeard.

When Jeanette disentangles herself from this castration fantasy, it is significant that the fetish provides her with the means of doing so. The mother's hateful relationship to the (female) body gives Jeanette the idea that the body is imperfect, unlovely, and unlovable. This body is inadequate to signify desire. On first seeing Melanie, Jeanette becomes aware of the faults of this view. She is captivated by Melanie's physical activity, namely, her boning of kippers (O 78). Jeanette returns to watch week after week, for Melanie's swiftly moving hands fascinate Jeanette (O 80). The hands and later Melanie's whole body hold her spellbound: in her eyes this body appears self-possessed and lovable (O 86, 101). The lovable body – or portions of it or objects associated with it – has a specific function in lesbian castration fantasies, which, argues Teresa de Lauretis, radically diverge from the psychoanalytic conception. She explains that in lesbian subject formation, a negative body image reveals a strongly felt failure of narcissism, and this experience is linked with the castration fantasy. It is 'associated with a failure of narcissism as the lack of a female body the mother can love. Failing the mother's narcissistic validation of the daughter's body image, castration means the lack or loss of the female body' (242). The lesbian body is inscribed in a fantasy of dispossession, and this is the original fantasy of castration. What occupies the position of the phallus in them is *not* the paternal phallus or a phallic symbol, but a *fetish*, signifying at once the absence of the object of desire (the female body) and the subject's desire for it (de Lauretis 222). The lesbian subject says, as it were: 'I cannot love myself, because the (m)other does not love me. I want another to love me and to love me sexually. This lover must be a woman – and not a faulty woman, dispossessed of her body (like me), but a woman embodied and self-possessed as a woman, as I would want to be and can become only with her love' (de Lauretis 249). The other woman's body, functioning as a fetish, signals difference between the lesbian lovers, thus inscribing and sustaining desire. As the mediating term and the signifier of desire, the fetish is any object or sign marking difference and desire between lovers (de Lauretis 229). Melanie's body serves as a fetish for Jeanette, enabling Jeanette to acknowledge sexual difference and to work through the Oedipus complex.

In Winterson's construction of the heterosexual castration fantasy, the fetish thus plays a key role. The mother's religious fetishes serve to deny sexual difference and castration. The direst consequence of the mother's castration fantasy is the fetishization of Jeanette. The daughter is, as it were, the mother's phallus, whose role is to realize the mother's ambitions. The mother desires through Jeanette, whom she smothers into her own body. Winterson's reconfiguration of this fantasy demonstrates that the fetishized female body can function in the same role as the phallus. Jeanette loves the fantasmatic image of a feminine body lost and denied by castration and recovered through the fetish. The fetish frees her to desire, independent of her mother's desire.

The emergence of autonomous desire raises the question of its foundation. Desire must be kindled and sustained in a child. The seduction fantasy accounts for the origin of (sexual) desire. Given that pregnancy and birth show the child the mother's role, fantasies target the father as the obscure player whose part needs explanation. Insofar as he is given a role, the father plays the part of a seducer: by seducing the mother, he calls forth (sexual) desire in her. He is the originator of desire. This fantasy establishes the figure of the man-father in order to make a sexual relationship possible in the first place (Verhaeghe 162, 165). In *Oranges*, the mother has an aversion toward men. She finds pregnancy distasteful, on one occasion referring to Jeanette's biological mother as a 'carrying case' (O 99). She sublimates sexual desire by desiring God. Desire is cut off from sexuality so that it can be represented as spirituality, totally dislodged from the body. Jeanette first shares this fantasy, for everything she finds out about heterosexual relations evokes her disgust (O 69–75). Again, her first love affair changes this inherited fantasy. Her initial disgust turns into delight, as it is the fetish, instead of the phallus, that seduces her. Jeanette finds out that Melanie's deftly moving hands, the triangle of muscle in her stomach, and the outline of her marvellous bones (O 101) kindle and sustain desire. The maternal fantasy of sublimated desire is replaced by fantasies lodging desire firmly in the body.

Jeanette learns that bodily contact has a spiritual dimension, which makes her reflect on God's significance. At the novel's end, she muses: 'I miss God. I miss the company of someone utterly loyal ... I don't even know if God exists, but I do know that if God is your emotional role model, very few human relationships will match up to it. I have an idea that one day it might be possible, I thought once that it had become possible, and that glimpse has set me wandering, trying to find the balance between earth and sky' (O 165). The lesbian relationship, firmly anchored in the body, enables Jeanette to experience reciprocal love uniting materiality and spirituality. Most significantly, her sustained attempt to balance the earth with the sky speaks of accepting desire as an unfulfilled and unfulfillable longing. It reveals the state of desirousness as the guarantee of desire's perpetual motion. Such a state consists, as it were, of two overlapping triangles: on the material plane, there is Jeanette, her lover, and the fetishized female body; on the spiritual plane, there is Jeanette, her lover, and God. Noticeably, the female fetish and God fuse, becoming two related ways of speaking about desire. As Maagaard points out, 'the forces of love and faith do not disappear, but are redefined and reemerge as experiences of religiosity felt as eros, whether physical or spiritual, for the other, whether human or divine' (157). Winterson's construction of the seduction fantasy targets the phallic father's privileged position, showing that for a woman, the mother's body may function in the same role. Simultaneously, she dislodges the notion that bodily love may only find its spiritual sublimation under the auspices of a markedly male God.

Jeanette sees her biological mother only once, while her biological father is never mentioned. The adoptive father too remains distant. According to the adoptive mother's version of the family-romance fantasy, Jeanette is the immaculate child of water and the word: her parents are God and a virgin mother who have conceived her for the special task of being a missionary. The mother's fantasy represents an early, omnipotent version in which the parents are seen as exalted beings whose unique offspring the child is. Jeanette at first cherishes this fantasy, but the discovery of her adoption papers collapses it; she, like everyone else, results from the sexual intercourse of two human beings. The family-romance fantasy she subsequently builds is based on her lesbian identity. Her sexuality is non-genital and non-reproductive, which lessens the significance of biological parents in her eyes. In fact, the fantasized parents are all she has.

Let us now return to *Jane Eyre*. In Hirsch's (182) view, Brontë singles out Rochester as the key to change. Jane's refusal to repeat his destructive amorous pattern compels him to acknowledge her as separate and independent from him. In Freudian terms, Rochester is forced to accept the fact of sexual difference, which, in turn, frees him to imagine for himself a new father in accordance with the family-romance fantasy.

This new-found freedom shows best in Rochester's role as father to his son with Jane in which he combines paternal potency with maternal nurturance. He becomes what Hirsch calls 'a male mother,' who exhibits an empathetic masculinity with no need to improve or correct.[5] Further, this modification of fatherhood, Hirsch argues, enables Jane to hand over their son to Rochester's care so that she can continue her imaginative labour and write her story. Hirsch points out that Brontë cannot reproduce female mothering or a female line of transmission. Thus, it is impossible for Jane to be simultaneously a mother, a sexual woman, and a writer (Hirsch 183–4).

We can begin the comparison of the alterations that *Jane Eyre* and *Oranges* make to the primary fantasies by observing Winterson's rejection of maternity as an option for Jeanette. It is even more impossible for Jeanette to be simultaneously a mother and a writer than it is for Jane. But unlike Brontë, Winterson envisions a strong link between maternity and writing. Jeanette's mother insists on the literalness of the family-romance fantasy: she *is* a virgin mother and Jeanette *is* her godly child. This fantasy allows the mother to challenge God as the source of all authority. Usually, such a conflict about authority and power, maintains Hirsch (171), occurs only within male family-romance fantasies. In *Oranges*, however, the mother sees herself up there with Him, almost as God's equal. She thinks her remarkable command of language comes directly from God: after her ear has been filled with God's voice, she has His authorization to speak. She sublimates earthly sexual relations into a religious erotic of the ear, justifying female creativity as springing directly from God, without male intervention. In spite of their mutual disagreements, the mother transmits a legacy of godly authorization to Jeanette, encouraging the daughter to fantasize, to imagine, and to write. Jeanette's authorial identity as a prophet springs from this legacy. She writes: 'The prophet has no book. The prophet is a voice that cries in the wilderness, full of sounds that do not always set into meaning' (O 156). Unlike the mother, she has no commanding book such as the Bible on which to ground her prophecies, yet she persistently represents writing fiction as resembling God's creative action.

Bollinger remarks that in parodying the Bible, Winterson fragments its originally tightly constructed narratives and makes room for her writing in the fracture – here, in other words, is an aperture out of Bluebeard's chamber. She observes further that the 'Book of Ruth' in particular has been 'fruitful' for the writing of *Oranges* (377). This sexualized metaphor, suggesting a textual mating, shows the wide range of application of primary fantasies. Winterson disagrees with notions that associate the writer's creative activity with heterosexual copulation and parenthood, emphasizing instead its godly nature. In concluding, I consider how the views she expresses in *Oranges* relate to traditional patriarchal notions of authorship, which make use of the terms familiar from primary fantasies, and how she associates male authors with God.

## Winterson's Fetishistic Writing Strategy

Hermansson claims that 'Bluebeard' has served women writers as a medium for dealing with their sense of Gothic imprisonment within male legacies of writing (9, 42, 59, 79). In writing their way out of Blue-beard's castle, women authors, like the surviving wife, counter male models of creativity. Women have used this tale in order to analyse and criticize the constraints of these models as well as to explore alternatives. In their turn, Sandra M. Gilbert and Susan Gubar show in their classic book, *The Madwoman in the Attic*, how primary fantasies have shaped these patriarchal notions of authorship, creativity, and the literary tradition. This book was published shortly before Winterson's debut novel; thus they share the same cultural space in which feminist notions of literary creativity were discussed. Traditional views of authorship metaphorically equate the penis with the writer's tool, the pen. According to these views, 'the male quality is the creative gift'; 'the author is a father ... an aesthetic patriarch whose pen is an instrument of generative power like his penis'; consequently, 'male sexuality is the essence of literary power' (Gilbert and Gubar 3, 6, 4). The ability to engender and to create powerfully equates male authors with God.

The literary father's patriarchal position triggers an Oedipal rivalry: fathers threaten sons with castration in order to guard themselves against the sons' attempted usurpation. Unlike daughters, sons can identify with the privileged paternal tool, eventually succeeding and even supplanting the father. The options open for women are few. Woman best serves in her 'natural' role of muse. If she writes, she acts on penis envy, imitating male authors. In both cases, the male literary tradition seduces her. As muse, she is the object of male desire; as a writer, she is the male-identified daughter. In traditional patriarchal theories of creativity, literary tradition is seen as the offspring of a literary family romance: male authors mate with female muses, producing literary children.

Retaining the metaphorical link writing has with the body, Gilbert and Gubar seize on various representations of the cave as emblems of femininity within patriarchal cultures, arguing that the womb is woman's privileged source of creativity. One such emblem is the Sibyl in the cave writing (upon) the Book of Nature. It is worth quoting Gilbert and Gubar's description of the female author's activity, because it contains key items that Winterson handles differently than the writers discussed by these scholars. They observe:

> This last parable [of the Sibyl in the cave] is the story of a woman artist who enters the cavern of her own mind and finds there the scattered leaves not only of her own power but of the tradition which might have generated that power. The body of her precursor's art, and thus the body of her own art, lies in pieces around her, dismembered, dis-remembered, disintegrated. How can she remember it and become a member of it, join it and rejoin it, integrate it and in doing so achieve her own integrity, her own selfhood? ... The female artist makes her journey into ... 'the cratered night of female memory' to revitalize the darkness, to retrieve what has been lost, to regenerate, reconceive, and give birth. (98–9)

A female artist's body is comparable to a cavern, and delving into it she finds her creative and aesthetic resources in a matrilinear artistic tradition. Other women before her have turned inward, discovering their artistic capabilities. A woman artist's closest model is a female precursor, a goddess-mother whose power lies in her ability to give birth. Gilbert and Gubar thus link maternity and creativity in order to turn woman's assumed intimate association with nature to her advantage. The Sibyl has, they write, 'a goddess's power of maternal creativity, the sexual/artistic strength that is the female equivalent of the male potential for literary paternity' (97). Throughout they emphasize metaphors of integrity, wholeness, and integration, for by grafting herself onto the matrilinear artistic tradition the female author achieves autonomy and authority. The woman artist is enticed to write by literary mothers with whom she identifies and whom she emulates. She finds her way out of imprisoning patriarchal notions of creativity in and through herself. Gilbert and Gubar's stress is on the family-romance fantasy, for they strive to demonstrate that female authors are creatively independent, autonomous, integrated mother-goddesses who must have an equal share in producing a literary heritage based on equality of the sexes.

Winterson concurs with Gilbert and Gubar's empathetic assertion that women are not castrated in the sense patriarchy insists they are.

She also endorses the view of the spiritual dimensions of writing. On most other points, however, she disagrees with Gilbert and Gubar. *Oranges* illustrates that for a woman writer, castration may mean the loss of a lovable female body, one that can in fantasy be recovered through the fetish. Given that the fetish may be any bodily fragment or even any object, sound, smell, or touch related to the lovable female body, creativity cannot be lodged in some specific body part such as the womb. What one might call fetishistic writing is markedly non-reproductive and non-heterosexual. It rejects representations of the literary tradition as resulting from heterosexual textual mating and of texts as a writer's offspring. Yet the fetish grounds writing in the body. Moreover, the fetish functions metonymically, as it always refers to an assumed whole, comparable to the fantasized, but absent and lost, mother's body.[6] Fetishistic writing prizes the dismembered and disintegrated 'sibylline leaves' of the previous literary tradition. This writing tactic does not and need not try to fit these leaves into a unified, integrated whole, as one can always reach for such a whole through the fragment – if one deems it desirable.

The discontinuous and palimpsestic narrative structure of *Oranges* illustrates Winterson's fetishistic writing strategy. Discontinuity serves to highlight the fact that the narrative is put together from fragments: she continually disrupts the main plot line with fairy tales, meditations on various matters, and brief asides. While following the main plot is easy, the novel's palimpsestic design emerges early on: both Old and New Testament stories are buried beneath Jeanette's story, yet even they are not referred to in their totality. Although Winterson names her chapters after the first eight books of the Old Testament, Bollinger observes that in each case she has chosen only fragments from the books alluded to. This narrative structure is further complicated by numerous intertexts such as *Jane Eyre*, 'Bluebeard,' and Christina Rossetti's 'Goblin Market,' which enter into the book's discussion of the biblical story of the Fall. Patchwork is the overall design of *Oranges*, testifying to an appreciation of fragments for themselves. This appreciation is akin to Roland Barthes's lingering lovingly over fragments in *A Lover's Discourse*, where he describes them as homages to texts that have seduced, convinced, and delighted him as a writer (9). This design, characteristic of all Winterson's novels, suggests a particular approach to desire. Normally, the phallus signifies the subject's desire to recapture through the heterosexual union the unity and plenitude the child presumably first enjoyed with its mother. In lesbian desire, provided that their fantasy scenarios are compatible, two female subjects can together find the originally lost, fantasmatic maternal body for themselves and in each other (de Lauretis 251). Jeanette briefly experiences such plenitude with Melanie. In *Oranges*, however, the emphasis falls on the necessity of leaving the garden; Winterson emphasizes loss rather than plenitude. Once the subject has undergone castration and desire is cut off from the maternal body, desire can never be totally filled. This characteristic actually safeguards and sustains desire.

Jeanette grows up on the Bible and *Jane Eyre*, and *Oranges* is built on these sources. They seduce Winterson, kindling her desire to write. What are they, if not her literary father and mother? The narrator of *Oranges* describes narration in terms of what she calls sandwich making: 'And so when someone tells me what they heard or saw, I believe them, and I believe their friend who also saw, but not in the same way, and I can put these accounts together and I will not have a seamless wonder but a sandwich laced with mustard of my own ... Here is some advice. If you want to keep your own teeth, make your own sandwiches' (O 93). Throughout her oeuvre, Winterson replaces familial and genital metaphors of literary creation with metaphors of orality and food. Suzanne Keen ('I Cannot' 167) characterizes her as 'a prolific and devouring poetic genius who consumes and transmutes her materials.' This devouring of literary materials is potentially a problematic feature, however, because it associates Winterson with Bluebeard. As mentioned earlier, Bluebeard crushes his victims into his body, reducing them to undifferentiated components of himself. Similarly, Keen observes that the co-presence of food, body, and word portrays Winterson's relationship to the literary tradition as incorporation. She chews up fragments taken from other writers, and, after having digested them, makes of them her own sandwich. What differentiates Winterson from Bluebeard, however, is the sacramental reciprocity her voracious appetite involves. 'The metaphors employed to describe the writer's reading, her art, and her relationship to her reader,' writes Keen, 'invoke Eucharist and transubstantiation, placing the writer first in the position of communicant, then (mystically) in the role of the host' ('I Cannot' 173). Winterson gulps down texts by others but only in order to offer subsequently her own texts for readers to devour. This writer-prophet puts great faith in the ability of her words to transform readers, but in doing so, she first willingly offers herself as the text to be savoured in the reader's mouth – and this action Bluebeard can never perform.

Winterson uses the religious associations of both *Jane Eyre* and its

'Bluebeard' intertext for multiple purposes in *Oranges*. In the context of a young girl's *Bildungs* narrative, she recounts the Fall, Christ's passion, crucifixion, and redemption through love. Simultaneously, she reconfigures the primal fantasies with whose help we make sense of ourselves and our place in the world. Finally, she adapts these fantasies to notions of authorship. At each turn, she suggests alternative ways of conceiving and narrating *Jane Eyre* and its 'Bluebeard' intertext. This constructive reconfiguration provides her way out of Bluebeard's chamber.

I now turn to examine Sarah Waters's *Fingersmith* in order to ponder how mimetic rivalry leads to ritualistic behaviour that engenders the sacred. What motivates the discussion of these two writers in conjunction with each other is the fact that Winterson is of an earlier generation of contemporary lesbian writers to whom Waters, of a younger generation, is indebted. Waters provides a new perspective on writing Bluebeard Gothic, one in which pastiche plays a key role. Although she has a different approach from Winterson, the two writers are nevertheless united by shared concerns.

## Bluebeard Persecutors and the Mechanism of Sacrifice in Sarah Waters's *Fingersmith*

*Fingersmith* rests on the changeling motif of Victorian literature: a sexually fallen aristocratic woman, Marianne Lilly, leaves her baby, Susan, with the poor and crooked Mrs Sucksby and takes Mrs Sucksby daughter, Maud, with her when the Lilly men track her down. By exchanging babies, Marianne Lilly wants to spare Susan from her cruel male relatives, while Mrs Sucksby sees an opportunity for Maud to acquire a lady's education. As a reward, Marianne Lilly agrees to split her fortune between the babies when they come of age. The Lilly men place Marianne in a madhouse, where she soon dies; Mr Lilly, Marianne's brother, brings up Maud. Meanwhile Mrs Sucksby draws up a complicated plan to rob Marianne's handsome fortune. She enlists a rogue called Gentleman to help her. Together they persuade Susan to help Gentleman to woo and clandestinely marry Maud. Maud, however, is to be placed in a madhouse, and Gentleman is to collect her fortune with a share going to Susan. Mrs Sucksby's real plan, however, consists of dressing Susan up as Maud, leaving Susan in the madhouse, having Maud back, and collecting both girls' share.

The main events of *Fingersmith* are prompted by Marianne Lilly's plight at the hands of her treacherous lover and cruel male relatives, and her proposal to Mrs Sucksby to exchange babies and share her fortune. This root event stands behind two plot lines: it feeds Mrs Sucksby's greed, giving rise to her plot against Susan, which would imprison Susan in a madhouse; as an uncle to Marianne's (assumed) baby, Mr Lilly has the right to get hold of Maud and subjugate her to his pornographic study. The unscrupulous ends of both plotters make them mirror images of each other: Mrs Sucksby is the reflection of Mr Lilly, who is explicitly compared to Bluebeard (F 204). My first task is to examine how their plots rely on the mechanism of sacrifice familiar from 'Bluebeard' and how the manoeuvres of the novel's Bluebeard figures exemplify the persecutor's perspective.

Christopher Lilly has dedicated his life to compiling an annotated index of pornographic literature. This scholarly devotion makes his habits mechanical. The Lilly mansion, Briar, runs according to an unchanging order, measured by a chiming clock. Nothing may intervene with his pursuits. Only occasional visits from publishers, collectors, and consumers of pornography break the monotony of Briar. Mr Lilly holds a special place among these men, for his knowledge of the subject, his dedication to it, and the extent of his collection are supreme. His possession of Maud – a childishly dressed young woman whom he has taught to read pornography aloud in an innocent fashion – crowns his achievements. In Girard's terms, Mr Lilly models desire in this closed community of perverts: he serves as an exemplary figure by showing others what is worth desiring and in what particular manner. He has perfected perversity by making it a purely scholarly undertaking. 'Here is work, not leisure. You will soon forget the substance, in the scrutiny of the form,' he tells Maud (F 200). In his view, this emphasis on formal study transcends the boundaries of the merely physical: 'I am a curator of poisons ... this is their Index. This will guide others in their collection and proper study. There is no work on the subject so perfect as this will be, when it is complete' (F 198–9).

More than any other Bluebeard in my corpus, Mr Lilly relies on the structure of perversity as the seal that locks his chamber. While Bluebeard keeps his chamber under lock and bind, Mr Lilly's library is ostensibly open to everyone, but he actually guards it carefully. He has installed a pointed finger on the floor marking the point beyond which everyone except Maud is forbidden to enter (F 76, 188). Having first consulted an oculist before installing the warning hand, Mr Lilly has placed it in a spot from which it is impossible to read the revealing names of the volumes. Thus the servants are unaware of the nature of his scholarship and the contents of his books. The perverse structure is grounded on a triangular configuration: Mr Lilly and Maud together share a secret of which the servants and the village community are ignorant. As long as he manages to convince Maud of the dangers of telling anyone, his chamber remains safe: 'Keep this from others. Remember the rareness of our work. It will seem queer, to the eyes and ears of the untutored. They will think you tainted, should you tell' (F 199). Maud is well aware that this enforced bond of secrecy keeps the library sealed; in fact, she sees herself as one of Bluebeard's wives:

> And in the yellow paint that covers the glass of the windows of my uncle's library I one day, with my finger-nail, make a small and perfect crescent, to which I afterwards occasionally lean and place my eye – like a curious wife at the keyhole of a cabinet of secrets.
>    But I am inside the cabinet, and long to get out ... (F 204)

Maud is like Bertha, buried alive in Bluebeard's chamber. This burial has been gradual, for it has taken Mr Lilly time to educate Maud in his pornographic undertaking. Maud's training has maimed her mind, amounting to a kind of murder. On the pain of severe punishment, she may not express herself or her needs in any way (F 188–99). She has had to learn to be an object and a tool. Mr Lilly thinks of her as a book among other books whose innocent covers reveal nothing of the lewd contents (F 194, 218, 250–1). He purposefully poisons her mind in order to turn her into a perfect instrument, an extension of himself: 'my aim has been to make you immune, that you might assist me ... Your sight shall save my own. Your hand shall be my hand. For you come here with naked fingers, while in the ordinary world ... the men who handle vitriol and arsenic must do so with their flesh guarded' (F 199). Mr Lilly forces Maud to wear gloves at all times outside the library. She can take off her gloves only when handling his books. This way her hands will not sully, tear, or otherwise damage them. Maud's hands and eyes function as substitutes for Mr Lilly's. For him, hands especially serve as stand-ins for the phallus. When Maud is ordered to take off her gloves in the library, her naked hands abolish woman's castration. They provide Mr Lilly with an exclusive view of the non-castrated woman, proving to him that there is no castration and hence no sexual difference.

In imprisoning his sister, Marianne Lilly, in a madhouse and Maud in his cabinet of secrets, Mr Lilly exemplifies what Girard (*Scapegoat* 50) calls the persecutor's mentality and perspective. The persecutor is convinced of the victim's guilt and of the justification of violence against this person. Mr Lilly hates his sister, who succumbed to sexual desire and sullied the Lilly name with an extramarital pregnancy; the mother has handed down this distasteful sexuality to the daughter. In Mr Lilly's thinking, Maud and her mother are both guilty of being women: as women, they are simultaneously lustful by nature and emblematic objects of lust. As all persecutors, Mr Lilly sees himself simply reactive and passive, controlled by the scapegoat who brings her fate upon herself. This fate includes the persecutor's belief that because the victim is the cause of trouble, she can and must also serve as its cure. Mr Lilly punishes Maud for being a woman, but makes her redeem her womanhood by imitating his scholarly attitude to pornography.

Mr Lilly's activities have a communal side too. This aspect emerges when his acquaintances visit him. Together, this community of perverts performs rituals of sacrifice that keep their mutual rivalry in check. After all, they are in the same business and share similar, if not the same, goals. Maud's presence controls their rivalry, preventing this community from sliding to chaos, because Mr Lilly's possession of Maud confirms his status as representative of the ideal pornographer.[7] He is thus the group's uncontested leader. This persecution mechanism functions in the following fashion. The men gather around Maud in a (semi)circle, forcing her to face the victim's fate: she must read aloud obscenities in a clear, sweet, childish voice. 'I place the book upon a stand and carefully weight its pages. I turn a lamp so that its light falls bright upon the print' (F 212), observes Maud of these readings. The lamp strengthens these sessions' link with sacrifice, as typically sacrifice takes place in the vicinity of a fire or its equivalent (Girard, *Scapegoat* 60, 62). Although the men repeatedly sacrifice Maud, their practice makes her seem what Girard (*Scapegoat* 43, 46) calls an omnipotent manipulator. 'When I have finished, Mr Hawtrey claps, and Mr Huss's pink face is pinker, his look rather troubled. My uncle sits with his spectacles removed, his head at an angle, his eyes screwed tight' (F 212–13). Because the words issue from Maud's mouth, she appears as their source and thus responsible for the listeners' sensual reactions. She is turned into a high priestess of lewd erotica, made sacred thanks to her double role as the cause of sexual trouble and its temporary cure. These reading sessions amount to a pedophilic gang rape of Maud. Given the fact of sexual difference, the trouble itself may never be permanently redressed. Thus the scene of sacrifice is turned into a ritual, a theatrical performance (*Scapegoat*

169). Because the victim's action is beneficial for the group, it must repeat this ritual (*Scapegoat* 55).

It was already mentioned that Mrs Sucksby, Susan Trinder's foster mother, serves as Mr Lilly's pale reflection, a female version of Bluebeard. In the Lant Street community of crooks and thieves upward mobility directs everyone. All want a place higher up with more money, opportunities, and comfort. Yet they share the same model of an ideal crook whose characteristics include cunning, daring, and courage. Mrs Sucksby and her partner, Mr Ibbs, serve as masterful imitators of this model, which explains why everyone vies for favour with them. Susan's supposed mother, allegedly hanged for murder, also proves a courageous disciple of this model. In encouraging Susan to participate in the plot against Maud, Mrs Sucksby evokes this false mother as a shared model: 'I know *she* would have done it, and not given it a thought. And I know what she would feel in her heart – what dread, but also what pride, and the pride part winning – to see you doing it now' (F 47). Mrs Sucksby, however, singles Susan out as a victim for different reasons than Mr Lilly chooses Maud. Girard (*Scapegoat* 166) maintains that mimetic desire is fuelled by envy, jealousy, and greed. Mrs Sucksby's actions illustrate this claim. Marianne Lilly's plea for help awakens mimetic desire in Mrs Sucksby. She is envious of the other woman's social position and financial opportunities, coveting them for herself and her daughter Maud. As a persecutor, Mrs Sucksby can safely plot to rob the Lilly women of station and money because she imputes all blame on them: they are the cause and cure of her crisis. If it were not for the exchange of babies and Susan's presence in her home, Mrs Sucksby would need not yearn after Maud; yet Susan will eventually put right this situation by replacing Maud. The night before Susan embarks for Briar Mrs Sucksby prepares a feast for her, which encapsulates her mercenary plan for the girl. The meal consists of a pig's head (a typical sacrificial animal), foreshadowing the fate of 'her lamb.' Contrary to Susan's beliefs, the feast marks her as one of the infants Mrs Sucksby farms of whose fate she is not particular. In one character's words, Mrs Sucksby 'loses children all the time. I don't think she will trouble very hard over one child more' (F 227). Indeed, once Mrs Sucksby gets Maud back, she never gives Susan another thought.

Both Bluebeard-like master plotters of this novel rely on a persecution mechanism in pursuing their own good, but each sacralizes the scapegoat in a different fashion. Because Mr Lilly's interests necessitate the mechanism's unending continuation, Maud is turned into a simultaneously profane and sacred scapegoat whose repeated sacrifice consecrates pornography. Pornography is the only ritual enabling the perverts to deal with sexual difference, and their rites lend sacrifice a theatrical quality. Mrs Sucksby, in contrast, believes that Susan's sacrifice dissolves the mimetic crisis once and for all. A worldly woman, she does not view her plan in religious terms, but sacrifice nevertheless plays a transcendental part in her designs. For her, it is a one-time affair, meant to put her out of reach of mimetic desire for good – but she is proven fatally wrong.

Thanks to its 'Bluebeard' intertext, much of *Fingersmith*'s drama arises from the clash of perspectives between persecutors and victims. Not only does the tale show persecutors and the sacrificial mechanism at work but also it illustrates how persecution affects scapegoats. Girard (*Scapegoat* 126) points out that 'one may talk about the same murder without talking about it in the same way.' By this he means that scapegoats may succumb to the persecutor's perspective by either agreeing with it or by desiring revenge, or they may disengage themselves altogether from complicity with violence. Such disengagement shows that the scapegoat has learned to understand and reject the mechanism in which she has been caught (*Scapegoat* 126). Next I discuss the effects of this sacrificial mechanism on the victims, Susan and Maud, and the choices they make once they realize their situation.

### Pearls in the Dust: The Victim's Perspective

The Briar episode links *Fingersmith* with *Jane Eyre*. Briar and Thornfield are Gothic mansions plagued by madness. Bertha haunts Thornfield, while Marianne Lilly's assumed madness taints Briar, casting its shadow on Maud.[8] Both settings witness the formation of an unlikely, socially disparate couple; equally, in both novels a mock courtship complicates things. By wooing Blanche Ingram, Rochester hopes to make Jane reveal her love for him. Although Susan is kept in the dark about Mrs Sucksby's real plot, she knows that Gentleman's courtship is sham – but unbeknown to her, so does Maud. Both girls secretly hope that the other would stop the game. Unlike in *Jane Eyre*, however, no one speaks out at the wedding, and Mrs Sucksby almost achieves her goal. What further unites the two books is the notion of love's power to break the mechanism of sacrifice and still mimetic desire, although the terms in which this takes place exhibit numerous differences, too.

Maud is the more experienced and cynical of the two girls, thanks to a childhood in a mad house and an apprenticeship to Mr Lilly. Like Rochester, she thinks herself thoroughly corrupted morally. This conviction and the desire to escape make her agree to Gentleman's plans. She cannot think of any other escape than having someone replace her: 'I remember the Bible story, of the child that was placed in a basket and was found by the daughter of a king. I should like to find a child. I should like it, not to keep it! – but to take its place in the basket and leave it at Briar to grow up to be me' (F 204).[9] Maud's decision to sacrifice another girl in her own stead shows that she understands the scapegoat mechanism. She realizes that for Mr Lilly any girl who performs the tasks of indexing, reading aloud in a certain manner, and conforming to a child's role will do.[10] Maud as a unique individual has no significance, for, as Girard (*Scapegoat* 132) remarks, the mechanism of sacrifice destroys individuality, making people interchangeable and substitutable. Mrs Sucksby's plot, of course, prohibits any sympathy between deceiver and victim, and this restraint applies to herself and the assumed deceiver, Susan. Maud knows of this plot: Susan has come to Briar to deceive her, but eventually Susan will be the real victim. In this context of evil intentions, Maud is surprised by Susan's kindness to her, which prompts her, in turn, to review the contents of Mr Lilly's forbidden chamber, the library. Falling in love with Susan brings alive its subject matter for her. She experiences sexual desire for the first time (F 274, 277), which greatly perplexes and confuses her, for, like her Uncle, she has thought herself immune to any other than academic interest to sexuality. Consequently, Maud is changed. Jane instils in Rochester the desire for a better life. Similarly, Susan awakens compassion in Maud, making her believe moral amelioration possible: 'I am not good. But I might, with you, begin to try to be' (F 284).

The forbidden chamber's existence in a building always radiates throughout the household, affecting everyone in some way. While its presence is a physical fact, its effects are intersubjective. Soon after her arrival, Briar's gloomy atmosphere makes Susan look for mystery. Scrutinizing her room, she sees 'the shut door at the head of the bed, and at the key-hole in it ... I wondered what I would see, if I went and bent and looked – and who can think a thing like that, and not go and do it?' (F 62). Next day she probes Maud's room, finding a wooden box, whose lock she picks. It holds a miniature portrait of a lady whom she takes to be Maud's dead mother (F 73). The box is a miniature cabinet of secrets: it alludes to the deal made by Marianne Lilly and Mrs Sucksby

whose victims are Susan and Maud; the picture is of Susan's real mother – the room with its furnishings actually belongs to her. Significantly,
however, Susan never learns any of Briar's secrets while staying there.
She never suspects the portrayed woman's true identity as her own
mother. The library's collections and Maud's role in Mr Lilly's life are
never revealed to her. Susan soon finds herself sleeping beside Maud,
who needs the presence of another in order to sleep. Susan assumes she
is sleeping beside an innocent girl whom she must instruct on matters
of love before her wedding, while Maud certainly knows, technically
at least, these issues much better than Susan. This mix-up leads to a
scene of mutual seduction during which the girls make love (F 281–3).
In the heat of passion, Susan calls Maud 'pearl' (F 238); this (biblical)
endearment encapsulates the girls' mutual surprise at finding a treasure where they only expected to find trash.

As in *Oranges*, this experience of physical love between women
proves decisive for both. Its significance emerges most clearly in Susan's handling of Maud's glove.[11] It turns into a fetish for Susan. The
glove demonstrates the lovability of a woman's body as well as marking its capability to bear and signify desire. This fantasy is familiar from
*Oranges*: the fetish marks at once the absence of the object of desire (the
female body) and the subject's desire for it. The female lover represents
an embodied and self-possessed woman with whom the lesbian subject
herself can become whole (de Lauretis 222, 249). The fetish functions
for the girls in a slightly different way, however. It validates the general
worth of the female body for Maud, while it enables Susan to distance
herself from the mother's body and yet love it. Not even the revelation
of Maud's treachery can change Susan's gut experience. She bites and
tears the glove but nevertheless keeps it as her dearest treasure. She
continues to dream of loving Maud in spite of her hateful feelings toward her, in a similar manner as Jane continues to have erotic dreams
of Rochester while separated from him.

As Mrs Sucksby's plot proceeds, Maud collaborates with Gentleman, feeding Susan delicacies so that eventually the plump Susan is
mistaken for Maud, while the diminished Maud is taken for Susan.
Simultaneously both girls ponder whether to reveal their treacherous
intentions to each other, but mimetic desire hinders them from doing
so. The model's influence is particularly evident in Susan's case. She is
checked by the scorn the Lant Street community would show her and
by Mrs Sucksby's false accounts of her murderess mother: 'I was meant
to make Mrs Sucksby's fortune ... They would say my nerve had failed

me. They would laugh in my face! I had a certain standing. I was the daughter of a murderess' (F 135). In contrast, Maud claims that it is 'love – not scorn, not malice; only love – that makes me harm her' (F 285). Because Susan does not reciprocate Maud's cautious profession of love, Maud thinks Susan is ashamed of their lovemaking. Maud has entertained the notion of turning Gentleman's plot to their mutual advantage, but now she withdraws, resolving to save only herself. In this sense, there is no malice, for Maud harms Susan impersonally; Susan is not her target, but simply an enabling agent for gaining freedom. Although both girls understand that they are about to sacrifice the other, mimetic desire makes them adopt the persecutor's perspective, collaborating with it. Therefore, both remain imprisoned within Bluebeard's chamber.

Maud tries to break free from the sacrificial mechanism before quitting Briar, however. She commits symbolic suicide by lashing out at the model under whose control Mr Lilly has forced her. As was observed before, Maud has been turned into one of Mr Lilly's books. She steals from him the library key, wreaking havoc there by slicing his books. She begins with *The Curtain Drawn Up*, the first book Mr Lilly made her read. 'I am almost afraid the book will shriek, and so discover me ... Rather, it sighs, as if in longing for its own laceration; and when I hear that, my cuts become swifter and more true' (F 290). Maud attempts to disrupt the sacrificial mechanism by destroying the model she has been made to imitate as well as the scene of sacrifice. The ensuing events suggest, however, that unless intersubjective relationships change, this mechanism keeps on feeding itself.

Towards the end of the novel it seems as if Mrs Sucksby manages to achieve her goals. Maud is with her, while Susan, committed to the mental hospital as Gentleman's wife, is dead to the world. One girl has replaced another, a substitution that conforms to the fact that mimetic desire makes subjects interchangeable. *Fingersmith* highlights this feature to the point of parody: Susan is actually Maud, Marianne Lilly's daughter, while Maud is really Susan, Mrs Sucksby's daughter. Moreover, the girls exchange dress, abode, and fate during the course of events: Susan becomes Maud, and Maud becomes Susan. In the world *Fingersmith* depicts, people desire to install themselves higher up in the social hierarchy. For Mrs Sucksby it is vital to have Maud back, because she wants the Sucksby women to replace the Lilly women. From this desire ensues a sacrificial crisis that compels the Lant Street community to scapegoat someone, a process I examine next.

## Sacrificial Crisis and the Maternal Bluebeard as the Voluntary Scapegoat

After Susan has escaped from the madhouse and found her way back to London, mimetic desire inflames to a point of murderous crisis. Spying on the Lant Street house, she sees that Maud has usurped her place. The conviction of Mrs Sucksby's genuine affection has sustained Susan amid her hardships, making her doubly determined to banish the double-crossing Maud. On returning to her Lant Street home, Susan brings along a sharpened knife with which to kill Maud. The presence of the knife makes it evident from the start that someone must be sacrificed in the Lant Street kitchen in order for the situation to resolve. The fast-paced confrontation revolves around this knife. Susan wounds Maud's hand with it, but then the knife is passed from one person to another, until it is placed on the table. The community is gathered around a fire – Mr Ibb's kiln – which strengthens the premonition of sacrifice. The unequal distribution of knowledge of the real state of things affects the choice of victim. In the beginning only Mrs Sucksby and Maud know all the details, but as the face-off proceeds, Gentleman correctly recognizes the crucial piece of information Mrs Sucksby has kept from everyone else, the fact that she is Maud's real mother. The plotters form allegiances in the heat of the crisis: Mrs Sucksby and Maud unite against Gentleman, while Susan acts as the unwitting catalyst that prompts the events.

Susan's role as a catalyst derives from her unwavering, childlike conviction of Mrs Sucksby's steadfast love for her. This blind faith joins Mrs Sucksby and Maud in a mutual attempt to safeguard Susan from the truth (Mrs Sucksby's betrayal of Susan). Gentleman, however, refuses to forgo his share of the Lilly fortune for sentimental reasons. It is in his interests to play the women against each other. In situations of communal sacrifice, remarks Girard (*Scapegoat* 135), the whole community is implicated in the actual deed. So it is with the stabbing of Gentleman, because it is not certain who actually kills him. Everyone is involved: Susan has sharpened and brought in the weapon, while both Mrs Sucksby and Maud fly at Gentleman, but no one can say who wielded the knife. One thing is clear, though. Gentleman turns the tables against himself with his snide remarks about love between women: 'Then [Gentleman] smiled. "You may get your daughter to do it [feel your heart], however. She's had practice"' (F 502). Given that a woman's love for another woman, be it a child or a lover, is the only good, selfless value these women acknowledge, they resolve the crisis by killing Gentleman. This act, however, does not abolish the sacrificial mechanism. He is a scapegoat in all respects, a reflection of the guilt the women share. After all, they are just as entangled in the harmful plot as is he.

When the police arrive at the scene, another foster child, John, hurries to name Mrs Sucksby as the culprit. This is his revenge at Mrs Sucksby for favouring Susan over him. Mrs Sucksby willingly acknowledges her guilt, because the confrontation has opened her eyes. By admitting responsibility, she concedes that it was wrong to exchange babies, wrong to hanker after more than her share, and wrong to betray Susan. She accepts her fate because she wants to stop the escalation of mimetic desire for which she is largely responsible. She becomes a voluntary scapegoat.[12] Like *Jane Eyre*, *Fingersmith* departs from 'Bluebeard' by making one of its Bluebeards reform morally. Mr Lilly, however, never relents, but dies cursing Maud for her treachery. Both girls concur in accepting Mrs Sucksby's offer of taking on all the blame. Their mutual mother buys her daughters freedom; by playing along, the girls let her protect them from the law. Mrs Sucksby's act alone, however, is not enough to break the sacrificial mechanism.

Susan learns of Mrs Sucksby's treachery against her only after Mrs Sucksby's hanging, when she finds Marianne Lilly's will in a secret pocket of Mrs Sucksby's taffeta dress. Susan falls gravely ill when she understands that Mrs Sucksby and Maud tried to protect her from knowing the worst in the Lant Street kitchen. She now fully acknowledges her share in the events and realizes that her love for Maud is stronger than hatred. Determined to find Maud, Susan begins her search at Briar. Jane was guided to Rochester by his voice sounding over half England, while Susan finds Maud by following sounds issuing from Briar's library. The novel's closure employs scenes familiar from *Jane Eyre* but changes their significance. During a confrontation in the library, Rochester confirms his identity as Bluebeard. There he vows that he will reform morally, if only Jane becomes his mistress. In *Fingersmith* the library serves as Bluebeard's chamber and the scene of confession. At last Susan learns the truth about Mr Lilly's library when Maud shows its books and tells Susan of what Mr Lilly made her do. During this scene, both girls frankly admit their share in Mrs Sucksby's plot. This mutual admission of guilt harnesses mimetic desire and frees them from complicity with the persecutor's perspective. This act finally breaks the sacrificial mechanism and frees the girls from the clutches of the two Bluebeards. The stilling of mimetic desire brings the cycle of interchangeability to rest, allowing the girls' separate identities to consolidate. The book's narrative organization provides proof of their having achieved distinct identities. Susan narrates the first and last parts, while Maud is responsible for the second part. Each has a distinctive manner and style of narration, emphasizing that the narrator-protagonists are two separate characters.

Unlike Rochester, however, Maud neither makes apologies for what she is nor promises to reform. Instead, she reclaims the library, making it her own place. Having realized that familiarity with pornography is the only training she has received, she has begun to support herself by writing pornographic literature. Now she promises to teach Susan to read and write. Together they will repossess Bluebeard's chamber, and the whole of *Fingersmith* is their joint proof of having done so. A happy ending is a disappointment in many Bluebeard adaptations, explains Tatar ('Bluebeard's' 23), because, having passed beyond the door, the woman has nothing left to investigate. *Fingersmith*'s ending departs from this convention, for the two women turn the library into a site for creativity, love, and eroticism. Mr Lilly is a mere scholar-collector in comparison to these women, while they have developed into creative and eloquent narrators. This ending suggests that women should not leave erotic literature to male authors, but make it express their own concerns. This is one of the issues I turn to when I consider the role narration and pastiche play in the portrayal of mimetic desire and sacrificial logic in *Fingersmith*.

## Narrative Imitation, Mimetic Rivalry, and Deliverance

*Fingersmith* is set in the Victorian period. Its characters, perspectives, and textual production all take place in the Victorian past. As is typical of postmodern neo-Victorian pastiche, *Fingersmith* imitates the generic conventions of its predecessors. It is helpful first to summarize the key nineteenth-century novelistic conventions *Fingersmith* draws on in its seriously playful reworking of nineteenth-century material. It places a premium on the twists and turns of the plot as well as on pseudo-autobiographical narrative voices. The novel's structure unites features of mystery, scandal, and changeling plots. The hidden mystery concerns the scandals toward whose revelation the plot strives: Marianne Lilly's extramarital affair and her illegitimate pregnancy, the mercenary exchange of babies, and the plots ensuing from this act as well as the lesbian sexual orientation of its two female protagonists. In the words of William Cohen, scandal structures the plot of sensation fiction in the Victorian period in the following way:

> The typical story of a Victorian novel involves the loss and eventual recovery of a fortune, benefactor, parent, child, sibling, or spouse. The course of recovery necessitates the disclosure of a secret, which has been hidden because it is in some way immoral or illegal; most often, it involves adultery or illegitimacy. The plot of the novel unfolds by threatening and finally effecting the exposure of this secret to the community, and once this revelation has occurred, the goods (property, family) are redistributed, now more justly among those who survive. The novelistic plot, distilled in this way, is analogous to the form of the scandal. (17)

Susan alias Maud loses her fortune, parent, and (pseudo)sister thanks to Mrs Sucksby's and Marianne Lilly's contract. Maud alias Susan also loses her parent and (pseudo)sister for this same reason. In the end, however, both property and family are justly distributed among Susan and Maud, who have suffered the most from their mothers' scheming. In accordance with the conventions of the scandal plot, the organization of the novel highlights episodes with strong narrative shock value. This emphasis necessitates a narrative strategy that foregrounds surprises and seduction: readers are enticed with suspense and titillation. Yet Waters's imitation of Victorian sensation fiction cannot be mistaken for a genuine nineteenth-century novel; it suggests, instead, strife between model and imitator. Many of the novel's features would have been impossible during the Victorian era. The narrators occasionally resort to coarse language and use sexually explicit expressions that could not have been used back then. The community of perverts and their actions are described with unprecedented openness, and so are lesbian desire and lovemaking. These divergences draw the attention of readers to the underside of the Victorian world, claiming that the era's sexual restraint and prudishness hid various sexual phenomena that, nevertheless, did exist. This exposure is not without sensationalism, as the aristocracy and the criminal underworld – the two extreme poles of the society – are shown to be the realms where these phenomena flourish. The more serious side of the book's pastiche draws attention to the manifold ways of ill-treating girls and women, to poverty and lack of opportunity, as well as to the various ways in which wealth allows the rich to abuse the poor. One may thus argue that Waters presents the

Victorian sensation novel in the role of the persecutor and that her authorial perspective lies with the persecuted. If this is so, then the goal of
her pastiche is to illustrate the workings of the mechanism of sacrifice
on the intertextual level. As we know, these positions tally with those of
Bluebeard and woman in 'Bluebeard.' Let us now examine how far this
analogy is applicable to Waters's pastiche practice of intertextuality.

The Notes section appended to *Fingersmith* names some of the historical studies (for example, on madhouses and execution) and other material that provided Waters with historical detail and inspiration. Readers
learn that Christopher Lilly is fashioned after a historical figure, Henry
Spencer Ashbee, who collected three annotated bibliographies of 'curious and uncommon' books under the pseudonym of Pisanus Fraxi.
Further, the pornographic texts cited by Maud come from real sources,
the publishing details of which can be found in Ashbee's books. What
the Notes section of the novel implies is that the phenomena and events
*Fingersmith* describes have for decades been hidden in Bluebeard's
chamber of Victorian literature and culture. Sarah Waters is like the curious wife who – together with her two narrator-protagonists – pries
open Bluebeard's closets. In so doing she brings out to the open the un-
derground business of libertine literature as well as homosexual desire.
By openly siding with her narrator-heroines, placed in the position of
Bluebeard's wife, Waters as an author adopts the same role. Pastiche is
her way of arguing that Victorian literature has always included hints
and insinuations, serving as invitations to readers to read between the
lines. Simultaneously, she suggests that this precursor tradition has always already been shot through with the fairy tale and same-sex desire.
In the case of Winterson and Waters it is as if both identified another
person in *Jane Eyre* worthy of the heroine's love, namely, Helen Burns.
Both expand the scene in which Jane crawls in Helen's bed and cradles
her fondly – only to find Helen dead in the morning (JE 68–70). Neither
contemporary author wants to assign such a dire fate for the female
love object. Their reading strategy amounts to acting the role of Bluebeard's wife – as a courageous explorer of both past and contemporary
taboos.

The author's adoption of the persecuted woman's perspective is
meant, I think, to uncover the mechanism of sacrifice functioning in
Victorian literature and show how it works. This literature typically
scapegoated all kinds of minorities such as ethnic and sexual 'others'
by assigning them the roles of villain and moral degenerate. By banish-
ing or killing these characters, the Victorian literary community purged

itself of the tensions teeming behind its surface: these scapegoats were made sacred, because they served as both the cause of sickness and its cure. While Waters's novel illustrates how this persecution mechanism works, she takes care not to replicate the role of scapegoat. Instead, by seizing on the sexual hints of Victorian literature and by opening up their meaning, her pastiche shows that lesbian characters and writers did exist in the past, but were hidden between the lines. Pastiche becomes a means of reclaiming the past and restoring former victims to their full humanity. Gutleben explains that the present-day fascination with Victoriana is accompanied by an awareness of the injustices experienced by its ill-treated or forgotten representatives. Resuscitating Victorian voices involves breaking free from and challenging Victorian norms and restraints (10–11). Yet in homage to that tradition, Waters's pastiche ensures that the sacrificial victim does not turn the mechanism of scapegoating onto the imitated model. Instead, the novel admits the strengths of the imitated model while correcting its shortcomings. Simultaneously lesbian literature is included in the continuity of the British literary tradition, including *Jane Eyre*.

Unlike Bluebeard's wife, who by probing secrets risks her life, Waters faces no dangers in imitating and criticizing a former literary tradition. Quite the contrary, neo-Victorian novels sell well. Gutleben argues that the neo-Victorian polarity between nostalgia and subversion often hides an opportunistic strategy. Although siding with the suppressed and restoring their stories is ethically commendable, the novels themselves tread beaten paths. The scandals they expose and the injustices they unearth are already familiar to readers from other sources. The secrets of the past are neither shocking nor seditious today; instead, they are what the public wants to read (Gutleben 11). Neo-Victorian literature thus smacks of opportunism, of taking advantage of today's climate of political correctness, and of commercial exploitation (Gutleben 37). Girard reminds us that such ambivalence is a sign of mimetic rivalry. The mixed attitude of reverence and critique, of imitation and critical correction, suggests that pastiche may never be completely clear of mimetic rivalry that leads to sacrifice. This observation applies to *Fingersmith* too.

The previous chapter discussed examples of how the Brontëan Bluebeard Gothic was exploded from within. Such books as *Rebecca* and *Charlotte* criticize *Jane Eyre* for sugarcoating its 'Bluebeard' intertext as romance. In spite of their criticism, the books treated in this chapter express much more faith in the viability of this classic and its literary-cultural legacy. For them, this legacy still allows authors to deal in meaningful ways with love, the search for transcendence, and the sacred. One may wager that the goal these particular authors have of changing the terms within which these issues are approached and depicted makes the rewriting of this legacy a pressing business for them.

# 5 Farewell, Charlotte Brontë! Angela Carter's 'Bluebeard' Tales and the Anxiety of Influence

'Outside, above, in the already burning air, see! the angel of death roosts on the roof-tree' (FRAM, 317). With this exhortation ends one of Angela Carter's many 'Bluebeard' stories, 'The Fall River Axe Murders' (1985). In this short story the angel of death is associated with Lizzie Borden's mother, who was subject to 'fits of sudden, wild, inexplicable rage' and who, the narrator wages, might have 'taken the hatchet to Old Borden on her own account' (310). Lizzie's gradual identification with the mother leads to a violent escape from her horrible father. She kills him, thus replacing the male relatives who usually punish Bluebeard. By making the victim play the role of rescuer Carter suggests that women also may undertake extreme action. In her essays on the Brontë sisters ('Introduction' and 'Love') Carter lauds Charlotte and Emily for creating heroines whose capacity for passion is unusual. By focusing on all-burning passion they struggled to find linguistic expression for sexuality, gender, and the emotions where no precedent language existed. Carter gives them special credit for this attempt. Of *Jane Eyre* she has this to say: 'It remains the most durable of melodramas, angry, sexy, a little crazy, a perennial bestseller – one of the oddest novels ever written, a delirious romance replete with elements of pure fairy tale' ('Introduction' v).

In spite of this professed admiration, Carter also sees Charlotte Brontë as a negative model. Unlike Emily, Carter claims, Charlotte was unable to sustain her passionate vision, thanks to *Jane Eyre*'s conventional closure. In Carter's view, 'there is a dying fall, a sadness, to the last chapter ... Marriage is not the point of their relationship, after all' ('Introduction' xv). And she adds (somewhat condescendingly?) that, middle-aged as she is, she feels tender embarrassment about rereading the novel: 'one wants the world to be kind, not to Jane, but to the girl who invented Jane, and, in doing so, set out so vividly her hopes and fears and longings on the page' (xvi). The Brontë essays place Carter as their descendant, but one who succeeds where Charlotte in particular failed.[1] It is Carter's commitment to passion, pushing her to stretch the expressive capacities of language, that gives her this position.[2]

Significantly, among the three fairy tales Carter identifies in connection with *Jane Eyre* is 'Bluebeard' ('Introduction' vi), the tale she kept rewriting during her career. The most obvious and strongest link between these two authors is the shared intertext of Bluebeard Gothic. Stephen Benson characterizes this relationship by remarking that Carter draws on *Jane Eyre* 'as a source text for its "Bluebeard"-inflected suggestion of the darker undercurrents of the utopian romance narrative' (234). In handling this Gothic intertext, Carter associates both Bluebeard and woman with winged creatures. For example, in 'The Fall River Axe Murders,' Bluebeard resembles a tyrant rooster lording over his coop; in *The Magic Toyshop* (1967) Uncle Philip's alter ego is a swan puppet; in *Heroes and Villains* (1969) the magician Donally dresses up in feathers; in 'The Bloody Chamber' the Marquis casts the wife in the role of Saint Cecilia, whose symbol is the dove, while in *Nights at the Circus*, Fevvers is a bird-woman. These tropes of winged figures, I suggest, situate Carter within literary tradition and express her relationship to literary ancestors.

Harold Bloom (38–9) calls such tropes *covering Cherubs*, explaining that they stand for literary continuity. Barring a writer's entry into (art's) Paradise, the Cherub imprisons the present in the past and victimizes the writer by trying to destroy his desire. (All writers are, for Bloom, male.) The writer must wrestle with this Cherub, an expression of his anxiety over being influenced by his forebears. He swerves away from them by creatively misreading them, which leads to his own artistic flight. Only by correcting and completing that which the predecessors got wrong or left incomplete in their work; only by instituting a personalized counter-sublime can a writer engage in a match to the death with the dead. If successful, he achieves the independent status of a strong poet, a shaper of the ways in which we see and understand the world. His forming influence extends even to the past so that at times it appears as if he wrote the works of his predecessors.

In this chapter I analyse Carter's winged figures as covering Cherubs that express her relationship to literary ancestors. These figures are mostly animals (most often birds or felines), but they also include masked creatures. How and with what means does Carter swerve away from the preceding tradition? To what extent does she creatively misrepresent and misunderstand it in order to superimpose her own versions on the tradition? Carter's 'Bluebeard' stories provide a fruitful context for exploring these questions, because the tale's narrative structures propose a motivation for the author's use of the same trope for the antagonistic protagonists. These structures deal with artistic creation, for the enmity between Bluebeard and his wife consists of entangled writing and reading contests that are embedded within the global plot of the 'Bluebeard' tale controlled by the (implied) author (Lewis; Hermansson). Bluebeard is a criminal-author, writing his stories of murder in his secret chamber, while his (latest) wife is a detective-reader, whose reading enables her to write her way out of Bluebeard's deadly authorship. In this context the question of influence includes an author's relationship to literary fathers and mothers. This approach of considering both literary parents seems suitable, for while Charlotte Brontë drew on Bluebeard Gothic, associated with women writers, she dedicated the second edition of *Jane Eyre* to W.M. Thackeray, the author of numerous Bluebeard tales. And although Brontë's preface sings Thackeray's praise, the reverent dedication suggests that she also takes him on, implicitly placing herself on par with him.[3]

Bluebeard Gothic, however, is but one intertext in Carter's 'Bluebeard' stories. They draw on widely diverse textual materials such as various nameable authors (for example, Djuna Barnes, William Blake, Colette, E.T.A. Hoffmann, Franz Kafka, Marquis de Sade, William Shakespeare), literary genres (the fairy tale, fantasy, magic realism), literary movements (surrealism, modernism, postmodernism), other artistic media (the cinema, music, pictorial arts, the freak show, the circus) and critical discourses (feminism, structuralism, poststructuralism, psychoanalysis). It is possible to trace these connections to nameable sources, yet given the mind-boggling number of intertexts, the result is doomed to remain incomplete. In fact, this density suggests another approach, one focused on the *system* that governs Carter's use of heterogeneous textual materials. In this view, identifying intertexts is certainly helpful, but what matters more is identifying the patterns and principles of aesthetic creation directing their use. The strong allegorical bent of Carter's writing supports this approach by turning the intertextual material into tropes of systems of thought and creation. Further, allegory and tropology imply a connection with myth as an explanatory framework within which allegorical elements and tropes acquire meaning. If there is a 'master' system governing Carter's use of various, mutually conflicting intertexts in her 'Bluebeard' stories, it is locatable, I argue, in her particular way of understanding *myth* and *mythical thinking*. No matter what the material is, she probes it in order to see how it founds a world; this founding elucidates its aesthetic principles. In my analysis, then, I approach the question of the anxiety of influence in terms of the system of Carter's intertextuality. Obviously, my research problem derives from Bloom's theory and its analysis of intertextual relations as an expression of the (Freudian) Oedipal drama. Although it is not known whether Carter ever read Bloom – given her theoretical erudition, she may well have – his theory's close links to myth make placing Carter's tropes of winged creatures in its context fruitful.

Carter invariably rewrote the 'Bluebeard' tale in the Gothic vein. 'The Bloody Chamber' (1979) closely follows Charles Perrault's 'La Barbe Bleue,' while *The Magic Toyshop* (1967), *Heroes and Villains* (1969), *Nights at the Circus* (1984), and 'The Fall River Axe Murders' (1985) are more loosely modelled on Bluebeard Gothic. They form my corpus. Becky McLaughlin (420) characterizes such a rewriting strategy as perverse, based as it is on literary disavowal in which both writer and reader pretend not to know a familiar story and its outcome. The present context suggests disavowal as a way of dealing with the anxiety of influence. Bloom maintains that a writer's struggle with ancestors necessarily involves perversion. The successor must be perverse in relation to the precursor by deviating from the precursor's work. Yet he cannot regard his own imagination as perverse, for its inclination must be health. Consequently, the successor's work shows the precursor to have been perverse thanks to the precursor's artistic failures (Bloom 85). Bloom represents the history of literary creation as one of 'disciplined perverseness' (95) that is imbued in aesthetic criticism. Carter literalizes this idea in her 'Bluebeard' stories by representing Marquis de Sade as an Ur-Bluebeard. I begin with Carter's criticism of the sadistic Bluebeard as a male literary forebear and then move on to discuss the ways in which her female artists respond to his models of aesthetic creation. In these sections this book's focus on *Jane Eyre* recedes to the background, thanks to a sustained focus on male literary ancestors. But when I move on to ponder how Carter's relationship to literary mothers may be modelled, Brontë's version of Bluebeard Gothic again plays a major role. In concluding this chapter I show how Carter's critical handling of myth and mythical thinking explain her departure from

Brontëan Bluebeard Gothic. Thus, as the heading of this chapter suggests, she bids farewell to the tradition associated with Brontë in order to direct the 'Bluebeard' literary legacy into new directions. While we can detect a similar goal in some of the other books discussed in this study, such as Winterson's *Oranges*, I nevertheless think that no other British author explores these new avenues in as sustained a manner as Carter does, thanks to her continued interest in 'Bluebeard.'

### Bluebeard's Anxiety of Influence

Carter portrays Bluebeard as an artist (a puppeteer-toy maker, a myth-maker, a connoisseur of art, a collector) labouring under the anxiety of influence. The 'artistic' display of wives in 'The Bloody Chamber,' for example, presents the Marquis's aesthetic response to his father's practice of hunting down girls with a pack of dogs (BC 135). This anxiety comes across forcibly in Uncle Philip's Christmas puppet show in *The Magic Toyshop* (MT 163–7).[4] It re-enacts the mythic encounter between Jove and Leda, resulting in the birth of a child.[5] Uncle Philip plays the role of Jove by manipulating a puppet he has designed, while he casts his niece, Melanie, in the role of Leda. The show involves a clever use of the trope of the Covering Cherub. The figure of Jove-metamorphosed-into-swan represents the mythic tradition Uncle Philip wants to transcend, and he accomplishes this goal through his own metamorphosis.

Uncle Philip's puppet show exhibits each stage in Bloom's description of an artist's coming to terms with the anxiety of influence (14–6). It corrects (*clinamen*) and completes (*tessera*) the myth by making 'art and nature combine with Philip Flower to bring you a Unique Phenomenon' (MT 163). In Uncle Philip's view, the myth consists of a single world, inhabited by gods and humans. What it lacks is art. 'Flower's puppet microcosm' swerves away from this world through aesthetic creation; the scene it depicts consists of two incompatible layers, art and nature. This turning away marks *kenosis*, Uncle Philip's break with the continuity of the mythic tradition. It leads to the *daemonization* of the artist and the humanization of the mythic Jove. Because Jove functions within the 'natural' world of myth, he is simply following his sexual urges in accosting Leda, as is any man in his relationship to a woman. Uncle Philip, in contrast, by sublimating those urges, turns mere copulation into an aesthetic parable of the artist's encounter with his Muse: 'Leda attempts to flee her heavenly visitant but his beauty and majesty bear her to the ground ... Almighty Jove in the form of a swan wreaks his will' (MT 166).

Uncle Philip reaches *askesis*, a match to the death with the dead ancestor, coming out a winner. He, not Jove, possesses a fully developed poetic will, capable as he is of aesthetic creation. The result is *apophrades*, a return of the Dead, in which not only does it seem as if Uncle Philip wrote the myth of Jove and Leda but also this myth now has to be understood in the terms he has set. He retains the myth's elements, but inscribes them with a new, superior meaning of aesthetic creation.

At the heart of Uncle Philip's rendition is the artist's encounter with Leda as his Muse. Bloom remarks that what the Covering Cherub veils over is the poet's primal scene, his birth as a poet, the discovery of which demands of the artist 'persistence, remorselessness, constant wakefulness' (36). The failure to uncover this scene accounts for an artist's inability to rise to the status of a strong poet. This act consists of (the latecomer's fantasy of) his Poetic Father's coitus with the Muse, in which they *fail* to conceive the latecomer. The strong poet 'must be self-begotten, he must engender himself upon the Muse his mother' (Bloom 37). This imperative directs Uncle Philip's performance: given that the mythical Jove merely copulated, he must give birth to himself as an artist by wreaking his will on Leda. As an artist he is the child ensuing from this union.

This analysis expresses, in a nutshell, the artistic endeavours of all Carter's Bluebeards. Now the pressing question is: what we can make of Carter's relationship to Bluebeard as the Covering Cherub representing her literary fathers? Another concern is the extent to which she is in agreement with Bloom's model of aesthetic creativity as a means of depicting this relationship. It is useful to begin answering these questions by dwelling further on Uncle Philip's puppet show, for there we begin to see how Carter swerves away from Bluebeard's aesthetics. She represents it through the Muse, Melanie cast as Leda: 'She was hallucinated; she felt herself not herself, wrenched from her own personality, watching this whole fantasy from another place ... She screamed, hardly realising she was screaming. She was covered completely by the swan but for her kicking feet and her screaming face. The obscene swan had mounted her' (MT 166–7). By depicting the artist's moment of self-begetting from the Muse's viewpoint, Carter draws attention to the violence in Bluebeard's artistry. To be sure, creation may involve aggression, but here it erupts into ferocity, reducing the Muse to nothing. She becomes alienated from herself, turning into a puppet in her uncle's aesthetic fantasy. From Melanie's perspective, the swan's advances are solely frightening; the very idea that she would feel honoured in being ravished by a feet-splattering, rubbery puppet is grotesque. She would find the notion of the sublime nature of this encounter ridiculous, if she managed to catch on to it from her fright. The primal scene of a poet's self-begetting manifests itself, for her, as a father substitute's manhandling of his niece: '[Uncle Philip] looked huge in his dinner jacket and striped trousers, a bull. Perhaps he was a bull. Fire spurting from his nostrils, he was going to turn into Jove as a bull' (MT 163). In Melanie's eyes there is only animal lust suggesting Uncle Philip's transgression of the incest taboo.

Representing Bluebeard's aesthetic fantasy from a female Muse's perspective implies Carter's *clinamen*, a deliberate poetic misreading, of this fantasy. The suggestion that what this perspective uncovers is a violation of the incest taboo provides a clue of her *kenosis*, the kind of discontinuity she initiates as regards this fantasy. It involves a double use of *exaggeration* as a means of dealing with Bluebeard's aesthetic practice. Not only does Carter complete (*tessera*) Bluebeard's art through exaggeration but also she uses exaggeration to criticize it. These moves are unusually explicit in 'The Bloody Chamber,' largely because this short story equates Bluebeard with Marquis de Sade. I now trace how Carter's exaggerated representation of Bluebeard's sadistic artistic practice brings out her criticism of the male aesthetic legacy when placed in the context of Bloom's theory.

## Bluebeard as a Sadistic Literary Forebear

In 'The Bloody Chamber,' the forbidden room, with its 'aesthetic' display of wives, represents the Marquis's truest artwork. The wife's role is to act as his Muse. In order to make her take up this role, he instructs her with pictorial representations, which function as self-portraits (BC 112, 121) that depict his birth as an artist. I look at one representative etching titled 'Reproof of curiosity.' The covering cherub trope takes here the form of a masked figure, which, as we shall see, is a variation of the winged creature trope. The scene of the etching is linked with Sade's work, standing for what Roland Barthes in his *Sade/Fourier/Loyola* calls a *posture*, a minimal unit of Sade's erotic grammar (28). Uniting one action and its bodily point of application, this particular posture with a man beating a girl places Bluebeard's artistry within the Freudian beating fantasy.

This etching shows a 'girl with tears hanging on her cheeks like stuck pearls, her cunt a split fig below the great globes of her buttocks on which the knotted tails of the cat were about to descend, while a man in black mask fingered with his free hand his prick, that curved upwards like a scimitar he held' (BC 120). The picture singles out the masked man as a beater, the Muse as the beaten, and the current wife as the onlooker. (She is leafing through books in the library.) The clue of this picture's aesthetic significance comes from the fact that the beating fantasy springs from a child's incestuous attachment to the father, which he must suppress.[6] In a similar fashion, according to Bloom, a writer's first love is his literary father, whom he must surpass. The portrait represents Bluebeard's strategy of renouncing the homosexual desire that fuels his art. It has, as it were, two layers. Its first layer consists of the artist's desire for the father and its suppression. In beating the Muse, the masked man is beating himself, for if he persisted in his desire, he would occupy the female position vis-à-vis the father. The mask veils this homosexual desire. The second layer consists in the externalization of this inner drama, which, Gilles Deleuze suggests, is typical of sadism: the feared female position is cut off. The beating man projects his guilt onto, and externalizes it as, a female figure. He evades incestuous desire by identifying with the agency forbidding it: the superego associated with the father (Deleuze 124).

The masked man fingers his scimitar-like penis with his free hand, while the other hand is raised to whip the Muse. Related to the beating fantasy, this scene reads as 'I, the father, beat you, my daughter, in order to experience sexual pleasure.' Normally, the father does *not* – and is not supposed to – take any kind of pleasure whatsoever in the beating: he performs it solely for the child's own good. Here, as in sadism in general according to Deleuze, the prohibition becomes the source of sexual pleasure, suggesting a resexualization of the Oedipus complex (104). This turn carves out a specific role for the Muse in Bluebeard's creative act, because it betrays his aim of annihilating her – and the fetish he attaches on her strengthens this aim.[7] In psychoanalytic terms, the fetish is a means of disavowing the mother's lack of penis by avowing its existence either in some other part of her body or in an external object. In Carter's 'Bluebeard' stories Bluebeard initiates his creative process by giving the woman acting as his Muse something to wear such as clothing or jewellery. The Marquis, for example, dresses his betrothed in a Poiret shift and a ruby choker. The gift is a fetish he attaches on the Muse's body. This act prefigures the result of his creation, for it is Bluebeard's knowledge of the fetish's eventual annihilation that arouses him. Deleuze points out that the intimate link between the fetish and

its destruction divests the fetish of its usual relation to disavowal and
suspense, transferring it into an altogether different context of negativ-
ity and negation (31–2). The Marquis goads his wife, clad in the shift
and choker, to embrace her role as Muse with the words 'Run to me,
run! I have a place prepared for your exquisite corpse in my display of
flesh!' (BC 141). His art would unite artist and Muse in mortal ecstasy,
provided that she succumbed to ecstatic self-annihilation.

Why does Carter represent Bluebeard's artistry as necessitating the
annihilation of the Muse? Bloom identifies a basic ambivalence in the
artist's relationship to the Muse: 'The poet thinks he loves the Muse out
of his longing for divination ... but his only longing is a homesickness
for a house as large as his spirit, and so he doesn't love the Muse at all'
(61). In specifying the kind of castle large enough for Bluebeard's artistic spirit, it is worth noticing that Bloom divides literary history into
the time before modernity and after it. 'The poet of any guilt culture
whatsoever,' he writes, 'cannot initiate himself into a *fresh chaos*; he is
compelled to accept a lack of priority in creation, which means he must
accept also a failure in divination' (61; my italics). The meaning of Bluebeard's fetish in Carter's fiction, always attached to a Muse, emerges
against this background. In sadism, explains Deleuze (19), destroying
the fetish serves as a conduit from a personal level of violence to an
impersonal one. The Muse stands for a human being's secondary, personal nature, while the father-poet represents primary, impersonal nature. The latter embodies pure negation overriding all foundations and
laws. This nature is freed from creation, preservation, and individua-
tion: it describes an original and eternal chaos (Deleuze 26–7). Carter's
Bluebeard annihilates his Muse because she provides him a conduit to
this state of original chaos.

The bloody chamber represents Bluebeard's magnum opus, dramatizing the last stages of aesthetic struggle that prove his standing as a
strong poet. Describing it, Carter's nameless narrator emphasizes it as
a locus of atrocious transgression (chaos) and perverse worship: 'At
the four corners of the room were funerary urns, of great antiquity,' the
narrator describes, 'and, on three-legged ebony stands, the bowls of in-
cense he had left burning which filled the room with a sacerdotal reek.
Wheel, rack and Iron Maiden were, I saw, displayed as grandly as if
they were items of statuary' (BC 131). This hell-like room (BC 124, 132)
literalizes the stages of Bluebeard's *daemonization* and *askesis*, his fight
to the death with the precursor. Bloom (64) emphasizes envious aggressiveness rather than phallic fatherhood, with stress on priority. Given

this stress, the strong poet's formula of daemonization takes this form: 'Where my poetic father's *I* was ... there my *I* is, more closely mixed with *it*' (Bloom 110). Bloom's explanation is worth quoting verbatim: '*Where it, the precursor's poem, is, there let my poem be*; this is the rational formula of every strong poet, for the poetic father has been absorbed into the id, rather than into the superego' (80; see also 71). Daemonization leads to the 'final product of the process of poetic askesis' that Bloom describes as the 'formation of an imaginative equivalent of the superego, a fully developed *poetic will*,' the poet's 'maturely internalized aggressiveness' (119). Simply put, the son shows that the law of castration applies to the father's but not to his own poetry: his poetry exposes the father's work as insufficient and imperfect.[8] As an expression of 'a fresh chaos' where divination again is made possible, the hellish chamber suggests that for Carter's Bluebeards a fully developed poetic will signifies merging with the legislating instance, the law. Indeed, Bloom says that the late comer only plays at castration, at a loss of power, because the Oedipal phase develops backward in the imagination (110). Now, the only father who is his own law is the primal father of Freud's *Totem and Taboo*. Only this one man stands outside castration; he has not succumbed to it. Because the law of castration does not apply to him, he is, as it were, chaos himself: he neither knows nor has limits. This is the father who owns all women – including mother and sisters – and who can really 'enjoy' a woman. While all the other men can only have a relationship to woman as object, the primal father is able to get off a woman as woman. All Carter's Bluebeards are versions of this primal father, who, as artists, refuse to undergo castration. The autoeroticism of the Marquis's self-portrait suggests as much. The phallic symbols of the cat's tail whip and the scimitar-like penis stand for the fullness of his being, his non-castration, which enhances the Muse's all too apparent castration ('split cunt').

In Carter's interpretation, then, Bluebeard's artistry revolves around a homoerotic fantasy about the (primal) father. It draws attention to the fact that any theory of castration, including Bloom's, logically necessitates the postulation of a predecessor outside its law. In its exaggeration it reveals the author's critically parodic stance towards such an intertextual model as Bloom's. Read through Carter's 'Bluebeard' stories, this model appears to be supported by what Bruce Fink calls a perverse structure. Fink elucidates this structure in the following fashion: 'The sadist, for whom the law has not operated, plays the part of the Other in his scenario in order to make the Other exist, and seeks to isolate for his victim the object to which the law applies' (*Clinical* 191). Bloom says that 'in his purgatorial *askesis* the strong poet knows only himself and the Other he must at last destroy, his precursor' (121). Carter's Bluebeards stage scenes of castration in which they play two parts: legislator and subject of the law; that is, the lawgiver, and the one on whom the exaction or limit is imposed. Thus they risk the threat that the father's bloody remembrance subsequently justifies filial rebellion against them.[9] Indeed, the anxiety of influence leads to an ongoing cycle of violence, as if strong poets were stuck on repeating the murder of the primal father of Freud's *Totem and Taboo*.

Carter's quarrel with such a model is, of course, that it leaves for woman only the role of Muse through whom the male artist safeguards his subjectivity and self-representation. Only the roles of a masochistic beaten or the sadistic accomplice are available to her, roles which Carter associates in her essay *The Sadeian Woman* (1979) with the masochistic Justine and the sadistic Juliette, respectively. In Bloom's model the phallus passes through the medium of woman as Muse from one man to another. In Gayle Rubin's words, 'in the cycle of exchange manifested by the Oedipal complex, the phallus ... is an expression of the transmission of male dominance. It passes through women and settles upon men' (192).

Analysing Carter's Bluebeard as a trope of the Covering Cherub reveals exaggeration leading to critical parody as her means of swerving away from the male literary legacy. I already mentioned that Carter also associates female characters with winged creatures, who, in order to escape death, must find a way out of the Muse's role. Given that Bloom does not grant women a role as artists, how does Carter model her female artists' relationship to male forebears in her 'Bluebeard' stories? As a way of examining this question, I analyse Bluebeard's female consorts as Covering Cherubs who express Carter's conception of a woman writer's affiliation to the male literary tradition. What does Bloom's model look like when viewed from this angle?

## Carter's Insurgent Cherubs

In 'Fitcher's Bird' the third clever sister exploits the conventions of totemic society by disguising herself as a bird. Given the totem's taboo nature, her outfit grants her immunity from the witch's clan, who meet her on the road on their way to the witch's wedding. The disguise suggests that the clever sister usurps the totemic father's place in order to ensure her escape and take revenge on her captivator. (Her clansmen later kill the witch and his clan.) As the 'Bluebeard' tale cycle's central phallic symbol (the key, the egg, the finger) suggests, this tale typically casts gender relationship in terms of mimetic rivalry over the phallus. This phallic object structures Bluebeard's relationship to woman, explains Lewis, thanks to its power to signify castration as the one difference that persists between them once she has returned the tarnished key or egg (225). Because the phallus, as the object that supposedly makes up for the woman's lack, remains a man's object, Lewis (229) points out, it is also for her what continually makes the lack by remaining what cannot be hers. In the context of artistic creation, Bluebeard assigns the female artist the place of an imitator who, by mimicking the male artist, is granted use and share of the phallus, but never control or full possession. This issue is pressing in Carter's case, for she undeniably draws on the patriarchal literary legacy. 'It in no way diminishes Angela Carter's achievement,' Susan Suleiman writes, 'to suggest that she may have learned a few tricks from Robert Desnos' (162). Suleiman describes Carter's approach as one of a *double allegiance*: like many other experimental female writers she adheres to the formal experiments and some of the cultural aspirations of the historical male avant-gardes, while at the same time voicing a feminist critique of dominant sexual ideologies, including those of the very same avant-garde (Suleiman 162–3). I would now like to show that this double allegiance leads to a specific way of struggling with the anxiety of influence, embodied by what I call Carter's insurgent Covering Cherubs. I trace the cherub's change from a Muse into an Artist by focusing primarily on *Nights at the Circus* and 'The Bloody Chamber.'

In the first part of *Nights at the Circus* ('London') the bird-woman Fevvers and Lizzie, her foster mother, together recount her evolvement into an artist, a fate of which she is aware from early on: 'there was one picture [in Ma Nelson's whorehouse] I shall always remember, for it is as if engraved upon my heart. It hung above the mantelpiece and I need hardly to tell you that its subject was Leda and the Swan.' In this picture, Fevvers explains, she 'always saw, as through a glass, darkly, what might have been my own primal scene, my own conception, the heavenly bird in a white majesty of feathers descending with imperious desire upon the half-stunned and yet herself impassioned girl' (NC 28). Significantly, the depicted scene is the same as in Uncle Philip's puppet show; also, the painting (or its reproduction) is by a man, namely Titian. A woman, however, interprets its import. In this picture Fevvers sees the origin of her bodily and artistic singularity, born from the passionate union of a divine spirit and a responsive girl, that is further underscored by her use of biblical language ('as through a glass, darkly'). I have already argued that Uncle Philip uses this scene in order to enact his own primal scene. Given that the Poetic Father's coitus with the Muse fails to conceive the later writer, the latecomer 'must engender himself upon the Muse his mother' (Bloom 37). He as an artist is the child ensuing from this union. Fevvers's interpretation of her primal scene departs from Uncle Philip's in two crucial respects. First, it is the Jove-Swan who functions as her Muse, with whose help she gives birth to herself as an artist. There is thus a switch in what are taken to be typical gender roles. Second, Leda's response is impassionate: although 'half-stunned,' she nevertheless actively participates in the scene, desiring to be impregnated by the Muse. Yet because the myth of Jove and Leda has no place for a female artist, she has no other choice than the grotesque in swerving away from it. (This union engendered the beautiful Helen, who, however, remained trapped in battles among men.) Insisting on her role as an artist, Fevvers retains the mark of her transcendent origins in her body: her wings. She is a bird-woman, an anomaly, which underlines her artist's role.

Carter explicitly links Fevvers with Lucifer, one of Bloom's strong poet figures par exellence. As with Bloom's strong poet, Fevvers's artistic career begins with her awareness of being in the *process of falling*. In order to perceive the differences between Bloom's and Carter's models of aesthetic creation, it is worth comparing Bloom's description of the poet's first realization of his falling with Carter's representation of it. In Bloom's view, the poet is a chosen man, and his consciousness of election comes as a curse: 'I *was* God, I *was* Man (for to a poet they were the same), and I *am* falling, from myself' (21). Carter has Fevvers climb up the mantelpiece and contemplate 'the grand abyss ... that would henceforth separate me from common humanity' (NC 29). Hearing behind her the strenuous beating of great white wings upon the wall, she jumps. 'Like Lucifer, I fell,' she says, recounting her first attempt to fly. 'Down, down, down I tumbled, bang with a bump on the Persian rug below me, flat on my face ... And then I knew I was not yet ready to bear on my back the great burden of my unnaturalness' (NC 30). This ungraceful flight, ending with a bump and a bleeding nose, not only mocks the strong poet's heroic descent but also makes fun of his tragic sense of himself as a chosen, cursed, lonely genius. Fevvers is unique, to be sure, but her special talent does not isolate her in the same way as it does Bloom's strong poet. Instead, the whores nurture her singularity, and eventually Lizzie helps her reach her full potential. Fevvers learns to fly by observing and imitating birds and by Lizzie's guidance: 'But do not think I carried out these studies on my own; although she was flightless herself, my Lizzie took it upon herself the role of bird-mother' (NC 32). When she has learned enough, Lizzie acts her role by pushing Fevvers off the roof (NC 33–5). During this second flight Fevvers is wedded to her singularity. What draws attention is, of course, that her ability to fly is the result of not only hard work but also the joint efforts of these two women. Her unique artistry is fostered by friendly cooperation.

Learning the trade is, however, but one step in becoming an artist. The true test comes only when the artist's 'consciousness of self is raised to an absolute pitch,' which leads to the struggle to the death with the predecessor (*askesis*): '*then* the poet hits the floor of Hell, or rather, comes to the bottom of the abyss, and by his impact there creates Hell' (Bloom 21). Having stopped falling and being fallen, he appraises his situation, choosing 'the heroic, to know damnation and to explore the limits of the possible within it,' describes Bloom. Now his task is to rally everything that remains, a comprehensive and profoundly imaginative task (Bloom 21), in order to surpass the precursor. This effort borders on solipsism, for the poet has nothing but himself to execute it: 'I have not but I am and as I am I am' (Bloom 22). The 'Bluebeard' tale typically represents the scene in the bloody chamber as the woman artist's fall into Hell. It dramatizes her artistic dilemma: she labours under the influence of male predecessors who refuse to acknowledge her as an artist. Unless she 'rallies everything that remains' she will most certainly be killed.

The woman artist's fall into Hell in Carter's 'Bluebeard' stories invariably results from mimetic rivalry, from her desire to seize the phallus and thereby achieve sameness and full equality. Witnessing Bluebeard's sadistic spectacle, she reappraises herself. In 'The Bloody Chamber' she suddenly finds herself infused with her mother's spirit and will: 'Until that moment, this spoiled child did not know she had inherited nerves and a will from the mother who had defied the yellow outlaws of Indo-China. My mother's spirit drove me on, into the dreadful place, in a cold ecstasy to know the very worst' (BC 131). This spirit fosters the activities of looking (scopophilia) and finding out (epistemophilia) in her that are traditionally taken to be male prerogatives. Looking at the Marquis's defilation of femininity, the wife finds out that what she was looking for was right under her nose all along: it was (hidden) in her, achieved through her first maternal identifications. Her infusion by the maternal spirit suggests a girl's very first triadic relationship. Sensing her sexual organs from early on, argues psychoanalyst Judith Kestenberg, the girl develops a triadic fantasy relationship including the mother, herself, and a child (usually a doll), signifying her awareness of her inner space and her identification with the mother.[10] This experience enables the girl to value what she has and, later on, when she encounters the reality of sexual difference, to hold her own ground. Contrary to Freud, Kestenberg claims that female castration anxiety has nothing whatsoever to do with envious regret over a lack of penis. Instead, it arises from the fear of damage done to this creatively pulsing inner space together with its concrete and symbolic offspring. The wife confirms and consolidates this identity through music. Once out of the chamber, she erects 'a pentacle of music' (BC 133) to solace and protect her, thus recreating her inner creative space. In 'The Bloody Chamber' music equals child in a girl's first triadic fantasy. It is the symbolic offspring expressing a sense of generativity and creativity the protagonist has crafted in conjunction with her mother who, as the narrator emphasizes, has scrimped and saved in order to enable the daughter to develop her musical talents (117).[11]

The last section of *Nights at the Circus* ('Siberia') further elaborates the notion of a female bond underlying female artistry. Because their train has been blown up by anarchists, the circus troupe finds itself disbanded in 'the hearts of limbo' (NC 225) and 'nowhere' (NC 280), which multiplies in various ways Fevvers's initial fall. Sighting a silver-bearded Jack Walser whom she has been looking for, Fevvers tries to fly to him with one broken wing: 'I fluttered lopsidedly a few yards more, until I could no longer sustain myself aloft upon it and crash-landed on my face in a snowdrift' (NC 251). This repetition of her first flight underlines her decline, pressing on her this icy Hell as the severest test of her artistry. When she locates Walser in a shaman's sacrificial hut, he begins chanting to her 'Only a bird in a gilded cage' (NC 289), the same song with which the Grand Duke proclaimed his intention of trapping Fevvers within his collection of golden eggs (NC 190). In a moment of horror, she sees Walser fuse into all the Bluebeards she has encountered along the way: 'Fevvers knew in her bones his song was meant to do her harm' (NC 289). Fixing her with his phosphorescent eye and his mad voice, Walser makes Fevvers diminish: 'She felt her outlines waver; she felt herself trapped forever in the reflection in Walser's eyes. For one moment, just one moment, Fevvers suffered the worst crisis in her life: "Am I fact? Or am I fiction? Am I what I know I am? Or am I what he thinks I am?"' (NC 290). The wording of her questions echo Lucifer's self-scrutiny: 'I have not but I am and as I am I am.' Significantly, as in 'The Bloody Chamber,' it is the (foster)mother who helps Fevvers to assert herself – as I am I am – and regain self-confidence: '"Show 'em your feathers, quick!" urged Lizzie' (NC 290). Given that Lizzie has helped Fevvers reach the knowledge of who she is and what she has, Lizzie can help her recreate herself as a winged spectacle. Again, Fevvers succeeds together with others: 'She cocked her head to relish the shine of the lamps ... like stage-lights; it was as good as a stiff brandy, to see those footlights, and, beyond them, the eyes fixed upon her with astonishment, with awe, the eyes that told her who she was' (NC 290). When Walser sees Fevvers with her wings spread out, he snaps out of his trance.

Carter's 'Bluebeard' tales emphasize female bonding – rather than biological mother–daughter relationships – as the sustaining springboard for female artistry. In *Nights at the Circus* Mignon's alliance with the Princess of Abyssinia turns her from a 'fleshy phonograph,' transmitting music of which she has no consciousness, into a woman who 'seized hold of the song in the supple lassoo of her voice and mated it with her new-found soul' (NC 247). The until-then-mute Princess, in turn, begins to speak (NC 248). In 'The Fall River Axe Murders' Lizzie Borden takes stock of her situation by opening up to her mother's aggressive legacy. In killing her father, she puts into effect what her mother dared only to dream of (FRAM 310). These examples point not only to Carter's criticism of the Freudian model underlying Bloom's schema of artistic creation but also to her creative corrections to it. Given that the role of the phallus in Bluebeard's aesthetic practice is to position sexuality as a function of representation – of an order in which man's phallic aggression consists in denying to woman his rights of vision and representation – Carter's women artists reject this ideology, because they cease to see themselves as lacking or castrated in the way Bluebeard does. Witnessing the extreme consequences of his fantasy, they give up idealizing and hankering after the phallus. It no longer represents an overpowering, awesome totem for them, largely because they realize that they need not exchange the daughter's initial relation of desire for the mother for the castration that makes her the opposite of the boy. What this realization means, in turn, is that the father, with his penis, does not have to stand at the origin and as the object of their desire.

In examining these female artists as expressions of Carter's swerving away from Bloom's aesthetic model of literary creation, we need to consider whether she is involved in a similar recuperation of the mother and the maternal as were, for example, Helene Cixous and Luce Irigaray in the 1970s, when they elaborated what Suleiman calls 'the maternal metaphor' for women's writing and cultural politics. Their attempts were directed against the notion that the mother is always patriarchal. Suleiman (166) points out that 'here is the mother who, as metaphor ... allows the woman to oppose both the Name-of-the-Father and the father's parsimonious economy.' Critics agree, however, that Carter does not accept the essentializing slant of these theorists (Kestenberg included). She neither proposes a new maternal space nor institutes some sort of a pre-Oedipal sublime. In her essay *The Sadeian Woman* Carter firmly rejects all such notions as so many myths of Woman, arguing that they are used for making actual differences among women fit one mould and precluding women from seeing the historical-material conditions of their subjugation. Yet Carter's repeated emphasis on female relations as the starting point for female artistry does suggest that she subscribes to such a notion as feminine structure of sexuality, one that models a woman's symbolizing activities. This concept is familiar from Lacan's work, who argues that there are two different, incompatible structures of sexuality.[12] (Both women and men can situate themselves within these structures.)

Feminine and masculine structures are determined separately with respect to a third term: the symbolic order, language. In Fink's words, 'masculinity and femininity are defined as different kinds of relations to the symbolic order, different ways of being split by language' (*Lacanian* 106). What characterizes the feminine structure is that it does not subject woman wholly to the symbolic order, which, although operative, does not reign absolutely in her case (*Lacanian* 107). Yet Carter insists that the bond between mother and female artist be eventually severed. In her 'Bluebeard' stories artistic creation involves accepting an authority *beyond* the mother figure. In order to help Fevvers learn flying, Lizzie first observes birds, and then she turns to graphs and mathematics to figure out the differences between a small bird and a large bird-woman (NC 31–2). The Marquis's wife plays J.S. Bach's *The Well-Tempered Clavier* to soothe her nerves; Lizzie Borden embodies her mother's legacy of rage in the form of a '*dark* man, with the aspect, yes of death upon his face' (FRAM 311). In so doing, the female artists draw on a symbolic element, a third term, one that applies to each and everyone. Traditionally, of course, this term has been linked with the paternal function which names, represents, and embodies – metaphorizes – the mother's desire and her sexual difference. Carter persists in stressing that this symbolic function is *not* to be associated with the father's phallus in the sense that constructs woman as lacking in comparison to man's assumed fullness. Given that the third term serves a symbolic function, it need not be the biological father, or even a man. It is the symbolic function itself that is essential (see Fink, *Lacanian* 196).

Carter modifies Bloom's model in one further significant way, for her female artists' *askesis*, the fight to the death with the precursor, involves a specific kind of epiphany: their re-encounter with, and realization of their responsibility for, their fundamental fantasy. This is the fantasy of their birth as an artist. In 'The Bloody Chamber' the wife describes how she 'seemed reborn in [the Marquis's] unreflective eyes, reborn in unfamiliar shapes ... I blushed again, unnoticed, to think he might have chosen me because, in my innocence, he sensed a rare talent for corruption' (BC 123–4; see also 115). In the hellish crypt she concedes that she married the Marquis because she was fascinated with luxury, power, perversion, and death (BC 132, 137). She assumes responsibility for her role in Bluebeard's game, acknowledging that she participated in it of her own volition (BC 132, 137). This acknowledgment motivates her narration as a way of dealing with her involvement in his fantasy (BC 115, 123–4, 132, 137). When Fevvers, labouring under Walser's annihilating gaze and chanting voice, manages to spread one good wing, the narrator describes her as 'a lopsided angel' who is 'no Venus, or Helen, or Angel of the Apocalypse, not Izrael or Isfahel ... only a poor freak down on her luck' (NC 290). The gap between a Venus and a Helen – to both of whom Fevvers has been compared – and a poor freak is marked by the artist's acceptance of her reduction. It is surprising to notice that in both instances of *askesis* the female artist *submits* to castration. Here it needs to be emphasized that Carter represents this notion as the letting go of narcissistic aspirations. Unlike Bluebeard the artist, the woman artist does not play at castration, but accepts it. In re-encountering the fantasy of her primal scene, Carter's female artist re-explains the Other's desire as the origin of her being in order to be free to desire on her own terms. This interpretive reassessment represents what in Lacanian psychoanalysis is called subjectifying the Other's desire and one's own share in it. It means taking responsibility for one's *jouissance*, which changes one's relationship to the Other's desire. In Carter's fictional world the woman artist's realization of her complicity in Bluebeard's fantasy marks a moment of beginning to work through the Other's desire. It involves her affirmation of 'I am that' – the drive, craving that landed her in Bluebeard's chamber (see Fink, *Clinical* 214–15). If, as Bloom claims, the Oedipal phase develops backward in the imagination of a strong poet, with Carter's female artists it proceeds forwards, because subjectifying the Other's desire is the only way one has of ever moving beyond castration.

Carter's female artist is engaged in a struggle with her male precursors, but hers is not the same struggle as that between father and son. In giving birth to herself, the woman artist needs communality and cooperation as the means for doing so. The artist is a unique figure, singled out by her talent, yet her genius is placed within a communal context that alleviates solitude and mocks any sense of tragic, cursed fate the artist might harbour. Also, Carter swerves from Bloom's model by representing the woman artist as one who is not to be placed within the Freudian model of castration that constructs woman as lack or absence. Approaching the symbolic register from her own structural vantage point, she holds her ground. This place ensures that she need neither be victimized by the father's artistic legacy nor merely repeat or imitate it. In fact, what the notion of the two incompatible sexual structures suggests is that artists working within the female structure are bound to swerve from the male legacy, because it constructs a different relationship to the symbolic order from the masculine one. Finally, Carter's stress on the necessity that the artist work through the fantasy of her primal scene opens up the possibility of moving beyond castration.

*Apophrades*, the last stage of Bloom's model, needs yet to be considered. This moment confirms the latecomer's victory, for when the dead ancestor returns, it seems as if the latecomer wrote his work. What do the dead fathers look like after Carter's female artists emerge through their struggle? Carter's criticism of Bloom's model of aesthetic creation suggests that one cannot characterize the dead ancestor's return as the latecomer's 'overwriting' of his work. Instead, the rupture between the ancestor and the latecomer, the space of complicity and critical distance, implies that Carter's female artist writes 'besides' and 'in between' the male ancestor. The question of diminishment thanks to the female artist's learning 'tricks' from male authors to which Suleiman refers subsides – of course, Carter takes from, say, de Sade and Desnos. These authors are part of her artistic legacy for which she takes responsibility. Yet the past remains the past; the ancestor wrote his own pieces, while Carter's female artists write their own. The latecomer, Carter suggests, is freed from the pressuring need of toppling the ancestor; instead, she can propel herself toward the future.

If the woman artist had a place in Bloom's model, the focus would lie on the father–daughter connection. The nurturing bond between Carter's female artists and mother figures makes this scheme useless in charting her relationship to literary mothers. How, then, should we model this relationship so that structuring and exploring it become possible? It is now time to return to Brontë and Bluebeard Gothic.

## The Woman Artist and Her Maternal Predecessors

In considering Carter's relationship to literary mothers I turn to Anne Williams's *Art of Darkness: A Poetics of Gothic*, where she proposes that the male Gothic plot employs the Oedipus myth, while the female Gothic plot draws on the myth of Psyche and Eros. This myth subtends animal groom tales, the best known of which is 'Beauty and the Beast.' (For an analysis of *Jane Eyre* in terms of 'Beauty and the Beast,' see Ralph.) Williams associates the male Gothic plot with 'Bluebeard,' arguing that this tale includes all the genre's basic ingredients (see her ch. 2). In contrast, the female Gothic plot empowers female authors and readers by presenting them with a model of subject formation that is not created through conflict, division, and abrupt separation. *Jane Eyre*, Williams (160) argues, belongs squarely in this tradition. The female heroine has a different relation not only to her own mother but also to that cultural (m)other repressed in her access to the Symbolic and to 'Mother Nature' (Williams 139). Williams (160–1) claims that 'this tradition of authorial mothers and daughters even implies an alternative to Bloom's Oedipal theory of literary influence: a model not founded on conflict but on accretion.'

Although one cannot place Carter's work within one comprehensive generic framework, she undeniably wrote female Gothic fiction. This genre stresses connections to romance, and Carter is no exception. A number of Carter's modernist female precursors such as Djuna Barnes in *Nightwood* (1936) wrote in this vein (Horner; Horner and Zlosnik; Tyler-Bennett). Carter follows in Barnes's footsteps in giving a prominent role to the grotesque freak show as a critical means of examining the Gothic legacy. One may query the usefulness of Williams's model, for I argued previously that Carter rejects notions linking aesthetic creation with Woman, maternity, and femininity. I nevertheless defend this chosen context, thanks to its mythical basis that serves the present purposes of analysis: 'Psyche' brings out Carter's simultaneous proximity to and divergence from myth. Her aesthetic model emerges from this double allegiance of following a pattern in order to break away from it. Of all her 'Bluebeard' stories, *Heroes and Villains* is the most extended meditation on 'Psyche' as Bluebeard Gothic. This novel organizes the following discussion, but I also refer to Carter's other 'Bluebeard' stories.

*Heroes and Villains* emphasizes the difficulty of distinguishing reality from fantasy that Anne Williams holds typical of female Gothic. Its theme of discerning appearances applies in particular to Marianne's relationship to two male Covering Cherub figures, Jewel and his tutor Dr Donally. Indeed, Donally warns her to 'mistrust appearances, they never conceal anything' (HV 60). The novel's opening describes a world split into warring sections. Marianne is a member of the tribe of Professors and Soldiers, while the men are Barbarians. Jewel, characterized as 'the Prince of Darkness' (HV 61), dons feathers in his hair and clothing, while Donally is 'a grotesque bird' (HV 71) in his feathery shaman's garment. Jewel corresponds to the romantic hero in female Gothic, while Donally is its sinister character, a Bluebeard. Carter cues readers with the help of mottoes as to her perspective on the Gothic tradition. One is from Leslie Fiedler: 'The Gothic mode is essentially a form of parody, a way of assailing clichés by exaggerating them to the limit of grotesqueness.' Marianne is a twentieth-century Psyche, for exaggeration and parody suggest the author's compliance with and departure from Gothic fiction, inviting readers to read the novel self-reflexively.[13]

The plot of *Heroes and Villains* follows in many respects that of 'Psyche' and female Gothic. Like Jane, Marianne is alone in the world, separated from her parents, her home, and her tribe. Jane longs to be acquainted with the wider world, and so does Marianne. Although Marianne voluntarily leaves home, she is nevertheless impelled forward by forces beyond her control, and her trials confront her with the cruel circumstances of both nature and culture. Psyche encounters Eros twice; this applies to Jane and Marianne too. Jane's first meeting with Rochester at Thornfield leads to disaster, while the second encounter at Ferndean puts things right. As a child Marianne sees Jewel kill her brother. The first glance she exchanges with him plants the seed of curiosity in her mind: what is a Barbarian (like)? Then Jewel disappears. Psyche is piqued about Eros; similarly, curiosity arising from both fear and desire draws Marianne to Jewel (Williams 153; HV 147). Haunted and obsessed, Jewel becomes the only dream she ever has (HV 6, 10, 137, 148). This feature is in keeping with the female Gothic plot, which represents the heroine first dreaming of terror and darkness, and then the subsequent narrative realizes her nightmare when she experiences the imagined in literal, concrete terms. This characterization applies to Jane and Marianne equally well. Ten years after her brother's murder Marianne leaves her tribe with a Barbarian whom she does not recognize as Jewel. When the heroine is reunited with the hero, Williams explains, she struggles with the fear that he is too strange, not the man she first saw. Marianne, however, wants Jewel to stay 'the marvellous, defiant construction of textures and colours she first glimpsed marauding her tranquil village' (HV 147). If Jewel remains a mysterious yet desire-instilling other, then Marianne need not change. The extradiegetic narrator's exaggerated treatment of Gothic conventions suggests that the whole genre is the 'furious invention' of the female artist's 'virgin nights' (HV 137). As Gerardine Meaney points out, the events may be regarded as Marianne's fabrication, which makes her an artist figure (quoted in Gamble 65). 'Psyche' as an intertext elaborates this motif of woman as an artist by linking female creativity with Psyche's pregnancy.

In the myth Psyche's jealous sisters persuade her to believe that Eros is actually a monster, a suggestion that in *Jane Eyre* becomes actuality when Rochester's planned bigamy is revealed. Given that Marianne's tribe holds the Barbarians a lower form of life, she sees Jewel through the filters of her culture: he is stupid, violent, and cruel. In a manner typical of female Gothic, *Heroes and Villains* confronts the heroine with the task of distinguishing the real from the imaginary, analogous to Psyche's sorting of the seeds. In 'Psyche' the goddess Aphrodite personifies the female principle, representing the individual mother, Mother Nature, and all that is associated with the culturally female, including irrational passions (Williams 153). This goddess is Psyche's contender, and their antagonistic relationship teaches the heroine to regulate outbursts of emotion. In *Jane Eyre* Helen Burns and Bertha Mason respectively teach the temperamental Jane to eschew not only fatal self-abandonment but also excessive passion. In *Heroes and Villains*, however, emotional excess is associated with the nomadic Barbarians living off nature. Superstition and ignorance reign among the tribe, and the tribesmen are prone to fits of passion and gratuitous violence. Marianne detests emotion as she also abhors motherhood. She guards herself against the feminine by resorting to rationality and indifference. Marianne's primary antagonist is the female principle that Aphrodite embodies in 'Psyche.' This antagonist is identified early on, when Marianne's nurse predicts that 'one day the Barbarians will get you and sew a cat up inside you and then you'll know, all right' (HV 10). As is typical of Carter's fiction, the brutal expression links motherhood with biology, reproduction, and death. Williams maintains that Psyche's task is to wrest Eros away from Aphrodite so that she may herself become a mother – in other words, a creator. This prospect is in keeping with the domestic ideology of *Jane Eyre*, whose happy end, argues Williams (157), implies that marriage ought to be understood as affirmation of identity rather than its obliteration. The female self develops and flourishes in interaction with others. Maternity expresses this idea of cooperation and reciprocity. In the myth of Psyche, erotic love serves as a metaphor for maternal love, and vice versa: birth is a metaphor for erotic gratification, for *jouissance* in all its senses (Williams 158). This affirmation takes place at the end of *Jane Eyre*, when Jane, clad in a pale blue dress – the colour associated with the Virgin Mary – has achieved all she ever wished for: marriage, motherhood, and the creativity of being capable of narrating her own story (JE 384). As is to be expected, Carter places these ideas under scrutiny.

The female Gothic plot transforms the heroine's apprehension about the unknown into learning and recognizing realities (Williams 149, 155), yet Bluebeard makes this process difficult. In *Heroes and Villains* the shaman Donally plots Marianne's marriage: he orders Jewel to rape Marianne, after which she must marry him ('Donally says ... Swallow you up and incorporate you ... I've nailed you on necessity' [HV 56]). The shaman manipulates the couple by forcing them to conform to the tribal power structure he creates. Like a god, he creates this structure ex nihilo. He has had the temptation scene from the Bible tattooed on Jewel's back. This tattoo reveals the link between creativity, coercion, and pain in Donally's artistry, for he treats the tribesmen as mere material. As Bluebeard, Donally resembles the cold, rational missionary St John Rivers rather than the passionate Rochester. There is a similar coercive tension between Donally and Marianne as between St John and Jane. Both recognize in the other an intellectual equal and a possible contender. The aphorisms Donally coins and hangs on the castle's walls are meant for Marianne, as she is the only one besides him who can read; these aphorisms comment on her situation, implying that he knows what is going through her mind. This strategy echoes St John's education of Jane. Both men aim to force a woman into a role they have chosen. Driven by curiosity, Marianne explores the forbidden secrets of patriarchy. Carter makes this process self-reflexive, for instead of dead bodies Marianne scrutinizes the patriarchal structures and mechanisms of Donally's fabricated myths, which draw on Christian mythology and primitive shamanism. In order to place Marianne in her role of 'our lady of the wilderness,' and 'the virgin of the swamp' (HV 50), Donally warns the tribesmen that 'Professor women sprout sharp teeth in their private parts, to bite off the genitalia of young men' (HV 49). He reasons that if he succeeded in installing her in this role then she would provide a focus for 'the fear and resentment [the tribe] feel[s] against their arbitrary destiny' (HV 51). Marianne resembles Jane in that she does not violate explicit rules laid down by Bluebeard. According to the conventions of female Gothic, the heroine does not subvert cultural rules by rebelling, but by trying to understand them. Thanks to this genre's emphasis on reason, she is involved in a process of enlightenment. For all her infatuation with Rochester and reverence of St John, Jane keeps her wits about her. Similarly, Marianne's intellectual upbringing enables her to recognize the structures Donally creates for what they are: wilfully constructed patterns of mystification and manipulation. In this respect, both *Jane Eyre* and *Heroes and Villains* fit the 'Psyche' plot in which a female self, by relying on her reason, makes her way in patriarchal society.

Bluebeard's manipulation makes the heroine's task of distinguishing between fantasy and reality doubly difficult. Typically, Bluebeard's abode reflects this complexity. I have already discussed at length how Rochester's manipulation of the public and private spaces of Thornfield confuses Jane. In *Heroes and Villains* too the Gothic mansion inhabited by the Barbarians becomes a space that perplexes Marianne. During the wedding ceremony Jewel recognizes Marianne as the sister of the man he has once killed. Ever since, Jewel has believed that this woman will eventually be the death of him. Later on, Marianne finds out that she is wedded to her brother's murderer. In this impossible situation they can only act according to ritual, that is, go to bed together (HV 80). Unexpectedly, the Gothic tower becomes the 'dark paradise of sensation' familiar from 'Psyche' (Williams 153). Williams (153) observes that when Psyche gazes upon Eros, she is pleasantly surprised by his beauty and desirability. So also is Jane, who holds Rochester more than beautiful to her, although he is not handsome according to rule (JE 149). Marianne is wedded to 'probably the most beautiful man left in the world' (HV 61), but her eye refuses to confirm what the other senses teach her. As darkness ascends, the bed becomes a 'silent world [in which] its inhabitants were denied all other senses but those of touch, taste and smell' (HV

88). What the narrator describes as 'this third thing,' an eyeless, formless erotic beast (HV 88) welds Marianne and Jewel together, although animosity reigns between them once morning breaks. For Marianne, the sensuous experience provides an unexpected perspective on Jewel, making her wonder whether Jewel is something other than a collation of her prejudice and spiteful, desirous curiosity, 'the invention of [her] virgin nights' (HV 137).

Marianne experiences the same difficulty as regards Jewel that Jane faced with Rochester: neither can make the hero's various facets cohere. Jewel is cruel, violent, ignorant, but also compassionate, gentle, and steadfast. This ambiguity is in keeping with female Gothic in which 'the female gaze recognises that appearances may deceive and that the identity of the other is complex' (Williams 149). Williams even claims that duality is the privileged condition of hero and heroine in female Gothic (149); such ambiguity challenges both to personal growth. In the myth this growing process is initiated when Psyche's gaze wounds Eros; likewise, Jewel is cut to the core by Marianne's first look: 'she converted me into something else by seeing me' (HV 122).[14] For both, the acts of looking and being looked at lead to a nascent sense of a subjectivity defined in conjunction with and against another person. Jewel is out of ken for Marianne, jolting her into self-reflection through the recognition of a wholly alien other, while Marianne makes Jewel realize that he may be something other than a painted warrior, an implement for killing people (HV 122). It is surely significant that the presence of both Jane and Marianne evokes a sense of guilt in the lover. Both men recognize the moral dimensions of their actions, which, in turn, alert them to the necessity of personal change (HV 80). Marianne's eyes are opened to the suffering of the tribal women (HV 103), while Jewel begins to protect her. She makes Jewel aware of Donally's manipulations so that near the end of the novel he banishes Donally.

As can be expected, Donally's mythico-patriarchal system assigns a specific function for female creativity. Jewel disrupts the gratifying sexual relationship by telling Marianne to conceive; moreover, 'shoving a little me up you' would prove his mastery over her (HV 90). Jewel's fantasy of planting 'a little me, furred, plaited and bristling with knives' inside Marianne (HV 90) turns a woman's private space into the locus of male fantasy. Marianne's disgust at maternity kills all pleasure because pleasure is made ancillary to procreation (HV 91). In this respect *Heroes and Villains* departs from the 'Psyche' myth in which motherhood is valued positively. Marianne has a terrifying vision: 'But now the room was full of faces floating bodiless on darkness like cream on milk, faces of diseased children shrieking raucously from warped mouths that she was their mother' (HV 91). The fearful connection between motherhood, biology, the child feeding on the mother's body, and death gains strength in Marianne's mind. It is concretized when Marianne encounters Donally's retarded son by the river. He jumps at her, and Marianne learns from him that she is pregnant. This scene juxtaposes copulation, pregnancy, and mothering, for the narrator describes Donally's son as a child feeding on Marianne: 'she wanted to fold him into her, where it was warm and nobody could harm him, poor, lucid, mindless child of chaos now sucking her as if he expected to find milk' [116]). Afterwards she engages in a ritual cleansing that signals her reluctant reconciliation to the idea of becoming a mother. Yet her 'desolating sorrow' (117) at becoming a mother highlights the disjunction between her creativity as dreamer and as woman. She has never considered the possibility of having a child (90), so alien is the idea of associating creativity with motherhood to her.

When Marianne visits a submerged city, she reviews her notion of maternity. There she sees a statue of a monstrous woman: 'It was the figure of a luxuriously endowed woman scantily clad in a one-piece bathing costume which, at the top, scarcely contained the rising swell of mountainous breasts ... The head, equipped with exuberant, shoulder-length curls, was thrown back in erotic ecstasy and ... the face clearly displayed a gigantic pair of lips twisted in a wide, joyous smile revealing a fine set of plaster teeth' (HV 138). This figure stands for the mother's body and the maternal (Aphrodite in the myth), a connection Elizabeth Mahoney explains in the following fashion. 'For this figure is the maternal body,' she writes, 'signifying a subversive, "monstrous" version of feminine desire. This space is symbolized by the sea, out of which the statue rises' (quoted in Gamble 62). Like *Jane Eyre*, *Heroes and Villains* refers to the Virgin Mary by associating woman with the colour blue. The statue's suit and flash-bulb eyes are blue. This links the statue to Donally's plan to make Marianne play the role of the 'Virgin of the swamp.' Seeing in the statue that which she fears, Marianne realizes that mother is actually an aggressively, powerfully sexual being; she represents self-sufficient erotic pleasure not linked with the phallus. The witnessing of this mother-goddess suggests for Marianne a new way of uniting maternity and creativity, and the designed role begins to take another shape in her mind than the one Donally envisioned.

The female Gothic's resolution shows the fruit of the heroine's learning process: she now distinguishes real from apparent, makes valid discriminations, and trusts in the validity of her perceptions (Anne Williams 170–2). The conclusion of *Heroes and Villains* questions this resolution. During her visit to the seaside Marianne sees the twin tower of her childhood in the submerged city, which instructs her, as also a tower instructed Psyche before her last task. 'This tower glimpsed in darkness symbolized and clarified her resolution; abhor shipwreck, said the lighthouse, go in fear of unreason. Use your wits, said the lighthouse' (HV 139). Marianne also sees how a lion sniffs at the sleeping Jewel: '[Marianne] watched it and was instructed' (HV 140). Briefly put, she thinks that the tower confirms her trust in reason as guide and that nature has no inherent structures of signification. The lion is no symbol and it abstains from devouring Jewel simply because it is not hungry (HV 145). This lesson enables Marianne to cut through Jewel's justifications when he decides to try saving the banished Bluebeard, Donally. Marianne sees beneath the warrior's mask: 'it had vanished as if an illusion which could not sustain itself in the white beams of the lighthouse' (HV 147). Jewel puts his faith in appearance. Because the warring tribes share this faith, it cuts out roles for each and everyone: 'One cannot escape the consequences of one's appearance' (HV 145). Jewel regards his rescue from the lion as a sign that he is destined for the role Donally designed: 'He'll make me the Tiger Man' (HV 146). Marianne rejects these explanations as mystification, for a belief in appearances turns one into a 'metaphysical proposition' (HV 145), while accepting a preset role signifies falling for the lure of power (HV 146). Yet Marianne's academic rationality crumbles at a crucial point. Angered by her reasoning, Jewel hits her. Infuriated, she reciprocates by proclaiming that the prediction will now come true: she will be the death of him (HV 147). In so doing, she resorts to the tribe's mythical reasoning. This move pushes her into a new stage, the inception of which was marked by staring at the female figure in the sea. Waiting for Jewel's return, Marianne catches sight of herself in a cracked mirror: 'there also stood Marianne, unrecognisable to herself.' She also sees her father, 'who merged imperceptibly with the image of the blind lighthouse' (HV 149). This mirror experience teaches Marianne the ineffectiveness of academic rationality among the tribe, but it does not mean that she abandons reason altogether. She now inserts herself in Donally's role, for academic rationality enables her to manipulate mythical reasoning as a means for both survival and ascension into power.

Marianne's rationality does not, however, solve the problem of emotion and the senses. Overtaken by emotion after having cursed Jewel, Marianne runs after him. In this last meeting she concedes that the murdered brother never meant much to her, while he obsesses about her. This concession leads to the novel's epiphany:

> He raised his eyes and they looked at one another with marvelling suspicion, like heavily disguised members of a conspiracy who have never learned the signals which would reveal themselves to one another, for to neither did it seem possible, nor even desirable, that the evidence of their senses was correct and each capable of finding in the other some clue to survival in this inimical world. Besides, he was so much changed, so far fallen from that magnificence bred of sophistication and lack of opportunity, and so was she, now in rags and haggard with sleeplessness and her condition, dirty also. (HV 148)

Already at Thornfield Jane believes that Rochester is akin to her (JE 149), and such a conviction is part and parcel of female Gothic, where the heroine realizes that the threatening and attractive hero is of her own kind. Yet simultaneously he retains his identity as 'other' (Williams 157). In contrast, in *Heroes and Villains* the male protagonist remains thoroughly 'other.' While, for example, Marianne thinks she understands her situation and Jewel (HV 138–9), the narrator observes that she never considers that Jewel might perceive this situation in another fashion, for 'the psychology of the outcast was a closed book to her' (HV 139). This novel suggests that information acquired by the senses and the body is correct, while reason appears in a problematic light, aligned as it is with learned ways of seeing and thinking. Culture with its signifying apparatuses lays down interpretive grids that distort, even fail to transmit, what the senses convey. These distortions harden into a culture's myths, explaining the origin of its members and their place within the sociocultural network. In its questioning of reason, irreparably linked with myth, *Heroes and Villains* departs from female Gothic, in which the heroine, thanks to her rationality, ultimately perceives an orderly, sensible world. She can trust the senses to give accurate information about it. As in *Jane Eyre*, the heroine's reward of marriage, children, and a place within society results from her gradual personal growth and rationality (Ralph 61). Carter rejects this pattern by representing reason and culture as sources of oppression. Reason is a product of culture whose processes are tied to its conceptual systems. All the warring fractions have their own systems of rationality. In the novel's world, the academic system of Marianne's father makes no better sense of the senses than the Barbarians' system: academic rationality has its own distorting myths. Neither system of rationality allows unmediated access to the senses, and in order to express and reflect on what they convey Marianne and Jewel would have to devise a new way of linking sense impressions with a new language. Gilbert and Gubar (368–70) argue that by ending *Jane Eyre* at Ferndean Brontë emphasized the utopian quality of Jane's union with Rochester, one not capable of flourishing under the strictures of a hierarchical society. As for Carter, her departure from Bluebeard Gothic emerges well at the moments of epiphany between her lovers.

These epiphanies recur in Carter's 'Bluebeard' stories, invariably taking place at the *limit* when characters' capacities are put under the severest tests; for example, in the midst of an all-engulfing fire (*The Magic Toyshop*), under the imminent threat of death ('The Bloody Chamber,' *Heroes and Villains*), or the danger of losing one's bearings for good (*Nights at the Circus*, 'The Fall-River Axe Murders'). The following two examples facilitate our understanding of what happens in this illuminating situation. The first scene, from *Nights at the Circus*, comes right after Fevvers has spread her damaged wings in order to guard herself against Jack Walser's inimical chanting, making him snap out of his trance:

> And then [Fevvers] saw [Jack] was not the man he had been or would ever be again; some other hen had hatched him out. For a moment, she was anxious as to whom this reconstructed Walser might turn out to be.
>
> 'What is your name? Have you a soul? Can you love?' he demanded of her ... When she heard that, her heart lifted and sang. (NC 291)

A diminished Fevvers encounters an amnesiac Jack Walser. Stripped of their previous pretensions and prejudices, both really see the other for the first time. During this fleeting moment they recognize the other as both radically different and as familiar; surprisingly, the impossibility of deciphering the other in terms of the self offers them solace and hope. In order to highlight the centrality of this epiphany in Carter's fiction, here is another example, from *The Magic Toyshop*, describing the reactions of Melanie and Finn after a fire has engulfed their family as well as all their belongings:

> (Melanie) 'My bear. He's gone. Everything is gone.'

(Finn) 'Nothing is left but us.'
At night, in the garden, they faced each other in a wild surmise. (MT 200)

Melanie and Finn literally lose everything – except each other. Although they are together, the reference in the novel's last sentence to John Keats's poem 'On First Looking into Chapman's Homer' suggests that each stands before the other as an explorer before an alien continent: 'Then felt I like some watcher of the skies / When a new planet swims into his ken; / Or like stout Cortez when with eagle eyes / He stared at the Pacific, and all his men/ Looked at each other with a wild surmise – / silent, upon a peak in Darien.' Coming to the fore at these key moments is what Jean-Luc Nancy (*Inoperative* 58) calls *compearance*: singular beings are exposed to one another *as* singular beings who share no common mythical ground. In order to grasp fully what Carter's departure from the conventions of Bluebeard Gothic means, it is worth comparing the moments of epiphany between her lovers with how Jane describes her marriage to Rochester: 'I am my husband's life as fully as he is mine. No woman was ever nearer to her mate than I am; ever more absolutely bone of his bone, and flesh of his flesh ... we are precisely suited in character – perfect concord is the result' (JE 384). Jane couches her fulfilment in mythical terms familiar from the Bible: marriage restores paradise lost with its emphasis on unity. Williams expresses this idea in the following fashion: 'the erotic fantasy organized around the Female Gothic hero reveals the structure of the Psyche myth. [Eros's] love promises to restore, in a different mode, the early, lost paradise of infancy' (156). In contrast, for Carter's lovers there exists neither a myth nor a community in which they could ever find a mutual(ly acceptable) mode of being. Yet nevertheless the strong bond between them suggests a passion of and for community that demands of them that they 'pass beyond every limit and every fulfilment enclosed in the form of an [immanent] individual' (Nancy, *Inoperative* 60).

Compearance refers to Nancy's notion of singularity as something that is in itself inherently plural. Simply put, Being is *being-with*; it is the 'with' that *constitutes* Being (instead of merely supplementing it). Being is *singular plural* (*Being* 30).[15] This concept overlaps with notions of alterity familiar from Lacanian psychoanalysis, according to which one appears to oneself as one is already an other for oneself. Yet the emphasis lies on being-with rather than on alterity as such. At the core of being is a primordial plurality that co-appears. Such compearance is 'not a question of coming out from a being-in-itself in order to approach others ... It is to be in the simultaneity of being-with, where there is no "in itself" that is not already immediately "with"' (*Being* 67–8). Carter's epiphanies arise from this insight of singular plurality: the characters are awakened to the 'with' in being that is not explicable in terms of 'I' or 'you' or a harmonious 'us.' Marianne, Fevvers, and Melanie have entertained the idea of 'hatching' their partners, of making the lover adopt their systems of understanding the world so that they could relate to him. Epiphany commits them to the 'with' in being as something that neither unifies nor reconciles. For example, Fevvers sings inwardly, for she is awakened to this awareness. Compearance, Nancy claims, puts singular beings in communication with one another because they appear to one another as singular beings – as an other irreducible to self, yet as someone with whom one shares being. This insight of the 'with' of being is contagious, because it awakens in a character the passion to be exposed to another, that is, to yield one's being to another, to place oneself in another's hands, without desiring a merger.[16] The difference to *Jane Eyre*, with its emphasis on a fusion of the lovers, could not be greater.

The conclusion of *Heroes and Villains* not only makes apparent the coercive power of a culture's myths, when the couple falls on the track the Bluebeard figure has laid out for them, but it also presents the link between maternity and female creativity in a new light. Lured by the prospect of power, Jewel rides off in order to become the 'Messiah of the Yahoos,' while Marianne, learning of his death, gives in to the same lure, deciding to become 'the tiger lady' who rules the tribe with 'a rod of iron' (HV 150; see also 144). In the end she unites creativity with motherhood, inscribing her role differently than Donally, for her encounter with the statue enables her to play a terrifying mother-goddess. Anne Williams treats the myth's conclusion – Psyche's immortality, marriage to Eros, and birth of their child – as so many signs of Psyche's access to the symbolic register. Carter criticizes this conclusion, for Marianne's ascension to the tribe's symbolic register means that she and her tiger child will perpetuate a violent and mystifying power structure together with a mythical mode of reasoning. Meaney sums up this view by stating that 'the renewal promised in the conclusion may be the establishment, not the removal, of a "repressive and authoritarian superstructure"' (quoted in Gamble 65). In this novel the female Gothic's valorization of family connections acquires a sinister hue, for it points back to the cyclical, mythical violence of the tribal culture of Freud's *Totem and Taboo*. Carter's contribution to Freud's analysis is to introduce the notion of the mother goddess into this mythical scheme, something that Freud ignored, because he could not fathom her relevance (Williams 132–3). The conclusion of *Heroes and Villains* suggests, however, that viewing this structure from the perspective of a myth such as 'Psyche' does not ameliorate a female artist's position. What is dangerous is forging creativity with sex and gender, for it invariably results in some sort of mother-goddess myth.[17]

Carter uses irony, exaggeration, and parody to highlight the impossibility of rectifying one myth with another. The epiphanies provide a fruitful starting point for exploring her alternative model of creativity, one that constitutes a break with the female Gothic, including Brontë's *Jane Eyre*. Carter's epiphanies suggest that what Nancy (*Inoperative* 47) calls the interruption of myth serves a key function in Carter's relationship to literary forebears. In this view, neither authorship nor the literary community (as a succession of literary generations) is based on myth. This reading implies that myth, including the myth of literature and of the author, represents the ultimate Covering Cherub with whom Carter contends. But does this struggle return her to myth, inevitably turning her into a mythographer?

## Myth as the Covering Cherub

Carter invariably depicts Bluebeard as a mythographer whose forbidden chamber stages what Nancy (*Inoperative* 44) calls the scene of myth. This space articulates the invention, recital, and transmission of myth, highlighting its role as a narrative of origins and an explanation of destinies. In Carter's 'Bluebeard' stories this scene of myth concerns sexual difference and its consequences. The mythographer Bluebeard positions woman as the specular opposite of man within the sexual economy of the same. Through the castration complex he forces on woman man's relation to the phallocratic origin (Lewis 228). Carter's Bluebeards seek the vengeful pleasure of absolute castration, which, in Lewis's words, 'punishes woman for abusing and contaminating man's protophallic image of his dominance' (236). Carter stresses myth's role in instituting community. She constructs claustrophobic households where an oppressive Bluebeard holds his family in an iron grip. The household's placement at the fringes of the community exposes the manner in which the myth of sexual difference sustains this community's normality. Bluebeard's household articulates an extreme version of this myth, and by so doing it suggests how the shares and divisions among the sexes within the community ought to be organized. In this sense myth addresses the community, who recognize one another in this myth, communicating and communing in its terms. Nancy claims that 'myth arises only from a community and for it: they engender one another, infinitely and immediately' (*Inoperative* 50). It includes a pact of recognition that says what myth is and says that we agree to say that this is. (For this reason myth is *tautegorical*, as it has nothing other to communicate than itself.) Through this mutual agreement myth communicates the *being-common* of what it reveals and recites (*Inoperative* 50).

The 'Bluebeard' tale, however, contests Bluebeard's mythography. His fantasy of masculinity collapses under its own impossibility, as first the woman, and then community, is awakened to the myth of sexual difference as a founding fiction (see Nancy, *Inoperative* 52–3). In 'Mr Fox' and 'The Robber Bridegroom' the fiancée's narrative of the bridegroom's cruelty interrupts myth by revealing to the community his perverse interpretation of sexual difference. Jolted into recognition of this fact, the community kills him. All variants of 'Bluebeard' culminate in this interruption.[18] Carter never fails to seize on this moment of collapse, during which '"*myth*" *is cut off from its own meaning, on its own meaning, by its own meaning*' (Nancy, *Inoperative* 52). In Carter's 'Bluebeard' stories this awakening takes place when the heroine becomes aware of Bluebeard's demand that she comply with his deadly desires, which leads her to recognize the mythical foundation she is supposed to accept. She understands that they share no common ground for being: Bluebeard's myth of sexual difference is not woman's foundation.

What does it mean to maintain that Carter seizes on the moment of myth's interruption? It means, as I now try to show, that the interruption of myth models her relationship to both readers and literary forebears. It is the 'system' governing her work – if we can talk of the interruption of myth as one. In order to make my argument concrete, I focus on one particular narrative strategy in her aesthetic arsenal: the grotesque, spectacular freak show. This choice is motivated by the fact that such a show tallies with how Bluebeard understands woman. In his chamber he represents her as a freak, a fact that Rochester's treatment of Bertha in *Jane Eyre* well exemplifies: 'What it was, whether beast or human being, one could not, at first sight, tell: it grovelled, seemingly, on all fours; it snatched and growled like some strange wild animal: but it was covered with clothing; and a quantity of dark, grizzled hair, wild as a mane, hid its head and face' (JE 250). Jane depicts

Bertha as an oddity, as a mongrel poised between categories, but she does not query the categories themselves, like Carter does. I discuss the basics of Carter's representational tactic by scrutinizing two examples, the Marquis's *enfer* in 'The Bloody Chamber' and the tattooed bodies in *Heroes and Villains*.

The Marquis displays the murdered wives as a freak tableau (BC 130–2): the first wife is placed on a catafalque, the second is strung from the ceiling, while the third is inside an Iron Maiden. Put on view in order to 'solve' woman's enigma by proclaiming the truth of castration as a fact of nature, this spectacular show ends up further mystifying sexual difference. The Marquis's setup betrays the impossibility of reaching his end. In searching for the proof of castration in a wife's body, he has strangled the opera singer, flayed the model, and pierced the Romanian countess. This 'artistic' correspondence between a wife's talent and her death only reveals the radical unknowability and impenetrability of her body, thanks to the fact that nature knows no castration. No natural law can prove castration; it can only be marked symbolically. Similarly, Donally turns the Barbarians into freaks by tattooing them, marking them as primitive, exotic, and bestial. Given that there is no direct access to bestiality or primitiveness, the result is, again, a body covered by language, a body that refuses to yield up its secrets. By using the representational technique of the grotesque freak show Carter highlights myth's role as a self-explanatory and self-enclosed system. The numerous freak tableaux in her fiction draw attention to the specific binary a given tableau is supposed to illuminate (such as man versus woman, life versus death, or human versus animal). In each instance, however, the binary illuminates the myth on which the tableau's existence depends as a tautegorical structure; it makes sense only in terms of the self-explanatory system of the given myth. This self-reflexive and critical approach to myth is missing from Brontë's *Jane Eyre*.

So far the focus has rested on Carter's fictional worlds, because understanding the interruption of myth in terms of mimetic illusion helps us to analyse its role and goals as regards narration and the relationship to literary forebears. Carter may be said to imitate Bluebeard's practice in that her narration makes ample use of the freak show. In this respect her 'Bluebeard' stories belong to the tradition of what Robin Blyn calls modernism's freak fictions. (Blyn identifies Djuna Barnes and Franz Kafka as significant practitioners.) Carter's narration focuses on the surfaces of bodies as they are put on display by the dynamics of spectacle. Borrowing Blyn's terms, we may say that Carter's 'Bluebeard' stories consist of strings of freak tableaux narrated by the voice of a *barker*. This narrative strategy interweaves *spiel* as the narrator's verbal and narrative performance with *tableau*, the fictional world presented as a series of freak shows. Within this framework, Blyn observes, narrative does not exist independently of the spectacular spiel performance. The intertextual density of Carter's 'Bluebeard' stories strengthens this interpretation of her narrators as barkers and of narration as a spiel performance. The interweaving of diverse textual materials creates a narration marked by the characteristics Blyn holds typical of spiel in modernist narrative fiction: 'exaggeration, exorbitant detail, rampant assertions, fraudulence, and claims to knowledge legitimated at different turns by science, theology, and mythology' (Blyn 139). It is in this role of barker that Carter's narrators approach the key binaries of the 'Bluebeard' tale such as the question of sexual difference, using the freak tableaux as the 'show case' with the help of which this difference is ostensibly tackled and explained.

This narrative strategy separates narration as spiel from the freak tableaux of the fictional world. It relies on the distance and distinction between characters and spectators (readers); the narrator's spiel sustains this separation (Blyn 136). We can use this distinctive distance in order to elaborate Carter's manner of interrupting myth. In *Nights at the Circus*, for example, the bird-woman Fevvers is a freak; as narrator her narration and speech are spiel. Her narrative performance addresses Jack Walser, and she maintains its purpose is to pass on knowledge about the boundary between human and animal. Although as narrator she dwells on her mysterious origins, she ends up articulating the self-imposed limits of narrative spiel. The excessiveness of her narration underlines the impenetrability of her body's surface as well as of the other bodies she narrates. Her aim is to throw light upon important boundaries, but she ends up mystifying them further, which, in turn, alerts Jack Walser – and readers – to the function of myth and mythical thinking within both the particular boundaries and the explanations accompanying them. Typically, the freak-show narrative spiels are rife with the essentialisms and the (quasi-)scientific language of various ideologies. They expand upon a cause-effect relation implicit in the freak displays. Carter uses the Western mytho-religious tradition and various critical discourses to explain the tableaux. Also, she employs fiction for this end by drawing on nameable authors as contexts that account for a given boundary. It would be wrong, I think, to say that the narrators' accounts explain nothing whatsoever. Rather, each narrator interrupts the explanation because it includes elements of mythical thinking. Nancy describes the basics of mythical thinking in the following manner: 'it consists in the thought of a poetico-fictioning ontology, an ontology presented in the figure of an ontogony where being engenders itself *by figuring itself*, by giving itself the proper image of its own essence and the self-representation of its presence and its present' (*Inoperative* 54). In Carter's case this means that narrators undermine the offered explanation, *before* it consolidates itself in a comprehensive auto-figuration – in a myth. For example, it was already mentioned that in 'The Bloody Chamber' the protagonist-narrator's return to mother remains ambiguous. The conclusion does not add up. The protagonist-narrator's marriage was partly motivated by her desire to separate from the mother. Does her return to home with her new lover (the piano tuner Jean-Yves) and life under mother's rule really represent a happy ending?

Carter's freak-show narrative strategy traces the temptation of explanatory systems to consolidate in myth. Making this temptation visible through narration as spiel and interrupting it prompts readers' epiphany in Carter's 'Bluebeard' stories. Is it the same as the characters' epiphany that we dealt with previously? The answer is, I think, twofold: readers are pushed to the limit as are characters, but the characters' epiphany is not the same as theirs. For one thing, readers are made aware that the endings are left open: we do not know, for example, whether in *Nights at the Circus* Fevvers and Jack Walser succeed in building their relationship on the insight of compearance; Lizzie strongly doubts it. Similarly, the narrator criticizes Marianne's return to myth in *Heroes and Villains;* and in *The Magic Toyshop* Finn may well be yet another Bluebeard (see Armitt). These open endings suggest that reading cannot ground itself in the mimetic illusion of fictional worlds. These worlds do not supply a new mythical foundation for readers: the characters' epiphanies offer them no shared model for building a better community, a new humanity, or a new subjectivity. While Gilbert and Gubar, for example, argue that a utopian vision characterizes the ending of *Jane Eyre*, Carter's open endings, in contrast, emphasize that readers cannot look for a message or a world view in her 'Bluebeard' stories.

It is the readers' awakened but disappointed expectation of a conclusive explanation to the freak show tableaux that carries them to the limit. This moment discloses neither a completed reality nor the reality of a completion. Rather, it reveals 'the mythless truth of ... being-in-common ... that is not a "common being" and that the community itself therefore does not limit and that myth is incapable of founding or containing' (Nancy, *Inoperative* 62). This difficult and obscure idea can be elucidated in the following fashion. Myth has nothing other to represent and communicate than itself. Literature has a stake and a principle beyond itself, because, by interrupting myth, it reaches beyond myth's self-enclosed auto-figuration and auto-communication. That literature arises from the singular relationship between singular beings precludes literature from consolidating itself in yet another myth. Writers and readers share literature on what Nancy calls the 'extreme and difficult limit.' Sharing exposes them to each other: it shows 'everyone's non-identity, each one's non-identity to himself and to others, and the non-identity of the work to itself and the non-identity of literature to literature' (*Inoperative* 66). Being-with cannot be given as a common experience, because no one experiences it in the same way. It opens itself up in a unique way to each and everyone, but its uniqueness does not rise from the individual as an immanent subject. Writers hear the passion inscribed in literature and they answer to it through their own writing. Literature courses through writers and readers; they leave on it their mark, but this mark does not originate in or belong to them. Literature inscribes being-with; that is, being for others and through others (*Inoperative* 66).

A good example of literature as a sharing of compearance in Carter's 'Bluebeard' stories is Mignon's song, 'Kensst du das Land wo die Blühmen bluhen,' in *Nights at the Circus*. When Mignon first performs it in the circus, the narrator relates it to a mythic scene: 'the Eden of our first beginnings, where innocent beasts and wise children play together under the lovely lemon trees, the tiger abnegates its ferocity, the child her cunning' (NC 155). The second time, Mignon sings it in Siberia; her voice makes native tigers congregate on the roof of the house where she is now living. On rehearing the song, the narrator reconsiders her previous interpretation: 'Mignon's song is *not* ... a plea,' the narrator states, 'she knows, oh! how well she knows [the land] lies somewhere, elsewhere, beyond the absence of flowers. She states the existence of that land and all she wants to know is, whether you know it, too' (NC 249). The land is not an Eden; it not a locatable place, but what Nancy calls an inavowable, mythless community. Although its members know of it, each interprets it in his or her way: 'when the tigers get up on their hind legs, they will make up their own dances – they wouldn't be content with the ones she'd teach them' (NC 250). This land brings humans and tigers together without inscribing being-with in a common model.

Mignon's song describes something that is happening to them in common. It is neither an origin nor an end, but something the participants share – but each in a different fashion. Nancy explains this sharing in the following way: 'we understand ourselves and the world by sharing this writing, just as the group understood itself by listening to the myth. Nonetheless, we understand only that there is no common understanding of community, that sharing does not constitute an understanding (or a concept, a schema), that it does not constitute a knowledge, and that it gives no one, including community itself, mastery over being-in-common' (*Inoperative* 69).

Given Carter's commitment to interrupting myth in her 'Bluebeard' stories, Bloom's mythical model of the anxiety of influence cannot describe her relationship to literary ancestors. For one thing, the interruption of myth interrupts the myth of the writer. The creativity Bloom (as well as Brontë) envisions is grounded in individual genius. The Bloomian writer believes he has the gift and the right to speak to, and on behalf of, his community who finds its being in his work. This is the standing Brontë herself would like to have. In contrast, Carter's authorship can fruitfully be related to a notion of the author whose writing is illegitimate, non-authorized, and risky, because it takes writers and readers to the limit where being-with is exposed (Nancy, *Inoperative* 70). This notion includes the writer as a unique, singular voice who inflects the plurality of being in a distinctive way in her writing. Further, the risk of writing arises from the author's refusal to deliver a founding speech; instead, the writer interrupts myth and mythical thinking and draws the reader's attention to this act. Paradoxically, as Nancy points out, there is something inaugural about such writing: 'It consists in coming to the limit, in letting the limit appear as such, in interrupting the myth. There is no sequel to it: this inaugural act founds nothing, entails no establishing, governs no exchange; no history of community is engendered by it' (*Inoperative* 68). Thus we can say that the interruption of myth does not make Carter a mythographer.

If there is no sequel to, and no exchange in, a writer's coming to the limit, how do we explain Carter's relationship to literary ancestors? Do writers experience an anxiety of influence? Taking my cue from Nancy, I would argue that anxiety is replaced by passion that is engendered by the author's experience of compearance at the limit. This experience orients the author toward the 'with' of being. Given that this plurality is both inside and outside of each singularity, passion turns the literary tradition into an arena of *sharing*, not of (Oedipal) struggle. An example elucidates this idea. Carter's freak-show narrative strategy and her freak tableaux are indebted to Djuna Barnes's *Nightwood* (1936). In order to elaborate on authorly relationships as taking place at the limit where singular beings share compearance, I briefly compare the ending of *Nightwood* with the endings of Carter's 'Bluebeard' stories.

*Nightwood* deals with Nora's anguished love for Robin. Tortured by Robin's rejection of her, Nora seeks counsel with their mutual friend, the sham doctor Matthew O'Connor. A long discourse on human nature and, specifically, Robin's nature, precedes the novel's ending. O'Connor's rich meditation is, as Blyn points out, undermined by the novel's final tableau in which Nora witnesses the meeting of Robin and Nora's dog. This grotesque sight makes Nora collapse on the floor. In this tableau, Blyn explains, 'Robin and the dog are poised for the very beast/woman embrace that defines Robin as a freak. In the end, the "beast turning human" comes to us as a picture of the "human turning beast," an evolutionary regression violently enacted' (Blyn 153). Rendered beyond knowledge and beyond possession, Robin's freedom, Blyn maintains, is purchased at the price of her exotic objectification (Blyn 153–4). This experience of the limit into which the interruption of myth pushes the readers of *Nightwood* emphasizes the freak's impenetrability. Robin is totally inaccessible to both Nora and readers. In contrast, Carter inscribes being at the limit in a different manner. Let us take 'The Fall River Axe Murders' as an example. Patricide isolates Lizzie Borden from her community; others see her as a mad freak. The story's narrator, however, shows compassion for Lizzie's despair, an empathy readers readily share, while it is also clear that Lizzie's story is neither the narrator's nor the reader's story. Yet both can experience some of the anguish Lizzie feels at her father's hands. If Barnes emphasizes impenetrability at the limit where she pushes readers, Carter typically leaves leeway for compassion and love. These two writers inscribe being at the limit in a different way, yet both are committed to safeguarding the passion that sustains writing.

In concluding, I want to return to the question of gender, because I believe it plays a role in the interruption of myth, although not in terms of a writer's androgyny, bisexuality, hetero- or homosexuality. Nancy observes that Freud's second model of psyche's construction (the mutual determination of id, ego, and superego) comes close to his notion of being-with, as does also Lacanian theory of significance, 'insofar as it does not bring about a return to signification [the symbolic Other], but a mutually instituting correlation of "subjects"' (*Being* 44–5). Nancy seems to allude here to Lacan's concept of *l'être de la signifiance* that Bruce Fink (*Lacanian* 119) translates as *signifierness*. This clumsy notion refers to the fact that the signifier's existence exceeds its significatory role: its substance surpasses its symbolic function, which is to signify. Lacan associates being with signifierness, the material, non-signifying face of the signifier. It has effects without signifying: *jouissance* effects (Fink, *Lacanian* 119). Another way of putting this idea is to say that this concept alludes to the signifier's existence beyond and outside of sense-making. Bounded by the paternal function, the masculine structure applies to the old notion of concentric circles, while the feminine structure is different, for the opposition between inside and outside is inapplicable to it. It is an open set that does not include its own boundary (*Lacanian* 124–5). The Other *jouissance* associated with signifierness stands apart from both the symbolic and symbolic castration. We can discern a place for it within our symbolic order, and even name it, but it nevertheless remains unspeakable. The Other *jouissance* is incommensurate, unquantifiable, and disproportionate (*Lacanian* 122). As I have argued, Carter draws on this notion of feminine structure and of signifierness in her fiction. It is there that we can look for new ways of dealing with sexual difference – and of being – that are not grounded in myth and mythical thinking. In trying to find a new language for passion, sexuality, and being, Carter pays homage to what she thought was the mutual goal of the Brontë sisters, yet she does so in a manner which breaks into alien territory that neither of her precursors could quite imagine.

# Conclusion: A Way Out

Tatar observes that 'one of the fatal effects of the Bluebeard story has to do with its habit of inspiring fascination and imitation rather than intervention and adaptation' ('Bluebeard's' 18). One of the guiding ideas of this book is the notion that the particular discursive layer which an author emphasizes has a decisive shaping influence on her or his adaptation. It is the chosen discursive register that largely accounts for the working of what I call the Brontë effect on a given adaptation of *Jane Eyre* as Bluebeard Gothic. When an author focuses on the symbolic register, her or his approach is closer to emulation and homage than to contestation. This is understandable, as the symbolic discourse emphasizes self-identity, control of signification, and cohesion. This observation applies even though an author introduces changes to the adapted text. Obvious examples in this book's corpus are Emma Tennant's *Adèle* and Diane Setterfield's *The Thirteenth Tale*. Tennant revises *Jane Eyre*'s point of view by shifting it to Adèle and elucidates characters and their actions with added hypothetical motivation. She also changes emphases, fills in gaps, and even alters certain key events. Setterfield, for her part, makes the Bluebeard Gothic legacy relevant to present-day audiences through updating. Yet their alterations are mostly embellishments, additions, and enlargements. Although Tennant criticizes Brontë for treating Rochester's ward dismissively and with prejudice, her book nevertheless reads like fan fiction. *Jane Eyre* still exerts influence on these adapting texts as a beloved national classic. Setterfield portrays Bluebeard Gothic as including the resources for containing Gothic excesses within its generic arsenal. This self-correcting ability of the genre largely accounts for its ability to lift readers above mundane concerns by immersing them in a good read. As the standing and value of *Jane Eyre* are neither questioned nor contested, its cultural status is reinforced in such rewritings. Having never really cut the umbilical cord, it is as if daughters fondly teased the mother about the latter's endearing foibles. Simultaneously such adapting texts attempt to gain increase in cultural capital by benefiting from the adapted work's cultural cachet (Hutcheon 91).

Another case altogether is exemplified by Leonowens's *Romance of the Harem*, which begins with a strong conviction in the appropriateness of the familial ideology only to realize its fatal flaws. An eager proponent of maternal imperialism like Charlotte Brontë and Jane Eyre – an ideology that consists of a mix of domesticity, feminism, and imperialism – Leonowens finds that this doctrine does not and cannot perform its task far away from home in the Siamese harem. It is the author's personal experience that compels her to question the underpinnings of the adapted text. What makes this book interesting is the fact that British imperialism, implicitly present in *Jane Eyre*, received very early its first sustained criticism, and that this critique came from a person whose initial stance toward the ideology Brontë relies on was favourable. In the family terms evoked here, Leonowens's book illustrates what can happen when a family member awakens to the shortcomings and inadequacies of her inherited legacy.

As is to be expected, adaptations prizing either the hysteric or analytical discursive layers of *Jane Eyre* typically highlight gaps, absences, and silences within it, which they then portray as troubling, even dangerous. Whenever authors hear the hysteric's questioning of the master's discourse, they are alerted to the interrogation of authority. As we have seen, the hysteric's basic query concerns gender identity: she is vexed by the question whether she is a man or a woman. In extension, employing the hysteric's discourse involves adapting authors to probe all those categories that an adapted text presents as organizing and subtending its signification system. In other words, the terms of operation of the adapted text are placed under scrutiny, probed, and contested. One might characterize this approach as one of wavering between categories and upturning them. Sanders points out that adaptations often have a joint political and literary investment, which typically emerges through the strategy of giving voice to those characters and subject positions that have been oppressed or repressed in the adapted text (19, 98). As the analyses in this book demonstrate, such critical strategies often arise from the adapting authors' experience of the adapted text as harmful, even traumatic. In these cases, the precursor text is seen to exert a damaging influence on culture by perpetuating, for example, questionable ideologies such as racism and imperialism. Many reinterpretations of *Jane Eyre* aim at exposing its questionable tenets as well as correcting them. Examples in this book's corpus include du Maurier's *Rebecca* and Waters's *Fingersmith*. *Rebecca* tackles *Jane Eyre*'s romantic assumptions, throwing doubt on Bluebeard's capacity and willingness to reform; instead, he is shown to be in the grips of deadly repetition that caricatures as love. *Fingersmith* also targets the novel's rendition of love. While it endorses the precursor's view of love's power of overcoming obstacles and providing transcendence, it contests the heterosexual orientation of such love.

Whenever adapting authors listen to the analytic layer of discourse in *Jane Eyre*, they are prone to explore the ways in which the precursor text meets the enjoyment feeding it, on one hand, and, on the other, misses its own meaning. This discursive layer remains always only partly heard, thanks to our inability to know and articulate fully the psychic dynamic that moves us and our texts. Adaptations such as Winterson's *Oranges Are Not the Only Fruit* and Carter's 'Bluebeard' tales consider the ways in which the Other's desire has shaped *Jane Eyre*. If an author's desire to write springs from her private and idiosyncratic experience of what Lacanian psychoanalysis calls the *objet a*, then no shared system can adequately express it. Writing, narrating, and reading can nevertheless be regarded as a persistent search for this object. Adaptors seizing on the analytic dimension consider the influence the symbolic system exerts on the adapted narrative together with its narrator's and author's way of dealing with this influence. Simultaneously, as the examples of Winterson and Carter show, these adaptors also probe how the precursor's novel feeds their own desire. In other words, these authors consider how *Jane Eyre* serves as a cause for their desire to write. To what extent are their aesthetic and ideational goals shaped by Brontë? Adrienne Rich exhorts women authors not only to know the writing of the past but also to know it differently from the ways in which this canon has been known before. In Rich's view, the purpose of gaining such knowledge is not to pass on a tradition but to break its hold over us (quoted in Sanders 9). While Rich refers to the stranglehold of the male literary canon on female writers, the corpus of this study shows that the classics of women's literature may also clothe successors in a straitjacket. In fact, Winterson's and Carter's examinations of the analytic discourse of *Jane Eyre* appear to lead to the conclusion that now is the time to move on: new times call for new artistic solutions.

Characterizing adaptations of *Jane Eyre* in terms of the discourse that governs the rewriting appears to suggest a concomitant aesthetic evaluation: the texts that prize symbolic discourse seem to score lower points than the other two. To some extent this is true; yet all studied texts certainly have merits. Hutcheon observes that unsuccessful adaptations often lack creativity and skill to make the adapted text one's own and thus autonomous (Hutcheon 20). This observation does not say, however, what appropriation and autonomy mean. The novels by Tennant and Setterfield can certainly be read as autonomous works in the sense that understanding and enjoying them does not require knowledge of *Jane Eyre*. Rather, it appears that they are weaker aesthetically than some other of the studied adaptations thanks to their authors' reluctance to deal in earnest with the thematic structures they borrow from Brontë. Both authors are aware of the criticism that has been levelled against *Jane Eyre*, but it is evoked only to be laid to rest without serious engagement.

Griselda Pollock ponders the staying power of 'Bluebeard' in cultural imagination, questioning whether it is explained by the tale's representation of masculinity as the psychological puzzle of desire linked to violence. Or does the tale fascinate us thanks to its representation of curious femininity as a necessary byproduct of patriarchal culture? Then again, she muses, perhaps the explanation lies in the tale's staging of the enigma of heterosexual difference as thrown into relief by marriage, the heterosexual social contract par excellence (xxviii). The adaptations discussed in this book, considered in light of the primary psychic fantasies, add yet another significant reason to Pollock's list. These fantasies emphasize that a subject processes his or her standing within a family by relating himself or herself to both parental figures: growing up involves dealing with mother and father. It is in keeping with this scenario that the figure serving as Bluebeard may, in fact, be either a man or a woman. *Jane Eyre* and the adaptations studied show that gender is not necessarily decisive, but a character's real or imagined position in a subject's life. Thus Tatar's interpretation of 'Bluebeard' as dealing with the dangers of sexual relationships that involve a threatening male and a timid female does not apply to all texts in this book's corpus (*Secrets*). A mother or some other authoritative female may just as well occupy the structural place and function of Bluebeard as happens in Winterson's and Waters's novels. In fact, flexibility about who threatens the protagonist's sense of self, including sexual identity, is typical of the Gothic, as Claire Kahane shows. Thus women also act as Bluebeards intent on trapping and sacrificing other women in order to reach various goals. Often the Gothic heroine must work through a contentious relationship to her precursor, usually a mother or the husband's former wife. Although at times female Bluebeards identify with the patriarchal position of male power, they by no means do so uniformly. For example, Aunt Reed in *Jane Eyre* installs herself in Uncle Reed's place, misusing his power, but in *Fingersmith* Mrs Sucksby operates on the basis of what she thinks are worthwhile aims in life. The lines are thus not drawn according to sex and gender but according to structural function and positions of power. Whenever characters have power over another, it opens up the possibility that they may use it in ways turning them into Bluebeard. Thus Bluebeard Gothic may fascinate us thanks to its dramatizing the perverted workings of power.

Another noteworthy finding concerns the question of who exactly is the heroine of 'Bluebeard' and *Jane Eyre*. The tale variants laud the latest wife (or fiancée) for courage and cleverness, as does Brontë by giving centre stage to Jane. Over the years the adaptations, however, have begun to shift the focus from the successor to the predecessor. Bluebeard's first wife, portrayed by Bertha in *Jane Eyre*, has gradually emerged as the true heroine: she has been wronged and abused, but has remained courageous and unyielding. Simultaneously the successor has begun to seem shady, if not downright mad. Adaptations have also changed the contemporary readership's approach to *Jane Eyre* by permanently affecting our perspective on it. In particular, as Sanders (158) points out, it is difficult to forget Jean Rhys's postcolonial appropriation of this novel. Indeed, Rhys's critique and feminist interpretations of *Jane Eyre* seem to play a role in almost all adaptations after the publication of *Wide Sargasso Sea*.

It is in keeping with Charlotte Brontë's mythic status as a canonical author that multiple and contradictory adaptations of *Jane Eyre* exist at the same time in the same cultural space (see Hutcheon xiii). What Sanders says of another canonical author, William Shakespeare, applies equally well to Brontë: the cultural value of such writers lies in their availability. Each new generation redefines them in contemporary terms, typically projecting its desires and anxieties onto their work. This strategy makes old texts fit new cultural contexts and different political ideologies than those of the author's own age (see also Schaff 34–5). Pollock expresses this same idea by observing that the narrative structure of 'Bluebeard' 'allows for endlessly renewed social and historical materials to find imaginative form through the limitless potential of its highly symbolic and freighted elements' (xxviii). Consequently, Brontë is constantly being remade by this process. To be sure, adaptations reinforce her position in the canon, but at each time it is a different Brontë that is at work (see Sanders 46, 48). The author's mutability indicates unfinished cultural business in the sense of continuing historical relevance. Yet as we have seen, some adaptations do suggest the need to leave the adapted text behind as either outmoded or unsuitable for the present age. Yet even then the adaptation cannot help but keep the adapted text alive. This process explains how *Jane Eyre* as Bluebeard Gothic 'has changed, created new versions of itself, and joined up with other stories to become yet other stories' (Tatar, *Secrets* 7).

# Notes

## Introduction

1 Variants of the 'Bluebeard' tale were in widespread circulation in Western
cultures long before their appearance in print. They are known to have
been disseminated, for example, in England, France, Italy, Germany, and
the Scandinavian countries. Often these oral tales are known in numerous variants. For example, Hermansson (17) mentions that the Norwegian
version, 'The Hen Is Tripping in the Mountain,' has been collected in fifty-
four variants. Tatar (*Secrets* 14) says that this tale found its way to Africa,
India, and the West Indies via trade routes. It is generally held that Charles
Perrault's 'La Barbe Bleue' in his *Histoires et contes du temps passé* (1697)
provides the first written version of the tale, followed by the variants
included in the *Kinder- und Hausmärchen* (1812) by the Brothers Grimm.
'Blaubart' was, however, dropped from the 1819 and later editions of
*Kinder- und Hausmärchen* because it was deemed too violent and too mark-
edly a French tale. It has been included in Ruth Michaelsi-Jena and Arthur
Radcliff's (ed. and trans.) *Grimms' Other Tales: A New Selection by Wilhelm
Hansen* (Edinburgh: Canongate, 1989) and in Jack Zipes's (ed. and trans.)
*The Complete Fairy Tales of the Brothers Grimm* (3rd ed. New York: Bantam,
2003). 'La Barbe Bleue' was translated into English in 1729 by Robert Samber; it was later included in one of Andrew Lang's widely circulated fairy-
tale collections, *The Blue Fairy Book* (1889; ed. Brian Alderson. New York:
Penguin, 1987). 'Mister Fox' and 'Mister Fox's Courtship' are included, for
example, in an edition by Katherine M. Briggs, *Dictionary of British Folktales
in the English Language* (Part A, vol. 2. London: Routledge, 1970). The variants included in Briggs's edition have been reprinted in *The Virago Book
of Fairy Tales* (London: Virago, 1990) and in *The Second Virago Book of Fairy*

*Tales* (London: Virago 1992), both edited by Angela Carter. The latter also includes an American 'Hillbilly' version of 'Mr Fox,' called 'Old Foster.' Hermansson and Tatar (*Secrets*) both provide an overview of the tale variants and their publication venues.

It has been claimed that the character of Bluebeard has a real-life counterpart in the fifteenth-century French nobleman Gilles de Laval Rais, a lieutenant of Jean d'Arc. Also other cruel historical persons have been assigned this role. In addition, many serial killers have been likened to Bluebeard, thanks to his serial femicide. Hermansson supplies information on these real-life connections.

2 One of the best discussions of *Jane Eyre* in this Gothic context is Michelle Massé's *In the Name of Love: Women, Masochism, and the Gothic*. Although most narratives Massé analyses are 'Bluebeard' tales, she never explicitly associates them with this tale cycle.

3 After its first publication, *Jane Eyre* has never been out of print (Schaff 25).

4 Shuli Barzilai argues that *Genesis Rabbah*, the midrashic commentary of the Book of Genesis, has significantly contributed to our understanding of the story of the Fall as a precursor of the 'Bluebeard' tale (see her ch. 1).

5 Thackeray's wife, Isabella, had suffered from a severe mental breakdown after the birth of their second child and she needed custodial care until her death. Later on, Thackeray fell passionately in love with an unhappily married woman called Jane Brookfield. Brontë was unaware of these similarities her novel shared with Thackeray's personal life and thus of the consternation her dedication caused him (Barzilai, 51–4 and fn18, 162).

6 In order to avoid confusion, I refer to the tale cycle by speaking of 'Bluebeard,' while when this name is used without quotation marks it refers to the tale's male protagonist.

7 Charlotte Brontë made her authorship public in her 'Biographical Notice of Ellis and Acton Bell,' published when she put out a new edition of *Wuthering Heights* and *Agnes Grey* in order to honour her dead sisters. Caroline Levine argues that Charlotte Brontë's pseudonym presented a case of literary cross-dressing – a woman posing as a man posing as a woman – the purpose of which was to make her audience consider their ideas and prejudices about authorship. If readers thought Currer Bell was a male author, then what were they to make of the unusually intimate description of a woman's mind? If, however, they wagered that the pseudonym hid a female author, how were they to respond to the book's 'coarseness' and passion? Levine concludes that the pseudonym enabled Charlotte Brontë to achieve emancipation from the confining trappings of both genders (Levine ch. 3).

8 There are transmedial adaptations of *Jane Eyre* as a 'Bluebeard' tale, for example, Jane Campion's movie *Piano* (1993), artist Paula Rego's *Jane Eyre: A Suit of 25 Lithographs* (Marlborough Graphics, 2003), and Polly Teale's two plays, *Jane Eyre* (London: Nick Hern, 1998) and *After Mrs Rochester* (London: Nick Hern, 2003).

9 Tatar's book compiles a useful and instructive sample of these versions.

10 Jane's letter reaches Uncle Eyre while Richard Mason is visiting him. These two men act the role of the heroine's brothers by intervening in Rochester's bigamous plans at the last minute. In so doing they protect both Bertha and Jane.

## 1 *Jane Eyre* as a 'Bluebeard' Tale

1 For similar scenes, see *Jane Eyre* (242, 253, 272).

2 Bronfen holds such a correspondence between physical spaces and mental states typical of Gothic heroines: 'The mind becomes a stage for phantasmatic presences at the same time that the somatic conversion of a psychic disturbance allows this mental phantom zone to be projected onto an external stage, so that the social space within which the hysterical heroine wanders emerges as the scene where unconscious phantasies can be materialised' (155).

3 Nothing explains why Jane narrates her tale at this particular moment. One possible reason has to do with the letter she has received from St John Rivers, in which he writes of his approaching death in missionary service in India. The novel concludes with St John's words welcoming Christ to take him to heavenly home. Written from a death bed, this letter serves as a powerful reminder of human vulnerability and mortality. Although St John and Jane believe in afterlife, as human beings they nevertheless die in and to this world. One may speculate that this letter provokes Jane to reminiscence about her past.

4 In examining Jane's and Rochester's red-room experiences I lean heavily on Bronfen's analysis of the fantasies with the help of which the hysteric attempts to deal with her psychic pain. It needs to be noted that Bronfen herself relies on Žižek's interpretation of Lacan in his *Looking Awry* (especially ch. 7). By drawing on both these studies, I hope to show Brontë's extensive use of the Gothic legacy in *Jane Eyre*. What is particularly striking in this novel is the unusually consistent manner in which psychic turmoil is projected onto external spaces, furnishings, and even objects.

5 Verhaeghe explains that 'these fantasies are constructed from a combination of things which have been experienced, heard, past events (history of

parents and ancestors), and things seen by oneself. The phylogenetic heritage is the family story into which the child is born, in which it already had a place before it was actually born, and in which it grows up' (162). Thanks to the child's slow maturation process, it has limited means of understanding gender identity and sexual relationships.

6  Thus the navel is, like the phallus, devoid of any direct reference to bodily reality (Bronfen 11).

7  Bronfen claims that behind hysteria is death anxiety, not sexual scenarios. Hysteric symptoms are protective shields with whose help the subject tries to ward off the traumatic knowledge of mortality (16–17).

8  The doleful ballad of the orphan child expresses Jane's situation, as her only conceivable home is with God: 'Still will my Father, with promise and blessing, / Take to his bosom the poor orphan child ... Heaven is a home, and a rest will not fail me; / God is a friend to the poor orphan child' (JE 18).

9  *Jane Eyre* alludes to an unsuccessful developmental trajectory during which 'a wild boy indulged from childhood upwards' (JE 185) fails to separate from the mother by subordinating to the father. This failure owes to the malfunction of the paternal figure.

10  As Rapaport points out, Bertha's name may ironically refer to (giving) birth. Ideally, she should give birth to Rochester's heir.

11  The pistols as emblems of the symbolic father emerge more clearly when Rochester's situation in Jamaica is related to a later incident. Finding out about the infidelity of one of his mistresses, he challenges his rival to a duel with pistols (JE 120–3). Rochester defends his honour according to accepted customs. Although keeping a mistress and getting embroiled in amorous tangles is not morally commendable, such relations are tolerated within Rochester's social circles (JE 147). This association of the pistol as an emblem of the symbolic father is also elaborated in Brontë's *The Professor* (1857). The protagonist-narrator William Crimsworth shoots his son's dog because it has been bit by a rabid dog. The son accuses the father: 'Oh, papa, I'll never forgive you! ... I never believed you could be so cruel – I can love you no more!' (*Professor* 252). The father explains the necessity of the act, and, after having been comforted by the mother, the boy 'came to me in my library, asked if I forgave him, and desired to be reconciled' (253). The novel's ending deals with the upbringing of William's son Victor and stresses the necessity of a boy's separation from the mother and his submission to the law of the father.

12  Rochester's transportation of Bertha to Thornfield supports the notion of her as his traumatic core. He could have provided for Bertha at Jamaica, or

he could have installed her with a nurse, for example, in some cottage far away from Thornfield. John Sutherland, for his part, wonders why Rochester did not place Bertha in one of the progressive asylums that were changing the treatment of the mentally ill in England in Brontë's time (69–70).

13 The pervert identifies with the imaginary object of his mother's desire, insofar as she herself symbolizes it in the phallus, not as a displaceable symbol, however, but as an unsymbolized and undisplaceable object. The pervert's lot is to be this imaginary phallus for her (Fink, *Lacanian* 175–6).

14 Hearing Adèle recite and looking at her dance, Jane is actually hearing and seeing Céline Varens, for Adèle has been carefully trained by Céline (JE 87).

15 Jane freely confesses that she does not understand enigmas and 'never could answer riddles in [her] life' (JE 168). As narrator, Jane highlights her density by foregrounding the younger Jane's timidity in drawing conclusions from Rochester's behaviour so that readers have an advantage over her in this respect.

16 Brontë is among the first novelists to make Bluebeard's sexuality an explicit issue. Davies remarks that it was only from the late nineteenth century onward that Bluebeard was associated with a potent, sexualized, and dangerous masculinity. Consequently, his murders were also understood as sexual in nature (Davies, 'Bluebeard' 39).

17 After bringing the house party to Thornfield, Rochester pushes Jane back into her familiar place of social exclusion, the window recess, from which he makes her watch his wooing of Blanche. Privately, however, Rochester continues to make Jane sit by his side, querying whether such placement is right (JE 145, 150, 155, 174, 185). This game of musical chairs confounds Jane, feeding the key question of her life: What should I be like to be loved? The situation is distressing, for the evening conferences led her to believe she was able to gauge Rochester's desire (JE 159). Jane cannot be secure in her assessment, however, for Rochester's stories about his escapades verify his sexual knowledge, identifying a different type of woman from Jane as the object of his desire.

18 At Gateshead Jane's family is a forbidden subject, for Jane's mother 'married down' in spite of her father's disapproval. The public story proclaims the benevolence of the Reeds, who provide for Jane, while stressing the inappropriateness of Jane's parents. The illicit nature of Jane's family legacy compels her to turn to the phantom romance associated with the Father-of-Enjoyment in order to construct clandestine knowledge about her origins.

19 On the eve of their wedding Rochester promises to reveal the secret in the future: 'I see you would ask why I keep such a woman in my house: when

we have been married a year and a day, I will tell you; but not now' (JE 243). This is the time period for fulfilment of various legal contracts as well as the conventional period for fairy-tale spells (*Jane Eyre* 243, fn3).

20 Presumably, Rochester plans to return to Thornfield after the honeymoon, in which case he himself, Jane, and Grace would be wedded to keeping the secret. This situation entails what Dor (145) calls a harvest of enjoyment, for all the parties involved know the secret, but no one can confess. Guilt shifts around; everyone is infected by it, but each must act as if he or she did not know about it. The pervert's aim in setting up this structure is to evade submission to the law (castration).

21 In contrast to Rochester's passionate wooing, Jane is reticent in physical and verbal expressions of love. To be sure, this strategy stems from her sense of propriety, but it is also closely related to hysteria. The hysteric seeks to keep her desire unsatisfied; she takes pleasure in simply being able to want it and in depriving herself of it. She has a wish for an unsatisfied wish (Fink, *Clinical* 126). Jane must keep Rochester's desire alive, not allowing him to garner too much satisfaction: 'Desire is sustained [in the person who incarnates the Other for the hysteric] only by the lack of satisfaction [the hysteric] gives him by slipping away as object' (Lacan, quoted in and modified by Fink 126). By orchestrating the circuit, Jane becomes master of the Other's desire – the cause of his desire – yet simultaneously she attempts to avoid being the person with whom he satisfies his desire. In other words, she keeps his desire unsatisfied in order to avoid being the object of his enjoyment (126).

22 Aunt Reed's confession contains new pieces of information about Jane's parents and her early childhood that help Jane to reconstruct the story of her origin (JE 197–8).

23 Again, Brontë provides an explanation for the woman's rescue, while in 'Bluebeard' the brothers simply appear on the scene. 'Magical help,' writes Menninghaus, 'disregards motivation and realism of the helping figure's powers, that is precisely what makes magical help in fairy tales probable, indeed "natural"' (66).

24 John Eyre is too ill to travel to Thornfield, so he sends a solicitor and Richard Mason to defend Jane. Soon afterwards, the Uncle dies. It is his death that confirms the existence of a dead symbolic Father for Jane; that is, the viability of the symbolic order.

25 In Bertha Jane faces the nauseous object she most fears (social annihilation), which explains why she cannot look at her. Being (socially) dead, Bertha, however, has no difficulty in looking at Jane.

26 That the famished Jane lands at the footsteps of her paternal cousins is a magical event straight out of fairy tale. Nothing has prepared us for it; the narrative logic, however, demands it if Jane is to find about her own family, receive her legacy, and be in the position to marry Rochester on her own terms (as an independent woman).

27 Right before Bertha's death Thornfield in its entirety has become an asylum-prison for two lunatics: Bertha and Rochester. His isolation and nighttime wanderings make him indistinguishable from her. Perhaps, then, by setting the place on fire, Bertha attempts to establish a double suicide as a grand finale to a thoroughly destructive marriage.

## 2 Testifying to Bluebeard's Atrocities: The Woman (Author) as Witness

1 Tuptim's case moves Leonowens so that she faints watching Tuptim suffer (RH 39). On waking up, she feels as if she were entombed alive. Her reaction recalls Bluebeard's latest wife, who almost faints from fright when she sees the contents of the bloody chamber.

2 Zlotnick explains the impact of maternal imperialism in this scene by observing that Leonowens presents her intervention as 'a moral reflex, one presumably arising from her domestic nature. It is this moral reflex which distinguishes her from the quiescent Siamese women attending the trial' (45).

3 For example, Leonowens communicates her empathy to the slave woman L'Ore by sitting by her side and asking kindly about the woman's child. She wins the woman's confidence by addressing her as follows: '"My sister," I said, "tell me your whole story, and I will lay it before the king"' (RH 47).

4 Linda Marie Brooks observes that typically *testimonio* records the witness's body language, apparel, surroundings, and so on, in order to provide information about the stage on which the act of giving testimony takes place. These details interact with the actual words of the witness, conveying a fuller picture, for example, of the consequences of her or his suffering (such as fatigue or vulnerability). *Testimonio* is thus a performance-based form of writing.

5 See also Joyce Zonana's similar argument in her 'The Sultan and the Slave: Feminist Orientalism and the Structure of *Jane Eyre*.' Zonana relates Brontë's views on the Orient to ideas put forth by Western feminists such as Mary Wollstonecraft.

6 Brooks emphasizes that *testimonio* is neither journalism nor legal testimo-

ny. It emerges through intercultural exchange, and its aim is to make available 'enactments of broader truths – performances of the dialogical process by which truths originate' (183).

7  I am aware of the importance of Rhys's decision to leave the male protagonist nameless. As Müller (70) points out, namelessness emphasizes the fact that this character is simply not to be identified with Brontë's Rochester, although he is obviously derived from Brontë's novel.

8  Sharon Wilson characterizes *Wide Sargasso Sea* as 'a dark postmodern and postcolonial metafairy tale' that shows 'Cinderella's' shadow side, the 'Bluebeard' or 'Fitcher's Bird' story (111).

9  In this instance, repetition corresponds with the notions of acting-out and melancholia, pathological responses to loss which seek to incorporate the other into the self as an act of preservation (Whitehead 86–7).

10  In this aspect repetition relates to the notions of working-through and mourning. It represents the discharging of emotion cathected to loss and the subsequent reformulation of the past (Whitehead 87).

11  Christophene explains Antoinette by saying that 'she is not *béké* like you, but she is *béké*, and not like us either' (WSS 128). Susan Meyer (98–9) observes that in Brontë's day the designation 'Creole' was ambiguous, because it could refer to either blacks or whites. While Brontë associates Bertha with blacks in order to underline her racial inferiority as regards the white Rochester, Rhys, in contrast, emphasizes that Bertha is neither.

12  Antoinette identifies the long stretch of poverty, loneliness, and Annette's realization that Antoinette was growing up like 'a white nigger' (WSS 109) as reasons for Annette's frenzied attempt to change their lives by remarrying. Antoinette also tells Rochester of her love for Coulibri, of being aware of the malicious gossip about her family, and about the 'cool, teasing eyes' with which they were viewed after the mother's remarriage. She recounts the traumatic incidents leading to the break-up between Annette and Mr Mason, Annette's total rejection of her, and subsequent madness. She even discloses to Rochester Annette's sexual abuse in the hands of her so-called caretakers.

13  Antoinette associates the white dress with her recurring nightmare, her mother (WSS 23, 51), as well as the 'breathless and savage desire' (WSS 78) it has once evoked in Rochester. In her mind these associations blend into a thematic dealing with (sexual) innocence, defloration, and threat of bodily and psychic harm.

14  Winterhalter (224–5) claims that Rochester actually narrates the section attributed to Antoinette. She justifies this argument by referring to the desperation of her voice in this part in comparison to the more controlled

voice in the other parts. Rochester's ventriloquism reveals how he remembers and imagines Antoinette's speech. Through such narrative embedding, argues Winterhalter, he underlines Antoinette's desire for him and the extremes to which she is willing to go to retain his affections. However, as Antoinette's embedded narrative refers to her present conditions at England (WSS 92) and specific childhood memories, it seems unlikely that Rochester would be acquainted with such details. Therefore, I interpret the embedded narrative as Antoinette's and regard the narrative design of Part Two as the (implied) author's doing.

15 Erwin (146, 153) links this pattern to novelistic conventions. The shift to Rochester's voice in Part Two suggests that Antoinette's own narrative is ended, having reached in marriage its proper nineteenth-century conclusion; however, as the marriage does not work out, the continuation of her narrative signals the two other options available to women: madness and death. Erwin remarks that Rochester's narrative serves as the copula uniting Antoinette's two narratives; this pattern may be written out as 'Marriage equals death,' an equation certainly not alien to 'Bluebeard.'

16 The comparison of woman with a bird echoes 'Fitcher's Bird,' and Brontë and Rhys play on this association. Frequently likened to a bird, Jane flies away from Thornfield in the dead of the night. In *Wide Sargasso Sea*, Rochester sings an old song to Antoinette: 'Hail to the queen of the silent night, Shine bright, shine bright Robin as you die' (WSS 70), an ominous lyric foreshadowing Antoinette's fate. Further, in this novel Mr Mason clips the wings of Annette's pet parrot, causing its death in the Coulibri fire. Later on, Annette identifies with this bird (WSS 39); in the end Antoinette too envisions herself as a bird, one who is then ready to fly away from Thornfield (WSS 155).

17 Whitehead characterizes the interpersonal witness's task in the following way: 'Interpersonal witnesses walk a tightrope: they must understand enough so that the traumatized person may convey a forgotten and excluded history while they must also take care not to understand too much lest the disruptive and resistant force of such traumatic historicity be lost' (160).

18 In 'Mr Fox' and 'The Robber Bridegroom' the groom asks the bride to visit his house in the forest. The fairy tale does not dwell on the bride's motives for visiting: she goes because she's been asked to and because her father has promised her to this man. Antoinette's dream follows this same logic.

19 Sharon Wilson observes that indigenous versions of 'Bluebeard' and 'Fitcher's Bird' are known in the West Indies (120, n10). Yet this tale is activated only with the arrival of the British colonists.

20 Much critical attention has been lavished on the ending of *Wide Sargasso Sea*, and critics differ on the nature and meaning of Antoinette's fate. Some argue that *Jane Eyre* preordains Antoinette to burn down Thornfield. Harrison, for example, thinks that while Rhys writes her way out of Brontë's text, Antoinette does not: she must remain, even if her story manages to get out. Antoinette must fulfil what Brontë has ordained for her (Harrison 147, 168). Sandra Drake, in contrast, argues that Antoinette carrying the candle is 'keeper, mistress and protector of the divine flame that brings freedom – [she] becomes a fit "daughter" of Christophene' (202). As death is understood in the Caribbean as another form of life, the ending marks Antoinette's return back to the West Indies (Drake 203).

21 Rochester is explicitly identified as Bluebeard on many occasions in *Adèle* (see 10, 24, 39, 63, 162–3, 187).

22 Tennant's approach also recalls Bruno Bettelheim's interpretation of 'Bluebeard' in his *The Uses of Enchantment*. Bettelheim claims that Bluebeard's violence is caused by his wife's infidelity. While her crime is adultery, his is over-possessiveness and the inability to forgive woman's innate sexual weakness. He argues that what makes Bluebeard's acts understandable, although not acceptable, is the archaic notion that a cuckolded man has the right to murder an unfaithful wife.

23 This romantic representation of Bluebeard affects the portrayal of the 'other woman' motif typical of this tale. These women are not depicted as victims predicting the heroine's fate; rather, they resemble the female helpers of the fairy-tale tradition. Living in Bluebeard's castle, Adèle must distinguish who among the many women there is a suitable substitute mother: Antoinette, Grace, Mrs Fairfax, Blanche Ingram, or Jane. She first opts for the French-speaking Antoinette, but slowly gravitates toward Jane, thanks to Jane's capability to hold her own ground and manage Rochester. Her mother Céline had this same ability. The right woman for this Bluebeard is an independent, headstrong, and passionate one who serves as a strong role model for his daughter. In the context of this tale, Davies (88) observes, such a woman overcomes her predicament and saves not only herself but also her oppressor.

### 3  Romance, Perversion, and Bluebeard Gothic

1 Hilary Bailey's *Mrs Rochester: A Sequel to Jane Eyre* (1997) and Kimberley A. Bennett's *Jane Rochester: A Novel Inspired by Charlotte Brontë's Jane Eyre* (2002) are fitting examples of adaptations where romance overrides serious consideration of gender issues. While such novels as these acknowledge

the importance of gender equality, they nevertheless stress conventional romance. Often they also include soft-pornographic scenes that portray contemporary habits of lovemaking. Margaret Atwood's *Lady Oracle* (1976) provides an extended and hilarious parody of romantic Bluebeard Gothic.

2 The game of power and domination illustrated in *Rebecca* has lately begun to shed new light on *Jane Eyre* too, as Lisa Sternlieb's analysis demonstrates. Sternlieb explains that as Rochester bullied Jane at Thornfield, Jane reverses the situation at Ferndean by not confiding in him. 'By lacerating his heart *deeper than she wished*,' Sternlieb writes, 'is Jane indicating that she fully intended to lacerate his heart, at least a little? She does not tame her man; she tortures him' (514).

3 *Rebecca's Tale* is an example of the kind of contemporary novel that Suzanne Keen (*Romances*) calls a romance of the archive. Novels in this genre depict characters doing archival research, interviewing people, and seeking solid facts in order to arrive at a judicious interpretation of the past and its significance for the present. Given that the past Beauman's researchers examine is fictitious, understandably the reassessment they are most interested in concerns the ethical makeup of characters and the ethical consequences of their actions.

4 Barzilai emphasizes that curiosity concerns both protagonists of 'Bluebeard,' although its interpretive tradition would have us believe that curiosity addresses only the wife. Barzilai differentiates between two types of curiosity: curiosity as self-preservation and curiosity as epistemophilia. While the wife's curiosity is largely motivated by self-preservation, Bluebeard's curiosity is whetted by an anxious desire for knowledge about whether the wife will submit to his disciplinary practices (6–7). Bluebeard nevertheless wants the wife to disobey: he would be sorely disappointed if he were robbed of the spectacle of punishment.

5 Auerbach nicely sums up the novel when she writes that the protagonist 'ends as she began, escorting Max to oppressively sunny watering places, soothing him out of his tyrannical moods as she had Mrs. Van Hopper' (107).

6 James undermines this literary tradition as does Jane Austen in her *Northanger Abbey*. 'Bluebeard' plays a major role in the delusions of Catherine Morland, Austen's heroine. It is the conjunction of Austen and Brontë that produces James's critical parody. James's gentleman Bluebeard commissions a young woman to care for two siblings, Miles and Flora, on a property he owns. She is fascinated with and sexually aroused by her enigmatic employer. A former governess precedes her, and, like Bluebeard's previous wife, she has died in strange circumstances. The Bly mansion holds a se-

cret, but unlike Bluebeard, the employer does not wish to verify the outcome of the governess's research in person. Instead, he asks that she never under any circumstances contact him about anything at Bly. He is content to spring the trap for her, knowing that she will not only enter the chamber but also be maimed by its secret.

7  Beauman depicts Lionel as a thoroughly nasty man. Not only does he seduce his wife's sister but also he is an inveterate philanderer. The retarded Ben who haunts the beach in *Rebecca* is turned into one of Lionel's 'byblows' in *Rebecca's Tale*, and the boy's condition is explained by Lionel's syphilis. Towards the end of his days, Lionel becomes a 'mad woman in the attic,' locked away from sight, thanks to an advanced state of syphilis. Incidentally, some critics have attributed Bertha Mason's illness to this same disease, acquired through the father.

8  The irony is that if Rebecca is Lionel's child, then the marriage has realized Maxim's fantasy of having a sexual relationship outside the bounds of the Oedipal prohibition.

9  The implication of the torn pages is that having found out about the cancer, Rebecca planned suicide and had written Max a final note. She, however, was then interrupted by Max; she changed her plans by making Max kill her. Most likely the second wife cannot bear the intimacy of the note, for *Rebecca's Tale* presents Rebecca as the only woman in Maxim's life.

10  As a reward for opening up the secrets of her past, Vida lets Margaret read the missing thirteenth story from her collections of stories, *Thirteen Tales*, later published as *Tales of Change and Desperation*, that no one has ever read. It is a concise version of her biography, an inverted 'Cinderella' tale, with rape, abuse, and an unhappy ending.

11  Miranda's novel includes the twelve-page pastiche of *Jane Eyre* she wrote when she was an adolescent. While on Martinique, the adult Miranda begins to expand the sequel, interweaving it with an account of her conference trip. Ben's journal is also most likely written, or, at least, edited by her, because in the night when Miranda attacks her father, she rages about being forced to edit Ben's 'fucking journals' (C 177).

12  Robert Rochester's letter supplies information on the birth of this masochistic couple. Robert's birth ruptured the marital harmony, for he was black. Not knowing that a Creole woman may give birth to a black child, Rochester thinks Bertha has been unfaithful to her. Bertha starts having lovers. Rochester finds himself aroused by her infidelity, asking her to mock and abuse him. The masochistic relationship has been formed.

13  Some scenes in *Charlotte* are lifted from *Rebecca*. In *Rebecca*, for example, the protagonist sits at Maxim's feet while he strokes her hair; a similar

scene takes place in *Charlotte*. In *Charlotte* Jane and Rochester visit Thornfield, where Rochester broods over the dilapidated house as does Maxim
over the damaged boathouse. The disastrous masquerade scene in *Rebecca*
has its parallel in *Charlotte* when Jane queries Rochester about his virility.
Rochester storms out of the house, leaving Jane to spend an agonizing
night alone.

## 4  Faith, Ritual, and Sacrifice: Rewriting the Religious Foundation of *Jane Eyre*

1  Fetishism supplies the congregation with a 'religious *écriture artiste*' (Apter
   130). The objects used in worship give the congregation colour, ornamen-
   tal style, and decor, enhancing their sense of being God's chosen people.
   Simultaneously, the fetishes hint at an idolatry that erases the difference
   between pagan and Christian realms. Like the pagans whom they try to
   convert, the congregation relies on these talismans in order to gain and
   sustain access to God.
2  Jeanette's ear infection illustrates both the mother's alienation from the
   body and the significance of aurality. The infection makes Jeanette deaf,
   but the mother never suspects that Jeanette is ill. Instead, she thinks the
   daughter is filled with the Spirit. To safeguard the daughter's assumed
   communion with God, she forbids others to speak to Jeanette.
3  Both Peter Allan Dale and Carolyn Williams claim that *Jane Eyre* ultimately
   rejects the religious script, opting for the romantic one; its conclusion is
   thus thoroughly secular. Williams nicely condenses this outcome by pointing out that 'Jane has heard the voice of her conscience, of God's will, of
   her own wish-fulfilment, and of her lover's need all in one' (241). I would
   nevertheless argue that Brontë's novel does not place the lover in God's
   position as does Winterson's *Oranges*. Instead, Jane and Rochester together
   serve God. Moreover, their union emphasizes sameness – Jane 'is bone of
   his bone, flesh of his flesh' (JE 384) – while Jeanette insists on difference
   and maintaining the separateness of lovers.
4  In Dale's view, the end of *Jane Eyre* rejects the religious structure: St John,
   instead of Jane, voices the confirmation of Christian beliefs; Jane's salvation is never depicted; Jane chooses Rochester instead of God and, to boot,
   depicts her marriage in terms of paradise on earth (216–24). It seems to me,
   however, that Lamonaca is correct in identifying the Victorian ideology
   of the home as the framework within which Jane negotiates her decision.
   Jane can justify her choice as inhering with what she assumes is God's will
   within this framework.

5 The conclusion of *Jane Eyre* reverberates with a religious association characteristic of the family romance: the blue-clad Jane is like the Virgin Mary; the first-born son has two exalted, godly parents (see also Lamonaca 256).

6 This lost object is not necessarily the breast with milk or the mother's womb, for which there may be a perceptual memory, but an entirely fantasmatic object. This fantasmatic object is the female body itself, whose original loss in a female subject corresponds to the narcissistic wound that the loss of the penis represents for the male subject (de Lauretis 231).

7 These pornographic sessions as scenes of sacrifice elucidate collective persecution in 'The Robber Bridegroom.' In this tale a bride witnesses a band of crooks, headed by her fiancé, rob, kill, and eat up a woman. This community of criminals resorts to sacrificial practice in order to bond the group together and to ensure its authority. The victim condenses the community's tensions and reprisals: killing the victim empties it of its poisons, stabilizing (temporarily) this community.

8 Contrary to general belief, Marianne Lilly was not mad. Her father and brother punished her for her extramarital relationship by shutting her in a madhouse. While in the madhouse, Susan learns that many of its inmates are not mentally ill but have been stowed away there by their relatives for various mercenary reasons.

9 Scapegoats are typically marked by some special feature such as being an orphan.

10 Mr Lilly takes special pleasure in the fact that he can continue punishing his sister through Maud. Whenever Maud displeases him, however, he threatens to replace her.

11 Maud cherishes a thimble as a memento of Susan. Rochester keeps the pearl necklace he gave to Jane as a memento of her (JE 380). These fetishes refer to the biblical allegory of the lost pearl – a variant of the lamb allegory – that the owner keeps searching for until he finds it.

12 Ironically, Mrs Sucksby now occupies the position of Susan's alleged mother. Throughout Susan's childhood Mrs Sucksby has fed her a fabricated story of a murderess mother hanged for robbery and manslaughter. When this story becomes Mrs Sucksby's story, the exchange of Susan for Maud has been completed.

## 5 Farewell, Charlotte Brontë! Angela Carter's 'Bluebeard' Tales and the Anxiety of Influence

1 Carter admires Emily Brontë's unwavering commitment to passion, best exemplified by the *amour fou* between Heathcliff and Cathy in *Wuthering*

*Heights*. Yet Emily's life, too, was beset by loss and grief; Carter wagers that Emily starved herself to death ('Love'). Although Carter explores passion, female self-destruction is rare in her fiction.

2  I have analysed the erotic poetics of Carter's 'Bluebeard' stories as a means of searching for new linguistic and literary expression in my essay 'Imagining the Impossible: The Erotic Poetics of Angela Carter's "Bluebeard" Stories.'

3  Benson characterizes Thackeray's 'Bluebeard's Ghost' (1843) as a droll social comedy that belongs to a tradition seeking to rehabilitate Bluebeard by presenting the female protagonist as either murderously over-curious or a manipulative adulteress (198–9). Sutherland's observation that *Jane Eyre* is the 'first adult, non-burlesque treatment of the Bluebeard theme in English literature' (68) is significant in this context.

4  Carter's portrayal of Bluebeard as a puppeteer has a precedent in Edgar Ulmer's film *Bluebeard* (1944). This film's Bluebeard, Gaston Morell, creates dramatic operas with self-made puppets.

5  Actually, Leda gives birth to twins, one fathered by Jove, the other by a human.

6  In his essay 'A Child Is Being Beaten,' Freud discusses how both sexes repress a childhood fantasy of being beaten by the father, which, for boys, means: 'I am loved by my father.' Boys and girls differ in the way they transform this unconscious fantasy into a conscious one. Girls envision that 'a child is being beaten' by an authority figure (a vicarious father), while she and other children look on. The boys' version holds 'I am being beaten by my mother.' Freud interprets this transformation as follows: 'the boy evades his homosexuality by repressing and remodelling his unconscious fantasy [of being sexually loved by his father]; and the remarkable thing about his later conscious fantasy [of being beaten by his mother] is that it has for its content a feminine attitude without a homosexual object-choice' (199).

7  This reading is in line with Deleuze's understanding of sadism, in which, when seen in the light of an individual's psychic development, a masculine coded superego beats an externalized, feminine coded ego. The sadist's goal is the expulsion and destruction of the ego and of the mother, for the ego is fundamentally associated with the maternal realm (Deleuze 124).

8  As in the Oedipus myth, a strong poet's self-knowledge depends on knowing who his father is. John T. Irwin elucidates the myth's father–son relationship. The father's recognition and acknowledgment of the son, however, makes the son dependent on the father's will. In order to create

a stable, independent personality, the son must free himself from this will. This situation leads to contrary impulses as regards paternal authority. The son wants what the father has: the father's authority. In principle, he can get it two ways, as a patrimony or against the father's will (ch. 23). In Bloom's model, weak and strong poets encounter the question of paternal authority differently. Achieving authority as patrimony is a weak poet's strategy, for the patrimony itself represents continued dependence on the father's will. He tries to make his parent a dead father whose honoured memory grounds an *orderly* patriarchal succession by submitting himself to symbolic castration.

9   It is surprising that Bloom does not mention that if the son refuses to acknowledge the father's authority and seizes his position by force, he actually destroys what he set out to seize.

10  Kestenberg maintains that from birth onwards, girls have all kinds of sensations of their sexual organs, especially of the womb and the vagina. Among the first sensations is the satisfaction of a full stomach, a feeling which reverberates to the genitals. Similarly, sucking produces low-amplitude contractions, giving the girl intimations of her inner space. The acquisition of this sense of inner space culminates in what Kestenberg calls the *inner genital phase*, responsible for the formation of the basic kernel of femininity understood as maternity.

11  In her essay 'Of Souls as Birds,' Margaret Atwood associates the egg with the witch's testicles, arguing that it expresses a man's fear of being sexually betrayed by a woman (33–4). Carter, however, suggests that it is the one organ both sexes share (egg, testicle). It symbolizes the notion that both genders approach the third term from their own vantage point. Because the third sister is in touch with her own creative generativity as symbolized by the egg, she is not diminished by the witch's destructive interpretation of femininity.

12  Lacanian psychoanalysis hypothesizes the existence of masculine and feminine structures that situate the genders differently as regards the phallus as a master signifier. While within the masculine structure the subject must reconstitute his relationship to the object, the feminine one necessitates a new relationship to the signifier (see Fink, *Lacanian* ch. 8).

13  Indeed, Carter says that for *Heroes and Villains* she 'consciously chose the Gothic mode with owls and ivy and ruins and a breathtakingly Byronic hero' (cited in Gamble 49).

14  Likewise, Rochester is transformed by his first meeting with Jane: 'When once I had pressed the frail shoulder, something new – a fresh sap and sense – stole into my frame' (JE 266–7).

15 This notion is grounded in etymology, for in Latin the term 'singuli' is plural in nature, for it designates the 'one' as belonging to 'one by one.' 'The singular is primarily *each* one and, therefore, also *with* and *among* all the others. The singular is plural' (Nancy, *Being* 32).

16 Epiphany as an interruption of myth propels Carter's characters to the limit. The extreme circumstances place them on the verge of birth and death: their old lives are gone and the future demands that they change. Part and parcel of this change is the realization of death as the *other's death*, no longer one's own death. The thought of the other's death evokes in them a deep sorrow. In *Nights at the Circus*, for example, Walser realizes that his '"self" would never be the same again for now he knew the meaning of fear as it defines itself in its most violent form, that is, fear of the death of the beloved, of the loss of the beloved, of the loss of love' (292–3). Committed to the 'with' of being, Carter's characters now exist, as it were, simultaneously inside and outside themselves. Being-with erases indifference and engenders commitment: '[Marianne] saw [Jewel's] face in the transfiguring firelight and felt a sharp, extreme, prolonged pain as though the lines of his forehead, nose and jaw were being traced upon her flesh with the point of a knife' (HV 118).

17 *The Passion of New Eve* (1977) presents Carter's extensive dismissal of the myth of femininity. If Bluebeard's chamber metonymically represents the incest prohibition that turns mother into a forbidden object, then this novel lifts the prohibition ('Kill your father! Sleep with your mother! Burst through all the interdictions!' [64]). A self-appointed matriarch of 'Amazons' and a plastic surgeon, Mother operates on the novel's protagonist, Evelyn, in order to create the perfect Woman. Mother's association with the Christian God is apparent; she is the Creator-cum-Holy-Spirit who wants to impregnate her daughter immaculately: 'In the most pure womb of Mary, there was sown one whole grain of wheat' (66). This attempt may be characterized as *transsexual*, for Mother turns a man into a perfect woman. It relies on what Joël Dor (183) calls a 'frantic idealization of femininity,' which is concerned with moral purity, for the notion of an ideal woman has as its corollary the idea of being without a sex. (Also, the transvestite-transsexual Tristessa turns out to be asexual: 'his cock stuck in his asshole so that he himself formed the uroborus, the perfect circle, the vicious circle, the dead end' [173].) In this fantasy, argues Dor, the Ideal Woman is made to resemble and replace the Name-of-the-Father that maintains structure by introducing a limit. Yet this new structure can only hold together the Imaginary and the Symbolic, while the Real remains free (Dor 186). That a *man* needs to be surgically corrected in order to create

an Ideal Woman implies that Mother has to adjust the Real of the genital to the Imaginary and the Symbolic. Ultimately Mother remains just as tied to phallic structures as each and every one of Carter's Bluebeards, for the Name-of-the-Mother turns out to be simply one version of the Name-of-the-Father. In fact, Mother appears to understand this mechanism, for when Tristessa wanted her to turn him into a woman, she refused to operate on him, because his test results struck her 'by what seemed to her the awfully ineradicable quality of his maleness' (173).

18  What ensues thereafter, however, remains open. Perrault's 'La Barbe Bleue,' for instance, ends in the wife's remarriage that Lewis (245–6) interprets as a return to patriarchy.

# Works Cited

**Primary Texts**

Anonymous. 'Mr Fox.' In Tatar, *Secrets*, 185–7.
Barnes, Djuna. *Nightwood*. New York: New Directions, 2006 [1936].
Beauman, Sally. *Rebecca's Tale*. Toronto: HarperCollins, 2001.
Brontë, Charlotte. *Jane Eyre*. Ed. Richard J. Dunn. New York: Norton, 2001 [1847].
– *The Professor*. London: Penguin, 1995 [1857].
Carter, Angela. 'The Bloody Chamber.' *Burning Your Boats: The Collected Short Stories*. London: Penguin, 1995.
– 'The Fall River Axe Murders.' *Burning Your Boats: The Collected Short Stories*. London: Penguin, 1995.
– *Heroes and Villains*. London: Picador, 1969.
– *The Magic Toyshop*. London: Virago, 1967.
– *Nights at the Circus*. London: Penguin, 1984.
– *The Passion of New Eve*. London: Virago, 1982 [1977].
– *The Sadeian Woman: An Exercise in Cultural History*. London: Penguin, 1979.
Du Maurier, Daphne. *Rebecca*. London: Arrow, 1992 [1938].
Grimm, Jacob and Wilhelm. 'Fitcher's Bird.' In Tatar, *Secrets*, 182–5.
– 'The Robber Bridegroom.' In Tatar, *Secrets*, 179–82.
James, Henry. *The Turn of the Screw*. Ed. Deborah Esch and Jonathan Warren. New York: Norton, 1996 [1898].
Leonowens, Anna. *The Romance of the Harem*. Ed. and with an Intro. by Susan Morgan. Charlottesville: UP of Virginia, 1991 [1872].
Perrault, Charles. 'Bluebeard.' In Tatar, *Secrets*, 175–9.
Rhys, Jean. *Wide Sargasso Sea*. London: Penguin, 1968 [1966].
Sacher-Masoch von, Leopold. *Venus in Furs*. In *Masochism*. Trans. Jean McNeal. New York: Zone, 1989 [1870].

Setterfield, Diane. *The Thirteenth Tale*. London: Orion, 2006.

Tatar, Maria. *Secrets beyond the Door: The Story of Bluebeard and His Wives*. Princeton: Princeton UP, 2004.

Tennant, Emma. *Adèle: Jane Eyre's Hidden Story*. New York: HarperCollins, 2002.

Thomas, D.M. *Charlotte*. London: Duckbacks, 2000.

Waters, Sarah. *Fingersmith*. London: Virago, 2002.

Winterson, Jeannette. *Oranges Are Not the Only Fruit*. London: Vintage, 1985.

**Secondary Works**

Anderson, Victoria. 'Introduction: A Perrault in Wolf's Clothing.' *Bluebeard's Legacy: Death and Secrets from Bartók to Hitchcock*. Ed. Griselda Pollock and Victoria Anderson. London: I.B. Tauris, 2009. 3–13.

– 'Investigating the Third Story: "Bluebeard" and "Cinderella" in *Jane Eyre*.' *Horrifying Sex: Essays on Sexual Difference in Gothic Literature*. Ed. Ruth Bienstock Anolik. Jefferson, NC: McFarland, 2007. 111–21.

Armitt, Lucie. *Contemporary Women's Fiction and the Fantastic*. London: MacMillan, 2000.

Apter, Emily. *Feminizing the Fetish: Psychoanalysis and Narrative Obsession in Turn-of-the-Century France*. Ithaca, NY: Cornell UP, 1991.

Atwood, Margaret. 'Of Souls as Birds.' *Mirror, Mirror on the Wall: Women Writers Explore Their Favorite Fairy Tales*. 2nd ed. Ed. Kate Bernheimer. New York: Anchor Books, 2002. 21–36.

Auerbach, Nina. *Daphne du Maurier: Haunted Heiress*. Philadelphia: U of Pennsylvania P, 2000.

Bacchilega, Cristina. *Postmodern Fairy Tales: Gender and Narrative Strategies*. Philadelphia: U of Pennsylvania P, 1997.

Barthes, Roland. *A Lover's Discourse: Fragments*. Trans. Richard Howard. New York: Hill and Wang, 1978. [*Fragments d'un discours amoureux*, 1977.]

– *Sade/Fourier/Loyola*. Trans. Richard Miller. Baltimore: Johns Hopkins University Press, 1976. [*Sade/Fourier/Loyola*, 1971.]

Barzilai, Shuli. *Tales of Bluebeard and His Wives from Late Antiquity to Postmodern Times*. New York: Routledge, 2009.

Beaty, Jerome. *Misreading Jane Eyre: A Postformalist Paradigm*. Columbus: Ohio State UP, 1996.

Benson, Stephen. *Cycles of Influence: Fiction, Folktale, Theory*. Detroit: Wayne State UP, 2003.

Bettelheim, Bruno. *The Uses of Enchantment*. Vintage: London, 1989.

Bloom, Harold. *The Anxiety of Influence: A Theory of Poetry*. 2nd ed. Oxford: Oxford UP, 1997 [1973].

Blyn, Robin. 'From Stage to Page: Franz Kafka, Djuna Barnes, and Modernism's Freak Fiction.' *Narrative* 8.2 (2000): 134–60.

Bollinger, Laurel. 'Models for Female Loyalty: The Biblical Ruth in Jeannette Winterson's *Oranges Are Not the Only Fruit*.' *Tulsa Studies in Women's Literature* 13.2 (Fall 1994): 363–80.

Botting, Fred. *Gothic*. London: Routledge, 1996.

Brinks, Ellen, and Lee Talley. 'Unfamiliar Ties: Lesbian Construction of Home and Family in Jeannette Winterson's *Oranges Are Not the Only Fruit* and Jewelle Gomez's *The Gilda Stories*.' *Homemaking: Women Writers and the Politics and Poetics of Home*. Ed. Catherine Wiley and Fiona R. Barnes. New York: Garland, 1996. 145–74.

Bronfen, Elisabeth. *The Knotted Subject: Hysteria and Its Discontents*. Princeton: Princeton UP, 1998.

Brooks, Linda Marie. '*Testimonio*'s Poetics of Performance.' *Comparative Literature Studies* 42.2 (2005): 181–222.

Brown, Susan. 'Alternatives to the Missionary Position: Anna Leonowens as Victorian Travel Writer.' *Feminist Studies* 21.3 (1995): 587–614.

Carter, Angela. 'Introduction.' *Jane Eyre* by Charlotte Brontë. London: Virago, 1990. v–xvi.

– 'Love in a Cold Climate.' *Nothing Sacred: Selected Writings*. Rev. ed. London: Virago, 1992. 165–80.

Carter, Keryn. 'The Consuming Fruit: Oranges, Demons, and Daughters.' *Critique* 40.1 (Fall 1998): 15–23.

Caruth, Cathy. *Unclaimed Experience: Trauma, Narrative, and History*. Baltimore: Johns Hopkins UP, 1996.

Cawelti, John G. *Adventure, Mystery, and Romance: Formula Stories as Art and Popular Culture*. Chicago: U Chicago P, 1976.

Chase, Karen. *Eros and Psyche: The Representation of Personality in Charlotte Brontë, Charles Dickens, and George Eliot*. New York: Methuen, 1984.

Ciolkowski, Laura E. 'Navigating the *Wide Sargasso Sea*: Colonial History, English Fiction, and British Empire.' *Twentieth Century Literature: A Scholarly and Critical Journal* 43.3 (1997): 339–59.

Cohen, William. *Sex Scandal: The Private Parts of Victorian Fiction*, Durham, NC: Duke UP, 1996.

Copjec, Joan. *Read My Desire: Lacan against the Historicists*. Cambridge, MA: MIT, 1994.

Cosslett, Tess. 'Intertextuality in *Oranges Are Not the Only Fruit*: The Bible,

Malory, and *Jane Eyre.' 'I'm Telling You Stories': Jeannette Winterson and the Politics of Reading*. Ed. Helene Grice and Tim Woods. Amsterdam: Rodopi, 1998. 15–28.

Dale, Peter Allan. 'Charlotte Brontë's "Tale Half-Told": The Disruption of Narrative Structure in *Jane Eyre.' Jane Eyre: Contemporary Critical Essays*. Ed. Heather Glen. Houndsmills: MacMillan, 1997. 205–26. [Originally published 1986, in *Modern Language Quarterly* 47.]

Davies, Meredid Puw. 'Bluebeard, Hero of Modernity: Tales at the *Fin de Siècle.' Bluebeard's Legacy: Death and Secrets from Bartók to Hitchcock*. Ed. Griselda Pollock and Victoria Anderson. London: I.B. Tauris, 2009. 31–50.

– *The Tale of Bluebeard in German Literature: From the Eighteenth Century to the Present*. Oxford: Clarendon, 2001.

De Lauretis, Teresa. *The Practice of Love: Lesbian Sexuality and Perverse Desire*. Bloomington: Indiana UP, 1994.

Deleuze, Gilles. *Coldness and Cruelty*. In *Masochism*. Trans. Jean McNeal. New York: Zone Books 1989. [*Le Froid et le Cruel. Presentation de Sacher-Masoch*, 1967.]

Dor, Joël. *Structure and Perversions*. Trans. Susan Fairfield. New York: Other Press, 2001. [*Structure et perversions*, 1987.]

Drake, Sandra. 'Race and Caribbean Culture as Thematics of Liberation in Jean Rhys's *Wide Sargasso Sea.' Wide Sargasso Sea* by Jean Rhys. Ed. Judith L. Raiskin. New York: Norton, 1999. 193–206.

Emery, Mary Lou. 'Modernist Crosscurrents.' *Wide Sargasso Sea* by Jean Rhys. Ed. Judith L. Raiskin. New York: Norton, 1999. 161–73.

Erwin, Lee. '"Like in a Looking-Glass": History and Narrative in *Wide Sargasso Sea.' Novel: A Forum on Fiction* 22.2 (1989): 143–58.

Felman, Shoshana. *Jacques Lacan and the Adventure of Insight: Psychoanalysis in Contemporary Culture*. Cambridge, MA: Harvard UP, 1987.

Fink, Bruce. *A Clinical Introduction to Lacanian Psychoanalysis: Theory and Technique*. Cambridge, MA: Harvard UP, 1997.

– *The Lacanian Subject: Between Language and Jouissance*. Princeton: Princeton UP, 1995.

Finke, Michael C. 'Sacher-Masoch, Turgenev, and Other Russians.' *One Hundred Years of Masochism*. Ed. Michael C. Finke and Carl Niekerk. Amsterdam: Rodopi, 2000. 119–38.

Freud, Sigmund. 'A Child Is Being Beaten.' *Standard Edition*. Vol. 17. Trans. James Strachey. London: Hogarth, 1919. 175–204.

– 'Family Romances.' *Standard Edition*. Vol. 9. Trans. James Strachey. London: Hogarth, 1909. 237–41.

– *Moses and Monotheism*. Trans. Katherine Jones. New York: Vintage, 1939.

– On the Sexual Theories of Children. Standard Edition. Vol. 9. Trans. James Strachey. London: Hogarth, 1908. 209–26.

– Three Essays on the Theory of Sexuality. Standard Edition. Vol. 7. Trans. James Strachey. London: Hogarth, 1905. 125–246.

– Totem and Taboo: Some Points of Agreement between the Mental Lives of Savages and Neurotics. Trans. James Strachey. London: Routledge Classics, 2001 [1913].

Gallagher, Susan VanZanten. 'Jane Eyre and Christianity.' Approaches to Teaching Jane Eyre. Ed. Diane Long Hoeveler and Beth Lau. New York, MLA, 1993. 62–8.

Gamble, Sarah, ed. The Fiction of Angela Carter: A Reader's Guide to Essential Criticism. Houndmills: Palgrave, 2001.

Gilbert, Sandra M. 'Jane Eyre and the Secrets of Furious Lovemaking.' Novel 31.3 (1998): 351–72.

Gilbert, Sandra M., and Susan Gubar. The Madwoman in the Attic: The Woman Writer and the Nineteenth-Century Literary Imagination. 2nd ed. New Haven: Yale UP, 2000.

Girard, René. Deceit, Desire, and the Novel: Self and Other in Literary Structure. Trans. Yvonne Freccero. Baltimore: Johns Hopkins UP, 1966. [Mensonge romantique et vérité romanesque, 1961.]

– The Scapegoat. Trans. Yvonne Freccero. Baltimore: Johns Hopkins UP, 1986. [Le Bouc émissaire, 1982.]

Gutleben, Christian. Nostalgic Postmodernism: The Victorian Tradition and the Contemporary British Novel. Amsterdam: Rodopi, 2001.

Harrison, Nancy R. Jean Rhys and the Novel as Women's Text. Chapel Hill: U of North Carolina P, 1988.

Hennelly, Mark M. 'Jane Eyre's Reading Lesson.' ELH 51.4 (1984): 693–717.

Hermansson, Casie. Reading Feminist Intertextuality through Bluebeard Stories. Lewiston: Edwin Mellen, 2001.

Hirsch, Marianne. 'Jane's Family Romances.' Nineteenth-Century Women Writers of the English-Speaking World. Ed. Rhoda B. Nathan. New York: Greenwood, 1986. 162–85.

Horner, Avril. '"A Detour of Filthiness": French Fiction and Djuna Barnes's Nightwood.' European Gothic: A Spirited Exchange 1760–1960. Ed. Avril Horner. Manchester: Manchester UP, 2002.

Horner, Avril, and Sue Zlosnik. Daphne du Maurier: Writing, Identity and the Gothic Imagination. London: Macmillan, 1998.

– 'Strolling in the Dark: Gothic Flânerie in Djuna Barnes's Nightwood.' Gothic Modernisms. Ed. Andrew Smith and Jeff Wallace. New York: Palgrave, 2001. 78–94.

Hutcheon, Linda. *A Theory of Adaptation*. New York: Routledge, 2006.

Huyssen, Andreas. *After the Great Divide: Modernism, Mass Culture, Postmodernism*. Bloomington: Indiana UP, 1986.

Ingham, Patricia. *The Brontës*. Oxford: Oxford University Press, 2006.

Irwin, John T. *The Mystery to a Solution: Poe, Borges, and the Analytic Detective Story*. Baltimore: The Johns Hopkins UP, 1994.

Jagose, Annamarie. 'First Wife, Second Wife: Sexual Perversion and the Problem of Precedence in *Rebecca.*' *Intimacy*. Ed. Lauren Berlant. Chicago: U of Chicago P, 2000. 352–77.

Jameson, Fredric. 'Postmodernism and Consumer Society.' *The Anti-Aesthetic: Essays on Postmodern Culture*. Ed. and with an Intro. by Hal Foster. Port Townsend, WA: Bay Press, 1983. 111–25.

Kacandes, Irene. *Talk Fiction: Literature and the Talk Explosion*. Lincoln: U of Nebraska P, 2001.

Kahane, Claire. 'The Gothic Mirror.' *The (M)other Tongue: Essays in Feminist Psychoanalytic Interpretation*. Ed. Shirley Nelson Garner, Claire Kahane, and Madelon Sprengnether. Ithaca, NY: Cornell UP, 1985. 334–51.

Kamel, Rose. '"Before I Was Set Free": The Creole Wife in *Jane Eyre* and *Wide Sargasso Sea.*' *The Journal of Narrative Technique* 25.1 (1995): 1–22.

Kaplan, Carla. 'Girl Talk: *Jane Eyre* and the Romance of Women's Narration.' *Novel: A Forum on Fiction* 30.1 (1996): 5–31.

Kaplan, Cora. *Victoriana: Histories, Fictions, Criticism*. Edinburgh: Edinburgh UP, 2007.

Keen, Suzanne. '"I Cannot Eat My Words But I Do": Food, Body, and Word in the Novels of Jeanette Winterson.' *Scenes of the Apple: Food and the Female Body in Nineteenth- and Twentieth-Century Women's Writing*. Ed. Tamar Heller and Patricia Moran. Albany: State University of New York Press, 2003. 67–82.

– *Romances of the Archive in Contemporary British Fiction*. Toronto: U of Toronto P, 2001.

Kendrick, Robert. 'Edward Rochester and the Margins of Masculinity in *Jane Eyre* and *Wide Sargasso Sea.*' *Papers on Language and Literature* 30.3 (1994): 235–56.

Kestenberg, Judith. 'The Inner-Genital Phase – Prephallic and Preoedipal.' *Early Female Development*. Ed. D. Mendell. Lancaster: MTP Press, 1982. 81–127.

Lacan, Jacques. *On Feminine Sexuality, The Limits of Love and Knowledge. Book XX. Encore 1972–1973*. Trans. with Notes by Bruce Fink. New York: Norton, 1999. [*Le Séminaire, Livre XX, Encore, 1972–1973.*]

– *The Seminar of Jacques Lacan: Other Side of Psychoanalysis. Book XVII*. Trans. Russell Grigg. New York: Norton, 2007. [*Le Séminaire de Jacques Lacan, Livre XVII, L'Envers de la Psychanalyse, 1969–1970.*]

LaCapra, Dominick. 'Reflections on Trauma, Absence and Loss.' *Whose Freud? The Place of Psychoanalysis in Contemporary Culture.* Ed. Peter Brooks and Alex Woloch. New Haven: Yale UP, 2000. 178–204.

– *Writing History, Writing Trauma.* Baltimore: Johns Hopkins UP, 2001.

Lamonaca, Maria. 'Jane's Crown of Thorns: Feminism and Christianity in *Jane Eyre.' Studies in the Novel* 34.3 (2002): 245–63.

Laplanche, J., and J.-B. Pontalis. *The Language of Psychoanalysis.* Trans. Donald Nicholson-Smith. London: Karnac, 1973. [*Vocabulaire de la Psychanalyse,* 1967.]

Laub, Dori. 'Bearing Witness or the Vicissitudes of Listening.' *Testimony: Crises of Witnessing in Literature, Psychoanalysis, and History.* By Shoshana Felman and Dori Laub. New York: Routledge, 1992. 57–74.

Levine, Caroline. *The Serious Pleasures of Suspense: Victorian Realism and Narrative Doubt.* Charlottesville: U of Virginia P, 2003.

Lewis, Philip. *Seeing through the Mother Goose Tales: Visual Turns in the Writings of Charles Perrault.* Stanford: Stanford UP, 1996.

Light, Alison. '"Returning to Manderley" – Romance Fiction, Female Sexuality and Class.' *Feminist Review* 16 (Summer 1984): 7–25.

London, Bette. 'The Pleasures of Submission: *Jane Eyre* and the Production of the Text.' *ELH* 58.1 (1991): 195–213.

Maagaard, Cindie Aaen. 'Jeanette Winterson: Postmodern Prophet of the Word.' *Literary Canons and Religious Identity.* Ed. Erik Borgman, Bart Philipsen, and Lea Verstricht. Aldershot: Ashgate, 2004. 151–61.

Mahoney, Elizabeth. 'But Elsewhere?: The Future of Fantasy in *Heroes and Villains.' The Fiction of Angela Carter: A Reader's Guide to Essential Criticism.* Ed. Sarah Gamble. Houndsmill: Palgrave, 2001. 58–62.

Massé, Michelle. *In the Name of Love: Women, Masochism, and the Gothic.* Ithaca, NY, and London: Cornell UP, 1992.

McLaughlin, Becky. 'Perverse Pleasure and Fetishized Text: The Deathly Erotics of Carter's "The Bloody Chamber."' *Style* 29.3 (1995): 404–22.

Meaney, Gerardine. '(Un)like Subjects: Women, Theory, Fiction.' *The Fiction of Angela Carter: A Reader's Guide to Essential Criticism.* Ed. Sarah Gamble. Houndsmill: Palgrave, 2001. 62–5.

Menninghaus, Winfried. *In Praise of Nonsense: Kant and Bluebeard.* Trans. Henry Pickford. Stanford: Stanford UP, 1999. [*Lob des Unsinns: Über Kant, Tieck und Blaubart,* 1995.]

Meyer, Susan. 'Colonialism and the Figurative Strategy of *Jane Eyre.' Jane Eyre: Contemporary Critical Essays.* Ed. Heather Glen. Houndsmills: MacMillan, 1997. 92–129. [Originally published in *Imperialism at Home: Race in Victorian Women's Fiction,* 1996.]

Mezei, Kathy. '"And It Kept Its Secret": Narration, Memory, and Madness in Jean Rhys's *Wide Sargasso Sea*.' *Critique* 28.4 (1987): 195–209.

Miller, Lucasta. *The Brontë Myth*. London: Vintage, 2001.

Modleski, Tania. *The Women Who Knew Too Much: Hitchcock and Feminist Theory*. New York: Methuen, 1988.

Moran, Patricia. *Virginia Woolf, Jean Rhys, and the Aesthetics of Trauma*. New York: Palgrave MacMillan, 2007.

Morgan, Susan. 'Introduction.' *The Romance of the Harem*. Ed. Susan Morgan. Charlottesville: UP of Virginia, 1991. ix–xxxix.

Müller, Wolfgang G. 'The Intertextual Status of Jean Rhys's *Wide Sargasso Sea*: Dependence on a Victorian Classic and Independence as a Post-Colonial Novel.' *A Breath of Fresh Eyre: Intertextual and Intermedial Reworkings of Jane Eyre*. Ed. Margarete Rubik and Elke Mettinger-Schartman. Amsterdam: Rodopi, 2007. 63–79.

Nancy, Jean-Luc. *Being Singular Plural*. Trans. Robert D. Richardson and Anne E. O'Byrne. Stanford: Stanford UP, 2000. [*Être singulier pluriel*, 1996.]

– *The Inoperative Community*. Ed. Peter Connor. Trans. Peter Connor, Lisa Garbus, Michael Holland, and Simona Sawhney. Minneapolis: U of Minnesota P, 1991.

Neck-Yoder, Hilda van. 'Colonial Desires, Silence, and Metonymy: "All things considered" in *Wide Sargasso Sea*.' *Texas Studies in Literature and Language* 40.2 (1998): 184–208.

Noble, Marianne. *The Masochistic Pleasures of Sentimental Literature*. Princeton: Princeton UP, 2000.

Nungesser, Verena-Susanna. 'From Thornfield Hall to Manderley and Beyond: Jane Eyre and Rebecca as Transformations of the Fairy Tale, the Novel of Development, and the Gothic Novel.' *A Breath of Fresh Eyre: Intertextual and Intermedial Reworkings of Jane Eyre*. Ed. Margarete Rubik and Elke Mettinger-Schartman. Amsterdam: Rodopi, 2007. 209–26.

Peters, John G. '"We Stood at God's Feet, Equal": Equality, Subversion, and Religion in *Jane Eyre*.' *Brontë Studies* 29 (March 2004): 53–64.

Petry, Alice Hall. 'Jamesian Parody, *Jane Eyre* and "The Turn of the Screw."' *Modern Language Studies* 13.4 (Henry James Issue) (1983): 61–78.

Pollock, Griselda. Preface. *Bluebeard's Legacy: Death and Secrets from Bartók to Hitchcock*. Ed. Griselda Pollock and Victoria Anderson. London: I.B. Tauris, 2009. xxi–xxx.

Pollock, Lori. '(An)Other Politics of Reading *Jane Eyre*.' *The Journal of Narrative Technique* 26.3 (1996): 249–73.

Pyrhönen, Heta. 'Imagining the Impossible: The Erotic Poetics of Angela Carter's "Bluebeard" Stories.' *Textual Practice* 21.1 (2007): 93–111.

Radway, Janice. *Reading the Romance: Women, Patriarchy, and Popular Literature.* Chapel Hill: U of North Carolina P, 1984.

Ralph, Phyllis C. '"Beauty and the Beast": Growing up with Jane Eyre.' *Approaches to Teaching Charlotte Brontë's Jane Eyre.* Ed. Diane Long Hoeveler and Beth Lau. New York: MLA, 1993.

Rapaport, Herman. '*Jane Eyre* and the *Mot Tabou.*' *MLN* 94.5 (1979): 1093–1104.

Reinhard, Kenneth. 'Lacan and Monotheism: Psychoanalysis and the Traversal of Cultural Fantasy.' 6 August 2009. http://english.chass.ncsu.edu/jouvert/v3i12/reinha.htm

Rhys, Jean. Selected Letters. *Wide Sargasso Sea.* Ed. Judith L. Raiskin. New York: Norton, 1999. 132–45.

Rich, Adrienne. 'Jane Eyre: The Temptations of a Motherless Woman.' *Jane Eyre.* Ed. Richard J. Dunn. New York: Norton, 2001. 469–83. [Originally published in *On Lies, Secrets, and Silence: Selected Prose 1966–1978,* 1979.]

Robbins, Bruce. 'Recognition: Servant in the Ending.' *The Turn of the Screw.* Ed. Deborah Esch and Jonathan Warren. New York: Norton, 1996. 238–40. [Originally published in *The Servant's Hand: English Fiction from Below,* 1986.]

Roberts, Doreen. 'Jane Eyre and "The Warped System of Things."' *Jane Eyre: Contemporary Critical Essays.* Ed. Heather Glen. Houndsmills: MacMillan, 1997. 34–51. [Originally published in *Reading the Victorian Novel: Detail into Form,* 1980.]

Rody, Caroline. 'Burning Down the House: The Revisionary Paradigm of Jean Rhys's *Wide Sargasso Sea.*' *Wide Sargasso Sea.* Ed. Judith L. Raiskin. New York: Norton, 1999. 217–24. [Originally published in *Famous Last Words: Changes in Gender and Narrative Closure,* ed. Allison Booth, 1993.]

Rubin, Gayle. 'The Traffic in Women: Notes on the "Political Economy" of Sex.' *Toward an Anthropology of Women.* Ed. Rayna R. Reiter. New York: Monthly Review Press, 1975.

Sanders, Julie. *Adaptation and Appropriation.* London: Routledge, 2006.

Schaff, Barbara. 'The Strange After-Lives of *Jane Eyre.*' *A Breath of Fresh Eyre: Intertextual and Intermedial Reworkings of Jane Eyre.* Ed. Margarete Rubik and Elke Mettinger-Schartman. Amsterdam: Rodopi, 2007. 25–36.

Skura, Meredith Ann. *The Literary Use of the Psychoanalytic Process.* New Haven and London: Yale UP, 1981.

Smith, Alan Lloyd. 'The Phantoms of *Drood* and *Rebecca*: The Uncanny Reencountered through Abraham and Torok's "Cryptonomy."' *Poetics Today* 13.2 (1992): 285–308.

Sternlieb, Lisa. 'Jane Eyre: Hazarding Confidencies.' Reprinted in *Jane Eyre* by Charlotte Brontë. Ed. Richard J. Dunn. New York: Norton, 2001. 503–15.

Stewart, Suzanne. *Sublime Surrender: Male Masochism at the Fin-de-Siècle*. Cornell: Cornell UP, 1998.

Su, John J. '"Once I Would Have Gone Back … But Not Any Longer": Nostalgia and Narrative Ethics in *Wide Sargasso Sea*.' *Critique: Studies in Contemporary Fiction* 44.2 (2003): 157–74.

Suleiman, Susan Rubin. *Subversive Intent: Gender, Politics, and the Avant-Garde*. Cambridge, MA: Harvard University Press 1990.

Sutherland, John. *Can Jane Eyre Be Happy? More Puzzles in Classic Fiction*. Oxford: Oxford UP, 1997.

Tani, Stefano. *The Doomed Detective: The Contribution of the Detective Novel to Postmodern American and Italian Fiction*. Carbondale and Edwardsville: Southern Illinois UP, 1984.

Tatar, Maria. 'Bluebeard's Curse: Repetition and Improvisational Energy in the Bluebeard Tale.' *Bluebeard's Legacy: Death and Secrets from Bartók to Hitchcock*. Ed. Griselda Pollock and Victoria Anderson. London: I.B. Tauris, 2009. 15–29.

– *The Hard Facts of the Grimms' Fairy Tales*. Expanded 2nd ed. Princeton: Princeton UP, 2003.

– *Off with Their Heads! Fairy Tales and the Culture of Childhood*. Princeton: Princeton UP, 1992.

– *Secrets beyond the Door: The Story of Bluebeard and His Wives*. Princeton: Princeton UP 2004.

Tyler-Bennett, Deborah. '"Thick within Our Hair": Djuna Barnes's Gothic Lovers.' *Gothic Modernisms*. Ed. Andrew Smith and Jeff Wallace. New York: Palgrave, 2001.

Verhaeghe, Paul. *Does the Woman Exist? From Freud's Hysteric to Lacan's Feminine*. Rev. ed. Trans. Marc du Ry. New York: Other P, 1999. [*Tussen Hysterie en Vrouw*, 1996.]

Warner, Marina. *From the Beast to the Blonde: On Fairy Tales and Their Tellers*. London: Vintage, 1994.

Whitehead, Anne. *Trauma Fiction*. Edinburgh: Edinburgh UP, 2004.

Williams, Anne. *Art of Darkness: A Poetics of Gothic*. Chicago: U of Chicago P, 1995.

Williams, Carolyn. 'Closing the Book: The Intertextual End of *Jane Eyre*.' *Jane Eyre: Contemporary Critical Essays*. Ed. Heather Glen. Houndsmills: MacMillan, 1997. 227–50. [Originally published in *Victorian Connections*, ed. Jerome McGann, 1989.]

Wilson, Edmund. 'The Ambiguity of Henry James.' *The Turn of the Screw*. 2nd ed. Ed. Deborah Esch and Jonathan Warren. New York: Norton, 1996. 170–3. [Originally published in *Hound & Horn* 7, 1934.]

Wilson, Sharon. 'Bluebeard's Forbidden Room in Rhys's Post-Colonial Meta-Fairy Tale, *Wide Sargasso Sea.*' *Journal of Caribbean Literatures* 3.3 (Jean Rhys Special Issue) (2003): 111–22.

Winterhalter, Teresa. 'Narrative Technique and the Rage for Order in *Wide Sargasso Sea.*' *Narrative* 2.3 (1994): 214–29.

Zipes, Jack. *Why Fairy Tales Stick: The Evolution and Relevance of a Genre.* New York: Routledge, 2006.

Žižek, Slavoj. *Enjoy Your Symptom! Jacques Lacan in Hollywood and Out.* New York: Routledge, 1992.

– *Looking Awry: An Introduction to Jacques Lacan through Popular Culture.* Cambridge, MA: MIT Press, 1991.

– *The Puppet and the Dwarf: The Perverse Core of Christianity.* Cambridge, MA: MIT, 2003.

Zlotnick, Susan. 'Jane Eyre, Anna Leonowens, and the White Woman's Burden: Governesses, Missionaries, and Maternal Imperialists in Mid-Victorian Britain.' *Victorians Institute Journal* 24 (1996): 27–56.

Zonana Joyce. 'The Sultan and the Slave: Feminist Orientalism and the Structure of *Jane Eyre.*' *The Brontës.* Ed. and Introduction by Patricia Ingham. London: Longman, 2003. 70–90.

# Index